Cash and Dash

Cash and Dash

How ATMs and Computers Changed Banking

Bernardo Bátiz-Lazo

OXFORD
UNIVERSITY PRESS

OXFORD
UNIVERSITY PRESS

Great Clarendon Street, Oxford, OX2 6DP,
United Kingdom

Oxford University Press is a department of the University of Oxford.
It furthers the University's objective of excellence in research, scholarship,
and education by publishing worldwide. Oxford is a registered trade mark of
Oxford University Press in the UK and in certain other countries

Published in the United States of America by Oxford University Press
198 Madison Avenue, New York, NY 10016, United States of America

British Library Cataloguing in Publication Data
Data available

Library of Congress Control Number: 2018935428

ISBN 978–0–19–878281–0

Printed and bound by
CPI Group (UK) Ltd, Croydon, CR0 4YY

To our children and godchildren
Aitor, Iker, Ignasi, Patricio, & Carmen

And to the loving memory of José Eduardo Rivero García (1965–2018)
schoolmate, compadre, citizen of the world, and most dear friend.

Foreword: On the Importance of Cash (and Cashless) Paleo-Futures

I think that we are on the cusp of a major change in the way that we pay each other, the way that money works in the connected economy, and, in fact, the very nature of money itself. When we went through the agricultural revolution we invented banking and writing. When we went through the industrial revolution we invented central banks and fiat currency. As we move through the post-industrial revolution, we are certain to invent new technologies that will be used for money and new institutions to manage that money. There is an inevitability to the change, even if most of us cannot predict what that change will be. So how we can go about formulating some worthwhile ideas?

Bernardo and I share a common interest in the often overlooked topic of "paleo-futures". Too often, people's incorrect predictions about the future of money and the technologies that help us make payments are simply forgotten. But to my mind, looking at these often ancient visions and trying to understand why the thinkers of the time were wrong is a very valuable discipline. We can learn as much from what didn't happen (e.g., EFTPOS UK, Mondex, television banking) as we can from what did happen (e.g. ATMs, PayPal, and Bitcoin). It is important to understand the context for visions, plans, and schemes for the future of money so that we can try to make more realistic projections looking forward from our time of rapid technological change. The long-term impact of the mobile phone on money, to choose an obvious example, is far from clear even as I write in the middle of a smartphone revolution that is changing the face of money in many countries. While it may well be that the mobile phone, rather than the credit card or the Internet, will turn out to be the technology that delivers cashlessness, will the global interconnection of smart devices mean that we converge on a single currency? A single kind of money? The elimination of ATMs? Or does the democratization and decentralization it engenders mean that we will all have our own kinds of money in the future?

Naturally, when people begin to think about these kinds of implications, they look to history to try to understand the dynamics and I, for one, am immensely interested in the history of money, the technologies around it and financial institutions in order to understand just how the interplay between business and society, banks and governments, technology and finance creates paradigms and, ultimately, products and services around new means of exchange, new stores of value, and new currencies. Looking at the results of the last industrial revolution and the long road to the 'Washington consensus', studying experiments in Europe, the USA, Latin America, and elsewhere, I believe helps us to be more informed in our speculation about new types of financial intermediaries, emergent institutions, and the impact of the technological changes.

I am fascinated by all aspects of the process, so I was glad to see that Bernardo has produced this work on ATMs and their impact on both financial institutions and people across the world, a work that touches on many of the aspects that I personally feel deserve further study and further understanding in order to help us navigate the coming economy and create a roadmap for the evolution of money. These include necessary discussions about politics and economic structures (see, for example, digital and cyber currencies), crime and cyber security, successes and failures that give a rounded picture of the path to our current world of fiat currencies, debit cards, and ATMs. Understanding where we are, and how we got here, is only a first step to understanding where we might go next, but it is a vital first step.

This book roams time and space to examine aspects of the evolution of money, and how ATMs and automation have changed our payment habits. Bernardo's focus is the comparison of Anglo-Saxon countries, America, and Britain; but also touches on countries that I wanted to learn more about (e.g. Sweden, Russia, and Mexico). His book is also about the big efforts to develop online, real time services, how these globalized, and aspects of retail payments that I wanted to know more about (e.g. building trust on new technologies), providing a wonderful tour of a topic that I think I know a lot about but really don't.

The trends in and around cash (and cashlessness), payment cards, mobile phones, and the pervasive connectivity we are just coming to terms with are central to the discourse on the post-industrial evolution of money and this book delivers valuable contributions to that discourse. I may be a little biased because the book contains contributions from a good friend of mine who I know sees both the wood and the trees, but a hearty well done to Bernardo for delivering a book that I will not only read from cover to cover but am sure to refer to time and time again.

Best regards,
Dave.
David G. W. Birch
Director of Innovation, Consult Hyperion.
Visiting Professor, University of Surrey Business School.
Author, *Identity is the New Money* (London Publishing Partnership, 2014) and
Before Babylon, Beyond Bitcoin (London Publishing Partnership, 2017).

Preface

On the face of it, with a very long list of failed innovations, observers of retail banking may question what makes a new banking product different and why banks have no research and development departments. Most people think that innovations have no past, that they occur in a vacuum, and that retail banking is a sleepy, uncompetitive world. But there is much to be learned by understanding the evolution of financial markets and the organizations that populate them, through tracing how groups of people (from diverse backgrounds and with opposing objectives) interact with one another and with technological applications in shaping innovation.

This book is partly backward looking. It also aims to dispute preconceptions and shed light on the challenges ahead for the financial industry, such as the use of applications of computer technology for financial inclusion, together with the emergence of mobile money, crypto currencies, digital wallets, and cashless payments. This book also shows that far more time and effort are invested in making a financial technology part of everyday life and maintaining it than in the white heat of innovation.

The discussion is informed by theory, since this encourages a conceptual understanding of how and why technological change in methods of payments is so slow. It moves away from the dominant narrative around cost structures in banking to emphasize managerial decisions, how customers' preferences evolve, explaining changes in the industrial organization of retail payments and changes in the corporate strategies of manufacturers and retail financial institutions. It includes explaining how financial institutions and their customers changed their practices, their skill set, their processes and procedure; how they dealt with legacy investments and how (and when) they met their strategic objectives. None of the chapters is dedicated to conceptual discussion. Instead I intertwine the conceptual part of the discussion with the narrative, for no single framework would capture the diverse features under scrutiny.

Nevertheless, the extant literature on ATM interchange fees, the industrial organization of banking, its economic and business history, and social studies of technology all influence and limit the questions driving the main theme of this book. These include whether computer technology changes payment habits or whether, on balance, banks respond with new applications to changes in consumer culture; how new start-ups in financial services solve the cash in/cash out dilemma; and whether 'bricks and mortar' branches are a barrier to potential new players in retail banking or costly legacy investments for established players. I do not claim to have solved every one of these debates. But I do claim to offer a fresh perspective on them while showing, at the same time, that technological change in retail banking is an essential characteristic of both late twentieth-century capitalism and globalization. As such, it needs to be understood through its local, grass-roots developments. Moreover, by documenting how genius and teamwork go hand in hand, I demonstrate the power of collaborative labour; and by detailing how conflicts between user groups and institutions can be beneficial, I demonstrate the interplay between banks and their broader ecosystem.

The title of the book hints at the cash dispenser. The common wisdom holds that the cash machine was born fifty years ago, in June of 1967. This was quite an eventful year—the same year as the 'summer of love'; The Beatles' manager Brian Epstein being found dead in his locked bedroom while the group launched the iconic *Sgt Pepper's Lonely Hearts Club Band* album, and the *Magical Mystery Tour* film and recording; *The Graduate* being watched in cinemas for the first time. In science and technology Christiaan Barnard carried out the first successful heart transplant operation in South Africa; the USA launched *Lunar Orbiter 3* while a cabin fire killed the whole crew of the *Apollo 1*; the first prototype of the Concorde was unveiled in Toulouse, France; and James Bedford became the first person to be cryonically preserved with the intent of future resuscitation. In sports, after beating Inter Milan 1–2 Celtic became the first British team to win a European cup; Gary Beban (UCLA) won the Heisman Trophy that the now infamous O. J. Simpson (USC) would win the following year; the Green Bay Packers won what was known retroactively as Super Bowl II; and the St. Louis Cardinals won baseball's World Series.

In feminism Margareta Arvidsson of Sweden won the Miss Universe pageant held in Miami, FL; while Labour MP David Steel sponsored an Abortion Law Reform Bill making abortion in most parts of Britain legal under certain criteria and with medical supervision. In politics and the economy the Mexican schoolteacher Lucio Cabañas began his guerrilla warfare in the state of Guerrero; Ronald Reagan was inaugurated as the new governor of California; Yuri Andropov became chief of the KGB; some half-million US troops were serving in Vietnam; Étienne Eyadama led a military coup in Togo; Thurgood Marshall was confirmed as the first African American Justice in the US Supreme Court while the same court declared state laws prohibiting interracial marriage to be unconstitutional; Israel fought the 'Six Day War' against the neighbouring states of Egypt (known at the time as the United Arab Republic), Jordan, and Syria.

The UK and Ireland formally applied for membership of the then European Economic Community or EEC (today the European Union); General Charles de Gaulle, the French President, vetoed the entry of the UK to the EEC for the second time in a decade; the British pound devalued from £1 = US$2.80 to US$2.40; Milton Keynes (the town where I live) and the Open University (my former employer and the reason that we came to Milton Keynes) were established; Barclaycard had been in operation for a year, while the Bank of England authorized 'roll over credit' thus transforming Barclaycard from a charge card to a bank-backed credit card; British banknotes were not yet decimal but decimalization had been announced while banknotes were bigger, had fewer security attributes than in 2017, and were all made out of rag paper.

Given those and many other events that took place in 1967, choosing the cash machine as an illustration of the process of innovation in banking could be seen as arbitrary. However, for many the credit card, magnetic ink characters on personal cheques, and the cash machine were the first tangible evidence that retail banking was changing. The credit card marked the advent of consumerism and the end of the hard work, discipline, and frugality of the Protestant ethos. The introduction of the cash machine marked the dawn of contemporary digital financial services, representing not only a form of automation but today's icon of the boundary between the ethereal and the physical in retail banking.

The 'hole in the wall' appears in a large number of systematic empirical studies that explore the economics of networks, the industrial organization of banking, changes in the cost structures of financial institutions, issues of competition and cooperation, and issues of social welfare and financial inclusion. Cashpoints even act as an index of technological change in banking. Most (if not all) of the previous, largely quantitative studies have engaged with technological change as if it was independent of its social context and external to retail financial institutions. They failed to consider technological trajectories, the changes in the underlying infrastructure, or user group dynamics. Empirical studies were most often blind to organizational change inside financial institutions or to the fact that what appeared to be an industry-specific innovation was in fact part of a wider process of globalization. Some even fell into the trap of assuming that US markets give birth to all innovations in banking.

I stumbled on the sparseness of research on cash machines from an historical perspective and the debate around 'the inventor of the ATM' accolade while researching a teaching case study on Barclaycard for the textbook edited by Gerry Johnson and Kevan Scholes (Bátiz-Lazo et al. 2002). This was surprising, given that a well-functioning market economy relies on the smooth running of its payment ecosystem. More so as two of the characters in the invention debate had been awarded honours by the Queen.

It was not that cash machines had been absolutely ignored but, apart from Jack Revell and Richard Coopey, no one had gone beyond collecting and analysing data on the number of machines in use (Revell 1983; Coopey 2004b). Indeed, we knew little of the genesis and evolution of this ubiquitous device, and how it had helped (or hindered) the globalization of retail payments.

In 2006, the British Academy (BA) was kind enough to give me a large grant so that I could look closely at the origins of what appeared to be a British invention (LRG-41806). I mostly made use of this grant while at Leicester and visited the main UK banking archives (Barclays, Lloyds, NatWest, Royal Bank of Scotland, Halifax, then at RBS, and Midland at HSBC). I was allowed frequent visits to the London Metropolitan Archives and their holdings from the late Abbey National Building Society, the Committee of London Clearing Banks, and Chubb & Son's. Ian Ormerod granted access to his personal collection on the NCR Corporation while Simon Rex and the Council of Mortgage Lenders gave me unlimited access to their records of building societies and the Building Societies Association.

In 2008 the Arthur L. Norberg Travel Fund enabled me to document the US experience through Burroughs and other collections at the Charles Babbage Institute. That same year a similar grant from the Hagley Museum and Archives allowed me to explore material from IBM and the Philadelphia Savings Fund Society. I was also supported by archival material from Citibank, IBM, and Diebold. Enrico Bandiera gave support by a long-distance search of the Archivio Storico Olivetti.

Collaborative work prompted more interviews and access to records elsewhere. Particularly useful were those from Hong Kong, Mexico, Sweden, and Spain.

I was fortunate that Tom Harper (NetWorld Media Group) came knocking at my door in 2012. He wanted to write a story for a wider audience and so we did. He was not only a great co-author, but instrumental in opening the door to a number of industry specialists. Chief among them were Mike Lee (ATMIA), Aravinda Korala (KAL ATM Software), and Dominic Hirsch (RBR London). Former IBM employees were another bunch of great informants that included Sir Anthony Davies, Larry Hirst, Philip Lippard, Jonathan Rosenne, and Robert Rosenthal. So were former TSB staff, including Michael McQuade, Harry Read, Ray Neal, and Hayden Taylor. Multiple sparring sessions on the more technical aspects of the DACS with Stuart McEwen Jenkins and the ATM with Robert Rosenthal were essential to clarify a number of engineering details.

Together all these inputs enabled to portray a mosaic evolution of the ATM and related computer applications, narrated through a changing mix of source material and selective emphasis on the business, technological, and social history of these devices.

Acknowledgements

My gratitude goes to the people from whom I learned the basic traits of researching banking organizations, notably the late Douglas Wood, Trevor Boyns, Robert Locke, and Peter Wardley—all of them my teachers, co-authors, and above all, good friends. Then my appreciation to those instrumental in and who supported my transition to the business history of banking, including (in no order but alphabetical): Hubert Bonin, Alan Booth, the late Phil Cottrell, David Lamond, Carlos Marichal, Dean Paxton, the late Derek Pugh, Andy Stark, and, in particular, Charles Harvey, Janette Rutterford, and John Wilson. To them, to the archivists who kindly granted access to their records, to the engineers and bankers who kindly shared their time, and to the many others with whom I have worked over the years, who have helped to shape my thinking on banking and computer history, I give my grateful thanks.

As in other similar enterprises, I get the credit and assume responsibility for the errors and omissions. But my point of view was considerably developed and refined through presentations and interactions at meetings of the Association of Business Historians, Business History Conference, European Business History Association, European Association for Banking and Financial History, ATM Industry Association, Monetary History Group, and SHOT's Special Interest Group: Computers, Information and Society.

A number of colleagues allowed me to present ideas in small and intense staff gatherings and thus, helped to shape results along the way. For that my appreciation to Bill Maurer's, Taylor Nelm's, and Lana Schwatrz's *Payment Parties* at the University of California, Irvine, Ross Anderson (Cambridge), Carlos Marichal (Colegio de México), Joost Jonker and Joost Danker (Utrecht), Lorenza Martínez, Sara Castellanos, and Biliana Alexandrova Kabadjova (Banco de México), Carlos Serrano (BBVA Bancomer), and Martín Monsalve (Pacífico).

Special thanks to those who were always ready to exchange ideas, including (in no order but alphabetical): Ian Bogost, Martin Campbell-Kelly, Albert Carreras, Chris Colvin, Jim Cortada, Barbara Hahn, Thomas Haigh, Lars Heide, David Higgins, Roger Horowitz, Richard John, Devendra Kodwani, Jeffrey Kutler, Ian Martin, Stephen Mihm, Tom Misa, Andy Russell, Susan Scott, Phil Scranton, Dave Stearns, Paul Thomes, Steve Toms, and Jeffrey Yost.

Tobias Karlsson and Carles Maixé-Altés were great colleagues who helped document Swedish and Spanish experiences, respectively. I was assisted by Robert Reid in, among other things, setting up a database to construct families of patents, while Claudia Reese helped with archival work in the UK and Germany (where we were denied access to the Nixdord/Wincor documents), as well as with oral histories and interviews with key players (which were later transcribed).

Sergio Castellanos (Bangor), a kindred spirit, was always willing to lend a helping hand, while Manuel Bautista (Columbia), Juan Felipe Espinosa (Andres Bello), and Leonidas Efthymiou (Intercollege Larnaca/UNICAF) enabled me to keep my head above water. The stellar performance of Prachandra Shakaya at Bangor to put the final manuscript together was priceless. Martin Gannon (Strathclyde), Alessio Reghezza, Marybeth Rouse, and Jungsik Son at Bangor provided valuable support.

I am indebted to the multiple colleagues and industry experts who took time to read extracts and draft chapters, and to comment and advise on the idea of book along the way. These included (in no order but alphabetical): Lars Arfvidson, Jim Bessen, Mark Billings, Jenny Campbell, David Cavell, John G. Chamberlin, Geoffrey Constable, Jim Cortada, Diane Coyle, Bhaskar Dasgupta (BD), Sir Anthony Davies, Gustavo del Angel, Ron Delnevo, Tony Gandy, Oscar Gelderblom, Sonya Hanna, Michael Heller, David Higgins, Bryan King, Alan Konheim, Michael Lafferty, Philip Lippard, Daniel Littman, Manuel Llorca, Stephen Mason, James McAndrews, David Miller, Joke Mooij, Malcolm Page, Andrew Paxman, John Reed, Jonathan Rosenne, Georgie Salcedo, Maria Sienkiewicz, Mark Tadajewski, Claire Tenzer, Aashish Velkar, Lee Vinsel, and Julio Zamora.

Lloyds Banking Group and there for Karen Sampson, Head of Archives & Museum, supported this project throughout the years. They graciously allowed the use of one of their trademarks in the title.

It was a pleasure to work with Clare Kennedy, Jenny King and Katie Bishop at The Press. My gratitude to Eve Richards for her help in producing a readable manuscript and to Alejandro Llaguno at All Design for assisting with graphs and diagrams.

Finally, Bangor University and there, Phil Molyneux, Kostas Nikolopoulos, John Thornton, Jon Williams, and Louise Hassan were always supportive and generous with this project. The final thanks to the undivided support of my parents, Yolanda and Bernardo, and my wife, Elena.

Contents

Contents

List of Figures

List of Figures

List of Tables

1

A Window to Internal and External Change in Banking

1.1 The Most Important Financial Innovation Comes Full Circle

'...the most important financial innovation that I have seen in the past 20 years is the automatic teller machine.'

—Paul Volcker[1]

'...and all the thinking came full circle to—you know what?—"It's cash and dash." That's all people want, is cash and dash.'

—Jenny Campbell[2]

In today's global economy most urbanites have interacted with the otherwise ubiquitous cash machine (also known as the 'hole in the wall', cashpoint, the bankomat, automated banking machine, and the automated teller machine or ATM). It facilitates travel and has helped to redefine urban and global space. The ATM is an expensive, industry-specific piece of capital equipment which also embodies the first step in multi-channel delivery strategies for the provision of retail banking services. Paul Volcker, of Federal Reserve fame, considers it the 'only useful innovation in banking'; while Jenny Campbell, former ATM specialist CEO turned TV celebrity, ponders on its importance for impromptu purchases. Cash machines have figured on most TV and printed news media because they represent an easily recognizable physical interface with today's otherwise ephemeral digital financial services.

Any doubt of the ATM's significant 'financial footprint' can easily be dispelled. This is illustrated by Figure 1.1, which is built on estimates by payments consultant RBR London. According to this source, by the end of 2016 there were 3.6 million automated teller machines (ATMs) deployed across the globe (a 30 per cent increase over 2013).[3] These enabled 109 billion cash withdrawals to be made (a 25 per cent increase over 2013), whose estimated

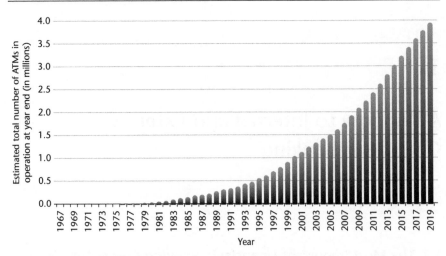

Figure 1.1. Growth to 2014 and forecast to 2019 of the global ATM stock (in millions of units at year end)

Source: Author's own estimates, based on data provided by RBR London.

total value was US\$14 trillion (a 4 per cent increase over 2013). Growth in ATM cash withdrawals worldwide included an impressive 10 per cent annual increase in 2015, the fastest annual growth rate since 2011.[4] According to the same source, financial inclusion was the key driver of this growth, particularly in the Asia Pacific region. These estimates suggest that there are approximately 100 billion US dollars residing in ATMs around the world at any point in time.[5]

On the trend of the ATM's global footprint, Mike Lee, CEO ATM Industry Association, reckons that: 'Fifty years on [in 2017], a new "cash robot" is added about every three minutes'. He continues:

> Five decades of monumental production, averaging roughly 165 terminals per day, have seen ATMs spread everywhere, from the frozen far north of Alaska to McMurdo's Antarctic research station near the South Pole; from Los Angeles to Lagos; from Cape to Cairo; from a desert aboriginal community in Western Australia to remote villages in the high-lying Himalayas.[6]

There is also evidence that the cash machine is deeply embedded in our culture. Think of the British independent rock band Hi-Fi and world popstar Britney Spears who have recorded whole songs about them. The 'hole in the wall' also features in Radiohead's 'Fitter Happier' hit single, and poems about ATMs have been part of National Poetry Month celebrations in the UK.[7] How to break into an ATM was the secondary plot in a Hollywood movie and in some of the episodes of the iconic *Breaking Bad* television series, while in a movie called *ATM* three co-workers end up in a desperate fight for their lives when on a late-night visit to withdraw cash they become trapped in a bank branch's lobby by an unknown man.[8]

The ATM represents a complex technology and, as such, has been shaped by numberless groups of people and organizations. As an industry-specific invention, it initially responded to a desire to offer 'after hours' cash distribution in Europe, while in the USA its adoption related to the securing of new retail deposits. However, as shown in Figure 1.2, most British people today make use of an ATM around lunchtime, with transaction volume declining as the day proceeds.

The data in Figure 1.2 show that 63 per cent of the total cash withdrawal transactions *circa* 2015 took place between 09.00 and 16.00 hrs, an average of a million transactions (13 per cent) per hour during this period, as opposed to 150,000 transactions (2 per cent) per average hour at any other time of the day or night.[9] In this regard, responding to an article celebrating the 50th anniversary of the ATM, Tom from Adelaide remembered how, when the machines first came out, he was driving a truck and saw ten or so people standing outside a bank in very heavy pouring rain waiting to get their cash.[10] He could not but laugh because, due his high position in the truck, he could see over the frosted window into the bank where four or five bank clerks 'were doing nothing'. So even if 'after hours' cash distribution was what motivated the invention of the ATM, this no longer holds good because people's payment

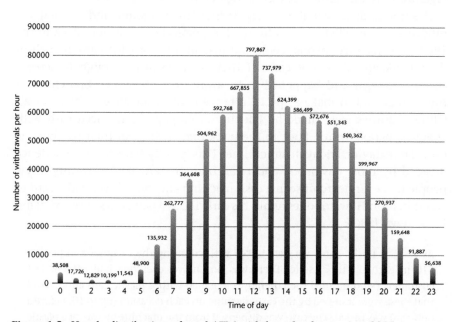

Figure 1.2. Hourly distribution of total ATM withdrawal volume, circa 2015
Source: Author's own estimates, based on data provided by LINK.

habits have transformed during the last fifty years. As Figure 1.2 and Adelaide Tom's anecdote show, these days people mostly withdraw cash when bank branches are open!

The pattern of withdrawals in Figure 1.2 also suggests that if a machine fails during a period of peak demand (797,867 transactions during 2015 between 11:00 and 12:00 hrs), the impact will be almost eighty times greater than if it happens during a low-traffic period (10,199 transactions between 02:00 and 03:00 hrs). Hence these patterns not only debunk the idea of ATMs associated with 'out of hours' cash, they also support the role of the ATM in the modern economy as the main point to distribute banknotes.

Yet in the 1960s no one foresaw the transformation of the cash machine into the ATM, or the success of the ATM as a self-service banking technology. It took twenty years' worth of trial, error, and redesign to reach the tipping point in worldwide adoption. Originally the ATM was one of a number of alternatives to 'bricks and mortar' banking. Yet today for many banks it remains an important part of their distribution strategy. Most bank customers (i.e. ultimate users) habitually visit an ATM, most commonly with a Visa or MasterCard marquee plastic card, in any one of five preferred locations, yet expect this token to work and the transaction to be finalized within 30 seconds, regardless of geography, time of day, day of the year, or national border. For this to happen, a great many individuals, public and private organizations, and groups of technologies have had to interact.

The trends discussed above suggest that the economic and cultural significance of the ATM resulted from a long period of evolution. Back in the 1960s, for instance, people could not just simply walk into any branch of their bank and draw out cash. If they were wealthy enough to have a current account and happened to be away from their own branch, then they either had to make a special arrangement in advance or had to wait while enquiries were made by telephone. As payrolls replaced cash with cheques, people would flock to the bank branch to cash their pay cheque on a Thursday or Friday at lunchtime. This rapidly became an experience dreaded by most customers and retail branch staff. By 1971, only a few people had ever heard or seen a cash machine and even fewer had a card to access it. John Howard-Jones recalls his early life as a bank clerk at the Midland Bank (now HSBC):

> As cashiers in the bank, we were tasked with counting the £1 notes and placing £10 in each plastic cassette. There was no choice; everyone had £10.00. The customers (who fulfilled the criteria) were issued with a plastic card and I recall that these were stamped by the cash machine on each occasion (up to 10) before a new card was issued. The cash was dispensed from the machine by way of a plastic clip, with the pound notes folded neatly inside... How times change.[11]

Fifty years on, things have indeed changed for retail financial institutions, their customers, and for people in general; banking is no longer exclusive but widely available. Cash machines are to be found in every nation, and, most importantly, they are usually in working order and conveniently located. This means that bank customers can have the access to their liquid balances that they want, where they want, and whenever they want. The ATM has been integral to this process of change, characterized by the co-evolution of technology, banking practices, and society.

And here is my conundrum: eyes glaze over when I tell of my interest in researching ATMs. Yet most people will remember an anecdote about interacting with one of them: some positive (a chance encounter with a long-lost friend), some negative (a theft), and many private (like the feeling when 'Insufficient funds' is displayed on the screen). So as well as their financial and cultural significance, the cash machine represents a small fraction of our everyday life and therefore, few people stop to reflect how it became the backbone of today's retail payments ecosystem; how technology has changed payment habits; how, when, or why technological change in banking leads to changes in consumer culture; and why innovation in banking is inconsequential unless it is widely adopted.

This book is as much about technological change in retail banking since the 1960s as it is an exploration of cash machines. The invention, evolution, and globalization of the cash machine forms the unifying thread that helps to answer why innovation in retail banking is so slow and so seldom disruptive. There is indeed widespread agreement that technology has played a key role in the development of capitalism since the start of the Industrial Revolution in the mid-eighteenth century. Under this lens, technology and its evolution are seldom the neutral and external forces described by economists. Instead, applications of technology result from social interaction and are often articulated to reproduce such interaction.

It is a cliché to say that technology, particularly the application of digital computers, has modified the activities inside productive units, and gone on, through market transactions, to reshape the relationships in these units and the ways in which they are structured. However, a great many routine activities within and around financial institutions that accept financial deposits (henceforth 'banks') remained largely unchanged until the advent of electronic computers in the 1960s. But bankers did not sit idle all this time. Starting in the inter-war years and certainly throughout the 1950s, many attempts were made to find alternatives to retail bank branches as distribution channels. Indeed, there has been a steady migration from 'bricks and mortar' to self-service channels (supported by landlines, mobile telephones, the Internet, and, of course, ATMs); while today's bankers, regulators, and others with an interest in financial technology (FinTech) expect the migration to continue.[12] This book, therefore, aims to help the reader understand the origins and evolution of these trends in some depth.

1.2 Researching the Cash Machine

The ATM has been heralded as a typical software application, 'on which a customer presses a sequence of buttons that causes the computer network to perform a complex set of operations correctly . . . the customer is programming the bank's computer'.[13] But as the research in this book illustrates, a large number of things had to happen before the ATM achieved 'software status'.

As suggested by Revell and McAndrews, the ATM uses technology for banking services; it is a machine incorporating a video display unit (VDU), keyboard, printer (to provide a record of the transaction or a summary statement), and other software and hardware that enables individuals using debit cards, credit cards, or certain paper or plastic tokens to make cash withdrawals and/or deposits, balance enquiries, balance transfers (between the accounts of the same customer, the customer and the bank, or the customer and a third party) as well as other services, for which users may be charged a transaction fee.[14] The ATM is thus seen as much more than a simple cash withdrawal device: it is an integral and essential part of a self-service offering.

There are other interesting features of ATMs. For instance, a machine must be fitted with a miniature strong-room to enable it to store and supply banknotes. The workings of any ATM include encryption capabilities to safely process and transmit user information. A stainless-steel fascia mediates between user and hardware to protect electronic equipment from adverse weather, vandalism, and theft. A full-service ATM offers all the features already mentioned and many others, such as accepting cash for deposits, in some instances recycling banknotes for other withdrawals; accepting personal cheques for deposit; and even communicating via closed-circuit television (CCTV) with an adviser at a central location. Today's ATMs, therefore, provide practically all the straightforward services a customer may need from a retail bank branch.

One important exception is that regular payments and credits have to be arranged separately. So do most cross-border transactions. A second important distinction between ATMs and banks appears in the case of deposit facilities; in some countries these are rarely more than a conventional night safe, leaving the bank to verify the amount deposited when the machine is cleared. Automatic currency exchange devices at airport halls suggested some time ago that it was technologically possible for machines to identify and count notes and coins, but it was until *circa* 2005 that cash and coins were counted and credited to customers' accounts alongside cash distribution through self-service machines in the high street.[15]

Coopey has questioned whether the ATM embodies a single technology.[16] He considers that the 'ATM is best viewed as the consolidation of a series of technologies and systems, developing independently, and some picking up impetus in turn from the development of the ATM itself'.[17] The potential coexistence of different technological solutions highlights the fact that senior managers of financial intermediaries can (and do) choose between alternative technological configurations. Having a choice of configuration, make, and model, empowers individual organizations to influence the evolution of these devices rather than having to accept the technological solutions determined by manufacturers. With these ideas in mind, British banking offers a particularly good example of user-driven change, given that a highly concentrated market and densely populated retail branch network resulted in individual orders being large by North American standards. Indeed, throughout the twentieth century the likes of IBM, Burroughs, and NCR worked hard to keep the custom of British banks, savings banks, and building societies. At the same time, developments in British banking often replicate those of their US-based counterparts.

The importance of cash dispensing technology in US banking was perhaps first noted by Richardson's pioneering contribution.[18] But neither Richardson's nor other systematic studies on the evolution of ATM networks within the business and technological history of US banking challenged the conventional wisdom on the creation and diffusion of different versions of cash dispensing technology.

Hopton, Kirkman, and Howells and Hine summarize developments in the British payment system.[19] Coopey and Barrie touch on the emergence of the ATM in the UK from an historical perspective.[20] Coopey offers evidence of the emergence of cash machines and its business and technological links with credit cards as the backbone of British electronic funds transfer systems (EFTS) and electronic point of sale terminals (POS). Some elements of this story are also found in Ackrill and Hannah's authoritative history of Barclays Bank.[21] Meanwhile, Barrie positioned the ATM within the overall process of technological change in UK banks. In a previous journal article, I provided a first detailed account of the transformation of cash machines into ATM networks in the UK.[22] Some attention to ATMs also appears in comparative studies of UK, Spanish, and Nordic banking.[23] The corporate histories of a number of banks often note the adoption of the first ATM and sometimes their growth as symbols of modernity and innovation.

Alongside systematic studies from an historical perspective, there is an extensive body of cross-sectional analyses by scholars who have explored the marketing dimensions of the ATM, industrial policy dimensions, and the ATM as a computer network. A survey by Vázquez-Alanís identified two areas that group academic contributions in the broad areas of economics and management, namely performance effects and networks effects.[24] Studies of performance effects aim to tell us how investments in ATM relate to greater operational efficiency, which in turn relates to changes in market share, interest and non-interest income. A central claim is that possibilities of informational asymmetries can be exploited through the early adoption of new information technologies such as ATM networks and can result in first mover advantage.

Contributions dealing with network effects focus on changes in the number of locations from which users are able to access bank records using an ATM. It is claimed that there are location-specific costs and that fixed specific costs (i.e. sunk or irrecoverable costs) are not important in explaining the growth of ATM networks. These contributions are further divided in two sub-categories. One involves studies dealing with the size of the network. Of particular importance are network externalities, the role of participants, the role of 'switches', economies of scale or scope in the provision of services, and density (i.e. number of devices per capita or km^2). A second sub-category deals with interchange fees, that is, sharing the costs of proprietary networks. This involves competitive dynamics between financial intermediates, pricing of the fee itself and customers' willingness to pay for the fee. In the USA, recommendations for public policy concerned with interchange fees have received substantial attention from legal scholars and those versed in the economics of industrial networks.[25]

Beyond Vázquez-Alanís' performance and network effects, there may be two other substantial areas of research. Both of these are in need of empirical and analytical attention. First, the effects of the computerization of banking on the money supply and monetary control. This is an area that considers the interaction of banks' corporate strategy and bank regulators in the creation of network standards. This would explore how the development of EFTS was influenced by the decisions of banks' senior managers, changes in customer behaviour and preferences, as well as the policy goals of monetary authorities. Second, the role of ATMs in interpretative studies of organizational change and information technology.[26] However, both of these alternative research agendas are beyond the scope of this book.

In summary, the use of standards and the creation of networks around ATMs have been documented. These studies have too strongly emphasized technology and market-based solutions while overlooking the corporate strategy motivating investments in expensive and highly industry-specific devices such as cash machines. Archival-informed analysis of similar, but previously undocumented, developments on the part of American and British retail financial institutions, the emergence of EFTS, and the creation and growth of ATM networks are the focus of the present research. A history of ATM networks offers an opportunity to explore both technological and strategic aspects of retail banking—an area comparatively neglected in the discussion of post-1945 British economic performance. Moreover, it gives us the chance to demonstrate how the history of technology must consider its users, in as much as business histories of the late twentieth century will be incomplete without attention to developments in information and communications technologies.[27]

1.3 The Context of Change: Technological Know-How and Bank Strategy

For most of the twentieth century, financial intermediaries working in retail markets, in particular those active in loans and deposit taking, were the main channel for monetary control. This presupposes the absence of secondary markets for government debt, while governments anticipated changes in the business cycle by introducing qualitative and quantitative criteria to allocate credit. In tandem, European, Japanese, and Latin American business organizations financed themselves primarily through bank credit rather than open market transactions.

The decades that followed the Second World War saw cheques rather than bills and coins in countries such as France and the USA becoming the predominant medium of retail payment.[28] A significant and sustained increase in the number (but not the value) of cheques to be cleared has been identified by a number of studies as one of the key motivations for banks on both sides of the Atlantic to automate.[29] The automation of internal processes during the late 1950s and the 1960s together with innovations in products and services (e.g. credit cards), eventually led to the creation of EFTS in the 1970s and 1980s as intermediaries brought retail branches online at a time when computers and computer networks were increasingly being used for inter-bank payments.[30] A key element in the implementation and expansion of EFTS was the creation of networks of self-service cash withdrawal machines commonly known as cash machines and ATMs.

The genesis of the first cash machines as the earliest form of ATM should be seen in the context of long-term processes of technical change seeking to be more than short-term responses for reducing cost structures. This view is strengthened by reflecting that mechanization and automation permeate the evolution of American and British retail financial intermediaries in the course of the twentieth century.[31] For retail financial institutions, the 1960s saw the introduction of computer technology to alleviate growing pressures in the labour market to recruit (cheaper) female clerical workers, antagonistic government officials, growing inflation, and a greater variability in interest rates.

In Europe and particularly in Sweden and Britain, banks began to grapple with ways to ease physical overcrowding in retail branches and an increasingly unionized workforce, which was demanding the end of Saturday mornings at work. Indeed, how to articulate Saturday closing was a top concern in the early and mid-1960s for the Committee of the London Clearing Banks.[32] But it came about in 1969, though only after the introduction of cash machines. Meanwhile many deposit-accepting mortgage specialists, called building societies, became active in developing retail branch networks while their mortgage loan portfolio expanded rapidly.[33] The trustee savings banks (TSBs) also used computer technology to tackle the decimalization of sterling and reduce back office work at branches as they amalgamated into a single provider in 1985.

Apart from a handful of exceptions, such as the development of an online, real-time retail branch network by the TSB, or Barclay's fiasco with the Burroughs B8500, retail financial intermediaries usually resisted the uncharted novelties of the latest technology.[34] Most banks and building societies selected career staff (typically from accounting or operational methods departments) to be trained in and head their computerization efforts. As a result, the speed of computerization was often 'conservative' but despite a few obviously inappropriate decisions made with regard to the adoption of technology, it appears that building societies, savings banks, and clearing banks in particular, got things about right.[35]

Research thus considers that executives of financial organizations had a degree of choice in adopting ATM and other applications of computer technology to solve specific problems. These choices were influenced (but not determined) by a long-term process of technological change in which the most recent episode had required approaches to the adoption of mainframe computer technology. However, other contextual forces should not be underestimated, including the government's view of an increasingly inefficient banking sector, the government's 'buy British' computer policy, the reluctance of staff and unions to continue with Saturday opening hours, staff shortages, internal and external pressures to reduce staff costs, limited space in retail branches when increased business had to be processed, the great and incessant varying of interest rates, the introduction of decimal currency in 1971, membership of the European Economic Community in 1973, and the dynamics of the Cold War.

A new period marked by intense changes in retail banking took off in the 1980s where the ATM industry was no exception. The 1980s was one of the greatest periods of diffusion for the ATMs both in and across nations. At this point it is worth recalling that a network of cash machines entailed ever larger irrecoverable investments (i.e. sunk costs) to develop, while most banks populated their own branch locations with both lobby and 'through the wall' installations.

The growth of the industry-specific ATM in the 1980s ensued in the context of, and in conjunction with other investments by, banks wishing to apply computer and telecommunications technologies. Between the late 1950s and the mid-1980s, retail banks all around the world used technology for five main things—albeit some earlier than others.[36] A first major application of computer technology was to simplify banks' book-keeping and record storage. This materialized, for instance, in the transfer of accounting and payroll from manual processes to tasks for the early mainframe computers.[37] Other instances included industry-specific computer terminals at teller counters as well as a drive to eliminate all forms of paperwork. The IBM S/360 (launched in 1965) quickly became the standard mainframe computer in the banking industry (and remained so after it was renamed S/370 and the Z Series).

A second major application was to automate the processing of payments. This was built up as a progression of office mechanization and took off with the American Bankers Association adopting Bank of America's and the Stanford Research Institute's magnetic ink character recognition (MICR) as the standard for cheque sorting in 1956.[38] Other innovations in the processing of payments included the introduction of direct to account payroll payments, direct debits, and small and large value electronic transfer systems such as CHAPS in the UK (1968), CHIPS in the USA (1970), and SWIFT (1974) for international payments.[39]

A third major application involved freeing customers from the shackles of the 'bricks and mortar' retail branch through applications such as ATMs but also home banking and terminals for the transfer of money at the point of sale (also known as EFTPOS).[40] Before cash machines, people who had access to a current account were very much banking with a single branch (as opposed to the branch network). When banks started to deploy cash machines during the 1970s, they were unwilling to issue credit cards (and/or cash machine activation cards) to people who were not considered creditworthy.[41] The result was that the first users of cash machines were largely business executives. It was easier for them to visit banks during the day than for manual workers.[42] The growing number of salary earners, however, plus the threat of competition, led commercial banks to react and include waves of new customers during the late 1970s and 1980s. New customers typically were of working-class origin, people who had perhaps some financial literacy thanks to their dealings with savings banks, or hire purchase or mortgage specialists but had hitherto not been much of a preoccupation for commercial banks.[43]

The banks managed the large pools of people joining the banking system in many developed countries during the late 1970s and 1980s first by ATMs and then by telephone banking. This strategy made use of the emerging service economy and growth in the size and diversity of business organizations. In turn, these caused the weekly cash payment of wages to manual and agricultural labourers to give way to the stability of a monthly salary paid directly into a current account. As the latter accelerated, retail banks found that the ATM was a device that could help ease congestion at 'bricks and mortar' branches. Individual banks then aimed to develop their own networks of cash machines, expecting to generate sufficient transaction volume to support the fixed costs of managing a large and often geographically diverse proprietary network. In turn, this would give them the edge over banks with small networks or even with none at all.

Bankers also intended to use technology to increase the diversity in the customer base, by breaking down information from the transaction oriented systems to yield more useful and meaningful data that could reveal in detail the group characteristics of their customers—in order to find new customer groups and design new products and services. A fourth application of computer power, therefore, was making new products and services possible while marketing more selectively. For instance, in the allocation of loans, automated credit scoring replaced the judgement of the retail bank manager, which opened the door wider to personal unsecured loans.[44] Meanwhile, though customers often felt their loyalty was not appropriately rewarded, in many countries they were prone to inertia and endured long-term relationships with their main account provider.[45] It is widely believed that people are more likely to get divorced than to change their bank.

Throughout the 1980s and 1990s senior bankers believed that applying computer technology, ATMs in particular, could be a competitive weapon in their struggle to protect households' financial assets from the threat of other depository institutions (such as savings banks), insurance companies, security trading houses, and even retailers.[46] A contemporary survey of European bankers by Arthur Andersen found broad patterns of agreement on this topic but with national differences: French banks were confident of retaining over 50 per cent of deposits, while British and (West) German bankers believed that other depository institutions would take at least an equal share to theirs.[47] Banks' responses to these threats varied according their size, location, and geographic scope. In England, for instance, Barclays reopened retail branches on Saturdays in 1983. In Germany, Dresdner Bank, attempting to remedy its late adoption of the technology compared with German savings banks, invested heavily in 'state of the art' ATMs.

Yet another application of computer technology by banks related to managing the business better, by using computer models and computer-generated information in the everyday management practice of a financial institution. According to a contemporary study cited by *The Economist*, between 1980 and

1985 big American banks (in terms of assets) spent close to US$7 billion on electronic banking technology.[48] The same source estimated that between 11 and 15 per cent of non-interest expenses were assigned to automation every year. Banks were spending another 2 to 3 per cent on voice and data telecommunications. All this meant not only the biggest non-interest expense item for the banks but was also the biggest expenditure on the broad areas of automation and telecommunications of any industry except data-processing itself, and twice as big a share as that observed in banking in the early to mid-1970s.

Admittedly, few senior managers in the early 1980s were happy with their systems.[49] Operating costs and payroll disbursement as a proportion of total non-interest expenditure remained high, while management accounting in financial institutions remained an obscure science.[50] Banks, in particular those that pioneered the adoption of mainframe computers in the 1960s, began to deal with legacy systems. This was not limited to hardware. Software applications were particularly tricky, expensive, and not always delivered as promised while proven reliability and trustworthiness began to inhibit new developments. At the same time, bankers began to recognize that innovation on the back of computer applications was (and continued to be) heterogeneous because the effects from improving communication are distinct from those that improve the storage and processing of information.

Some empirical evidence suggests that, given banks' greater efficiency in information processing the limited economies of scale to be captured in banking could be associated with improvements in the application of computer technology.[51] This made scaling up more profitable. At the same time, however, improvements in information technology seem to have had little impact on attempts by the banks to save costs for multiple activities and capture economies of scope.[52] This was rather disappointing because banks from the 1980s on had actively pursued diversification across markets, customer groups, and geographies.[53]

1.4 How Times Change: A Map to the Book

As argued in section 1.3, location and time period are important for understanding social and technological change. As a result, this book emphasizes American and British experiences in exploring the origin, development, and globalization of the cash machine. Evidence emerges primarily from banking in industrialized nations. It is based on an eclectic and rich collection of archival business records, patents, photographs, videos, emails, internal bank magazines, specialized newspaper articles (e.g. *The Economist, Financial Times, American Banker, ABA Banking Journal, ATM Marketplace*), social media (e.g. contributions to Linkedin, Twitter, Facebook), and interviews with key players and former bankers and engineers (see appendix 1). It is framed by a conceptual discussion exploring innovation in the forms of retail payment. The content of the chapters will together provide a multi-layered analysis combining a clear chronology and detailed discussion of a specific aspect of operation; each chapter discusses the influence of a specific user group in shaping this technology. The ATM then serves as an anchor point from which to explore the interaction between changes in computer technology and banking practices, because the ATM embodies digital markets. It allows customers to program central computers of banks, proliferates all over the world, and is very much part of everyday life; but above all, it marks the physical and organizational boundaries of the bank. Figure 1.3 illustrates the recurrent themes and flow of ideas through this book.

As Figure 1.3 suggests, our story is embedded in a larger process of automation which sees bankers, engineers, and cash converging to produce a self-standing, offline device called the cash machine. The chapters following this introduction explain the origins of the technology, namely, its immediate predecessors and its invention as a stand-alone machine in Sweden (Chapter 2) and the United Kingdom (Chapter 3). Chapter 4 documents the early online versions. These explanations focus on the interaction of bankers and engineers. Alongside the genesis of the technology, you will find details on the mushrooming industrial organization of its European and American manufacturers.

Here it should be noted that lazy journalism created a myth around the origins of the ATM and widely diffused it through the Internet. In its different versions Luther Simjian, John Shepherd-Barron, James Goodfellow, or Donald Wetzel should receive the accolade of 'inventor of the ATM'. However, the historical record fails to identify a hero inventor; rather multiple independent versions of it were launched at more or less the same time in different countries. There is no evidence the engineers responsible for them knew of each other's existence before this launch, although in the space of weeks in 1967 or

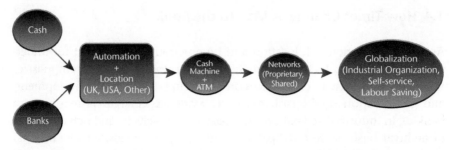

Figure 1.3. A basic model of the genesis and globalization of the ATM
Source: Author's own design.

even days, three different devices were set running. In spite of the great fanfare, there was no real race to market. Moreover, there was no single personality or competition to be the 'inventor of the ATM' before 1997, the 25th anniversary of the first launch in Barclays' Enfield (London) branch. The notion of a Eureka moment, an epiphany or the like emerged only after TV reporters found it too tempting to resist.[54] Yet, regardless that the celebration of a specific device as the first to be operational is germane to the process of invention and the maintenance of a complex technology, it is mentioned here in order to provide some clarity to that myth.

More damaging for the current myth was that, in their thirst for fame, none of these white, mostly Christian, middle-class men ever acknowledged the work of the others. In radical opposition, the narrative underpinning my story is not only empirically based but emphasizes teamwork and collaboration in and across business organizations, and as a result devalues the figure of the inventor as 'lone wolf'. This does not ignore important personal contributions—indeed the individuals named in this story were carefully chosen—but it highlights the increasingly intricate business and technological web required to capture any modern, successful, retail payment technology. Even then I feel my review to be incomplete, and to have done justice to none but the essential spinners.

From the outset, the evolution of designing a cash machine had to overcome a number of technical challenges. For instance, the early cash machines were single, integrated pieces of machinery—as opposed to today's multi-component ATMs—and thus more intolerant of failure, even in their minor parts. Failure was unsatisfactory, not least because it impacted on legal and operational requirements. Engineers on both sides of the Atlantic and in Japan worked hard to improve the machines' security and reliability and, more important, to develop online, real-time connectivity with central computers. This required changes in design and the development of communication and message encryption protocols; it also meant digitalizing customer records. In short, the online devices described throughout Chapter 4 are only the initial step in the monumental task of providing real-time banking.

Chapters 5 and 6 describe the local underpinnings of the globalization of cash withdrawal services through the evolution of proprietary shared ATM networks. During the 1970s, bankers expected that a proprietary fleet of ATMs could become a source of competitive advantage over stand-alone small and medium-sized banks, who could not lay out the cost and expertise needed to deploy and maintain such a fleet. By the early 1980s, however, the ATM had passed the 'proof of concept' stage. Chapter 5 tells how regulation (in some states of the USA), plus the economics of shared networks, led to a process whereby in the ten to fifteen years after 1980 shared ATM networks became the norm in retail baking.

Alongside this process, changes in functionality and the potential to reduce queues quicker than human tellers could enable banks to allocate low value, high volume services such as balance enquiries to the ATM, at the same time as giving branch staff the duty of selling high value, low volume services such as mortgages and car insurance. This reallocation opened bank doors to a great many people who had previously gone without a current/checking account, not to mention self-service banking.

The advent of so-called 'non-stop' computer systems and the personal computer were two developments in the 1980s; although they began by changing the fringes of banking they ultimately revolutionized it. However, fault resistant computing was essential before small and mid-size banks could share ATM networks and thus successfully contest the apparent advantage of the proprietary networks set up by their larger rivals. Equally instrumental, the operating system of micro-computers was needed to enable the ATM to work as a terminal of the bank's central computer system.

Chapter 6 details the competitive dynamics leading to the formation of a global shared network of ATMs, while analysing the trends of ATM adoption in different countries. Another theme in this chapter is the politics behind the formation of a global ATM network (on the back of protocols set by Visa and MasterCard). This part of the story therefore describes the interaction of banks, payment card companies, and other firms managing ATM networks.

Chapter 7 considers the rise of the independent ATM deployers (IAD) which depended on a transformation in the industrial organization of cash withdrawals. This transformation could not have taken place without the ending of the surcharge ban, and a new breed of ATMs. Innovations in design and operation, that opened the door to new 'lighter' devices enabled them to be placed in a number of non-bank branch locations, such as casinos on Mississippi paddle boats and even in Antarctica. These were often managed by specialized, non-financial companies (also known as IADs) which further changed the competitive dynamics of the industry.

As in many other industries, people around the ATM formed trade associations. In Chapter 7 we draw attention to the most widespread around the world, called the ATM Industry Association (ATMIA).[55] Industry associations allow communities of practice to meet and discuss new system requirements (both formally and informally), as well as to lobby executive and legislative powers (particularly in the USA) to defend members' interests. Through its twenty-year history, ATMIA has become the prime location for meetings of like-minded people working with ATMs in banks, IADs, security companies, cash distribution companies, etc.

The rise of the IAD and the miniaturization of the machines, therefore, made for a much broader set of possible locations for ATMs, arguably increasing their penetration and usefulness. British and American consumers, however, were diametrically opposed in their attitudes to surcharging: while in the USA surcharging was welcome as the price for convenience, in the UK surcharging, perceived as a 'tax' on the poor, has largely disappeared. Whether these attitudes explain the much greater number of ATMs per capita in the USA than in the UK remains an open question.

The advent of the IAD and low-end ATM, together with surcharging, needed large numbers of individual consumers who would trust technology and develop self-service habits. However, as noted in Chapter 8, ATM networks in the 1990s were still error prone and this gave rise to a growing number of withdrawals (aka 'phantom withdrawals') for which neither client nor bank wanted to take responsibility. These were mostly associated with low value transactions and hence consumers (certainly in Britain) had few incentives to fight them through the courts. Instead, they mostly decided to bear the loss and stop using the technology. For the financial institutions which had made substantial investments in developing ATM networks, persuading customers to accept the 'new' technology and limiting the chance of fraud by fictitious claims of 'phantom withdrawal' were equally important.

It is argued that a feature of innovation in retail payments is the striking of a balance between, on the one hand, unexpected responses by users, adoption, and maturation cum customer trust and, on the other, investments in infrastructure. It is also argued in Chapter 8 that building the infrastructure for ATM networks, together with the required organizational learning and competencies tied into ATMs, enabled banks to successfully roll out other self-service alternatives, most notably telephone, Internet, and mobile banking. In other words, the ATM effectively laid the foundation of the cashless society.[56] But this only became possible when, first, the technology permitted it and, second, when the details of the rights and responsibilities surrounding the use of digital devices for self-service banking had been ironed out, thanks to the popularity of the ATM.

Chapter 9 looks at the impact of automation on staff at branches. This comparison of UK and US experiences rehearses the long debate over the destruction of jobs by automation. But there is a twist. Rather than focusing on the trade-off between capital expenditure and labour costs, I introduce Chandler's 'throughput' (i.e. transaction volume) as a key variable for decision-making.

To conclude, 'after hours' cash dispensing was the *raison d'être* for the origins of the cash machine. Whether this remains the case is debatable. Nonetheless, one could construct a straightforward narrative arc that links the first devices in 1967 to the proliferation of self-service banking and electronic payments in the twenty-first century. Such a narrative, however, would obscure important discontinuities in the history of retail payment technology, as well as the transformation of retail banking in the late twentieth century.

Such a narrative would also overestimate the importance of innovation in reducing cost structures, while disregarding both the need for the broader adoption of technology and the ways in which the process of adoption comes about (one that often has to negotiate conflicting objectives between users). Such a narrative would also assume that globalization is a force levelling the playing field for one and all, although retail payment systems are characterized by discontinuities outside of national borders and have strong national roots.

This book aims to address these themes while, at the same time, offering an opportunity to better understand the efforts and investments required to create and maintain ubiquitous self-service technology. Another theme of importance is the way in which payment systems shape patterns of consumption, just as much as the reverse.

Notes

1. 'Paul Volcker: Think More Boldly', *The Wall Street Journal*, 14 December 2009, accessed 24 October 2017, <http://www.wsj.com/articles/SB10001424052748704825504574586330960597134>.
2. Interview (telephone) with Jenny Campbell, former chief operating officer and managing director of Hanco (2006–10) and CEO and Chairman of YourCash (2010–16), by B. Bátiz-Lazo, 22 February 2017.
3. 'Global ATM Market and Forecasts to 2019', *RBR London* (2014 and 2017, London).
4. 'Payment Instruments in Profile: The ATM', *ATM Industry Association*, 16 March 2017, accessed 7 October 2017, <https://www.atmia.com/news/payment-instrument-in-profile-the-atm/4628>.
5. Tom Hutchings, RBR London, ATM & Cyber Security Conference, London, 10 October 2017.
6. Mike Lee, 'The ATM at 100, A Forecast for 2017–2067: Part 1', *ATM Marketplace*, 8 September 2017, accessed 7 October 2017, <https://www.atmmarketplace.com/articles/atms-at-100-a-forecast-for-2017-2067-part-1/>. See also 'Extreme ATMs Dossier', ATM Industry Association, accessed 7 October 2017, <https://www.atmia.com/files/50th%20Anniversary/Extreme_ATMs_Dossier_-_PUBLISHED(1).pdf>.
7. 'National Poetry Month', *Rosecantine*, accessed 9 June 2014, <http://rosecantine.com/2009/04/15/national-poetry-month-poem-the-atm/>.
8. *Barbershop*, directed by Tim Story (2002, Beverly Hills, CA: Metro-Goldwyn-Mayer), Film. *Breaking Bad*, 'Peakaboo' (Series 2, episode 6), directed by Peter Medak, written by Vince Gillian and J. Roberts (24 December 2009, New York, NY: AMC Network Entertainment), TV series. From the same series 'Green Light' (Series 3, episode 4), directed by Scott Winant, written by Vince Gillian and Sam Catlin (11 April 2010); 'Sunset' (Series 3, episode 6), directed by John Shiban, written by Vince Gillian and John Shiban (25 April 2010); and *ATM*, directed by David Brooks (2012, Santa Monica, CA: Gold Circle Films), Film.

9. A similar pattern is shown for average daily transactions in Europe by Shepherd-Barron (2017, 181), although the latter failed to disclose the source of the data and calculation method.
10. 'The ATM Turns 50', *Daily Mail (Mail Online)*, 21 September 2017, <http://www.dailymail.co.uk/news/article-4906962/ATM-50-An-oddity-changed-consumer-behavior.html#ixzz4uqKOPNYq>.
11. Personal communication (Linkedin message) from John Howard-Jones, former branch clerk Midland Bank, with B. Bátiz-Lazo, 7 October 2017.
12. Bob Meara, 'Bemoaning the Decline in Branch Foot Traffic', *Celent blog*, accessed 11 August 2014, <http://bankingblog.celent.com/2014/02/05/bemoaning-the-decline-in-branch-foot-traffic-it-could-be-worse/>.
13. Ceruzzi (2003, 80).
14. Revell (1983, 42); McAndrews (1991, 4).
15. Bátiz-Lazo and Reese (2010).
16. Coopey (2004b).
17. Coopey (2004b, 175).
18. Richardson (1970). Other efforts include McAndrews (1991), Sienkiewicz (2002), and Hayashi et al. (2003, 2006). Others who have written on the emergence and diffusion of ATMs in the USA include doctoral dissertations by Hopkins (1986), Lane (1989), Lee (2000), Lozano (1987), and Peffers (1991).
19. Hopton (1979); Kirkman (1987); Howells and Hine (1993).
20. Coopey (2004b); Barrie (2006).
21. Ackrill and Hannah (2001, 214 and 332–4).
22. Bátiz-Lazo (2009).
23. For instance Bátiz-Lazo and Maixé-Altés (2011a, 2011b); Maixé-Altés (2012, 2013).
24. Vázquez-Alanís (2007).
25. McAndrews (2003).
26. Coombs et al. (1992).
27. Haigh and Paju (2016).
28. e.g. Effosse (2017); Jaremski and Mathy (2017).
29. Bátiz-Lazo and Billings (2007); Bátiz-Lazo and Boyns (2003); Bátiz-Lazo and Wood (2002); Bonin (2004); Booth (2001, 2004); McKenney and Fisher (1993); Wardley (2000); Yavitz (1967).
30. Bátiz-Lazo and Wood (2002); Richardson (1970).
31. Bátiz-Lazo and Wardley (2007); Bátiz-Lazo and Wood (2002); Wardley (2000). Note that by 1911, a process of amalgamation left some 80 per cent of deposits in the hands of five banks (Midland, Barclays, Lloyds, Westminster, and National and Provincial). These plus some six others controlled access to the cheque clearing system. Hence the name 'clearing banks'. Amalgamations also had the effect of providing clearing banks with a national web of offices and retail bank branches. Building societies are mutual organizations which for most of their history specialized in deposit taking and mortgage provision. Societies used agents and developed retail branches more organically than clearing banks did. Other participants in British retail finance included insurance companies, trustee savings banks, and hire purchase companies. After the 1970s, these were joined by the National Giro Bank and the Co-operative Bank.

32. Bank of England Archive (henceforth BoEA), C54/10 Chief Cashiers Duplicate Letters, Committee of London Clearing Banks (henceforth CLCB), Meetings of 2 July, 30 June 1964; C. Webb, 'Never on a Saturday', *The Times*, 28 June 1969: 8; A. Thomas, 'Problems Ahead as Saturday Banking Ends', *The Times*, 28 June 1969: 11.

33. Davies (1981); Bátiz-Lazo and Billings (2007).

34. Bátiz-Lazo et al. (2014b); Martin (2011); Wardley (2000).

35. Bátiz-Lazo and Wardley (2007).

36. Bátiz-Lazo et al. (2011a); Bátiz-Lazo and Wood (2002).

37. e.g. Bátiz-Lazo and Haigh (2012); Bátiz-Lazo et al. (2011b).

38. On office mechanization see Bátiz-Lazo and Wardley (2007); Heide (2009); Wardley (2003); Wootton and Kemmerer (2007). On the collaboration between Bank of America and Stanford Research Institute see McKenney (1995); McKenney and Fisher (1993).

39. On SWIFT see Scott and Zachariadis (2014).

40. Chemical Bank (New York, NY) launched a service called 'Pronto' in 1981. It allowed customers to use home computers to check their balances and make payments. This is the first recorded home banking service. Within a year similar experiments were on the way in California, Texas, and Florida. A similar but earlier service was launched in (West) Germany using videotext. Source: 'Banking on the Inhuman Factor', *The Economist*, 27 March 1982: 85; and 'Cash from the Other Fellow's Tap', *The Economist*, 18 September 1982: 94. See further Bátiz-Lazo and Woldensenbet (2006); Pennings and Harianto (1992).

41. The indiscriminate mass mailing of credit cards in the late 1950s and 1960s in the USA and Britain is well known and documented, e.g. Ackrill and Hannah (2001, 187–8). However, this changed partly as a result of regulation in the USA and also as business practices in other countries became more selective as they adopted the US model of bank-issued credit cards (Bátiz-Lazo and Del Angel 2016). See also Essinger (1987, 4).

42. As late as 1974 the highest-volume cash machines in the USA—in downtown Chicago—processed 2,000 transactions per month, which paled in comparison with the average 4,000 by a human bank teller at this time (Essinger 1987, 4).

43. Bátiz-Lazo et al. (2014b); Booth (2007).

44. Poon (2011); Vik (2017).

45. This continued to be an issue as late as 2016. That year a survey of 1,000 US consumers by NGData found a negative correlation between age and satisfaction in its sample, with 51 per cent of respondents aged 18–34 saying they would be happier if their banks understood them better, compared to just 27 per cent of those aged 35 or more. Source: 'Customers Want their Banks to Know Them Better—Now and Into the Future', *Businesswire*, accessed 19 July 2016, <http://www.businesswire.com/news/home/20160719005183/en/Customers-Banks---Future>.

46. 'Beating Back the Outsiders', *The Economist*, 22 March 1986: 59.

47. 'Banking in Europe: The Next Ten Years', Arthur Andersen (London, n.d.), cited in 'Beating Back the Outsiders'.

48. 'Wiring Main Street (Survey International Banking)', *The Economist*, 29 March 1986: 15.

49. Channon (1978); McFarlan et al. (1983); Revell (1983).
50. Studies critical of management accounting in banking include Drury (1994, 1998); Soin et al. (2002).
51. Marinc (2013). See further Lescure (2016) and references therein.
52. Mitchell and Onvural (1996).
53. Canals (1993, 1997).
54. Shepherd-Barron (2017, 85).
55. Other important industry associations include Asociación de Operadores de Transferencias Electrónicas de Fondos y Servicios de Información de América Latina (ATEFI) or Association for Electronic Funds Transfer and Information, which brings together like-minded people in Latin America and the Caribbean. Source: 'ATMIA y ATEFI Anuncian Acuerdo de Cooperación para el Mercado de Cajeros Automáticos de América Latina', *Businesswire*, 6 May 2017, accessed 13 October 2017, <http://www.businesswire.com/news/home/20150506005264/es/>.
56. The term 'cashless society' was originally coined in the USA in the mid-1950s to describe a future state of the economy in which a system of electronic transactions replaced the use of coins, cheques, and banknotes as a medium of exchange. See further Bátiz-Lazo et al. (2014a).

2

Was There a White-Heat Moment of Invention?

2.1 About Bankers (the Users) and Engineers (the Producers) of Technology

Here we detail the roles of engineers and bankers in the conception and initial deployment of cash machines in the 1960s. These two groups, as well as the organizations where they worked and the forums where they interacted, have always been the most active users shaping the complex technology that is today's ATM. The interaction between bankers and engineers is evident in the details of making purchases and the way in which this technology fitted the overall drive of banks to computerize administrative systems. The deployment of the first cash machines marked a new stage in the long-term process of mechanization of retail banking because the cash machine increased the minimum capital investment necessary to compete within retail banking. In this sense, cash dispensing technology was perceived by individual banks as a potential source of competitive advantage.

It has been claimed that the development of cash machines in the USA was influenced by learning gained from introducing punched card tabulators and early computer technology;[1] and that geographical restrictions on retail branch banking also played an important role.[2] However, most accounts fail to acknowledge that the growth of cash machines and ATMs in the 1970s and 1980s marked the first time since the start of computerization in the late 1950s that technology was seriously modifying services for retail customers. Changes went beyond the superficial use (from a customer's perspective) of pre-printed stationery, mechanical annotations, or magnetic characters in cheques, while supporting an increasingly mobile yet urban population that no longer had to rely on any single bank branch. It has also seldom been acknowledged that the advent of automatically dispensed banknotes coincided with the growth of stand-alone contraptions to automatically sell sweets, petrol, access to public transport, and even dry cleaning. As an industry-specific invention, the cash machine initially responded to a need for an 'after hours' currency distribution service in the UK and Sweden, while its adoption in the USA related to securing new retail deposits. From the outset the evolution of its design had to overcome a number of technical challenges including two notable features: first, the overall security of devices storing currency that guaranteed off-hours service; and, second, ensuring that the accounts that were debited belonged to the people taking the cash. These two features were technical preconditions for 'industrializing' the large-scale, unmanned provision of retail financial services such as banking by telephone, mobile and Internet banking.

By documenting the interaction between banks and engineers that led to the introduction of currency dispensing equipment, this chapter also tells how bankers largely disregarded the patent system. Bankers aimed to gain competitive advantage from cash machines by securing exclusivity agreements for the domestic market from a particular manufacturer (e.g. De La Rue for Barclays or Speytec-Burroughs for Midland). Bankers' attitudes to innovation were in stark contrast to those of engineers. As shown below, patents on cash machines were secured owing to the initiative of engineers (e.g. Chubb, Smiths Industries, Speytec). For engineers the patent system remains an institutional outcome of history through which society recognized and legitimized creative activity, as well as a vehicle for diffusing innovation and rewarding intellectual property.[3]

Retail finance is a market where patents are an 'imperfect measure of invention'.[4] Bankers overlook the possibility of a unique or proprietary element in innovation, for several reasons. First, retail financial markets are largely confined to national boundaries, thus limiting the scope for any long-term investment. Second, any innovation in service, or with the potential to increase productivity, can easily be replicated by direct competitors. Third, before the 1990s, retail banking was a market difficult to contest without the physical elements of logistics and distribution. In most countries, banks had sole access to wholesale cheque clearing facilities and the cost of developing a 'bricks and mortar' branch network was beyond the financial capacity of many potential competitors.

Fourth, 'banking [was] a business of people, and thus economies of scale [were] not really something you could aim to achieve'.[5] For most of the twentieth century, retail transactions for financial intermediaries in Europe and the USA were initiated at the counters of retail branches while staff inside these branches relied on manual processes to conduct their business. The introduction of computer technology in general and cash machines in particular began a trend of doing more work centrally and less at retail branches—with the subsequent loss of autonomy for the branch as a 'self-sufficient production unit'.[6] Hence, bankers' strategic priority, which disregarded the patent system and innovation, had less to do with the ability of individual banks to retain an advantageous market position as with their ability to control and reduce the potential costs of doing so.[7]

Fifth, the result of bank runs and the financial crises of the nineteenth century was that banking had to continually portray values of 'trust' and 'confidence'.[8] But embodying these values often made banks 'conservative' and 'dull' in the eyes of the general public. Hence the need to incorporate the otherwise opposing values of 'modernity' and 'innovation'. Indeed, mechanization and, more often, applications of computer technology were widely advertised by retail banks as a way of achieving 'modernity'.[9] However, such an achievement led to yet another apparent contradiction: on the one hand, the financial intermediaries at the vanguard of technological change explored and adapted new applications to exploit existing functions and also developed new capabilities. On the other, directors and senior managers of these intermediaries preserved many of their internal practices largely unchanged; although mechanization and applications of computer technology were altering the speed at which routine practices could be followed, no one was redefining practices and routines from first principles.

The reminder of this chapter deals in chronological order with the steps in the genesis of currency dispensing equipment. These are summarized in Table 2.1.

Section 2.2 briefly discusses early and unsuccessful attempts in Japan and the USA. Section 2.3 outlines trailblazer banks in Sweden and Chapter 3 those in the UK, both of which deployed devices in 1967. The Swedish and British experiences deserve greater attention because they both had significant impact on the international market. In this process we focus on some of the engineering challenges that different teams faced in order to deliver what is now a ubiquitous and yet industry-specific technology. This aids our understanding of the way that cash machines appear alongside the drive to automate operations in retail counters, both responses to pressures in the labour market. The result of this process is a wholly different conception of the cash machine, because it challenges the predominant descriptions of a currency dispenser in the conventional wisdom (which often portrays it as having originated from a single isolated inventor) and moves towards a description that incorporates a multiplicity of concurrent events, highlighting the feedback in the innovative process between inventor, manufacturer, and user.

2.2 Early Attempts at Cash Automation

The history of automation in banking through industry-specific devices is long and colourful. For instance, one can easily find references to devices at

Table 2.1. Milestones in the invention of the cash machine, 1960–1975

Date operational (Country)	Financial services firm	Manufacturer/ applicant (Patent no.) (Priority date)	Model (Moniker)	Inventor (according to patent when available)	Description of device in patent (description in the media)	Comment
April 1961 (USA)	First National City Bank (Citibank)	Reflectone Electronics (US 3079603) (June 1960)	Bankograph	Simjian	Depository machine combined with image recording means	First patent for a 'subscriber control apparatus' with priority of April 1959 (US 3039582)
July 1966 (Japan)		(Possibly Omron-Tateisi JP 4279966A) (July 1966)	(Computer Loan Machine)	(Yamamoto, Mizuta, Tanaka, Asada)	Accepting credit card and advancing cash on loan	
Oct. 1966 (USA)	American Bankers Association	Diebold			(Automatic cheque deposit and cash distribution device)	Prototype
June 1967 (UK)	Barclays Bank	De La Rue	DACS or De La Rue Automatic Cash System (Barclaycash)	Sheppard-Barron (team leader) and undisclosed	(Customer operated cash dispenser)	First confirmed multiple device deployment worldwide
July 1967 (Sweden)	Swedish savings banks	Asea-Metior	Bankomat Mark 2 (Minuten)	Arfvidson and undisclosed	(Customer operated dispenser)	First confirmed multiple device deployment in Sweden
July 1967 (UK)	Westminster Bank	Chubb/Smiths Industries (GB 1197183) (May 1966)	Chubb MD2	Davis, Oliveira, and Goodfellow	Customer operated dispensing system	First patent on PIN/PAN
Sept. 1968 (USA)	Citibank				(Cash station that responds to card in conjunction with a secret code issued to customer)	Prototype
Sept. 1968 (UK)	Midland Bank	Speytec/Burroughs (GB 1329964) (Sept. 1969)	RT2000 Remote Teller	Edwards, Perkins, Newcome, and others	Dispensing items in response to security card	First activation card with magnetic stripe
Sept. 1969 (USA)	Chemical Bank	Docutel (US 3761682) (Oct. 1971)	Total Teller	Barnes, Chastain, and Wetzel	Credit card automatic currency dispenser	First confirmed multiple device deployment in the USA
Dec. 1969 (Japan)	Sumitomo Bank	Omron-Tateisi (GB 1300848) (April 1969)	Kei YM4050	Tateisi, Mizuta, and Ano	Cash dispensing and receiving system	First confirmed multiple device deployment in Japan
Dec. 1972 (UK)	Lloyds Bank	IBM (US 3798359) (June 1971)	2984 cash machine (Cashpoint)	Feistel	Block cipher cryptographic system	First confirmed multiple deployment of online device
August 1973 (USA)		Diebold (US 3949364) (July 1972)	TABS 300	Clark, Barone, and Kinker	Automatic remote banking system and equipment	First reference to automatic teller machine (ATM) in the patent record

Source: Own estimates.

the turn of the twentieth century. Examples include a 'sales pitch' in 1904 for an 'automated coin-counting and coin-wrapping' device published in *Bankers Magazine*.[10] In 1914, Alfred Ilg was granted patent US 1094073 envisioning an automatic identification device for unmanned financial transactions. It is not clear if Ilg's and many other such devices found actual application. But, clearly, the possibility of bringing in machines to help retail financial services was there.

Many popular accounts of the first attempt at a mechanical currency dispensing technology point to the 'Bankograph' developed by Luther George Simjian (1905–97), allegedly in 1939.[11] Over his lifetime Simjian secured over two hundred patents,[12] but an apparent typographical error seems to have been perpetrated regarding Simjian's first patents relating to the Bankograph: these were US 3039582 filed on 9 April 1959 and US 3079603 filed on 30 June 1960. Simjian secured some twenty other similar patents during the 1960s and his efforts are acknowledged throughout the patent record as a 'Prior Art Device'. However, there is no evidence to suggest that he engaged in anything related to the Bankograph before the late 1950s.[13]

The Bankograph (see Figure2.1) was an automated envelope deposit machine that had no currency dispensing features. Work on this device seems to have emerged out of Simjian's preoccupation with automatic photographic vending machines and is part of a larger concept of customer-orientated automation, which swept the USA and elsewhere, as reflected by contemporary attempts at the self-service provision of sweets, petrol, transport, dry cleaning, and currency. The New York City press advertised the trial of two Bankograph machines in 1961 at First National City Bank, New York, NY (henceforward Citibank).[14] It is unclear why these trials went no further, although the threat of legal action by the regulators seems to have influenced the decision.[15] The Bankograph, however, embodied the anxiety of US banks to find alternative means to capture core deposits; while the concern of British and Swedish bankers, as will be evident below, was cash distribution.

A more intriguing cash dispensing device appeared in Japan in 1966.[16] Customers activated it with a 'special credit' card, and rather than accessing current account balances, it dispensed ¥20,000 (about $55) on a three-month loan. Like the British and Swedish inventions described below, this Japanese device, after checking for authenticity but without directly verifying the user's account balance, issued banknotes when prompted by an activation token. Tokens for British, Japanese, and Swedish devices were issued to creditworthy customers. The main difference was that British and Swedish banks debited the whole amount of the withdrawal within three working days, whereas the Japanese spread it out to three months at 5.5 per cent annual interest.

The existence of this technology challenges the British claim to have made the first operational cash machine, but it is unclear exactly how it worked.

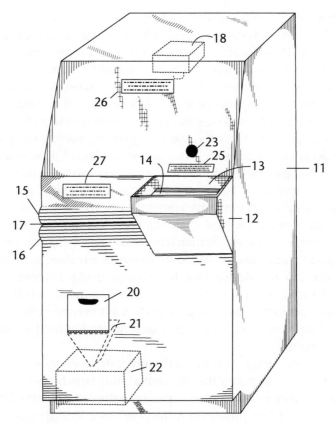

Figure 2.1. Simjian's early concept of a currency dispenser, 1959
Source: Patent US 3039582 (filed 1959, granted 1962).

Moreover, Japanese sources seem to coincide in marking 1969 as the year when a machine was first deployed in Japan from which customers could withdraw cash (but of course not online). They did so in the offices of the former Sumitomo Bank, but the technology had no immediate impact on the international market, whereas British and Swedish devices were very soon operational, licensed, or replicated elsewhere in Europe and North America.

2.3 Metior's Bankomat: One of the Hottest Swedish Models

The origin of the Swedish technology dates back to the late 1950s when the Technical Committee of the joint purchasing company Sparfrämjandet responded to a group of savings banks wishing to introduce direct-to-account payroll services to compete with commercial banks.[17] Thanks to the savings

27

banks' links to the unions, the number of payroll accounts in them increased.[18] However, so did the associated administrative costs, because the savings banks had to expand their workforce to deal with an increased volume of transactions at retail branches. Sparfrämjandet wanted some type of machine that could dispense banknotes, and discussed the issue with Securitas—which had experience in the development of automatic passage systems and the use of coded personal identification numbers (PINs).

As the name suggests, Securitas, was a Swedish engineering company, specialized in developing alarm systems and access solutions.[19] Prior work around relevant technologies started in 1964 with a gate control device that combined pressing four digits on a keyboard while inserting a coded punched-hole plastic card. Another relevant development was a system (called Tankomat) that combined a card reader and a four-digit personal number for self-service at petrol pumps, which was operational in 1965.[20] Following the approach by Sparfrämjandet, Securitas understood that a significant investment had to be made to develop the device that the savings banks required and thus approached the Rausing Company (now called Restello), which supplied coin-sorting machines to the savings banks.[21] A joint venture company called Metior was formed in 1966, for which engineering staff moved to Lund and a year later to Malmö.

Engineers from Metior collaborated with staff from Sparfrämjandet to design what was to be called the 'Bankomat' (this later became the generic brand name for currency dispensers throughout the Baltic region). The first of these was installed in Uppsala on 6 July 1967 (see its activation token in Figure 2.2). Two days later, a similar device was shown by the commercial bank Svenska Handelsbanken in Stockholm. Serial production began in 1968, thanks to an order for twenty Bankomats from Sparfrämjandet, which also made a number of requirements—further indicating that the savings banks actively contributed to the shaping of the new technology. By February 1970, Metior had produced 178 cash machines, of which 37 were destined for the domestic market (24 were delivered to the savings banks) and 141 were for export. Through the early 1970s, Metior continued to expand foreign sales to include devices deployed throughout Scandinavia, the Netherlands, Germany, France, Israel, Spain, and even the former Soviet Union.[22]

In its early years Metior developed four generations of cash machines. The first generation was not sold commercially. The second and third were developed for the savings banks and the fourth was designed for the commercial banks and the French market. The cards used to activate Bankomat Mark 2 and Mark 3 were made of steel and used perforated holes for identification. The Mark 2 and Mark 3 limited each card to one withdrawal per day, but this was unsatisfactory in that it left open the possibility of withdrawing cash immediately before and immediately after midnight. The Mark 4 abandoned the

Figure 2.2. Activation token for Bankomat, 1967
Source: Author's scan of Lars Arvidson's card.

punched-hole cards and replaced them with information embedded in a magnetic stripe that had been developed by the French Société Générale d'Automation. This technology ensured that withdrawals were made only from accounts with positive balances, as demanded by French banks. The Bankomat was then poised to become the dominant machine in the French and Swiss markets.

But while Metior had success in foreign lands, it lost its market share in Sweden (see also Chapter 4). This is connected with two events that took place in 1971. First, commercial banks, Kungliga Postverket (the Swedish Royal Post Office), and the rural credit societies together created a subsidiary called Bankomatcentralen (the Automatic Cash Dispenser Centre) with the mission of

29

installing and running currency dispensing equipment for its patrons. Managers of Bankomatcentralen had discretion over decisions regarding the location of cash machines, marketing (under the Bankomat brand), and the administration of card registration, data-processing, clearing, and statistical information. Soon afterwards, Bankomatcentralen abandoned Metior, having opted for different equipment.

The second event related to the appointment of Jan Rydh as the director of Spadab. Spadab, formed in 1961, was a company jointly owned by the Swedish savings banks to house their computer and data-processing activities. In 1971, shortly after his appointment, Rydh led a delegation of Spadab staff to attend the Automated Teller Machine Conference in Chicago. Impressed by what he and his colleagues had seen, once they returned to Sweden Rydh instructed the engineers at Spadab to start what became known as the 'Minuten project'. The aim was to discontinue stand-alone devices (such as the early Bankomats) and promote the large-scale adoption by the saving banks of currency dispensers connected online to Spadab's computers. In searching for potential suppliers, the firm made contact with a number of manufacturers, and ultimately three companies competed for the project. These were the Swedish company Asea-Metior (by this point Metior had lost its independence), the British company Chubb & Son's Lock and Safe Company Group (Chubb), and the US-based company Docutel. In 1975 the savings banks finally abandoned Metior machines instead choosing Docutel as their supplier of currency machines with the Swedish company Datasaab responsible for their installation and servicing.

There are at least three explanations for the savings banks' abandoning of Asea-Metior's machines. The first relates to Asea-Metior's engineers being unable to offer robust security for its devices. The second concerns the weakness of the US dollar against the Swedish krona, making the Asea-Metior dispenser expensive in relation to the Docutel machine. The third explanation is that the early 1970s saw the swift and widespread adoption across many countries of online terminals at retail branches. Independent producers of currency dispensers, such as Asea-Metior, faced difficulties when customers demanded wholly integrated systems, such as those offered by Burroughs, IBM, or NCR,[23] which could deliver a central computer, teller terminals, and cash machines.

Notes

1. David K. Allison, 'Interview with Mr Donal Wetzel', *National Museum of American History*, 21 September 1995, accessed 16 April 2007, <http://americanhistory.si.edu/comphist/wetzel.htm>.

2. Hayashi et al. (2003); McAndrews (1991, 5).
3. Cooper (1991).
4. Sullivan (1990).
5. Personal communication (telephone) with Sir Jeremy Morse, by B. Bátiz-Lazo, 19 October 1994. For a summary of economies of scale and scope in banking see Lescure (2016).
6. Ackrill and Hannah (2001, 328–9).
7. Wood and Bátiz-Lazo (1997, 36).
8. Schroeder (2003).
9. Bátiz-Lazo and Wardley (2007, 179).
10. 'Automatic Coin-Counting and Coin-Wraping (sic) Machine', *The Bankers Magazine*, 68 (1904): 661, accessed 3 July 2012, <http://ow.ly/bZpCU>.
11. 'Automated Teller Machine', *Wikipedia*, accessed 16 April 2007, <http://en.wikipedia. org/wiki/Automated_teller_machine> and 'Lamelson-MIT', accessed 16 April 2007, <http://web.mit.edu/invent/iow/simjian.html>.
12. 'Luther G. Simjian', *Engineering and Technology Wiki*, accessed 1 October 2014, <http://www.ieeeghn.org/wiki/index.php/Luther_G._Simjian>.
13. Bátiz-Lazo and Reid (2008, 2011).
14. 'Machine Accepts Cash Deposits', *The New York Times*, 12 April 2016. There are reports of another device that accepted deposits in the form of cheques and cash, and rejected counterfeits. There is no indication of its make or whether it was operational. See 'A Fascinating Teller', *ABA Banking Journal*, September 1956: 95.
15. See further Zimmer (1971).
16. 'Instant Cash via Credit Cards', *ABA Banking Journal*, January 1967: 99; 'Fast machine with a buck', *Pacific Stars & Stripes*, 14 July 1996: 7.
17. Unless otherwise stated, this section borrows freely from Harper and Bátiz-Lazo (2013, 11–12) Bátiz-Lazo et al. (2014b, 14–18). Savings banks were established as not-for-profit retail depository institutions in Scotland in 1810, with the aim of engendering thrift amongst the emergent proletariat. See further Bátiz-Lazo and Maixé-Altés (2011b); Fishlow (1961); Payne (1967); Ross (2002).
18. In Swedish there is no difference between 'salaries' and 'wages', hence the adoption of the term 'payroll'. In the 1950s and 1960s commercial banks were also in the process of attracting the direct-to-account payment of payrolls and, given their prior relations with large firms, they were having the same success as the savings banks, or more. On Swedish commercial banks see Husz (forthcoming).
19. I am grateful for the assistance of Lars Arfvidson in clarifying the origins of Metior. Source: Personal communication (email) from Lars Arfvidson, engineer at Securitas and Metior, with B. Bátiz-Lazo, 2 July 2017.
20. This system for unmanned petrol stations was introduced at an Esso service station in southern Stockholm on 10 December 1965. Personal communication (email) from Lars Arfvidson, technical manager Metior, with B. Bátiz-Lazo, 29 June 2017.
21. Coin supplying devices were common in mid twenty-century banking. For instance, Gustav Tauschek of Vienna, Austria and IBM were granted patent US 1976585 in 1934 for a contraption that supplied coins of different denominations when activated by a perforated card.

22. By 1975 exports included 90 devices each to Switzerland and (West) Germany, and a massive 700 to France ('Cash Dispensers—Swedish Style', *The Banker*, September 1975: 1138). Michaud (2004) documents the Bankomat in France.
23. Of greater success were Olivetti teller terminals, which could emulate a number of different computer manufacturers.

3

The British Are Coming!

3.1 British Banking in the Early 1960s

The simultaneous innovations that occurred in Britain are particularly intriguing because of the interactions between senior bank managers and independent groups of engineers. This process of innovation is rooted in the strategies of the ten-strong membership of the Committee of London Clearing Banks (CLCB). Known in the vernacular as the clearing banks, for most of the twentieth century the members of the Committee controlled the domestic payment system and were the biggest in terms of total assets and number of retail branches.[1] For example, Lloyds Bank, ranked fourth in terms of deposits, employed 17,470 staff and had some 2,000 retail bank branches in the UK in 1950.[2]

In 1955 the CLCB formed an Electronics Sub-Committee. This working party had a mandate to research the possibilities of bringing electronic computing to British banking and was pivotal in establishing banks that would become early computer pioneers. Under its leadership, the banks met at home and abroad with a number of existing and would-be electronic computer manufacturers and users, in order to discuss their common and specific requirements.

In 1961 Barclays Bank, Britain's biggest in terms of deposits, opened the first centre dedicated to housing a mainframe computer and the other clearing banks soon followed.[3] They were all motivated to reduce congestion for the tellers of retail branches. The combination of the First World War, the depression of the inter-war years, and high economic growth in the decades that followed the end of the Second World War, resulted in inadequate levels of male staff at the clearing banks.[4] Female clerical workers—who were paid lower wages—made up some of the shortfall.[5] As the peacetime economic recovery took hold, women found it more appealing to be employed in manufacturing because of the highly repetitive and demanding tasks at bank branches. This led to an increasingly high turnover rate of women and recently employed male staff at branches.

These pressures, combined with private and public initiatives to introduce the electronic payment of wages, antagonistic government officials (who were particularly critical of the clearing banks' labour inefficiency and who threatened nationalization), growing inflation and a greater variability of interest rates, led clearing banks to grapple with ways to automate their work.

Senior managers of banks also had to face an increasingly unionized workforce, which demanded an end to the Saturday morning opening of retail branches. Indeed, in the early and mid-1960s a top concern for the CLCB was how they could present Saturday closing to their customers.[6] However, the opportunity came about in 1969, and only after the introduction of cash machines.[7] Even then, the currency dispensers could not alleviate the problem of Saturdays, for 'the machines were expensive and clearly could not be provided to all the branches'.[8] Sir John Thomson, Barclays Chairman, commented on the eve of Saturday closing:

> By the 1st July [1969] we hope to have installed 150 cash machines and a further 100 by the end of the year. We shall then have a dispenser within 5 miles of the homes of 77 per cent of our customers.[9]

At the time, cheques and related services dominated the transactions at retail counters.[10] In retail payments, current accounts were the exclusive remit of high income and high net-worth individuals, as evidenced by Dicks, who estimated that 83 per cent of weekly-paid consumers did not have a bank account.[11] The hours of opening that suited traditional customers were much less attractive to working-class customers.[12] While the clearing banks may not have wanted individual working-class customers, the emergence of financial services that duplicated those offered by the banks threatened to exclude the clearing banks from this whole category of servicing.[13] However, attracting large employers in order to pay individuals by cheque or directly into bank accounts was simply out of the question until the staffing issues relative to retail counters had been resolved.

This is the context in which cash machines in the UK appeared and which saw three teams of engineers working independently of each other to manufacture a currency dispensing machine for the clearing banks. The teams came from Barclays Bank and De La Rue Instruments; Smiths Industries, Chubb, and Westminster Bank; and Midland Bank, Speytec, and Burroughs. The efforts behind each of these innovations are described in detail below.

3.2 De La Rue Automatic Cash System (DACS)

3.2.1 *The Heavens and the Earth*

It is common knowledge that the first cash machine to be deployed was one of six machines in a pilot project installed by Barclays Bank in its Enfield (north-east London) retail branch in June 1967;[14] beating the Swedish saving banks' Metior by nine days and Westminster's Smiths Industries-Chubb system by a month.[15] Sir Thomas Bland, Deputy Chairman of Barclays Bank, in a public ceremony to unveil the device, claimed that it was a 'major banking break-through', referred to its self-service attributes by describing it as a 'mini bank', and highlighted its greater 'efficiency' in servicing customers, letting the bank respond to the 'needs of modern society'.[16] In his speech, Bland also noted that the development had taken eighteen months.

Explaining the reasons why a suburb such as Enfield and not a large city centre in London, Glasgow, or Edinburgh had been selected as the first site, staff at Barclays argued that the town had a 'model cross-section community, fairly self-contained; it is not too far from London, the branch has a good pavement façade, sufficiently high windows and enough space inside for the safe, and town-planning permission was readily given'.[17] Five more Barclaycash machines were installed by the end of the summer in towns with similar characteristics, namely, Hove, Ipswich, Luton, Peterborough, and Southend.

The devices were developed by De La Rue Instruments, a division of the then diversified security printer, with a total of eight employees and a brief to develop systems for banking automation.[18] During the development process the devices were referred to as the 'De La Rue Automatic Cash System' or DACS. But they were advertised as 'Barclaycash' machines and were called 'robot cashiers' or 'mini banks' by the internal and popular press.[19] Pye Telecom of Cambridge, a radio manufacturer which became part of Phillips in the spring of 1967, was responsible for the assembling of the DACS, following designs from De La Rue and banking specifications from Barclays' Organization & Methods department.[20]

It is interesting to note that, at Barclays' insistence, the verification of the customer was at the heart of the DACS. Developing this interface can be seen as a spin-off technology from De La Rue's investment in verification systems. In the late 1950s and as had been the case for Metior in Sweden, De La Rue Instruments started to use radioactive material as a security device to help an oil company (Royal Dutch-Schell) in the distribution of fuel to unattended depots (called 'Tankomat' in the case of Metior). This entailed knowledge of the use of Carbon-14 in a token verification system (GB 990256)[21] and a mechanism for automated vending machines (GB 990255).[22] A third item of prior knowledge at De La Rue Instruments related to the research that led to a patent for an 'Apparatus for Feeding Sheets' which was essentially a banknote transport system combined with a counting system.[23] This technology, together with the Carbon-14 token verification system and the mechanisms for automated vending machines constituted the 'kernel' for retrieving and distributing money by its currency dispenser device.

Figure 3.1. Activation token for Barclays–De La Rue, 1967
Source: Courtesy of Barclays Group Archives.

Once in operation, the machines had to be activated by the vouchers issued to Barclays' customers. Figure 3.1 depicts one of these vouchers. Customers applied in advance and purchased the vouchers, valid for six months from the date of issue, from Barclays' retail branches during opening hours. Before activating the device, a manual signature was the first form of identification and authorization for individual customers. The initial electronic signature in the pilot devices was in the form of a six-digit identity number and it enabled the customer to open a drawer.[24] The voucher was then inserted into that drawer (of which the prototypes had two and subsequent machines only one). The sample voucher in Figure 3.1 shows two big perforations at each end (depicted as black dots). These holes helped customers to fix the voucher over two pins sticking out when the drawer opened.

Unknown to customers, the purpose of the specific location and orientation of the voucher was, once the customer closed the drawer, to allow a Geiger-Muller counter to verify the voucher was genuine by means of the voucher being previously impregnated with 'mildly radioactive ink when printing'.[25] Inside the machine a section of the voucher was guillotined to bring it to the standard size of a personal cheque.

Validation of the voucher was a second form of identification. It activated a mechanical arm that had two tasks. One involved picking up the cheque voucher from the drawer and placing it in a container. The second task involved rotating to drop a pack of banknotes on the drawer that dispensed the cash. This was a fixed sum of ten pounds (approximately £160 in 2014), in packs of one-pound notes tied together by a paper band.[26] When the voucher was retrieved by bank staff, the transaction was processed like a cheque during normal banking hours. It is worth noting that the ground-breaking internal logic of the DACS was designed by John Glenny at De La Rue Instruments.[27]

3.2.2 *The Gullibility of a Eureka Moment in a Bath-Tub*

By all accounts the DACS/Barclaycash is the innovation that, perhaps mis-guidedly, has received the most publicity and has been most prone to hyper-bole. Popular accounts have been fuelled by John Adrian Shepherd-Barron (1925–2010),[28] director at the time of Security Express. This was an armoured truck company resulting from a joint venture with Wells Fargo (San Francisco, CA), which had a monopoly in the UK on transporting money for banks.[29] Shepherd-Barron was also managing director of De La Rue Instruments.[30] Shepherd-Barron had a mandate to dissolve De La Rue Instruments, while his role in Security Express brought him into monthly contact with the various managers of the banks.[31]

As his own advocate (as a public speaker) and on a number of websites, Shepherd-Barron painted a rather esoteric development over the course of a weekend at his home in Cobham, Surrey, following an idea that emerged one Saturday when he could not get any money from the bank, having arrived after it had closed for the weekend.[32] This part of the story by Shepherd-Barron is somewhat inconsistent with the historical record. As stated above, it was not until 1969, well after cash machines had proven their effectiveness beyond a pilot project, that banks stopped servicing retail clients on Saturday mornings. Moreover, during our interview, Shepherd-Barron stated that he had initially conceived the idea of a currency dispenser from a joint project of the CLCB, to be offered to all the clearing banks equally so as to standard-ize the system.[33] It is plausible that this initiative was a response in 1964 to the establishment of a permanent committee within the CLCB to consider the issue of Saturday closing. The exact membership of this permanent committee and its relation to the Electronics Sub-Committee are unknown, but its existence does help to substantiate some of the claims by Shepherd-Barron; the involvement of the Midland Bank and Westminster Bank in the creation of alternative designs, as clarified below; and also explains why the DACS—built as a cheque cashing concept for internal installation (and then moved to an external installation)—had to be abandoned in favour of card operated systems.

Shepherd-Barron claims that he came up with a concrete idea, using a chocolate bar dispenser as the basis of the design, together with the con-cept of an identification number. He claimed that the next working day, in his capacity as the managing director of the armoured truck company, he had a meeting with Harold Darvill, Chief General Manager of Barclays Bank, to whom he proposed the concept. It was warmly received; within two days Derek Wilde, Chief Executive, or his Deputy 'arrived in the bank's Rolls Royce at twenty minutes' notice' to flesh out the idea and secured a contract.[34]

There are no surviving internal records at Barclays, De La Rue, or the CLCB relating to the genesis of the cash machine.[35] However, there is evidence that as early as 1956 the banks considered developing and financing machinery to support their drive to computerize cheque clearing and automate retail branches.[36] These specifications were discussed with foreign and domestic computer manufacturers and the National Physical Laboratory.[37] Surviving records at Barclays mention the discussion over cash machines only after their first deployment in June 1967. Thereafter they never appear in the minutes of team meetings by the top echelon of Barclays' management (unlike, for example, the introduction of credit cards, which dominated the strategic thinking of the group at this time). The absence of any mention in Barclays' Board records, together with Barclays' 'steadily earning a reputation as a technological innovator',[38] suggests that it was more likely that Shepherd-Barron met with Donald Travers, Barclays' Head of Mechanization and one of the three men from this bank in the CLCB's Electronics Sub-Committee, or with Ron Everett, Head of the Organization & Methods department at Barclays.[39]

3.2.3 Back to the Future of the DACS

The historical record is unclear on the sequence of two key events. First, at some point before 1966, Barclays broke ranks within the otherwise tight cartel around the CLCB and secured a contract with De La Rue for it to supply the DACS exclusively to Barclays.[40] There is evidence that Barclays made a contract ordering six of the devices as prototypes with a view to purchasing 250 further machines. Under the exclusivity clause, De La Rue never sold to other British banks, while Barclays replaced the fifty or so De La Rue machines in operation in 1974 with an order for 100 newly developed NCR 770 devices.[41] The other only known deployment of the DACS was at a retail branch of UBS in Zurich and to three local banks in the north-east of the USA.[42]

To deliver on those orders and other equipment developed by De La Rue Instruments (including a desktop banknote counting machine and a coin roll paper wrapping machine), the production of the DACS relocated in 1969 from the eight-staff strong factory at Watford, Hertfordshire (north of London), which was under the management of Stan Middleditch, to rented accommodation in Portsmouth.[43] Within three months of the relocation to Portsmouth, however, Shepherd-Barron was posted to a new assignment in the USA while Ken Wolf became managing director of De La Rue Instruments.

Brian Knight was appointed Chief Engineer in Portsmouth and was responsible for recruiting staff within the area (otherwise employed in engineering firms servicing the military or with experience in similar advanced systems). The people that came from Watford continued to be responsible for the DACS and its installations across the UK. At Portsmouth, the original design of the DACS, which 'had come from a consultant',[44] suffered some minor but important modifications such as reducing the personal identification number to four figures, reducing the vouchers to fit a standard personal cheque (so only a corner was cut inside the machine), and eliminating one of the drawers. Stuart McEwen Jenkins, engineer and project manager at De La Rue Instruments, remembers:

> By 1969 the single drawer DACS was operated by a swinging vacuum cup arm which picked up the customer voucher when the drawer had been pushed closed and then place the voucher into a storage container. The arm then moved to pick up a banded package of bank notes from the top of a vertical square shaped storage tube to drop the note bundle on to the closed drawer platform, in place of the voucher. When this action was complete the drawer automatically opened to present the banded notes to the customer.
>
> The customer was then expected to close the drawer to complete the transaction.
>
> The stored banded note packs in the square shaped container were then lifted by a servo operated support platform so that the next note bundle was in the correct position ready for the next transaction to occur.[45]

As overall production in Portsmouth expanded, staff grew to about fifty people while operations relocated again to its own, purpose-built premises a couple of years later. At this point the production of the DACS stopped. The DACS proved unpopular with the customers because, as mentioned above, they had to place their voucher on the two pins inside the drawer. This was difficult to do even in dry weather.

To prove a point regarding the potential for the drawer system to be vandalized, an apocryphal story circulated amongst branch staff where competitor Westminster Bank left some fish and chips overnight at the DACS in Barclays' Enfield branch, while in retaliation Barclays staff put superglue into the card acceptance slot of the Westminster's Chubb machine at the Victoria Station branch.[46] But this nibble of British humour aside, the fact remains that the DACS proved to be most unreliable and in consequence did not last long. To little surprise there was but one production batch.

3.2.4 *De La Rue Strikes Back*

De La Rue, however, went on to develop a teller assisting banknote-counter machine, marketed as 'Chequemaster'. The first of these was installed at the Chichester, West Sussex branch of the National Westminster Bank (NatWest).[47] The requirement specification for this device was provided by Bryan King, project manager at NatWest's Organization & Methods department and who had a mandate to look into ways of improving customer service, and the handling of cash and coins. The machine proved to be a success and soon many others were in operation across different banks in the UK and elsewhere. For instance, automobile manufacturer Renault used one in its plant near Paris for weekly wages payments.

The basic dispensing mechanism used in the 'Chequemaster' was based on the existing De La Rue note counting machine increased in width to allow for two note denominations to be dispensed side by side. This mechanism later became known internally as the cash dispensing module or CDM. An NCR coin dispenser was also attached to the CDM/'Chequemaster' with the purpose of delivering coins directly to the customer whilst the notes were handed over by the cashier when, for instance, a customer cashed a pay cheque.

The success of the 'Chequemaster' gained the attention of NCR and with the help of NCR engineers in Dayton, OH, the CDM was further developed for mass production. This unit became known as the 770 CDM and became a component of the NCR 770 'through the wall' ATM in 1975. A new request by NCR asked for a new smaller vacuum note pick-up CDM by De La Rue and this was designated the 1100 series CDM. This was primarily designed to suit and first used in 1977 by the NCR 1770 'In-Lobby' ATM, aimed to be located at the entrance of bank branches and which was about the size of a small washing machine with all customer access along its top surface. The result of this collaboration between NCR and De La Rue on the note dispensing mechanism is important as it helped the ATM to evolve from a banknote lengthwise dispenser to a banknote edgewise dispenser, that is, the point at which banknotes were fed short edge first to customers.

The 1100 CDM was later further developed to suit the next generation of NCR 1780 ATM. This cash dispense module was superior to what was on offer at most other contemporary cash machine manufacturers as it was the first to enable friction-based feeding of banknotes. The success of this friction-based dispenser is also important as it enabled De La Rue to remain in the ATM market for some years as OEM supplier to NCR and other US-based manufacturers such as Docutel, Diebold, and Citibank (via its California-based technology subsidiary).

During the period between 1978 and 1984, De La Rue went on to develop the first multi-note denomination dispensing machine which was designated the 1300 Series. This system utilized the first tamper-indicating currency cassette which could be pushed in like a filing cabinet drawer, one above the other. The feed module design for the 1300 system was based on the proven 770 CDM concept using many of the same components. Alongside this application, a delivery module was created that could dispense notes either to the front or to the rear for the bank clerk to assist application or to the front for ATM 'through the wall' application.

3.3 Smiths Industries and Chubb & Son's MD2

3.3.1 *Victorian Origins of Chubb*

A second key event which remains unclear in the historical record is the entrance of other British manufacturers of cash dispensers. One interviewee claimed that Chubb & Son's Lock and Safe Company had been working to develop a cash machine with the CLCB's Electronics Sub-Committee as early as 1959.[48] The discussion now moves to exploring this claim.

The story of Chubb & Son's Lock and Safe Company Group (Chubb) is typical of the rise and fall of English firms that originated during the Industrial Revolution.[49] Its roots date back to Charles and Jeremiah Chubb, who were ships' chandlers in Portsmouth until they developed the first detector lock in 1818. Later on, their operations relocated to Wolverhampton (near Birmingham) at the same time as the growing success of their patented lock and key. Their main manufacturing plant and headquarters were to remain in the Midlands for almost two hundred years, venturing into safes in 1835 and into sales operations in the USA in 1870.

By the 1960s, Chubb had decades of experience in providing security services, including the provision of safes and fire prevention equipment, to financial institutions all over the world. Chubb was a large company, trading on the London Stock Exchange with a consolidated turnover that reached £38 million in 1970 (£1,120 million or $1.8 billion in today's money), of which 41.2 per cent resulted from exports and overseas operations.[50] Chubb was run under the leadership of George Chubb (1911–2003), 3rd Lord Hayter, direct descendant of the founder, as its Chairman, and William E. Randall, its managing director.[51]

Exactly when and how Chubb got involved in the design of the cash machine is unclear. However, it seems that it did so at the request of one or more of the clearing banks. It is important here to note that work on this device started only once the banks defined the problem of allowing customers access to cash without the assistance of bank staff. Moreover, for the banks it was paramount to ascertain that only the rightful owner could debit an account by this means. This idea, of course, has permeated the delivery of self-service in retail finance to this day.

3.3.2 *First Prototype and Entry of Smiths Industries*

Chubb designed a first prototype, the 'money dispenser' or MD1. Chubb then marketed it to Westminster Bank and gave them first option to buy and install, but not exclusivity.[52] The MD1 did not perform as expected—in particular the cash dispensing mechanism. This is not altogether surprising when we consider that Chubb lacked the sophisticated skills to develop and market advanced electronics. As a result, in 1965 Kelvin Electronics, the renamed marine arm of Kelvin Hughes (owned by the specialist engineering firm Smiths Industries known today as Smiths Group) was asked to redesign the prototype which ultimately resulted in the Chubb MD2.[53]

David Miller was part of the development team at Smiths Industries.[54] According to Miller, it was the summer of 1965 when Peter Blair, Smith's public relations director, asked him to meet with Tony (Anthony I. O.) Davies immediately as there was something very important to discuss and to visit Kelvin Electronics in Hillington, Glasgow. There Miller and Blair were introduced by George Chubb (Chairman of Chubb), to Tom McMillan, general manager of the Management Services Division of the Westminster Bank (now part of the RBS Group and trading as NatWest). At the time McMillan was the most senior manager responsible for the development of computerization at the Westminster and the Organization & Methods team came under his jurisdiction.[55] Miller was also introduced to Chubb executives Bill (William E.) Randall, managing director, Harry Thorpe, and Alfred Markham.

After the meeting at Hillington, Miller was appointed manager of the project and asked to select a team of four people using production engineers from the Colindale (London) laboratory and the electronic design team in Cheltenham, Gloucestershire—which were involved in the development of advance electronics for the military.[56] Everyone was sworn to secrecy before work on the design began. Miller would report directly to Peter Blair. Engineering responsibilities was to be under Geoffrey Constable, then chief engineer at Kelvin Electronics in Glasgow, and Jeff Holter and Neville Whittney based in Cheltenham.

3.3.3 *Design and Operation*

Chubb was to design and build the safe to house the unit, the external fascia, and the cash stack.[57] Meanwhile, at Smiths Industries, Constable posed the problem of the cash machine to his staff, which at the time included a development engineer called James Goodfellow. Constable's brief called for a means of securing access to the machine to be devised. The fundamental element was that 'the system [would] dispense a pack of money only if there is correspondence between this number entered by the push-buttons and a number that is read by the card-reader from the card'.[58] This novel idea was the genesis of the common Personal Identification Number or PIN system that has become so familiar in all ATM equipment (see the activation token in Figure 3.2). Specifically, the idea was that a Primary Account Number (PAN) was to be combined with a Private Identification Number (PIN). This led to a patent for a 'Banknote Dispenser' being filed on 2 May 1966 by Anthony I. O. (Tony) Davies and James Goodfellow (GB 1197183/US 3905461). This

Figure 3.2. Activation token for Chubb MD2, circa 1967

Source: Reproduced by kind permission of The Royal Bank of Scotland Group plc ©.

patent is the earliest instance of a complete 'currency dispenser system' in the patent record.

The PAN was printed through perforated holes on a plastic card (as shown in Figure 3.2).[59] Note that the exact position of the first two holes on the card, which worked as entry gate, identified the issuing bank; while the remaining holes were purely a PAN.[60] The size of the card was a quarter that of a Hollerith card. This had the dual advantage that it could work within existing punched card technology while being of a convenient size—the card was close to the size of a personal presentation card and the recently introduced credit card.[61]

The card by itself, of course, could be forged. It would be easy to beat the system by anyone with a PIN creating counterfeits by simply copying the holes in the plastic card onto a Hollerith card. The key to securing the system was thus two-fold: on the one hand, a strong enough identification system to prevent anyone from working out the PIN from the PAN punched on the card and vice versa. This would secure access to the customer to the transaction alone. However, the card was coated with high coercivity magnetics—something that was revolutionary technology at the time. This coating meant that the card was magnetic and was the only thing that could be read and deemed legitimate by the machine in part authorization of the transaction.

In the MD2, then, a transaction began by inserting the card in a dedicated slot in the machine (which was different to the trapdoor for banknotes). The first two holes (see the top of Figure 3.2) were used to stop the card so that a magnetic head could read it. This confirmed that the card was made of the correct material and it had been issued by the bank that owned the cash machine. Second, the PAN was read into the 'AND gate'.[62] Third, the device requested the PIN from the customer. The successful conjunction of these three actions triggered the ejection from the dispenser of a plastic wallet with the cash. Finally, the device stored the plastic card for its retrieval and processing by bank staff, and reset for a new transaction.

Once Geoffrey Constable and his team in Glasgow finished the initial design work, all of the main engineering took place in the south of England as the project relocated to Colindale and the Aerospace Division in Cheltenham. Initially, Colindale was responsible for completing the control mechanism and card transport system, but continuing performance difficulties at Chubb meant that the construction of the customer instruction module and the redesign of the money dispensing mechanism also moved to Colindale. Previous expertise in electronics of flight landing systems at Cheltenham was then used to give integrity to the dispensing electronics.[63]

3.3.4 Deployment

Late in 1966, a demonstration of the PIN/PAN system in a modified confectionery dispenser was put together in Chubb's facilities in Wolverhampton. This demonstration was attended by, among others, representatives of the Midland Bank (today trading as HSBC in the UK) and the Bank of England.[64] Around this time, Midland Bank parted company with Chubb after failing to secure the exclusive supply of its cash machine. Instead it was to be the Westminster Bank that took the lead. In January 1967, Tom McMillan hosted a lunch at the Westminster Bank attended by engineers from Chubb and Smiths Industries, where the final MD2 concept was agreed, together with an initial order of ten machines on the understanding that the first of these would be ready to use by 31 July 1967.[65] Thus on that date the MD2 was first installed at the Victoria branch of the Westminster Bank, that is, within a month of its first deployment by Barclays/De La Rue in London and the savings banks/Metior in Sweden.

The Chubb machine resulted from months of joint development and collaboration with Smiths Industries and the Westminster Bank to bring it to market.[66] Initially, a further eight branches were to have the system installed, but Chubb was soon inundated with requests for other British and overseas banks. The Westminster, not wishing to have to wait in line for the innovation they had brought to the market, quickly altered the earlier agreed figure, proposing the supply of a further forty machines only five days after the launch.[67] This expansion was at a cost of £95,000 to the bank (about £2.8 million or $4.5 million in today's money).[68]

The 'Chubb MD2' 24-hour dispenser was quick to win praise outside the banking industry. For instance, Jack Howe (1902–2003), Bauhaus architect and industrial design consultant, received the prestigious 'Duke of Edinburgh's Design Prize' for its looks in 1969.[69] The MD2 design was also voted 'Best New Idea' in the *Sunday Telegraph*'s 'City Editor Awards'.[70] Although the inherently inclusive nature of the system clearly worried the paper's chauvinistic editor, he stated that, while the 24-hour system was the best new idea, the worst new idea was 'letting one's wife use one's Westminster Bank 24-hour Cash Dispensing Machine'.[71]

As mentioned, customers applied for and were given plastic cards the same size as credit cards. But while Barclays had limited the use of the DACS to customers of its own branch (such as Enfield), the Westminster allowed the issue of the £10 activation card throughout its nationwide branch network.[72] The customer keyed in a six-digit personal code and the Chubb MD2 dispensers delivered ten one-pound notes in a plastic wallet 'or cassette (as it was in effect a plastic box which was open ended, somewhat like a thin cigarette packet)'.[73]

If desired, the MD2 'could easily be arranged to dispense varying amounts of say £5, £10, £15, £20, etc.'.[74] This is not to say that the device could deliver any amount that the account holder chose. The MD2 could dispense only whatever amount of money was stored in the plastic wallet using crisp, brand new banknotes—and most ATMs would continue to do so until the 1980s. But back in the 1960s and early 1970s, the only way for a bank customer to have varying amounts of cash dispensed automatically from an MD2 was to acquire multiple activation cards. Actually, most customers who were offered the use of a cash dispenser typically received only one activation card, while the top earners received two or three cards per month.[75]

When in operation by customers it was found that the MD2's trapdoor opened and closed relatively slowly. In this regard, there was a credible account of a customer who, after receiving his own £10, had his fingers trapped in the trapdoor trying to extract the next £10 plastic holder in line for dispensing. This was a rather embarrassing event for the victim at a major branch in busy Oxford Street. A passer-by alerted the branch staff and the truant was released, saved from starving to a slow death in Oxford Street. The grounds for trusting this story is that the Good Samaritan who alerted the branch staff apparently wrote to Head Office claiming a reward.[76]

In response to the Westminster's request during the design stage, the customer's card was retained by the MD2, so that branch staff could debit the correct account when they retrieved the card from the machine and extract the account number and branch code from it.[77] The customer's name and branch were put on the reverse of the card by the card unit. When the cardholder transferred branches, branch staff would erase the account details from the card and then just type in the new account details by putting the card through an old-style, mechanical typewriter as the cards were pretty flexible.

Once retrieved, the cards were sent to the Clearing Department, which then returned the debits sheets with Chubb cards to the account holding branch via the 'IN Debit Clearing' for the customer's account to be debited £10, and for the card to then be sent by post to the customer by that branch. At the time, the Westminster's Organization & Methods department thought this was the most efficient available system to deal with the cards, albeit the customer would only get his or her card back in four working days at best. When the customer received the card through the post, it was ready for further use.

Grant Wells, a branch employee at the time, recalled how, to debit a cardholder's account, the cards were processed via the bank's internal cheque clearing system attached to a 'dummy cheque'.[78] The cardholder's branch would then receive the 'dummy cheque' with the card attached via the daily cheque clearing and debit the account with £10 and then post the same card back out to the customer for reuse. According to Wells, a good customer would have two or three cards at one time.

Given the exclusivity agreement signed between De La Rue and Barclays, in the late 1960s and early 1970s the Chubb MD2 became the machine of choice for British banks as well as spreading with international success (shown by its rapid deployment in Canada, Australia, and Singapore). For instance, Martins Bank installed its first machine in Liverpool in 1967.[79] The National Provincial Group did likewise in January 1968, at the District Bank's Piccadilly branch in Manchester.[80] In 1968, the Royal Bank of Scotland was the first to introduce 24-hour access to cash north of the border in twenty-five of its branches.[81] Meanwhile, within the first year of operation at the Westminster Bank, the service was no longer considered an 'experiment'; there was a device in place in thirty-six branches across England (with an estimated growth to sixty by December 1968) used on average for 150 withdrawals per week per device.[82]

In the absence of a video display unit (VDU), the Chubb dispenser communicated with the customer by fixed light signals (primarily to indicate that the card or voucher had been accepted).[83] From the outset, banks adopting the Chubb MD2 (and the DACS) chose to fix the currency dispenser to the outer wall of the branch rather than in the banking hall. This was safeguarded by the use of a stainless-steel exterior and interior cladding of thickened armour designed to withstand attack, making the MD2 operational 24 hours per day.[84]

Here it is important to note the number of engineering challenges the different teams faced. For instance, never before had any other machine positioned electronic circuits so close to changing weather conditions, requiring the development of metal alloys and sealants that would not easily succumb to the inclemency of seasonal changes and different climates within the British Isles. Another challenge concerned badly designed plastic wallets: replacing them was soon becoming an important part of the cost of the transaction; they easily stuck within the device, bringing it to a halt. Soon the wallets were replaced by paper bags.[85] Other parts of the mechanism were expensive, hard to come by, and in some instances tailor-made. A handful of engineers, most of them located in London, were able to service the device when it broke down. For instance, staff at Chubb did not at first have the expertise to look into complex electronic systems and thus, field engineers were sourced from Smiths Industries' Avionics Division.[86] The scarcity of replacement parts and engineering skills often meant that foreign banks had to wait for an engineer, a spare, or both to be flown over from England.

Having all this new technology meant that there was an unknown number of 'teething problems' waiting to be solved. But instead of holding back and eliminating all major shortcomings in the manufacturing and performance of the device, Chubb opted to expand and distributed 700 currency dispensers to fourteen countries by 1970.[87] As we will see, rapid growth exacerbated the weaknesses in the system, making the problems in the field worse with each new installation, while the constant breakdowns diverted engineers from thinking how to solve the problems once and for all.

3.3.5 Distribution Agreement with Diebold

Records suggest that during conversations and the ensuing correspondence between representatives of Chubb, Diebold, First National City Bank (Citibank), and Smiths Industries the term 'automatic teller' was first put forward. These conversations were even more significant as they led Diebold's Daniel Maggin, Chairman of the Board, and Ray Koontz, its President and Chief Executive Officer, to travel to England in July 1970 with the specific purpose of meeting (without prior notice) with Chubb's managing director, William Randall. Diebold wanted the exclusive right to distribute Chubb's cash machines throughout the USA.

Chubb had direct operation in the USA for its safe and other banking security equipment but had resisted the chance to spread its cash dispensers there. That was not the case in Canada, where MD2 cash dispensers were already operational. This development was rooted in the Chubb-Mosler & Taylor joint venture, which delivered an MD2 in 1969 to the Toronto office of the Canadian Imperial Bank of Commerce (CIBC). When offered the superior distribution capabilities of Diebold in the USA, Chubb believed that an association with Diebold offered better prospects than going it alone against the likes of Burroughs, Mosler, and other entrants to the emerging automatic currency dispenser market.

For its part, Diebold claimed to have spent resources exploring the possibility of developing a cash machine of its own, but considered that the Chubb machine was a better answer to the Docutel system (Diebold and Docutel are discussed in greater detail in Chapter 4).[88] But Diebold also pressed for a newer version of the Chubb cash dispenser, a returnable card machine that could be activated by the growing number of people carrying a bank-issued credit card rather than by a bespoke card, token, or voucher. Chubb and Smiths Industries acquiesced and developed the new device, while Diebold entered the cash machine market when it began distributing Chubb's MD4 (also known as Mark 4) machines to US banks in 1971.

The Chubb units, however, were found somewhat disappointing by the US market.[89] After repeated failures and a limited availability of spare parts and service engineers, Diebold engineers and customers thought the Chubb devices did not meet their service expectations. Not surprisingly Diebold finally stopped distributing Chubb devices in 1973 and at the same time, Diebold decided to develop and eventually launch its own Total Automatic Banking System (TABS) 500. This device was developed by Robert W. Clark, Phillip C. Dolsen, and Donald E. Kinker, and first installed in 1974.[90] It was described as a 'complete teller' concept because it had a depository mechanism, a selection of cash amounts (as opposed to a fixed amount such as the Chubb had), a check printer to issue balances (to help verify offline transactions at the end of the day), and could be fitted with a telephone and CCTV camera for two-way video off the screen (which could be used to help customers make a transaction during banking hours). Figure 3.3 depicts one of the ways in which the TABS 500 was deployed: as a through-the-wall, drive-up system.

The distribution agreement with Diebold, however, was transformed into some sort of arrangement for sharing and allocating markets. Unfortunately, in 1977 this agreement was deemed in breach of US competition rules by the US Department of Justice.[91] As a result, Chubb agreed to withdraw for three years from the lucrative US market and not to make contact with Diebold for five years.

3.3.6 Building Market Share but Losing Independence

Alongside the Diebold fiasco, William Randall, the managing director of Chubb, decided that the best course of action was for the firm to continue making inroads independently into the cash dispenser market. This was in

Figure 3.3. Diebold's TABS drive-in deployment, circa 1975
Source: Courtesy of Diebold-Wincor Inc.

spite of not having any senior people with a track record in the understanding and marketing of advanced electronics. Yet, still intent on growing in the cash machine market, Randall hired Ken Rankin as managing director of Chubb's cash machine operations;[92] Chubb also in August 1973 acquired from Smiths Industries all the manufacturing, assets, patent, and inventory related to cash machines for £218,000 (£3.5 million, or $5.6 million in today's money).[93] These assets were combined with Chubb's facilities to form a new subsidiary called Chubb Integrated Systems Ltd. Shortly afterwards, Chubb introduced a new generation of machines: a new 'online' version of the hole-in-the-wall MD4, and a brand-new and 'online' lobby machine called MD6000, both circa 1975.

In 1976 Chubb acquired Gross Cash Registers Ltd. to form a new subsidiary company called Chubb Cash.[94] The acquisition was made on the basis that it would provide in-house electronic expert capabilities together with the power to design the much-needed improvements in software that would upgrade the functioning of the cash machines.[95] But in spite of this acquisition the integrated circuits revolution continued to elude Chubb.

As the 1970s drew to a close, observers were aware that the demand for replacement cash registers, office machines, and cash machines was likely to benefit the likes of Chubb.[96] By the end of 1977, for instance, NatWest had issued 75,000 cards to activate its cash machines in the UK. These cards were accepted by 406 Chubb MD2 and MD4, which sat alongside 100 NCR 770 machines.[97]

But in trying to secure contracts, Chubb had been actively tailoring the operation of its machines to suit most of its customers. As the firm tinkered with its models and disregarded the increasing engineering costs, it was in fact missing the opportunities associated with greater scale. Indeed, 'Chubb never got to a final ATM design. Always changing it to suit this bank or another.'[98] This approach was different to that taken by firms such as NCR or IBM, who first surveyed the needs of the banks and then designed the specifications of their machines. Once off the production line, they underwent few or no adjustments to suit individual customers. Chubb was thus failing to secure any large contract because NCR or IBM consistently outbid it.[99]

Clearly, multiple and recurrent changes in specifications with a view to satisfying the customer increased development costs and delayed delivery. These also applied to an OEM agreement signed in November 1978 to supply Phillips with a modified MD7000 (to be designated SBF002 and 003 by Phillips). The agreement with Phillips also limited Chubb's opportunities to supply other OEM agreements.[100]

By 1980, Chubb Cash Ltd., the company that had manufactured and supplied electronic and electromechanical cash registers, automated tellers, and point-of-sale-systems, had weakened considerably; it reported operating losses of £4.7 million (£25.3 million or $41 million in today's money—a figure that includes research and development costs for manufacturing new cash machines).[101] Keeping hold of the cash machine market not only cost Chubb Cash a fortune but was also draining resources from elsewhere within the group and dragging down the parent company's trading performance.

In 1982, Chubb left the cash machine market for good.[102] But in spite of the move, trading conditions continued to deteriorate and a couple of years after, in 1984, Chubb was purchased by the Racal Electronics Group. Racal's directors kept Chubb and its management largely intact while adding its own expertise in electronics.[103] In 1989, Racal took Chubb back to the stock market and it was taken over by Williams Holdings, which engaged in a programme of asset stripping and sold all its divisions as independent businesses.

3.4 Speytec, Burroughs, and Midland Bank

Sometime in the summer of 1966, the Midland Bank (today HSBC) signed a contract, with exclusivity, to develop a cash machine with a small engineering outfit called Speytec.[104] Based in Croydon (south London), the company had been established by John Edwards, Len Perkins, and Messrs. Simons and Young (the acronym uses the initial letters of the group's surnames). Perkins had a background in radar technology. Edwards was the most entrepreneurial member of the group and had worked in the USA on various military projects. He came back and formed a company to exploit the then very active area of automation. An early contract was to deploy technology for depositing and retrieving dry cleaning after hours. The activation of this system required some form of secure token and a plastic card with a magnetic coating was proposed.

Speytec designed and manufactured these cards, though it was impossible to find such a device in England. Despite failing to get the dry-cleaning business off the ground, the resourceful Edwards, debating what other uses could be made of their card, is said to have contacted several managers of retail banking departments, finally getting the attention of one from the Midland. Midland was then the second biggest bank in the UK (after Barclays) in terms of deposits and, more importantly for customer relations, it had a 'larger number of units than [was] operated by any other financial institution in this country and the biggest branch system among the commercial banks of the western world'.[105] Surviving records from the Management Committee of the Midland Bank are consistent with their having been approached by, rather than seeking out, Speytec.[106]

Midland Bank commissioned W. G. Kneale, General Manager (Administration), to liaise with Speytec and the National Physical Laboratory (NPL) on 'developing an alternative approach' to those of Chubb and De La Rue.[107] It is interesting to note that, during our interviews, engineers at Speytec, Chubb, and De La Rue all claimed that they were working in isolation and that they became aware of alternative designs only when the competing cash machines were deployed and subsequently advertised in the press.

However, as early as March 1967, Kneale knew that at least three other banks were about to install 'small quantities' of cash machines by the end of the year.[108] He also understood that Barclays Bank had financed the De La Rue dispensers and that Barclays had gained exclusivity rights—something 'the manufacturer regretted'. De La Rue nevertheless provided Midland with 'basic information' that conveyed a broad understanding of its machine (including the use of encoding, mode of activation, and the fact that De La Rue had doubts about its security).[109]

The data storage capabilities of the Speytec magnetic card allowed Midland to develop a specification which allowed the card to be returned to the client as part of the cash delivery.[110] The machine dispensed fixed amounts of currency while the magnetic stripe recorded the number of withdrawals, thus obviating the need to enquire about the customer's liquid balance:

the issuing of a card was enough to imply the extension of a line of credit to its owner.[111]

Speytec's solution was clearly distinct from the Chubb and De La Rue systems where the cards and vouchers were retained and processed as cheques drawn on cash. However, the Speytec cards were limited to one use per day and twenty uses altogether. At the bank's insistence, the cards were marked with a dimple system to show how many times they had been used. This limit on reusability gave the bank a degree of control over the amount that the card could issue. In addition, the bank only issued cards to those customers with a balance of £200 or more (£3,200 or $5,500 in today's money),[112] thus limiting its potential for overdrafts.

Given the limited engineering experience from other sectors, Speytec embarked on designing the currency dispenser from first principles and with NPL reporting on improvements to the security systems. The prototypes had to solve a number of problems: for example the technology available necessitated the use of five power supplies. Equally, weather-proofing such components with metal alloys for the fascias that were both light and resistant to the UK weather and the effects of salt water (hence the Hastings branch was included in subsequent trials) were new issues generally to the field of electronics. Nevertheless, six trial machines were installed.

As part of the trial, the security of the system was investigated by the bank's Operations & Methods department. Working together with NPL's Autonomics Division they demonstrated that it was relatively easy to read Speytec's activation card. This was a common shortcoming of the punched card system. Following the release of the Chubb system, it was even easier, according to NPL, to copy their soft plastic cards, which were simply punched cards, although in this case the PIN itself could not be read from the card. Speytec responded to the NPL report by introducing several changes to the coding and moved to a token as big as a plastic credit card, resulting in four magnetic tracks to store the customer's six-digit secret number.[113] By making one head record information in one direction and a second head in the opposite direction, it made the security of the PIN redundant. As further security (the secure card property) the device was activated by a Carbon-14 dot hidden in an arrow ostensibly added to show where to point the card on introducing it. The magnetic dot was placed at random in the arrow and was measured inside the machine in each transaction.

Further trials at the NPL suggested that 'until a dispenser could be linked to a computer, there must always be a security risk'.[114] The desirability of interfacing a dispenser with the computer was in itself a major step forward from the asynchronous, stand-alone first-generation cash machines, such as those by Chubb and De La Rue. By September 1968 a total of £41,530 had been allocated to the project (approximately £1 million in today's money).[115]

Midland then purchased twelve machines for field testing from Speytec at a total cost of £80,000 (of which £15,200 was granted to Speytec in the form of an interest free overdraft to be repaid from future profits).[116] The first two machines were operational in October and the rest delivered by the end of December 1968.

In terms of technology, the Speytec machines represented a more advanced concept than the Chubb and De La Rue systems through the use of the now ubiquitous magnetic stripe (the Management Committee having bought Chubb machines for the purposes of comparison) despite the NPL criticisms of a weaker PIN system than Chubb had. However, it was policy and user decisions rather than elegance of engineering that led to the final outcome. Midland at this time began to consider moving the Speytec team to Burroughs. The Detroit-based manufacturer was the chief supplier of Midland's computer equipment.[117] This was seen as a way to step up the scale of the programme. In May 1969 Burroughs bought Speytec; the bank passed all the results of its research to Burroughs' engineers in the USA and Speytec became a division of the UK subsidiary, Burroughs Machines Ltd. In September 1969, Midland ordered 500 cash machines from Burroughs at a cost of £1.5 million (£21.6 million or $34.8 million in today's money).[118]

One of the conditions of the takeover was that the directors, Perkins and Edwards, and the key Speytec staff should stay with Burroughs for two years to ensure an effective handover of know-how. This was when a new factory was set up in Croydon to manufacture fifty machines using the Speytec technology whilst the Speytec design team (now enlarged) developed a cash machine using Speytec's cards and Burroughs technology. A separate design team was set up in Strathleven, Scotland, to develop a system using the standardized credit card magnetic stripe. No other British bank deployed Speytec/Burroughs cash machines until 1974. Then the first two non-Midland currency dispensing machines began use in Belfast where Burroughs had set up a mainframe computer for the local trustee savings bank in 1970.[119]

During this period, also, the Burroughs patent GB 1329964 was filed (9 September 1969) along with the US patent US 3697729 and French patent FR 2061005, for a 'Système de distribution et carte sécurité à utiliser avec celui-ci' (Distribution System with a Card Security System). Following US and French requirements, neither of these patents mentions Speytec or Burroughs but it was formally assigned to Burroughs by the inventors in return for one dollar each, merely stating the names of the original Speytec inventors (John David Edwards, Leonard Perkins, John Henry Donald, Peter Lee Chappell, Sean Benjamin Newcombe, and Malcolm David Roe). Once the two years were up, most of the Speytec team left Burroughs and formed a new company to exploit their expertise in magnetic card technology in text processing systems and automatic typewriters.

Burroughs, meanwhile, tried to sell its cash machines by capitalizing on its commercial links with banks around the world. However, surviving records suggest that the trustee savings banks (TSB) in the UK were the only large adopters of this technology.[120] As mentioned, the first Burroughs ATM for the TSB appeared in 1974 while the last of 552 RT650 ATMs, a through-the-wall machine at the Aberdare, Mid Glamorgan (Wales) branch, was decommissioned in 1992.[121] The source also mentioned that although initially the RT650 were considered 'the first of the modern ATMs, [they had their] fair share of teething problems'. The RT650 were replaced by NCR 5085 machines. In South America, Banco de Colombia bought several of Burroughs' machines and deployed them in Bogotà, where 'not only was there limited access to activation cards but the machines were found to spend large amounts of time inactive'.[122] This experience led Colombian banks to have 150 cash machines from other manufacturers operational by the end of 1985. To little surprise, Burroughs had little success in creating a significant market share and the company left cash machine manufacturing when it sold its operations to NCR in the mid-1980s.

3.5 Patents and Innovation in Retail Banking

The creation of an industry-specific innovation such as a currency dispenser resulted from the convergence of different technological configurations. This process of creation empowered individual banks, bank consortia (as in the case of the Swedish savings banks), and their staff to leave their mark on the design and evolution of the technology.

Here I must emphasize that the invention of the cash machine was neither an absolute secret nor a 'race to market', at least in Britain, as was made evident by a series of articles in the press. As early as October 1965—almost two years before the deployment at Barclays' Enfield branch—both the *Times* (9 October) and the *Financial Times* (11 October) broke the news that banks were in the process of developing 'automatic machines [that would be] giving cash at any time'. Both news items promised that the machines would be ready in Britain in 18 months' time. Neither of them mentioned the developments in Sweden. Only the *Financial Times* followed up the story of the machines 'developed for installation in the walls of banks' by describing and specifically naming De La Rue in March 1967 and, more importantly, by showing a picture of the Chubb fascia side-by-side with that of De La Rue in May of 1967. In other words, the general public had seen the cash machine at least a month before the 27 June 1967 launch by De La Rue in Barclays' Enfield branch. This was due not only to reports in the broadsheets but also to the distribution of brochures and face-to-face communication at the branches. Retail banking customers had to be taught how to operate the new devices, and had to apply in advance for either activation vouchers or plastic punched cards.

In terms of institutional arrangements, documenting the genesis of invention explains why bankers largely disregarded the patent system, in complete contrast to the attitude of the engineers. It also challenges the view of a single isolated inventor of the cash machine (e.g. Shepherd-Barron, Simjian, or Goodfellow) and provides evidence that its origins lie in teams of people working together in complex innovative networks (e.g. Midland/Westminster-Chubb-Smiths Industries, Midland-Speytec-NPL, Barclays-De La Rue). Furthermore, this story of invention shows that mechanical self-service technology works in retail finance only through the active involvement of the user, in this case, three of the biggest London clearing banks (Barclays, Midland, and Westminster). Documentary evidence suggested that it was the banks' insistence on high levels of security that crystallized efforts and opened up this new path of customer-focused automation in the banking sector, the key development being the Chubb-Smith PIN patent (GB 1197183). The essence of this system had a profound influence on the industry as a whole. Not only did such future entrants into the cash machine market as NCR and IBM license Chubb's PIN system, but a number of later patents reference this one as a 'Prior Art Device', to the extent that in an out-of-court settlement in the USA (circa 1982), NCR agreed to pay an undisclosed amount to Chubb for having infringed its PIN/PAN system.[123]

As mentioned, early cash machines retained the access card or voucher after every transaction. Customers' accounts were debited when the voucher or card was retrieved from the machine after use and the branch where the cash machine was located informed the customer's branch. Chubb cards were posted back to the customer together with a statement of account or returned the next time the customer's passbook was updated.[124] Barclaycash vouchers were non-returnable. The card and voucher were issued only if the customer had sufficient funds (or the manager of the retail branch wanted to extend credit). The mechanization of cash withdrawals meant that individual banks could, if they wished, continue with their system of accounting control of customers at retail branches. There was no need for centralized records since the cash machine was in effect a stand-alone device. As with accounting machines, cash dispensers offered greater efficiency rather than an alternative way of operation.[125]

Finally, the first generation of cash machines in the UK reached a peak of some 1,300 deployed units in 1977. Slowly but steadily they were replaced by devices which, as noted above in the NPL report, had some degree of 'online' security through a connection to a central computer. These devices grew into systems which did not require human intervention to finalize the transaction, thus 'allowing the customer to directly program the (bank's) mainframe computer'.[126] Introducing second generation machines posed a serious challenge to all the early entrants to cash dispensing technology, making demands on electronics, integrated, systems and online computer technology in their design and manufacture. Detailing the move to 'online' systems and the birth of the ATM proper are the topics of Chapter 4.

Notes

1. A payment clearing system existed in London from the 1770s. This evolved to a system where representatives of note-issuing banks met to exchange cheques, to transfer money between accounts at different banks, and to settle net positions with payments from balances at the Bank of England. The system grew to a limited liability company known as the Banker's Clearing House Ltd. (established in 1864). The company was owned and controlled by a group of banks called the Committee of London Clearing Banks (CLCB), which offered current account facilities and money transmission services as their core business. Non-member banks wishing to compete with current account facilities could do so only by outsourcing to one of the clearing banks. By 1900 the ten clearing banks controlled 46 per cent of all deposits in sterling by residents in England and Wales and by 1921, five of these banks held 97 per cent of all deposits. British monetary authorities consented to this high degree of concentration, amenable to 'gentlemen's agreements', because they considered that it offered greater flexibility than regulation would for controlling the money supply and inflation.
2. *Branch and Staff Numbers*, mimeo, Lloyds Group Archive, 2009.
3. Martin (2012).
4. Booth (2007).
5. Booth (2008); Wardley (2011).
6. BoEA, C54/10 Chief Cashiers Duplicate Letters, Letter to Sir Edward Dodd (H. M. Chief Inspector of Constabulary—London), 5 August 1964; BoEA, C54/10 Chief Cashiers Duplicate Letters, CLBC Meeting of 2 July, 30 June 1964.
7. C. Webb, 'Never on a Saturday', *The Times*, 28 June 1969: 8; A. Thomas, 'Problems Ahead as Saturday Banking Ends', *The Times*, 28 June 1969: 11. CLCB/B/029/MS32147/9, Bank Office Hours, Meeting of the Representatives of the Retail Banking Consortium, 3 February 1969, 1. Banking Hours, (ii) Cash Dispensers.
8. CLCB/B/029/MS32147/9, Meeting of the Representatives of the Retail Banking Consortium, 19 February 1969, 1. Banking Hours, 4. Cash Dispensers.
9. CLCB/B/029/MS32147/9, Bank Office Hours, Note for Mr Wilson (Saturday Closing), 31 January 1969.
10. In 1960 the clearing of retail payments was extended to include credit transfers and standing order payments but their volume was insignificant until the 1970s, when

the UK saw the widespread use of credit cards, store cards, cheque guarantee cards, and other substitutes for payment with bills and coins.

11. Dicks (1968, 3).
12. Booth (2008, 119–21).
13. Billings and Booth (2011).
14. Unless otherwise stated, this section borrows from Bátiz-Lazo and Reid (2008, 2011). See also Ackrill and Hannah (2001, 335–8).
15. 'In the Words of the ATM Inventor', *ATM Marketplace*, accessed 2 February 2018, <https://www.atmmarketplace.com/articles/in-the-words-of-the-atms-inventor/>.
16. Barclays Group Archives [henceforward BGA], Press and Information Department, Speech by Sir Thomas Bland, 27 June 1967.
17. Peggy Nye, 'Instant Case at Enfield', *Spread Eagle*, vol. 42 (August 1967): 326.
18. 'De La Rue Company History', *Funding Universe*, accessed 8 October 2014, <http://www.fundinguniverse.com/company-histories/De-La-Rue-plc-Company-History.html>. See also Pugh (2011).
19. Peggy Nye, 'Instant Case at Enfield', *Spread Eagle*, vol. 42 (August 1967): 326.
20. Here the record is unclear as to the role in designing the machine played by Dr John Westhead, the future Chairman of Pye, who had been at Cambridge with John Shepherd-Barron. There is a reference to Dan Stanley as the schoolmate and chairman of Pye in Shepherd-Barron (2017, 71).
21. 'Improvements In or Relating to Security Documents and Monetary Tokens' (GB 990256) were developed by Barry Birch Goalby, Stefan Klackowski, Roy Salter, and Charles Dennis Lowe with a priority date of 26 March 1962 and the patent was granted in 1965.
22. A patent for a 'Sensing Mechanism for Automatic Vending Machines' (GB 990255) was filed on 15 March 1963 and granted in 1965. Developed by Barry Birch Goalby, Stefan Klackowski, Roy Salter, and Charles Dennis Lowe, it focused on the automation of customer service rather than any specific goal of automating banking technology.
23. Developed by Frank Albert Richardson, Stanley William Middleditch, and Reginald Leslie Walker, it was filed on 30 June 1960 and granted in 1962 as GB 912215. This was later developed into a patent filed on 25 September 1964 entitled 'Sheet Feeding and Counting Apparatus' developed once again by Stanley Middleditch with Victor Richard Sels. It was granted in 1968 as GB 1109466.
24. 'Dough à la Mode', *ABA Banking Journal*, May 1968: 78.
25. Shepherd-Barron (2017, 48) and interview (video conference) with Stuart McEwen Jenkins, former project manager at De La Rue Instruments, by B. Bátiz-Lazo, 12 October 2017. Personal communication (email) from Stuart McEwen Jenkins, former engineer De La Rue, with B. Bátiz-Lazo, 24 October 2017.
26. Richard Browning, 'Historic Inflation Calculator', *MailOnline*, accessed 8 October 2014, <http://www.thisismoney.co.uk/money/bills/article-1633409/Historic-inflation-calculator-value-money-changed-1900.html>. It is also interesting that in 2014 the £10 note remained the minimum withdrawal for most British cash machines.
27. Interview (video conference) with Stuart McEwen Jenkins, former project manager at De La Rue Instruments, by B. Bátiz-Lazo, 12 October 2017.

28. Born in Shillong in Assam, India (now Bangladesh), on 23 June 1925, and died in Scotland, on 15 May 2011. He was educated at Stowe School and during the war he served in the Royal Air Force and attended the University of Edinburgh under military auspices before being admitted to Trinity College Cambridge as a pensioner in October 1948. He initially read for the Economics Tripos, and appears to have been allowed a pass in the first part of the examination in 1949, but did not complete his degree. Following his time at Cambridge he moved to De La Rue as a management trainee based in Surrey, where he eventually worked at the board level, for example, chairing an armoured truck company division (Security Express Ltd) and becoming managing director of De La Rue Instruments. For an alternative biography see Shepherd-Barron (2017).

29. 'The De La Rue Company Ltd', Monopolies and Mergers Commission, accessed 8 October 2014, originally at: <http://www.competition-commission.org.uk/rep_pub/reports/1960_1969/fulltext/054c03.pdf>. See also Pugh (2011, 166).

30. 'De La Rue Company History', *Funding Universe*, accessed 8 October 2014, <http://www.fundinguniverse.com/company-histories/De-La-Rue-plc-Company-History.html>. See further Pugh (2011).

31. Interview with John Shepherd-Barron, former director of De La Rue, by B. Bátiz-Lazo and R. Reid, 26 March 2008.

32. Brian Milligan, 'The Man Who Invented the Cash Machine', *BBC News*, 27 June 2007, accessed 24 October 2017, <http://news.bbc.co.uk/1/low/business/6230194.stm>.

33. Interview with John Shepherd-Barron, former director of De La Rue, by B. Bátiz-Lazo and R. Reid, 26 March 2008.

34. Interview with John Shepherd-Barron, former director of De La Rue, by B. Bátiz-Lazo and R. Reid, 26 March 2008 and Shepherd-Barron (2017, 72).

35. As noted by Booth (2007, 219) and corroborated by me at the London Metropolitan Archives, the papers of the Electronics Sub-Committee did not survive as part of the documents of the British Bankers Association (stored at the Guildhall Library). However, some scattered references are made in surviving records at HSBC Group Archives (HSBCGA, London, Acc 200/176 and Acc 200/677) and the Royal Bank of Scotland Archives (RBSGA, Acc WD/366/3 and WD/366/11).

36. RBSGA, WD/366/3, 6th Report of the Electronics Sub-Committee: Suggested specifications of equipment for bank automation (20 December 1956).

37. RBSGA, WD/366/3, 7th Report of the Electronics Sub-Committee: Visits to National Physical Laboratory, Master Printers, Solartron Research Laboratory (1 March 1957) and RBSGA, WD/366/3, 8th Report of the Electronics Sub-Committee: Meetings with manufacturers (1 June 1957). The list of manufacturers included foreign firms such as IBM, Burroughs, Remington-Rand, Olivetti, and NCR, as well as domestic firms such as Power Samas, Elliott Brothers, English Electric, and Leo Computers. Neither De La Rue nor Chubb appears on the list.

38. Martin (2011, 37).

39. Ron Everett is mentioned as a key actor in the specification, pricing, and development of the DACS prototype by Shepherd-Barron (2017, 71–2).

40. Beside Barclays Bank, the Bank of Scotland also made use of DACS devices in Britain in the 'Scotcash' system. At the time Bank of Scotland was part of the same group as Barclays.

41. In June 1974 Barclays placed an advance order for 100 NCR 770 devices. The order was made public in May 1975. The first retail branches to offer the new machines were in High Street and Cornmarket Street, Oxford. In September 1975 NatWest introduced its first NCR 770 (advertised as 'Servicetills'). The first two machines installed in January 1975 were for staff use only. Two more were operational in banking halls in April and May and therefore limited to banking hours. But the machine that came into operation in the Croydon branch in September was external and therefore provided service to the public all year round. By the end of 1977, NatWest had 100 NCR 770 machines in operation alongside 406 Chubb MD2 and MD4 dispensers while 75,000 cards had been issued to customers. Meanwhile, Barclays increased the order to 500 NCRs in 1979. The bulk of NatWest's and Barclays' NCR 770 machines were to be manufactured in Dundee, Scotland. During the move from Ohio to Scotland a new model was rolled out in 1978, the NCR 1780. This kept many of the features of the 770 except that it was the first NCR ATM to be fitted with a video display unit (VDU). Source: BGA, 'Barclays Fact Sheet—Cash Machines', undated. Note compiled by Barclays Group Archives; Royal Bank of Scotland Group Archives, press release, 9 September 1975; National Cash Register (NCR), *Annual Report and Accounts*, 1978; Ackrill and Hannah (2001, 335–6); Bátiz-Lazo (2009).

42. The DACS cash machines were used by three banking companies in the USA: First Pennsylvania in Philadelphia, PA; South Shore National near Boston, MA; and First National of Natick, MA also near Boston, MA. The thirteen machines deployed in the USA were the second design type with a single drawer. They were in service during the late 1960s and early 1970s. Source: Personal communication (email) and interview (telephone) with Jim Noll, service engineer, by B. Bátiz-Lazo, 1 April 2013. See also 'Show Him the Money: Collector Cashes In', *ATM Marketplace*, 17 March 2003, accessed 17 June 2017, <https://www.atmmarketplace.com/news/show-him-the-money-collector-cashes-in/>. The deployment in Zurich is evident in a promotional video: 'Geldautomat (Bancomat)', *YouTube*, 21 April 2013, accessed 27 June 2017, <https://www.youtube.com/watch?v=QYfBczC1FrU>, and corroborates part of the DACS story as told by Shepherd-Barron (2017, 62–4).

43. Unless otherwise stated, this paragraph borrows from the interview (video conference) with Stuart McEwen Jenkins, former project manager at De La Rue Instruments, by B. Bátiz-Lazo, 12 October 2017.

44. Personal communication (email) from Stuart McEwen Jenkins, former project manager at De La Rue Instruments, by B. Bátiz-Lazo, 16 October 2017.

45. The root to this device and others that became the 1300/1327 series multiple banknote dispensers by De La Rue was a patent for a 'Cash Dispensing Apparatus' filed 28 May 1971, granted 18 September 1973 to S. McEwen Jenkins and J. Whitehead as GB 3760158 (US 3760158A, CA 945520A, and DE 2127815A1). Source: personal communication (email) from Stuart McEwen Jenkins, former project manager at De La Rue Instruments, by B. Bátiz-Lazo, 26 October 2017.

46. Personal communication (email) from Bryan King, former member of the Organization & Methods department at the Westminster Bank, with B. Bátiz-Lazo, 19 October 2017.

47. The Westminster Bank and the National Provincial Bank merged in 1968 to form National Westminster Bank (commonly known as NatWest). Unless otherwise stated, the rest of this section borrows from multiple personal communications (email) from Stuart McEwen Jenkins, former project manager at De La Rue Instruments, with B. Bátiz-Lazo, 11 to 26 October 2017, and personal communications (email) from Bryan King, former member of the Organization & Methods department at the Westminster Bank, with B. Bátiz-Lazo, 19 to 21 October 2017.

48. Interview (telephone) with David Ibbs, former engineer at Chubb, by B. Bátiz-Lazo, 5 November 2013.

49. Unless otherwise stated, this section borrows from Bátiz-Lazo (2009); Bátiz-Lazo and Reid (2008, 2011).

50. Conversion using average earnings based on: 'Purchasing Power of British Pounds: From 1270 to Present', *Measuringworth*, accessed 18 October 2013, <http://www.measuringworth.com/ppoweruk/>, and a mid-market rate of 1 GBP = 1.61923 USD according to 'XE Live Exchange Rates', *XE*, accessed 18 October 2013, <http://www.xe.com/>.

51. Chubb & Son's Lock & Safe Company Group, *Annual Report and Accounts* (London, 1970): 16.

52. Personal communication (email) from Malcolm Page, former director NatWest, with Bryan King, 21 October 2017.

53. Interview (telephone) with David Miller, former engineer at Smiths Industries, by B. Bátiz-Lazo, 30 May 2017. See also: 'Was the ATM a Disruptive Innovation?', *ATM Marketplace*, accessed 30 May 2017, <https://www.atmmarketplace.com/articles/was-the-atm-a-disruptive-innovation/> and Nye (2014, 191–2).

54. Unless otherwise stated, this paragraph was sourced from personal communication (email) from David Miller, former engineer at Smiths Industries, with Micheal Lee, CEO ATM Industry Association, 9 February 2017.

55. Personal communication (email) from Bryan King, former member of the Organization & Methods department at the Westminster Bank, with B. Bátiz-Lazo, 19 October 2017.

56. See further Nye (2014).

57. Unless otherwise stated, this paragraph borrows freely from a personal communication (email) from David Miller, former engineer at Smiths Industries, with Micheal Lee, CEO ATM Industry Association, 9 February 2017.

58. Patent GB 1197183/US 3905461.

59. Unless otherwise stated, this paragraph borrows from interview (telephone) with David Miller, former engineer at Smiths Industries, by B. Bátiz-Lazo, 30 May 2017; and interview with James Goodfellow, Paisley, Renfrewshire, by B. Bátiz-Lazo and R. Reid, 27 March 2008.

60. A total of 60 digits were available on the quarter Hollerith card used by the system: six were used by the sort code, eight by the account number, and two for the entry gate; leaving 44 digits that could be used for a PAN.

61. The introduction of the credit card to the UK is well documented. For instance, Ackrill and Hannah (2001); Bátiz-Lazo and Del Angel (2016); Bátiz-Lazo and Hacialioglu (2005); Drury and Ferrier (1984); Mandell (1990).

62. An 'AND gate' is a digital logic gate with two or more inputs and one output that performs logical conjunction.

63. Interview (telephone) with David Miller, former engineer at Smiths Industries, by B. Bátiz-Lazo, 30 May 2017. See also: 'Was the ATM a Disruptive Innovation?', *ATM Marketplace*, accessed 30 May 2017, <https://www.atmmarketplace.com/articles/was-the-atm-a-disruptive-innovation/>. For an authoritative story of Smiths Industries see Nye (2014).

64. Files 8A129/1 in the Bank of England Archives (BoEA) contains a note dated 8 June 1967 that specifically refers to a recent meeting held at Chubb's in Wolverhampton where a new cash machine was demonstrated to the Bank of England's Deputy Chief Cashier, Richard Creighton Balfour, and Robert Catt, the Deputy Secretary for Organization & Methods and Head Office computer projects. A search of a series of Chief Cashier's Duplicate Letters (series ref.: C54/11 to 21), dating from 1964 to 1967 to help ascertain the exact date of this meeting proved fruitless. However, it is clear the representatives of the Bank of England were more interested in the technology for its own retail branch operations and the servicing of its own customers than in concerns over bank regulation or supervision of the money market (all these areas were at the time under the aegis of the Cashier's Department).

65. Personal communication (email) from David Miller, former engineer at Smiths Industries, with Micheal Lee, CEO ATM Industry Association, 9 February 2017.

66. 'Memorandum for Board', 1 August 1967 (RBSGA WES/595/14, File marked 'Mechanisation').

67. T. McMillan, General Managers' Committee: Administration Department, '24-hour Cash Dispensing Service', 4 August 1967 (RBSGA WES/595/14, File marked 'Mechanisation').

68. General Mangers Committee: Administration Department, 'Expenditure on Machines and Equipment', 26 January 1968 (RBSGA WES/595/14, File marked 'Mechanisation'). Conversion using average earnings based on: 'Purchasing Power of British Pounds from 1270 to Present', *Measuringworth*, accessed 18 October 2013, <http://www.measuringworth.com/ppoweruk/> and a mid-market rate of 1 GBP = 1.61923 USD according to 'XE Live Exchange Rate', *XE*, accessed 18 October 2013, <http://www.xe.com/>.

69. Chubb & Son's Lock & Safe Company Group, *Annual Report and Accounts* (London, 1970): 16; 'Jack Howe Obituary', *The Telegraph*, 16 December 2003, accessed 15 June 2017, <http://www.telegraph.co.uk/news/obituaries/1449526/Jack-Howe.html>.

70. 'City Editor's Awards 1967: Men of the Year', *Sunday Telegraph*, 31 December 1967; and RBSGA, WES/595/14, File marked 'Mechanisation'.

71. 'City Editor's Awards 1967: Men of the Year', *Sunday Telegraph*, 31 December 1967 (RBSGA WES/595/14, File marked 'Mechanisation').

72. Personal communication (email) from Bryan King, former member of the Organization & Methods department at the Westminster Bank, with B. Bátiz-Lazo, 19 October 2017.

73. Personal communication (email) from Bryan King, former member of the Organization & Methods department at the Westminster Bank, with B. Bátiz-Lazo, 19 October 2017.

74. RBSGA—WES/963, Westminster Bank, 'Technical Information, Chubb & Son's Lock & Safe Co Ltd', 1967.

75. Interview (telephone) with David Miller, former engineer at Smiths Industries, by B. Bátiz-Lazo, 30 May 2017.

76. Personal communication (email) from Malcolm Page, former director NatWest, with Bryan King, 21 October 2017.

77. RBSGA—DR/418, The Royal Bank of Scotland, Drummonds Branch, leaflet '24 hour cash service', circa 1968; and personal communication (email) from Malcolm Page, formerly of the Westminster's Organization & Methods, with B. Bátiz-Lazo, 27 October 2017.

78. Personal communication (email) from Grant Wells, Head of ATM & Projects, Travalex, with B. Bátiz-Lazo, 5 January 2017.

79. Personal communication (e-mail) from Nicholas Webb, Barclays Bank Archive, 'ATM Paper', with B. Bátiz-Lazo, 19 June 2007.

80. RBSGA—DIS/641, District Bank, photographs of Piccadilly branch cash machine on first day of use, 5 January 1968.

81. RBSGA—RB/150/2, The Royal Bank of Scotland, staff newspaper *Newsline*, February 1993. According to this article the actual date of operation was 28 December 1967: 'The first cash machine soon proved a hit!'.

82. 'Britain as Seen on ITV (S1 E1 Home & High Street)', *YouTube*, 9 April 2016, accessed 24 October 2017, <https://www.youtube.com/watch?v=Sb2_EuUy3FA>.

83. RBSGA—DR/418, The Royal Bank of Scotland, Drummonds Branch, leaflet '24 Hour Cash Service', circa 1968.

84. RBSGA—WES/963, Westminster Bank, 'Technical Information, Chubb & Son's Lock & Safe Co Ltd', 1967.

85. Interview (telephone) with David Miller, former engineer at Smiths Industries, by B. Bátiz-Lazo, 30 May 2017.

86. Interview (telephone) with David Miller, former engineer at Smiths Industries, by B. Bátiz-Lazo, 30 May 2017.

87. Chubb & Son's Lock & Safe Company Group, *Annual Report and Accounts* (London, 1971): 9.

88. 'How the ATM Revolutionized Retail Banking: Part II', *ATM Marketplace*, 10 June 2013, accessed 8 April 2016, <http://www.atmmarketplace.com/articles/how-the-atm-revolutionized-retail-banking-part-ii/>.

89. 'How the ATM Revolutionized Retail Banking: Part II', *ATM Marketplace*, 10 June 2013, accessed 8 April 2016, <http://www.atmmarketplace.com/articles/how-the-atm-revolutionized-retail-banking-part-ii/>.

90. Interview (telephone) with Jim Block, Chief Technology Engineer Diebold, by B. Bátiz-Lazo, 26 March 2013.

91. US District Court, N.D. Ohio, C76-49A (2 November 1977).

92. Interview with Bill Chubb, 4th Lord Hayter, by B. Bátiz-Lazo, 30 March 2010.

93. Chubb & Son's Lock & Safe Company Group, *Annual Report and Accounts* (London, 1974): 5. Conversion using average earnings based on: 'Purchasing Power of British Pounds from 1270 to Present', *Measuringworth*, accessed 18 October2013, <http://www.measuringworth.com/ppoweruk/> and a mid-market rate of 1 GBP = 1.61923 USD according to: 'XE Live Exchange Rate', *XE*, accessed 18 October 2013, <http://www.xe.com/>.

94. Chubb & Son's Lock & Safe Company Group, *Annual Report and Accounts* (London, 1977): 11. The cash register business, based in Hollingbury near Brighton, was sold shortly after amalgamation while the manufacturing of cash dispensing technology moved to Chubb Integrated Systems. The latter was eventually renamed Chubb Security Installations or CSI. CSI was subsequently divested in 2000 and acquired by the Gunnebo Group (of Sweden). Since then it has traded as CSI Gunnebo and retained some related products such as Armapod Plus, Citypod and Cityroom, all of which were designed to house the ATM machines and to protect those individuals who replenish or service them and may be at risk of physical assault or armed attack whilst doing so. Source: Personal communication (email) from Jane Garland, Marketing Communications Manager, Chubb Fire Limited (A UTC Fire & Security Company) with B. Bátiz-Lazo, 10 April 2007; Personal communication (email), from Alan Jacques, Design and Engineering Manager, Gunnebo CSI, with B. Bátiz-Lazo, 1 May 2007; 'Company Profile History', CSISEC, accessed 16 April 2007, originally at: <http://www.csisec.com/company_profile_history.htm> and 'Our History', Chubb UK, accessed 16 April 2007, originally at: <http://www.chubb.co.uk/chserver> and 'Our History', Chubb UK, accessed 16 April 2007, originally at <http://www.chubb.co.uk/chserver>. See also 'Chubb: Centuries of Innovation', accessed 2 February 2018, <http://www.chubbfiresecurity.com/en/uk/about/history/>.

95. Personal communication (email) from Bill Chubb, 4th Lord Hayter, with B. Bátiz-Lazo, 6 December 2009.

96. *Investor's Chronicle*, 3 March 1978. Note that in 1970, Chubb purchased ICC Machines Ltd., a specialist in devices for counting, issuing, and changing coins.

97. An estimate for 1974 reckoned that the fixed cost of purchasing and installing an ATM was between $25,000 and $30,000 while $200,000 should be added to cover the operating costs of armoured car services and data processing. At the time, NatWest had 6,000 customers with cash cards and nine Chubb machines (RBSGA—unpublished research note compiled by Group Archives). That is an average of 667 customers per machine. NatWest could have achieved economies of scale at a rate of 44,000 transactions per machine per month if each of NatWest's customers had made, on average, 1.2 withdrawals per week. See Walker (1980).

98. Interview with Bill Chubb, 4th Lord Hayter, by B. Bátiz-Lazo, 30 March 2010.

99. Interview with Bill Chubb, 4th Lord Hayter, by B. Bátiz-Lazo, 30 March 2010.

100. London Metropolitan Archives (henceforth LMA), CLCB 002: 01 07 035 'Phillips Agreement', Letter from A. A. Thomas to K. F. Rankin, dated 5 August 1980.

101. Conversion using average earnings based on: 'Purchasing Power of British Pounds from 1270 to Present', *Measuringworth*, accessed 18 October 2013, <http://www.measuringworth.com/ppoweruk/> and a mid-market rate of 1 GBP = 1.61923 USD according to 'XE Live Exchange Rates', *XE*, accessed 18 October 2013, <http://www.xe.com/>.

102. Chubb & Son's Lock & Safe Company Group, *Annual Report and Accounts* (London, 1980; 1981; 1982).

103. Interview with Bill Chubb, 4th Lord Hayter, by B. Bátiz-Lazo, 30 March 2010.

104. Interview with Sean Newcombe, former engineer at Speytec, by B. Bátiz-Lazo and C. Reese, 5 February 2008. Interview with Jack Donald, former engineer at Speytec, by B. Bátiz-Lazo and C. Reese, 4 June 2008.

105. Holmes and Green (1986, 232–41).

106. Circular No. S. HSBC 1493 119/1967—'Automated Cash Dispensers', *HSBC Group Archives*, ref. 0200/0677b (henceforth HSBC 0200).

107. 'Automated Cash Dispensers', 15 May 1967 (HSBC 0200/0677b).

108. 'Automated Cash Dispensers', 26 April 1967 (HSBC 0200/0677b).

109. The same source mentions trials by the First National Bank of Arizona of a machine which accepted, counted, and validated cash credits. No other record of this machine was found.

110. GB 1329964, filed in September 1969 (granted 1973) by John David Edwards, Leonard Perkins, John Henry Donald, Peter Lee Chappell, Sean Benjamin Newcombe, and Malcolm David Roe.

111. The intended sum was £200 per cash card ('Automated Cash Dispensers – Speytec Ltd', 20 September 1968, HSBC 0200/0677b).

112. Conversion using Retail Price Index as suggested by: 'Purchasing Power of British Pounds from 1270 to Present', *Measuringworth*, accessed 9 October 2014, <http://www.measuringworth.com/ppoweruk/> and a mid-market rate of 1 GBP = 1.61923 USD according to: 'XE Live Exchange Rates', *XE*, accessed 18 October 2013, <http://www.xe.com/>.

113. The magnetic stripe system was spread over a number of filings, all of which are based on the original GB 1329964 patent. The method for verifying the card was detailed in GB 1329965 (filed on 27 August 1970 by the Burroughs Corporation and granted in 1973) and the card itself was patented under GB 1329966 (also filed on 27 August 1970 by the Burroughs Corporation and granted in 1973).

114. 'Automated Cash Dispensers', 26 April 1967 (HSBC 0200/0677b).

115. 'Automated Cash Dispensers', 30 September 1968 (HSBC 0200/0677b). Conversion using Retail Price Index as suggested by: 'Purchasing Power of British Pounds from 1270 to Present', *Measuringworth*, accessed 2 February 2018, <http://www.measuringworth.com/ppoweruk/>.

116. Speytec machines were deployed in branches at Croydon, Glasgow (Clydesdale), London (Old Bond Street, Piccadilly, and Shaftesbury Avenue), Manchester (Deansgate), Belfast, Crawley, Eastbourne, Hastings, and Romford. This was done while the bank was working to identify 50 other possible sites.

117. Booth (2007, 155).

118. 'Contracts 500 Cash Dispensers for Bank', *The Times*, 10 September 1969: 22, col. G. Conversion using average earnings based on 'Purchasing Power of British Pounds from 1270 to Present', *Measuringworth*, accessed 10 October 2014, <http://www.measuringworth.com/ppoweruk/> and a mid-market rate of 1 GBP = 1.61923 USD according to: 'XE Live Exchange Rates', *XE*, accessed 18 October 2013, <http://www.xe.com/>.

119. B. R. Johnson, 'First Steps in Self-Serving Banking', TSB Gazette, vol. 37 (1974): 74–80.

120. On the deployment of Burroughs ATMs by the TSB see Bátiz-Lazo et al. (2014b).

121. The removal of the 'ageing machine' was done with great care as it was found it was holding up the wall. Source: 'Farewell to an ATM Dinosaur', *Lloyds TSB Banknotes*, October/November 1992: 8.

122. 'La máquina de hacer plata', *Revista Semana*, 11 February 1985: 33–4. I appreciate Beatriz Rodriguez-Satizabal pointing me to this source.

123. Konheim (2007, 509–11).

124. RBSGA—DR/418, The Royal Bank of Scotland, Drummonds Branch, leaflet '24 hour cash service', circa 1968.

125. Bátiz-Lazo and Wardley (2007).

126. Ceruzzi (2003, 80).

4

Building the Pipelines

4.1 Sluggish Take-Off

This chapter looks at the 1970s, a period of initial growth and dispersion while engineering concerns revolved around the critical issue of proving the viability of the cash dispenser (i.e. 'proof of concept' stage). The latter involved alternative designs by several manufacturing firms. Developing security and online capabilities was a key way for banks to make sure that the person who initiated the transaction had the right to do so. Towards the end of the 1970s the first standards for operation had been put in place, when IBM and Docutel had the potential to become the dominant players in the industry. But in spite of being in a position to lead the ATM market, they blew their chance by insisting on newer proprietary technology which was incompatible with the banks' substantial investments in older systems.

As noted in Chapter 3, there is no evidence suggesting that the genesis of the cash machine witnessed any race or extreme competition to be the first to market. But this was to change as more and more banks became interested in testing the technology. Table 4.1 summarizes the first deployment of cash machines across the world between 1967 and 1980. According to these data, 1973 was the average year of first installation in most countries, but this varied substantially (as suggested by a standard deviation of 4.16). It was also the case that in many of these countries individual banks deployed a small number of machines (sometimes as few as one or two). For many banks (and even countries) no devices were deployed in significant numbers until the mid to late 1980s, that is, ten or even fifteen years after the first of them. Indeed, until the early 1990s deployment worldwide remained below half a million units.

In its early days, few believed that the cash machine would make a difference to the average consumer. In context, this prediction might have seemed safe, since alternative technological solutions also appeared around this time. Some of them were successful (such as telephone banking, the electronic transfer of funds, and point of sale terminals) and many others that we have

Table 4.1. First adoption of cash machines in selected countries, 1967–1980

Manufacturer	Country (year of first deployment)
Asea-Metior	Sweden (1967), Germany (1968), the Netherlands (1968), Portugal (1968), Spain (1968), Switzerland (1968), Denmark (1969), France (1969), Israel (1970).
Chubb	UK (1967), Canada (1969—through Chubb Mosler) and Singapore (circa 1974).
Diebold	USA (1971)*, Mexico (1972), Ecuador (1975), Uruguay (1978).
Docutel	USA (1969).
IBM	UK (1972)*, Honduras (1980).
NCR	USA (1973)*, UK (1975)*, China (1980).
Olivetti	Peru (1979).
Omron-Tateishi	Japan (1969).
(Not Available)	Australia (1974), Colombia (1975), Finland (1975), Republic of Korea (1975), Cyprus (1976), Norway (1977), Hong Kong (1978), Puerto Rico (1978), Ireland (1980), Austria (1980).

* First deployment for manufacturer only.
Source: Own estimates.

forgotten (e.g. Minitel, TV banking, semi-automatic cheque cashing in retail stores, and videotexting). They all competed for attention and capital investment in the automation of retail banking. These inventions appeared before credit or debit cards were a popular alternative to banknotes and coins, at a time when most of the world's citizens worked in a cash economy.

Conditions in the global economy were also unhelpful. These were the early days of variable exchange rates, when millions of working days were lost as a result of militant action by organized labour, and high rates of inflation were common across industrialized economies (which, in turn, resulted in the highly volatile prices in other currencies for devices priced in dollars, sterling, or Swedish krona).

Together with restrictions in international trade, macroeconomic conditions and a lack of clarity over functionality helped various providers to develop a large number of alternative designs. Often they would limit their services to their home market while aiming to establish the long-term feasibility of the cash machine.

We now look at the early cash machine manufacturers. For clarity, we focus on the US market where the manufacturers will be divided into three different categories, namely, independent participants (Table 4.2), diversifying participants (Table 4.3), and foreign participants (Table 4.4).

Table 4.2 lists the indigenous entrants to the provision of cash machines in the USA, following the classification by Sarah Lane.[1] The 'indigenous' category identifies companies set up with the specific purpose of manufacturing devices for the distribution of cash, which were established roughly at the time the market was created.[2] As noted in Table 4.2, the average year of entry was 1970, while the average year of exit was 1978. Companies in this category

Table 4.2. Independent participants in the market for cash machines in the USA, 1967–1986 (alphabetical order)

Manufacturer (year of entry/exit) (Avg 1970/1978)	Model and features (as of 1974 or closest)	Genealogy
Bank Computer Network Corp (1972–76)	Lobby type machine. Keyed-in account number and PIN. Could accept credit card or one-time card.	N/A
Digital Security Systems (1971)	Check-$-Matic—Pay out varying amounts of bills and coins. Activated by ID number or voucher.	N/A
Docutel (1969–86)	Total Teller System—Automated terminal with pre-programmed buttons for 11 transactions. Also developed a drive-up version of the Total Teller called the T3.	Leading supplier until 1974. Merged with US subsidiary of Olivetti in 1982 following failure of acceptance of latter models.
Money Machine (1967–78)	Model 401 & 402—Could dispense money in 5 sec. Activated by credit card type token (401—card retained) or credit card with magnetic stripe (402—card returned).	N/A

Source: Own estimates, based on Lane (1989) and Zimmer (1971, 1974, 1975).

included Docutel, a subsidiary of Recognition Equipment Inc., a manufacturer of baggage handling equipment (which is often wrongly hailed as the inventor of the ATM).[3] Table 4.3 summarizes the domestic 'diversified' entrants. This category encompasses companies that offered cash machine equipment, building on their experience in cash-handling devices or security products, such as safes and vaults (e.g. Mosler, LeFebure). These were devices that mainly operated offline. Yet another group came largely from computer manufacturing (e.g. NCR, IBM, Honeywell, and Burroughs).[4]

The data in Table 4.4 outline foreign-based manufacturers of cash machines in the USA for the years between 1967 and 1986. This further illustrates how manufacturers alongside the British and Swedish pioneers emerged from a range of sectors—each with its own competitive dynamics. When compared to independent and domestic diversifiers, foreign manufacturers seem to have been the most ephemeral (with an average lifespan of two to three years). These included Omron-Tateisi from Japan, Datasaab from Sweden, and of course, Chubb and De La Rue from the UK.[5] Many other outlets emerged in Europe, such as Siemens and Nixdorf in Germany, Phillips in the Netherlands, and Italy's Olivetti; but many other smaller ones also; 'each individual manufacturer coerced their own governments and their own banks to be protective'.[6]

Taking the data in Tables 4.2, 4.3, and 4.4 together produces a mosaic of the early stages in the spread of cash machines. This results from a heterogeneous mixture of independent manufacturers competing with domestic diversifiers

Table 4.3. Diversifying participants in the market for cash machines in the USA, 1971–1986 (alphabetical order)

Manufacturer (year of entry/exit) (Avg 1975/1982)	Model and features (as of 1974 or closest)	Genealogy
Burroughs (1971–86)	Model TC750—Offered full compatibility with other electronic tellers, back-up of transactions in magnetic cassettes, customized operation. Dispensed cash in packaged clips (up to 9 per customer). Also offered table top version.	Built on Speytec design at the instance of Midland Bank. Sold auto teller operations to NCR in 1986. Years later it re-entered the market and in 2011 partnered with South Korea's Nautilus Hyosung.
Concord (1982–6)	N/A	N/A
Diebold (1971–6)	MD 200 & 400—Special card retained by the bank (200) and compatible with credit cards (400). Total Automatic Banking System (TABS) 500—Advanced reconciliation. Could be fitted with CCTV.	The MD models were originally designed and manufactured by Chubb in the UK. But given their poor performance, Diebold launched its own Total Automatic Banking System (TABS) 500 in 1973. Became and remained a leading participant.
Honeywell (1977–81)	N/A	N/A
IBM (1972–86)	Developed for Lloyds Bank as 2984. A second-generation model 3614 was part of IBM 3600 Finance Communication System family of products. This was followed by the 3624 model, which was the most popular ATM in the late 1970s and early 1980s.	Following the failure of acceptance of the 473x family, in 1984, Diebold and IBM created a joint venture called InterBold to leverage the former's expertise in self-service banking technology through the latter's international sales network. The joint venture ended in 1997.
LeFebure (1973–80)	724 Automated Customer Terminal.	Security products activities acquired by Mosler in 1998.
Mosler Safe Co. (1971–8)	Teller-Matic System 4000 included drive-up unit version.	Entered the industry through previous joint venture with Chubb in Canada. The automatic teller activities of Mosler were sold to TRW in 1978. TRW merged with Fujitsu in 1981.
NCR (1973–86)	Model 770—Had a modular design that enabled constant updating.	Design and manufacturing relocated from Ohio to Scotland in 1978 and became the leading supplier in the market following the IBM failure of acceptance.
SCI Systems (1985)	N/A	N/A
TRW (1978–80)	N/A	Automatic teller activities of TRW and Fujitsu merged in 1981.

Source: Own estimates, based on Lane (1989) and Zimmer (1971, 1974, 1975).

Table 4.4. Foreign participants in the market for cash machines in the USA, 1969–1986 (alphabetical order)

Manufacturer (year of entry/exit) (Avg 1979/1981)	Model and features (as of 1974 or closest)	Genealogy
Chubb—UK (1976–7)	MD 6000 lobby machine. MD4 'online' 'through the wall'.	Bankrupt in 1984. Divisions sold to different parties. Trade name remained but not in automatic tellers.
Datasaab—Sweden (1980–1)	N/A	Originally developed to service Docutel's European clients, it developed its own devices in collaboration with Omron.
De La Rue—UK (1969–71)	DACS—'through the wall' device activated by cheque-like token.	Deployed 13 machines in the Boston, MA and Philadelphia, PA areas. Exited the market in 1975.
Fujitsu—Japan (1981–6)	Introduced special features, such as a machine for drive-through banks that adjusted itself to the height of each passing car and machines for the blind with voice guidance and braille indicators.	Remained independent and grew to be one of the largest providers in the US market.
Interbank—N/A (1982–6)	N/A	N/A
Omron—Japan (1985–6)	System directly connected to the user's bank account to verify funds.	N/A

Source: Own estimates, based on Lane (1989), Thodenius et al. (2011), and Zimmer (1971, 1974, 1975).

and foreign providers. The average life of a provider in the US market was 7.6 years, but this fluctuated (as measured by a standard deviation of 5.6). Data in Tables 4.2, 4.3, and 4.4 suggest that the industry had a sluggish take-off between 1967 and 1972, in part due to the challenges presented to banks by any device interacting directly with the public. Early devices had many challenges, such as a poor customer interface, low security, being unable to operate throughout an extended day (and even then offering low availability), as well as issues around the handling of external media.[7] Thereafter sales enabled some eight to ten firms to remain in the market (standard deviation of 3).

Other sources also hint at the limited adoption of cash machines following their invention—in good measure, considering the limited capabilities of early devices, most of them were offline, kept the card or activation token inside the device, and supplied a fixed amount of cash in response to a pre-purchased card or token. In Spain, for instance, Banco Español de Crédito (Banesto), the country's biggest in terms of assets, installed one Bankomat at its head office branch in 1969.[8] It would be ten years before they deployed another. In the USA, one estimate was that in 1969 at least twelve banks in the United States had introduced cash machines;[9] whereas others reckoned that in 1971, only eleven banks (seven of which had more than $1 billion in assets) had an automatic cash machine in operation.[10] Linda F. Zimmer, the author of a number of annual estimates for the size of the ATM industry, calculated that in 1975 there were over 2,000 Docutel devices operational in some 500 banks across the USA.[11] In 1973, Money Machine Inc. claimed to have been 'the first to market cash machines in a big way in [the USA] . . . and second only to Docutel in the market [then], with 380 machines installed and on-order'.[12] These devices had generally been installed within retail bank branches, because many states in the USA restricted the number and distance of electronic terminals from the main office. But together these estimates suggest a staggeringly low penetration, in view of the almost 13,000 independent banks in the USA at the time.[13] Attitudes to the device differed sharply: some bankers saw the equipment as increasing customer convenience, while others considered automated cash dispensing a marketing gimmick, and an expensive one.

Cost was indeed one of the two greatest challenges faced by banks early on. To buy a cash machine in the mid-1970s cost between $24,000 and $35,000 or it could be leased for between $400 and $800 per month, with up to $10,000 more for installation;[14] in other words, a $30,000 to $40,000 price tag for 'through the wall' installation (with the necessary alarms) at a branch—this would have bought 'three vault doors, or six night depositories, or 10 teller stations, or a three kiosk pneumatic drive-in teller system'.[15] Most manufacturers also charged a monthly servicing fee of $130 to $350. Additional costs for supplies and internal processing could amount to another $800 a month. By comparison, the average wage of a teller at the time was about $900 a month plus benefits. 'Down time' of equipment that was prone to failure was also included in the considerations of many bankers while the additional cost of offering round-the-clock operation ('up time') was not trivial, especially because bankers in Sweden and the USA found that most customers used the dispensers initially during office hours (broadly 9 a.m. to 6 p.m.)—as alternatives to tellers.[16]

Getting customers to use the equipment for the first time was the other big challenge for banks.[17] It was found that if a customer used it once, he or she was likely to continue using it with increasing frequency. As a result, many banks fitted 'how to' instructions as a sticker alongside the machine for many a year—something that today we take for granted.

4.2 Challenges to Massification and Resilience

Alongside bankers' efforts to wrestle with costs and persuade people to actively use the device, engineers had to surmount significant technological challenges because, as mentioned, unreliability and limited functionality in its early days helped to keep its use down.[18] Among other things, engineering had to find solutions to the dominance of paper-based administrative systems within financial institutions, as well as emergent databases and database management systems and sequential (rather than random) access to digitalized records.[19] Inside the devices themselves, engineers had to deal with such issues as 0.1-millimetre-thick banknotes travelling individually inside the machine, the build-up of dust and dirt from external sources, including banknotes, paper, and magnetic stripes from customer cards, plus multiple moving parts that needed regular adjustment.[20] Never before had electronic equipment been so exposed to the elements. Early cash machines could erroneously dispense several banknotes instead of just one—all without the owner's knowledge. More important, they were a single, integrated piece of machinery, which meant that they were intolerant to the failure of even their smallest components. Magnetic stripes on the activation cards, for instance, were quite sensitive and could easily deteriorate—to the anger of customers.[21] Hence many banks often found machines idle for days or even weeks until an engineer or spare part became available. Security was also an issue, since the lack of online capability meant that the system could easily be abused; while other machines had simply a flawed design that was unable to withstand any serious attack. Geoffrey Constable, an engineer at Smiths Industries and familiar with the first design, remembers:

> The [Chubb] MD2 produced strong market feedback. The concept of a retained token, while sound from a security point of view, was not convenient for either the bank or its customers. A re-usable card machine was a necessity and, by this time, NCR had entered the market with just such a machine. Even more challenging, credit cards were now starting to be machine readable using an encoded magnetic stripe and the pressure for a normal credit card to work in an ATM was unstoppable. This situation raised enormous problems. Both Chubb and Smiths were acutely aware at that time that conventional magnetic stripe encoding was not secure, as the card could be 'skimmed' and replicated.[22]

Not only was security a concern, but the early devices were wired to a set number of activities, while the displacement of space by an often quite bulky object in a retail branch was significant. In short, early cash machines were stand-alone, clunky, unfriendly, unreliable, and inflexible. Given these constraints, it's not surprising that it took more than a decade for banks to deploy them except in a handful of experiments. By this time, the devices could identify a customer, check his/her balance, pay a variable amount of cash, update the balance accordingly, and provide other services (such as displaying the available balance or making a transfer) as the customer chose.

But however slowly and despite an uncertain future, bankers and engineers ploughed on. Automation on the back of computer applications inside financial institutions, together with possible networks for the electronic transfer of funds promised alternative ways to deliver customer services, greater cost efficiency, and potential new sources of income.[23] Thus the need for human intervention to credit and debit customer accounts in order to finalize a transaction in the early cash dispensing systems invited further automation. 'Many observers believed an on-line operation [could] more effectively control fraud.'[24] Critical to this process was developing capabilities for electronic data-processing technology, databases of customer information, applications to manage electronic repositories, and other hardware and software which would enable the device to credit or debit the customer's account without human intervention. In other words, it is electronic data-processing (EDP) which made the immediate and full updating of customer records, without any form of human intervention at the point of contact with the customer, the feature which distinguishes the early cash dispensing devices from the ATM—'a computerized telecommunications device that provides clients of a financial institution with access to financial transactions in a public place'.[25] This process of transformation required an intermediate state where the same device operated according to the context and choice of individual financial intermediaries, namely, stand-alone or delayed communication to a central computer.

Hence, many of the early 1970s cash machines were manufactured to work offline or 'batch' (that is, to transmit all transactions to be processed at the end of the day or some other fixed point). But this was not enough. The processes and procedures supporting the interaction between customer and bank also had to be digitized. For instance, point of sale terminals and magnetic card reading cash machines were available in the early 1970s, yet the manual input of purchases using credit cards (and later debit cards) remained in place until the late 1980s and early 1990s. In other instances, and far removed from the point of the transaction, the labour of human operators was required to initiate the programs and routines for updating records, performing control routines to verify the accuracy of these processes, or physically moving magnetic tapes and disks (with up-to-date records of transactions) between computers.

At the time these developments were taking place, the cash machine was also transformed from something set up and wired to a single form of operation to a more general platform, which allowed pre-programmed instructions to be stored (for operation to suit purchasing specifications and the emulation of alternative manufacturers). It is only when the device achieves online, real-time communication at the point of contact with the customer and can finalize the transaction without the involvement of any other human being that the ATM can be said to fulfil its function. That is, to serve as a remote device allowing individual customers to interact directly, easily, securely, reliably, and unobtrusively with the financial intermediary's central computer

Table 4.5. Competing claims in the development of the first online cash machine, 1968–1974

Year of claim	Engineering firm and bank	Country	Characteristics
1968	Asea-Metior & Swedish savings banks	Sweden	Cash dispenser in Malmö used an IBM 7714 interface to connect to an IBM 360 computer in Stockholm.
1969	Docutel & Chemical Bank	United States	Docutel US patents 3761682, 3651976, 3662343, and 368569 describe for the first time in detail a system that seems closer to the ATMs of today.
1972	IBM & Lloyds Bank	United Kingdom	IBM 2984 was a device linked to the central computer, able to check the customer's balance before withdrawal.
1972	Omron Tateisi Electronics Co. (later to be known as Omron) & Mitsubishi Bank	Japan	Omron's GB patent 1300848 described for the first time an 'online' method of transaction in which the system is directly connected to the user's bank account to verify funds and used a magnetic card as token.
1974	Diebold	United States	TABS 600 was an online version of the TAB 500, which included MICR printer and CCTV.

Source: Own estimates, based on Bátiz-Lazo and Reid (2008) and Harper and Bátiz-Lazo (2013).

and thus become a 'true' software application as proposed by Ceruzzi (2003, 80). It is this transition from attended to unattended services, resulting in truly self-service terminals, that opens up the possibility of 'McDonaldizing' retail finance.[26]

In this context IBM was the only provider who 'had a system [and] had the potential at that time to take over the market. [Because they] were truly international and because they had the mainframe control'.[27] IBM had the ability to provide mainframe-based software support for the ATMs plus leading encryption, key management, and online authorization which all helped address the security and fraud problems experienced in earlier systems.[28] The remainder of this chapter provides evidence to support this statement while documenting the genesis of online, real-time cash machines. The claims made for the various devices are summarized in Table 4.5.

4.3 Online Systems in the Patent Record

4.3.1 *The Relative Importance of Online Systems*

At least five independent claims assert the development of the first online cash machine. While these claims are not directly related to the original invention of the automated teller machine, they are significant in pointing to a further debate in the historical record, namely, 'Who developed the first online system?' and therefore paved the way for the second generation of cash dispensing machines.

As mentioned, the main difference between a cash machine and an ATM was complete absence of human intervention in the former. In this sense, a prerequisite in offering services other than mechanical aids for non-human involvement in cash withdrawals (or deposits), was the digitalization of customer records.[29] Even the ATM was possible only after solving hardware and software issues such as linking the device to a computer centre, programming the software to store records in a database, database management systems, and developing capabilities to handle high volumes of random transactions (unsystematic in their sequence yet standard in their nature). There were also organizational issues such as changing procedures to reconcile accounts, developing audit trails, and having adequate staff skills to rely on. The whole architecture of the banking organization had to change and it was a huge step from digitalizing specific activities to having fully operational online, real-time payment systems. These challenges, all expressed in smaller or larger measure by the emergence and dissemination of the automated teller machine, help to explains why it took so long to automate retail banking; hence the importance of looking at the early online systems in the history of the ATM.

Of the claims to be the first online machine three can be seen in the patent record, namely, Omron-Tateisi in Japan, and Docutel and Diebold in the USA. Then there is archival evidence supporting the claims of Metior in Sweden and IBM in the UK. These claims are now discussed in turn.

4.3.2 Omron-Tateisi in Japan, 1966–1975

The earliest claim for an online cash withdrawal device appeared in the context of the Tokyo Olympics of 1964.[30] This was some sort of account management system through which the customer interacted remotely with bank staff. Through the system the customer could withdraw cash not only in the branch where his/her account was, but in any other branches of the bank. The details of the operation of this system are scanty and therefore the validity of the claim remains unclear.

A more significant claim to have installed an early online cash withdrawal device in Japan emerges from the patent record. In this case by Tateisi Electronics (also known as Omron Tateisi or Omron).[31] As other innovators of cash dispensing technology, this Japanese company became involved in automatic vending machines. For the Tokyo International Fair in 1963, it set up a multi-function meal-ticket vending machine at the Daimayu department store in Kyoto. In 1964 its staff found another application for magnetic stripe technology through the development of an automatic ticket gate for railway commuters which handled both commuter passes and regular tickets. This technology was an essential part of the first automated (unmanned) train station, Hankyu Railway's Kitasenri station, which became operational in 1967.

Tateisi filed a patent in Japan on 1 July 1966 and published it on 15 October 1969 (JP 4279966A; also filed as US 3443675A in 1967 and granted in 1969). The patent named Mititaka Yamamoto, Yukio Mizuta, Toshio Tanaka, and Takeo Asada as inventors.

This patent for an 'automatic credit loan machine' described a system that bears a remarkable resemblance to De La Rue and Shepherd-Barron's system (see fascia in Figure 4.1) in that it used a 'credit card'-sized token to verify the eligibility of the user and retained it inside the machine (i.e. not returning it to the user) at the end of the transaction. The means of verification were magnetic, contained within a magnetic stripe on a card for accessing the relevant account. But as the name suggests and in contrast to the devices developed in the UK and Sweden, the Japanese machine did not aim to access liquid balances but to 'dispense a predetermined loan of cash'.

More significantly, this patent family developed into a system filed on 26 April 1969 by Omron Tateisi Electronics in Japan (in the UK it was filed in March 1970 granted as GB 1300848 in December 1972). It described for the first time an online method of transaction in which the system is directly connected to the user's bank account to verify funds.

The company's corporate history claims to have deployed an offline system using a plastic card with a magnetic stripe between 1966 and 1969. Called 'Kei YM4050' the first of these were in operation at the Shinjuku and Umeda

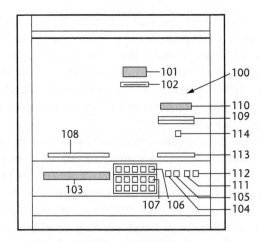

Figure 4.1. Fascia of Omron's automated teller system, 1966
Source: Patent JP 4279966A (filed 1966, granted 1973).

branches of the Sumitomo Bank in December 1969.[32] The system was not restricted to cash withdrawals and could be applied to other banking services because of the multiple types of transaction information that could be read and stored in the card. At the time, the price of a cash machine developed by the British maker De La Rue was about ¥7 million (approx. $32,000), whereas the domestic one cost ¥5 million (approx. $23,150).[33]

In May 1971 the company deployed an online system called 'Kei YM-LA-01' at the central office of the Mitsubishi Bank, where it was connected directly to the bank's main computer.[34] This seems to have been the start of automated cash withdrawals in Japan, where by 1974 there were 3.5 million activation cards in circulation and between 5,000 and 6,000 cash machines installed by thirteen 'city' banks and seventy-five local (commercial) banks.[35]

The rapid growth of cash dispensers led to the creation of joint companies to manage them (more on shared networks appears in Chapters 5 and 6). The first of these was the Nippon Cashing Service Co., established through the collaboration of fifty-four banks and the Nippon Telegraph and Telephone Public Corporation, to oversee all cash dispensers operating in the Greater Tokyo Metropolitan area, Kinki area, and Nagoya city.[36]

4.3.3 Donald C. Wetzel and Docutel, 1968–1974

Another claim to the original conception of the automatic teller machine dates back to 1969 and specifically the deployment in New York City of a device manufactured by the Docutel Corporation as conceived by Donald C. Wetzel.[37] Such is the strength of the claim of Docutel and Wetzel, that in 1995 the Smithsonian Institute named Wetzel the 'inventor of the ATM'.[38]

In 1968, when Wetzel started work at Docutel, it was a subsidiary of Recognition Equipment Inc. based in Dallas, TX. Recognition Equipment was the world leader in optical scanning technology, supplying devices to a number of financial service providers in the USA and Europe.[39] Docutel was not directly involved with financial institutions as its parent company had pointed it towards other areas of activity, including automated baggage handling and automated petrol pumps.[40] Wetzel joined as vice-president of product planning, after having worked as a salesman at IBM for a decade and a half since his graduation. His experience included servicing financial institutions in Texas, northern Louisiana, and New Mexico.[41] Shortly after his appointment, Wetzel came up with the idea that Docutel ' . . . could build a machine that would perform at least 90 percent, perhaps more than 90 percent, of all the transactions processed by a teller'.[42] This first prototype was offline and was activated by a customer PIN and encryption in the magnetic stripe of a plastic card.

According to Wetzel in the same interview, there were plans for a more advanced version with a number of self-service functions (e.g. envelope deposits, balance transfers between accounts, cash advances on the credit card, third party payments, etc.). This machine was much closer 'to the ATM we know today...So they didn't want just a cash dispenser alone.'[43]

But this terminal would have to be compatible with IBM, NCR, and Burroughs, the three main computer manufacturers, and its development would require a significant investment. In 1969 a venture capital consortium purchased Docutel with a view to introducing its cash machines without delay.[44] By 1974, Docutel had acquired a 70 per cent share of the cash machines installed in the USA while Wetzel had left the company, for personal reasons, and started his own business servicing financial institutions in Texas. Meanwhile, the combination of a worldwide recession in the mid-1970s and the focus on a single line of business in Docutel, led to the loss of its independence when it was acquired as the US subsidiary of Olivetti in 1982.

Perhaps the reason to support the Wetzel-Docutel claim is best summed up in the illustrations that accompanied its 1973 patents, which display for the first time in the patent record a full, free-standing automated teller system (see Figure 4.2), rather than an invention defined primarily by its verification/security system, as Chubb's or De La Rue's was.

But whether or not Wetzel conceived the system from first principles is to some degree open to doubt. The source of both the claim and the dubiety emerges from an interview given by Don Wetzel on 21 September 1995. In this interview, he claims total ownership for the concept of a complete ATM system: 'Finally I suggested the idea of this machine that would do most of the work of a teller. In Docutel it was well received.'[45] The patent record, US patent US 3761682, filed on 7 October 1971, cites Wetzel as an applicant and contains a detailed description of a fully-fledged cash dispensing system. However, the patent records contain at least three previous applications from Docutel which do not name Wetzel at all. These patent applications were filed on the same day as each other a year before Wetzel's, namely US 3651976, US 3662343, and US 368569 filed on 29 July 1970. These patents feature the names MR Karecki, TR Barnes, KS Goldstein, GR Chastian, and JD White. White has claimed that it was he and Goldstein who conceived the idea of a complete automated teller system.[46]

The Docuteller was installed in New York's Chemical Bank in 1969 and hailed as the first ATM, if not in the world, then certainly in the USA.[47] However, doubt over this claim by Docutel and Chemical Bank was thrown by trailblazer Citibank, which had not only tested Simjian's Bankograph in 1961, but in 1968 had also tested a 'money dispensing' device of unknown make, described as a 'cash station', which would provide 'an around-the-clock electronic substitute for the conventional check-cashing system...operated by a special Citibank card [which] responds only to that card in conjunction with a secret code issued [to] the individual customer'.[48]

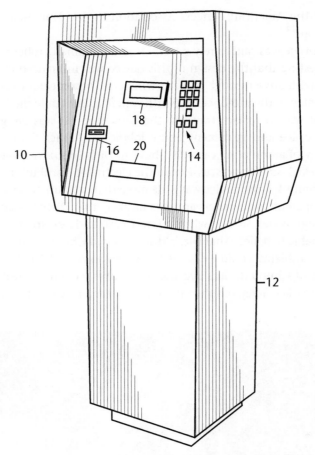

Figure 4.2. Docutel's currency dispensing machine, 1973
Source: Patent US 3761682 (filed 1971, granted 1973).

In short, the Docutel patents are significant, for they describe in detail a system that seems closer to that of today's ATMs, using a magnetic card for verification. However, it is clear from the patent record that the analogue nature of this device places it very much in the first generation of cash dispensing technology; claims to have designed the system from first principles, or to have been the first to be operational are also dubious.

4.3.4 *Diebold, 1966–1974*

As briefly mentioned in Chapter 3, Diebold had in the mid-1960s initiated independent research and development in regard to electronic cash dispensing equipment. Figure 4.3 provides photographic evidence for this claim: it shows Richard Glyer demonstrating a Diebold prototype at the annual meeting of the American Bankers Association in San Francisco, CA on 25 October 1966.[49]

The prototype was said to rely on CCTV and pneumatic tubes for its operation, suggesting that the design of this device was influenced by Diebold's experience with drive-through banking which had become quite popular with the ascendency of the motor car in North America. But while the idea behind the concept was to replace travel to the bank teller, it was designed to be located in 'office and apartment house lobbies'.[50] Rather than offering an effective way of automating cash distribution, Diebold's device was probably intended to kick-start the discussion on the electronic distribution of cash. As shown in Figure 4.3, the device was little more than a futuristic looking fascia. It has no apparent connections and it is unlikely that Diebold had solved its internal design issues, such as where to store cash and how to dispense it. It is then reasonable to believe that Diebold approached Chubb to learn first-hand how these problems could be solved.[51] In any event, Diebold ended the distribution of Chubb devices because their 'units were never really suitable for the US market. They didn't really meet customer expectations, based on

Figure 4.3. Diebold's early concept of a currency dispensing machine, 1966
Source: ERNEST K. BENNETT/AP/Press Association Images (ID 6610250174).

repeated failures and limited availability of parts. So not surprisingly, sales never really picked up.'[52] Instead, Diebold decided to continue developing its own device, resulting in the launch of the Total Automatic Banking System (TABS) 500 in 1973.

The TABS was developed as a 'complete teller' concept by a team composed of Robert W. Clark, Phillip C. Dolsen, Donald E. Kinker, and other development staff at Diebold. The machine included a depository mechanism and the possibility of selecting one of several amounts for withdrawal (the Citibank prototype of 1968 and the European machines had a fixed withdrawal amount). The TABS also had an internal MICR-printer to issue balance documents that helped reconcile offline transactions to the mainframe at the end of the day, and it could be fitted with a telephone and CCTV camera for two-way video on the screen (available during banking hours to help customers with transactions). It should be noted here that while early devices such as the TAB 500 automated cash dispensing to consumers, they still required manual back office work by banks to process the transaction slips.

Diebold's first patent foray into the technology was filed on 2 August 1974 (US 3949364), and encompassed an 'Automatic Remote Banking System and Equipment' which would involve either 'a blank drive-up or walk-up service unit served by a teller located at either the unmanned or the remote station during business hours'. This development from 'traditional' drive-through approaches to the technology quickly developed into a completely automated system for which a patent was filed on 3 September 1974. This became the TABS 500 machine, which was developed into an online version, the TABS 600.[53]

4.3.5 *The Swedish Claim to the First Online Device, 1967–1977*

Two important events support the Swedish claim to have made the first online cash machine. The first relates to their initial deployment. According to the original plan between the Swedish savings banks and Metior, the Uppsala machine of 1967 would have been connected online if IBM had delivered an interface that enabled the Bankomat to link up to a computer.[54] Instead, a claim to have made the world's first commercial application of an online cash dispensing technology dates this event as 6 May 1968, when a dispenser in Malmö was set up to service 1,000 accounts. Online teller terminals located on the counters of retail branches were connected through conventional telephone lines using modems to the centre in Malmö, which was equipped with a third-generation IBM 360/40 computer.[55]

The procedure for turning the Metior cash machine into an online device involved checking the customer's PIN locally, inside the Bankomat. When verified, the customer's card number and the amount requested were transmitted via the IBM 360 to the computer centre of the jointly owned company managing computers for the savings banks (a company called Spadab) in Stockholm. If the account had a sufficient balance the return signal was positive, enabling the Bankomat to dispense the money. The Bankomat had an internal counter where the correct notes were dispensed, and then it would send an end-of-transaction message back to Spadab.[56] Subsequent versions of the Bankomat were fitted with batch features to 'call' the system; the Bankomat Mark 4 was able to connect online via a modem. However, in spite of the possibility of online, real-time computing, most cash machines at the Swedish savings banks operated as stand-alone, offline devices; in fact few banks anywhere had an account database at the time to authorize online transactions.

As mentioned in Chapter 2, another important development in the history of Swedish cash machines began when a newly appointed director of Spadab, Jan Rydh, attended the Automated Teller Machine Conference in Chicago in 1971. Rydh reminisced that, during discussions on the conference fringe focusing on investments in offline dispensers, on impulse he made the sudden decision to treat investments in offline machines as a sunk (i.e. irrecoverable) cost. In 1975 the savings banks finally abandoned Metior and chose Docutel as their supplier of ATM devices (that is, online cash machines), with the Swedish company Datasaab responsible for installation and service.[57]

Chapter 2 also provided three possible explanations as to why the savings banks abandoned Metior. The first relates to Metior's previously mentioned problems with security. The second highlights the weakness of the US dollar against the Swedish krona, making the Asea-Metior dispenser expensive compared with the Docutel machine.[58] The third explanation is that the early 1970s saw the swift and widespread adoption of online terminals at retail branches across many countries. Independent producers of cash machines, such as Asea-Metior, faced difficulties, since banks demanded wholly integrated systems such as those offered by Burroughs, IBM, or NCR, which could deliver a central computer, teller terminals, and cash machines.[59]

The savings banks were the first to use this new generation of cash machines, known as mini-banks or 'Minuten'. The first machine was installed on 24 May 1977, and the fleet eventually grew to 600 units. From the outset, all the Minuten were connected to a central computer in online, real-time mode. Then in 1982, Spadab searched the market for a new generation of ATMs, looking to deploy 1,000 machines. By this time Asea-Metior had withdrawn from the market, and Datasaab offered an ATM of its own, developed in collaboration with Leif Lundblad's Inter Innovation Company and benefiting from Docutel technology. However, this machine could not fulfil the demands of Spadab. Instead, the savings banks chose the offer made by Ericsson (Sweden) and Omron (Japan) to deliver 900 ATMs, thus ending the presence of Swedish innovators within their home market.[60] Meanwhile, 1,100 units of Bankomat IV were sold in France between 1969 and 1977. Of these, 250 were manufactured in Sweden and the rest in France by Transac, where production had relocated.[61]

4.4 The IBM Cash Machine

4.4.1 *Digitalizing the Black Horse, 1962–1970*

The deployment of Lloyds Bank's first online dispensers in December 1972 and throughout 1973 is generally considered the keystone in the transformation from cash machines to ATMs. The acquisition of online cash machines resulted from a greater effort to control the cost of the expected growth in the number of transactions within Lloyds' retail branches as well as helping to prepare for the changeover to decimal currency.[62] However, the biggest driver in introducing automatic cash machines was the sight of long queues of people waiting at branches on Fridays to draw their weekly pay cheque or enough to support their weekend spending use.[63] The queues were so long that they often extended into the street and banks had to hire extra cashiers to deal with the rush. The problem was exacerbated when banks decided to close at the weekend. All in all, the transition changed processes and procedures that had been in place for almost fifty years.[64]

Automatic cash dispensing for Lloyds took root in 1958 when the bank became an IBM customer, deploying some small computer systems to help with the administrative control of large branches. At the time, the idea of using computers in banking was far from novel. By the end of the 1960s, all large banks in Britain, the USA, and across the world had developed plans or already implemented different devices that would completely computerize their activities.[65] But there was still no 'perfect' system that could provide branches of retail banks with easy access to the existing computer centres.[66]

The first system installed by Lloyds in 1958 was a 305 Ramac at the bank's Pall Mall (London) branch. This was at the time the biggest banking branch in Europe and serviced the accounts of officers in the Army and Royal Air Force. The Ramac model was chosen for its direct access capabilities, such as instant statements.[67] Preparations then started for a more ambitious project with the formation of a joint team staffed with representatives of Lloyds (C. P. T. Harvey and B. L. Martin) and IBM UK (C. D. Oswald and D. J. Lewis) in August 1962. This project aimed at 'developing and specifying a system and equipment for branch accounting'[68] which, in the team's view, was what needed most attention before 'overall system economy' could be increased. Their study stated that the bank had 3.2 million customers and 1.56 million current accounts (which had grown at an average rate of 3.6 per cent per annum between 1958 and 1962), serviced through 1,300 branch offices. It estimated that accounting work within the 677 largest branches (in the form of mechanical ledger operation)[69] relating to approximately 77 per cent of customer accounts could be handled by 'the centralisation of the greater part of the bank's accounting operations in a single multiple unit computer centre in London'.[70]

Deployment of the computer equipment was not immediate but progressive and continued throughout a six-year period, because there were several challenges to address. These included, first, the lack of automation within the clearing system.[71] British banks had not at this time agreed the standard for the application of magnetic ink to cheques; the centralized credit clearing operation was largely manual and in dire need of mechanization. Second, as the report noted, working on Saturday mornings was insufficient for the central computers to receive all the information until late on Monday mornings.[72] Third, the authors of the study estimated that two years would be required to establish a detailed installation programme and new procedures in the branches; procedures for the computer centre; the space to host the computer centre; a major computer programming effort (the aim of which was 'account posting', that is, the debiting and crediting of individual accounts);[73] leased telephone lines from the Post Office;[74] and the training of secure and appropriate staff to man the computer centres and train branch staff in the new procedures, the operation of the computer equipment, and the loading of information into computer tapes.[75]

Conversion then proceeded at a rate of one man-year per 2,000 current accounts or eight branches and 15,000–20,000 accounts per month (an estimated 200,000 current accounts or 310,000 accounts of all types per year).[76] By 1964 the 305 had been replaced by a 1401/1405 system, followed by a 1410/1302. An identical 1410/1302 installed in the City of London was dedicated to cheque clearing. In 1965 the 'successful partnership with IBM'[77] delivered 'the first teleprocessing network in British banking'[78] when a 1050 system together with 1460 equipment enabled Lloyds' Pall Mall branch to interact online with most branches around the south coast of England. This was followed by events in October 1968, when the IBM 3980 Bank Teleprocessing System became operational, thus 'allowing a greater number of remote terminals at teller branches to connect online with the central computer'.[79] Lloyds was already employing seventy IBM 3940 Bank Terminals when the 3980 came into being. The 3940 provided data collection facilities at branches (mainly for input) as well as the necessary experience in running a network on the back of Post Office modems and telephone lines. The original 3940 terminals located along the 'trunk route' between the London and Birmingham computer centres were too costly for smaller branches to run. The roll-out of the 3980 system aimed to address these and other operational shortcomings (in particular, the 3982 Keyboard Terminal was specifically designed for the requirements of British banks) while providing access to 'even the most remote branches'. The 3980 was a concentrator system where one hundred 3940s and one hundred 3981 concentrators in major branches connected with the four 360/65s. The 3981 Computer Concentrators contained circuitry and storage facilities for controlling the 3982 terminals and for transmitting data to and from the computer centre. The 3981 was connected to more than 800 terminals in smaller branches, with up to ten 3982s connected to each 3981 concentrator. Branches without a 3940 terminal would record their data on punched paper tape, which was then taken by a van either to a branch with a 3940 terminal or directly to a computer centre, whichever was nearer.

After years of effort to digitalize its back office systems, Lloyds was in November 1970 the first clearing bank to successfully move its customer accounting systems from its retail branches to a central computer.[80] Lloyds thus had its computer system ready in time for decimalization in February 1971, when larger banks such as Barclays could not.[81] At the time, Lloyds had 154 branches and 801 sub-branches, some five million accounts (including nearly three million current accounts), and four computer centres, each housing a 360/65, reflecting its core business areas, that is, one in London, one in Birmingham, one in Bristol, and a dedicated centre for cheque clearing in the City. These devices helped the bank to process between 650,000 and one million cheques daily in 1970. Lloyds claimed to have invested £25 million in computers[82] (£15 millions' worth already in use and the rest on order) as well as doing it 'less expensively' than others.[83] In spite of this success, the computerization of smaller and remote branches would continue until October 1973 when the bank could finally claim to have all its branches and sub-branches online.[84]

4.4.2 The Lloyds Bank 'Cashpoint', 1969–1976

Equipped with a database of customer records as well as processes and procedures to deal with them centrally, Lloyds Bank could consider online cash withdrawals. After all, commercial applications based on EDP such as airline reservation systems had been in use for several years. But the online cash machine network grew into 'the key project as far as [Lloyds] Bank's general management [was] concerned'.[85]

Cash machines first appeared in Lloyds' internal records in July 1969, just as Saturday closing had come into effect. As noted above, they aimed to solve the problem of the Friday queues for cash.[86] This reference to cash machines emerged in a progress report on the process of computerizing branch accounting and in the context of estimates for additional computer power by 1973.[87] The report was again co-authored by IBM and Lloyds staff and chiefly concerned the cash machines already deployed by Barclays and NatWest and the forthcoming installation of 3982 keyboard terminals in Lloyds branches. A section of the report then specified the bank's requirements for its cash machine as summarized in Table 4.6.

Table 4.6 shows the study made a point of emphasizing 'concise but clear' operating instructions, because there was dissatisfaction at Lloyds with the guidance for users of Barclays' and NatWest's cash machines, considered 'unclear and hard to follow'. Requesting multiple currency combinations in the dispensing method[88] also reflected Lloyds' concern with issuing policies for activating (and in the case of NatWest, retaining) tokens by its competitors, which people at Lloyds felt restricted the number of users to those in the highest income bracket.[89] It is noteworthy that the specifications in Table 4.6 assigned a budget of up to £4,500 per device for development purposes. This was equivalent to 2.8 times the median salary of a wage earner or the expectation

Table 4.6. Specification for the Lloyds Bank-IBM online cash machine, 1969

Specification	Features
Badge (i.e. access token)	• Embossed the customer's name, 6 digit branch sort code, 7 digit account number, 4 digit expiry date.
	• Magnetically encoded strip with customer's branch and account number, security number, monthly withdrawal limit, and expiry date.
Method of operation	• The machine will validate the customer's keyed in security number (PIN) against that on the access token (PAN). Also the amount required against the limit and will dispense up to that limit (an appropriate message will appear).
	• If both check the limit will be updated to account for the withdrawal.
	• A 'debit' for the customer's account and branch number will be generated in appropriate medium (i.e. paper tape, tape cassette, punched card, optical MICR or even human readable document.
	• The token will be retained after two failed attempts to input security number.
	• The transaction should take place in 10 seconds or less.
Keyboard	• Ten numeric keys (0 to 9).
	• Method for choice of amount obtained (£5, £10, £20, £50) while permitting combinations.
Operating instructions	• Concise but clear enough to be understood by the average consumer.
Location	• Branch lobby, through the wall, off bank premises.
Security	• Appropriate for location while the mechanism being 'fail safe'.
Note dispensing	• Avoid possible jamming (potentially distribute only new banknotes).
Badge validator	• A simple machine capable of magnetically encoding limits and date to the badge.
	• Operational after insertion of a key(s)—so only designated staff can activate this device.
Cost	• On the basis of replacing 1/2 or 1 cashier per device installed, up to £4,500 per device.

Source: Based on Lloyds Banking Group Archives, HO/IT/Pla/2, Outline for Development: Information Services, Lloyds Bank—IBM, 1969, pp. 51–5.

that an automatic teller could replace up to three branch employees.[90] A further point of interest is that the expiration (or revalidation) date implied that the device had to know the current month and year at any given time.

'Big Blue' was then responsible for finding the engineering solution. For unknown reasons IBM changed the leading person at its banking group (servicing the Midland Bank and the Bank of England alongside Lloyds—which was the main customer) and made Anthony Cleaver the project leader for the banking team, with a clear mandate to develop the cash machine.[91] He then had to make the case within IBM for building a prototype. In turn, a brief specification was circulated amongst IBM's banking salesmen around the world to estimate how many would be sold worldwide if it was produced. The result was not promising and Cleaver explained that there was a larger market for bank communication devices in general, in particular, for cash machines. About this incident Sir Anthony remembers:

> Presumably because [the salesmen] hadn't thought it through and had only a brief specification, [they estimated the sales volume] was 1,600 units. I was then summoned to New York to explain how I thought I could sell 1,500 to Lloyds. I eventually managed to convince [IBM] that I could.[92]

Around this time John Fairclough relocated from Hursley to the laboratory in Raleigh, NC.[93] Fairclough was clear about Cleaver's requirements for Lloyds and to little surprise IBM then assigned the Raleigh lab to lead the design of the prototype that would become the 2984 cash machine, and eventually be produced back in the UK. In this process, responding to the bank's concern for security, the resulting device was made capable of recognizing an activation token through a PIN/PAN protocol. This was somewhat conventional, in that it originated in the Chubb device of 1970 (US 3543904, a patent issued to Smiths Industries[94]) and also complied with the American Bankers Association standard for magnetic stripe content and embossed characters.[95] In this protocol the customer enters his/her Personal Identification Number (PIN) through the keyboard and the device reads the Primary Account Number (PAN) from the second track of the magnetic stripe. A cryptography algorithm validated the PIN to the PAN. The third track, which provided read and write capabilities, enabled offline systems to control daily withdrawals.[96] To the extent that there was a paper (and later a magnetic tape) record of transactions within the device, this could be tallied against the cash dispensed and reduce the possibility of a customer disputing the receipt of cash.

Thus, in the absence of a fully digitalized payments ecosystem, dispensing cash out of hours relied on solutions within the device to record the transaction or a combination of the device and the activation card. However, engineers believed that online, real-time operation raised further security considerations,[97] in particular, the possibility that a criminal might gain access to the data cable and cause a breach in the data handshaking between terminal and base; a specific hazard was that the handshaking might be recorded and replicated. If the instruction to 'dispense cash' was unvarying, it could be counterfeited with very profitable results for the criminal. It was therefore vital that the 'dispense' command, plus associated instructions should vary unpredictably from one transaction to the next. This could be achieved through an enciphering (encrypting) system.

IBM's Systems Communication Division (SCD), located on the Hudson River in Kingston, NY was assigned responsibility for the crypto-product development to the point where the customer had to be 'authenticated before any transaction [could] take place'.[98] Walter Tuchman was named project manager. As a first step, Tuchman needed to identify an appropriate encryption algorithm. He considered but found weaknesses in the so-called 'Hill Cipher'.[99] In its place, he proposed adopting research by Horst Feistel (1915–90), who had developed, without any direct commercial application, a reliable cipher algorithm (called Lucifer) that would secure privacy in the communication between computer systems. Feistel's research leading to Lucifer might just have been 'blue sky' and not found any application, except that IBM now entered the crypto-business.[100] IBM decided to modify Lucifer, referring internally to it as DSD-1, and incorporated it into the IBM 2984.

Here is worth digressing slightly from the story of IBM and Lloyds to note that it was the work of Martin Atalla (1929–90) in the early 1970s that led to the use of high security modules.[101] It was his so-called 'Atalla Box' of 1973 that protected offline devices thanks to an un-guessable PIN-generating key. But banks and international credit card companies were fearful that Atalla would dominate the market.[102] Hence when they were negotiating the international standards for credit cards in 1976, IBM passed on DSD-1 to the US government. This resulted in a significant turning point, first, because DSD-1 became from this point on an encryption standard for the Federal Information Processing Standard (FIPS).[103] Second, banks and credit card companies took advantage of this to adopt DSD-1 in 1978 as the basis for ISO 4909 or the standard detailing magnetic stripe data content for the third track on bank cards.[104] In this way it seems clear that the Lucifer code grew into a standard mechanism of encryption. It was not only the first commercial use of a cryptographic function but remained the standard for digital encryption until the year 2000, when it was replaced by the 'Advanced Encryption Standard' (AES), also known by its original name of Rijndael, a family of ciphers with different key and block sizes adopted by several standard setting institutions, some outside the banking industry.[105]

After this brief detour, let's go back to the IBM-Lloyds story. In tandem with advances to develop the cash machine prototype in the USA, Cleaver, back in the UK, had to wrestle with IBM's Systems Network Architecture (SNA)—the standard package for communication in its systems.[106] This was an attempt to impose a specific IBM protocol on all devices connected to IBM systems and reflected IBM's top brass strategy of selling complete computer solution packages. But as a general-purpose application SNA was 'all things to all people' and therefore too slow to meet Lloyds' specifications. Cleaver could not afford a slow system and instructed his team in the UK to side-step SNA. Programmers in the team spent eighteen months developing a new communications software package: about eight in development and ten to test it thoroughly to ensure that it was resilient and fast enough. When the prototype was ready in June 1971, Lloyds placed an order for 500 machines with IBM, costing nearly £3.5 million in total.[107]

As mentioned, the first 2984 cash machine made its public debut as Lloyds' 'Cashpoint' in December 1972 in its Brentwood, Essex branch.[108] Within a few months Lloyds had another 24 cash machines in operation and another 75 gradually going to retail branches through 1973 and 1974.[109] All of these were lobby machines, while another order for an additional 500 included 100 'through the wall' devices.[110] The machine was initially available only in the UK and was innovative, being the first widely deployed machine to be operated by a plastic card with a magnetic stripe on the back (containing the customer's account number and the branch sorting code).[111] There was still no video display unit (VDU); instructions to the customer were relayed on a separate panel lighted from behind, made out of plastic stripes. There were perhaps more moving parts than in the Chubb MD2, as the keyboard was exposed only after the card was validated, notes were first dispensed into a concealed cash tray (which was then lowered over the keyboard for the customer to collect the cash), and the card itself was returned to the customer to end the transaction. The device offered customers the novelty of choosing of variable cash sums to a maximum of £100 at any one time (one version offered up to £20 in one-pound notes and another up to £50 in five-pound notes).[112] The whole process of cash withdrawal took about 40 seconds.[113]

The 2984 'Cashpoint' automatic cash machine connected to the central computer in the same way and using the same 'rails' as the 3982 terminals, that is, directly to the computer centre in the large branches (which already had dedicated telephone lines) or via the 3981 concentrators in smaller branches. The drawback of this design, however, was that the bulk of the 2981 cash machines were operational only during existing banking hours, that is, when the central computers at head office were staffed and active.[114]

The 'Cashpoint' was thought to work within banking halls (known as 'lobby' machines), 'through the wall', and 'in locations away from banking offices'.[115] The IBM device was activated with a plastic card with magnetic stripe and, like all early cash machines, had a keyboard with pre-programmed functions rather than a video monitor displaying instructions. But the banknotes were dispensed in a way that present-day consumers would find unusual, that is, at 90 degrees to the keyboard and card insertion slot. Actually, most cash machines delivered banknotes vertically (i.e. short side foremost) until NCR in the early 1980s introduced a new customer friendly monitor (VDU) and also delivered the cash horizontally (i.e. long side foremost), thus reducing jams by increasing the contact and the control of individual banknotes.[116]

By December 1976, 630 'Cashpoint' machines were operational in 430 branches and included Lloyds' first 'through the wall' machine as well as a very successful non-branch installation at Lewis's, a large department store, in Birmingham in 1974.[117] At the time, customers found 'the cash dispenser was extremely useful',[118] while the deployment gave Lloyds the prestige of having operated the first cash dispenser in a non-banking site for almost ten years before any other bank.[119] It also encouraged the bank to think of seventeen more possible non-bank locations in stores, universities, and hospitals.[120]

Between 1972 and 1976, the number of offline machines in the UK grew 38 per cent from 883 at the end of 1972 to 1,220 in 1976.[121] Over the same period, online machines grew over sixty times from 12 in 1972 to 737 in 1976. But of all the 1,957 machines in operation in 1976, online machines represented 38 per cent, although they comprised 62 per cent of the total. In other words, in spite of the IBM-Lloyds innovation, offline machines remained the most common type of device in the UK in the mid to late 1970s.

The lengthy process of rolling out the 'Cashpoint' and other online machines is partially explained by the high cost, low reliability, and limited availability of adequate telephone lines for EDP. These hampered the possibility of the generalized and immediate updating of customer records on the scale that UK banks required. Indeed, Lloyds Bank waited for its 100th 'Cashpoint' until 1981, when it started operating at the Piccadilly branch in Manchester; but its 1,500th was functioning in August 1983 at the branch in Welling, Somerset.[122]

4.4.3 Second- (IBM 3614) and Third-Generation (IBM 3624) Devices, 1976–1991

The experience with Lloyds and in particular its multiple '39' and '29' requests, led IBM's top brass to decide that retail bank branch networks could be good business.[123] The idea crystallized with the launch of the 3600 Finance Communication system in 1976, which included the 3614 cash machine—the commercial application of the 2984 devised for Lloyds. This machine immediately had a number of commercial victories. For instance, the First International Bank of Israel deployed about half a dozen IBM 3614s in 1977.[124]

The 3614 was replaced in 1978 by the very successful 3624—which ushered in the online world of self-service banking for IBM. In 1979, Security Pacific National Bank, Los Angeles, CA had the largest IBM 3624 based network at the time, the very first of which was operational in its Westwood, CA branch, within walking distance of the UCLA Westwood campus.[125] The 3614 expanded the range of possible locations by considering a drive-through version, but retained pre-programmed keys. This model distributed banknotes vertically (i.e. long-side foremost) and included the possibility of envelope deposits—an important feature given the intensive use of personal cheques in the USA to this day.

The success of the second-generation 3624 was based on several features, such as enabling customization based on a series of IBM Mainframe BAL macros.[126] It also communicated via a binary synchronous (bi-sync) protocol or synchronous data link control (SDLC) protocol to the IBM mainframe, while allowing upgrades to be tested and certified easily. The 3624 was one of the first ATMs to accommodate differences between European and North American banks in an interchange network—differences in terms of the length of the account number and PIN (more on which later).[127] All in all, the 3624 was widely considered to be one of the first effective online ATMs. This effectiveness, however, seems to have been largely in urban networks—as IBM discovered when it found itself unable to satisfy the requirements of Iowa banks, which turned instead to NCR devices.[128]

At this point IBM seemed poised to overwhelm its competitors until executives at 'Big Blue' decided to deploy a new device family in 1981 (the same year as the personal computer). The 4700 Finance Communication System was a follow-on product to replace the 3600 but very much based on proprietary hardware and software incompatible with previous models, including the already successful and widely deployed IBM 3624.

Some financial institutions remained loyal to IBM as was the case of Lloyds Bank in the UK. Lloyds' first new generation 4731 ATM was also its 2,000th in-branch 'Cashpoint'.[129] However, it was deployed until November 1988 as part of the redevelopment of the Wallingford, Oxfordshire branch. This branch was piloting a new look and layout for the bank. The new ATM was a first 'Cashpoint' for the branch and the nearby area. It had a VDU instead of a single-line display, so customers would find it easier to use. Its safe had greater storage space to increase up-time (while reducing the likelihood of running out of cash). From the perspective of branch staff, operating the new ATM 'was a little more complicated', but not an insurmountable task.

Overall, however, the 4700 series was a disaster. Experienced people in the field had warned IBM's top management that they were about to make a huge mistake but to no avail.[130] According to a former top executive, the 473x marketing failure lay in its being 'designed by a committee and, in trying to be all things to all people, would not quite meet anybody's requirements'.[131] Whether or not this was true, the fact remained that 'designers were too clever by half and ignored the customers'.[132] James Adamson, long-time CEO of NCR in Dundee, Scotland, reflected on some of the things that enabled his company to come from behind and outdo IBM.[133] Adamson's recollection was that it was hard to gain access to the IBM machines as the space inside them was very tight and compact, so it was extremely challenging to service them. As a response, Adamson continued, NCR created a machine that 'almost anyone could build and take apart in half an hour'. He claimed the new concept was demonstrated on a stand at one of the ATM shows in the USA while the NCR ATM could easily interface with devices from other computer manufacturers such IBM, Burroughs, and Siemens. 'And the reason for that', he said, 'was NCR were [in other related business with the banks, such as] the point of teller terminals and cheque sorting machines, [which had to] have access to all these [other] banking systems'.

It was certainly the case that many banks evaluated the new IBM machine and refused to buy it because, at a stroke, IBM had made the banks' significant capital investment in the older computer infrastructure obsolete. The lack of a migration path away from the IBM 3624 did not help ensure a successful product line, for obsolescence extended beyond physical devices inside bank branches to other devices and software that supported communication across the bank's network, and even to standards for shared cashpoint networks. IBM's move soured banks' attitude to its products, inadvertently opening the ATM market to other manufacturers—which, in turn, transformed the ATM into a major enterprise.

Around this time, two Ohio-based companies, NCR and Diebold, were working on technology that would enable them to dominate the supply of cashpoints for the next two decades. As a result of the IBM 473x ATM failure, NCR built its business on software that emulated the IBM 3624. It also benefited from deregulation and the diversification of banks across retail markets.

Meanwhile, IBM and Diebold formed a joint venture in 1984, called Inter-Bold. Its aim was to unite Diebold's self-service technology with IBM's global distribution system. Seven years later, in 1991, in spite of growing sales, the decision was taken to end the joint venture in 1997. Diebold had not achieved the international market breakthrough it had hoped for and IBM's returns fell short of its expectations, in part due to the growth in local processing architectures, which invalidated IBM's strategy to link ATMs to its expensive mainframes. An industry insider commented: 'Diebold did not understand the non-US banking environment, and did not adapt its products well enough. IBM had a hard time selling Diebold machines against NCR competition because NCR was compatible with the IBM 3624 and Diebold was not.'[134] With the closure of InterBold, IBM abandoned payment technology systems entirely.

4.5 Traveller, Your Footprints are the Path

This chapter tells how the cash machine evolved into the ATM as the 1970s progressed. Slowly but steadily cash machines stopped being stand-alone devices and developed online, real-time capabilities while articulating proprietary ATM networks, as electronic data interchange networks, solid state memory, programming languages, integrated circuits, etc. became readily available. Financial intermediaries deployed mini computers as well as electronic fund transfer (EFT) terminals to tellers at retail branches to support further moves to EDP centralization. Manufacturers offered different modes of operation. Some models stored transaction information electronically in themselves (first on magnetic tape cassettes and later on floppy disks). This was transmitted for general clearing at the end of the day through an EFT terminal, such as the Burroughs RT500. Others informed a mini computer within the branch, which kept balances and corresponded with the central computer. The advent of storage within the machine also opened possibilities for customizing the device through software applications, as well as storing different types of record (such as a table of cancelled or overdrawn accounts). A combination of stand-alone and batch processing machines thus characterized the 1970s.

Here it is worth noting that the popular accounts of the emergence of cash machines often overlook the fact that their growth in the 1970s marked the first time that technology had modified services for retail customers to this extent since the start of computerization in the late 1950s. Changes went beyond the superficiality (from a customer's perspective) of pre-printed stationery, mechanical annotations, or magnetic characters in cheques; while supporting an increasingly mobile yet urban population that no longer wished to rely on a single bank branch location.

As is generally the case in most histories of computers and of computers in banking, this chapter concentrates on the most tangible aspects of the transition from attended to unattended self-service.[135] Histories of software are few and far between.[136] This is partly due to the ephemeral, incremental, and 'subterranean' nature of its applications, but also because the lack of research into the underpinnings of computer infrastructure.[137] Software systems are large and complicated, and represent a significant investment. Therefore, when Docutel came out with a new cashpoint model which was not compatible with its customers' precious software, banks would not buy the new devices. As a result, Docutel lost not only the leading share of the US market but also its independence.[138] When IBM did the same with the 473x ATM family, they failed for the same reason. NCR discovered (perhaps by pure chance or perhaps not) the value of IBM 3624 compatibility, and it quickly became the leading manufacturer. Nowadays, most ATMs are compatible with NCR's NDC self-service, secure transaction protocol, so this differentiator is no longer as significant.[139]

This chapter also highlights the difference in scope of invention between IBM and the early contributors to the ATM industry (e.g. Arfvidson and Metior in Sweden; Constable, Goodfellow and Chubb, Shepherd-Barron and De La Rue in the UK; Wetzel and Docutel in the USA, etc.). The early inventions worked alongside banks while aiming to make customers' money available when banks were closed. Building on the collaboration with Lloyds Bank, IBM scoped its ATM inventions to develop a machine with which it could sell computers and computer systems. But despite its potential for owning and controlling the ATM industry, this strategy ultimately proved unsustainable; the lack of a migration path resulted in IBM being unable to capitalize in the hugely popular 3624. However, IBM's footprint in the ATM industry is undeniable. Although the Primary Account Number (PAN)'s relationship to the Private Identification Number (PIN) was needed in any case, it was the achievement of IBM to produce a worldwide standard. It should be emphasized here how the magnetic card and its three tracks, together with the PAN, became not only a de facto standard but one of the three critical norms for the global working of the ATM. The other two were the cryptographic standard (developed by Feistal for IBM) and the ISO 8583 messaging standard for inter-bank ATM operations.[140] These made it possible for any bank to buy ATMs regardless of manufacturer, while bank customers could use any ATM, anywhere in the world.

Notes

1. Lane (1989).
2. Lane (1989) classifies a manufacturer as 'independent' if the firm was established in the USA at approximately the time of entry to the cash machine market.
3. Certainly the account that predominates in the US popular press see: *ATM Marketplace*, accessed 2 February 2018, <https://www.atmmarketplace.com/articles/rise-and-fall-of-docutel-part-ii-of-ii/>; Ellen Florian, Doris Burke, and Jenny Mero, 'The Money Machines', *Fortune Magazine*, 26 July 2004, accessed 18 April 2017, <http://money.cnn.com/magazines/fortune/fortune_archive/2004/07/26/377172/index.htm>; 'Interview with Mr Don Wetzel, Co-Patentee Automatic Teller Machine', *American History*, accessed 2 February 2018, <http://americanhistory.si.edu/comphist/wetzel.htm>.

4. By 2007, NCR had about 70 per cent of the world's ATM installations. In Britain it had about 90 per cent. Personal communication (email), from Ian Omrod, former engineer of NCR, with B. Bátiz-Lazo, 11 April 2007. Company documents claimed that by 1981 the ATM had made over 1.7 billion transactions in the USA alone and NCR was the world's leading manufacturer ('The History of NCR', 107).

5. The DACS currency dispensers were used at three banking companies in the USA namely First Pennsylvania in the Philadelphia, PA area; and South Shore National and First National of Natick, both located near Boston, MA. These three banks were responsible for deploying at least 13 machines in the late 1960s and early 1970s, all of them of the second design type with a single drawer. The same model also had some overseas locations. Source: Personal communication (email) from Jim Noll, former ATM service engineer, with B. Bátiz-Lazo, 27 March 2013.

6. Interview with James Adamson, former CEO of NCR Dundee, by B. Bátiz-Lazo and R. Reid, Edinburgh, 18 June 2008.

7. Personal communication (email) from Robert Rosenthal, former IBM engineer, with B. Bátiz-Lazo, 23 July 2016.

8. 'Memoria 1968', *Banco Español de Crédito* (Banesto), Madrid: 48.

9. Lane (1989, 29).

10. Sienkiewicz (2002).

11. Zimmer (1975).

12. 'New Money Machine Series Incorporates Instaposit Depository', *Autotransactions Industry Report*, March 1975: 12–13.

13. According to Janicki and Prescott (2006, 291): 'in 1960, there were nearly 13,000 independent banks. By 2005, the number had dropped in half, to about 6,500. In 1960, the ten largest banks held 21 percent of the banking industry's assets. By 2005, this share had grown to almost 60 percent. A great deal of these changes started during the deregulation of the 1980s and 1990s.'

14. Estimates in this paragraph were sourced in Sponski (1974), Zimmer (1974), and 'Rise and Fall of Docutel: Part II of II', *ATM Marketplace*, 17 March 2003, accessed 13 April 2016, <http://www.atmmarketplace.com/articles/rise-and-fall-of-docutel-part-ii-of-ii>.

15. Sponski (1974, 24).

16. Zimmer (1975). For the USA and for Sweden see 'Cash Dispensers—Swedish Style', *The Banker*, September 1975: 1138.

17. Zimmer (1971).

18. Interview with James Adamson, former CEO of NCR Dundee, by B. Bátiz-Lazo and Robert Reid, 18 June 2008.

19. Booth (2004, 2007); Campbell-Kelly (1992); Haigh (2006).

20. Personal communication (email) from Robert Rosenthal, former IBM engineer, with B. Bátiz-Lazo, 23 July 2006.

21. 'Banks Cash Dispenser that Would Not Deliver', *The Straits Times*, 21 December 1974: 7; and '"Instant Cash" Cards and Magnetic Stripes', *The Straits Times*, 16 January 1975: 10.

22. Constable (2015, 5).

23. Bátiz-Lazo (2017a); Bátiz-Lazo et al. (2011a); Knights and McCabe (1998).

24. Zimmer (1974, 74).

25. 'Automated Teller Machines', *The World Bank*, accessed 19 May 2016, <http://data.worldbank.org/indicator/FB.ATM.TOTL.P5>.

26. Ritzer (1995, 54–5 and 134).

27. Interview with James Adamson, former CEO of NCR Dundee, by B. Bátiz-Lazo and Robert Reid, 18 June 2008.

28. Personal communication (email) from Robert Rosenthal, former IBM engineer, with B. Bátiz-Lazo, 23 July 2016.

29. On the overall importance of this specific feature for US banking see Cortada (2006).

30. I am grateful for the assistance of Aravinda Korala, Bai Li, and Yoshi Sato from KAL ATM software to recuperate and interpret Takeshi Hosino, 進化する銀行システム (*Evolving Bank System*) (Tokyo, 2017); and Hisiao Nagoaka, 'ATM戦略の発展過程とその考察' (Development Process of ATM Strategies and its Considerations), Research Center for Socionetwork Strategies, Kansai University (May 2008). Personal communication (email) from Bai Li, KAL Japan, with B. Bátiz-Lazo, 26 July 2017. See also Harper and Bátiz-Lazo (2013, 11).

31. In 1950 Tateisi Electronics was renamed Omron Tateisi Electronics, with the trademark Omron established in 1959. In 1965 the company developed a vending machine capable of accepting credit cards in collaboration with Automated Canteen Co., then the largest vending machine manufacturer in the USA. See 'Enhancing Lifestyles in Japan', *OMRON Global*, accessed 7 May 2008, <http://www.omron.com/about/corporate/history/ayumi/innovation.html>; 'Development of the X-ray Timer', *OMRON Global*, accessed 7 April 2016, <http://www.omron.com/about/history/founder/02/> and 'Chronology', *OMRON Global*, accessed 7 April 2016, <http://www.omron.com/about/history/chronicle/#>.

32. I am grateful for the help of Masayoshi Noguchi (Tokyo Metropolitan University) in accessing '50 years of Omron-Tateisi' (1985, 111), '55 years of Omron-Tateisi Electronics' (1988, 234), and 'Will Cash Dispensers Change the Banking Business?', *Nikkei Business*, April 1970. Personal communication (email) from Masayoshi Noguchi with B. Bátiz-Lazo, 7 May 2008.

33. 'US dollar to Japanese Exchange Rate (1 / 215.991)', *Like Forex*, accessed 18 May 2016, <http://www.likeforex.com/currency-converter/us-dollar-usd_jpy-japanese-yen.htm/1970>.

34. 'The Beginning of Cashless Age', *OMRON Global*, accessed 8 April 2016, <http://www.omron.com/about/history/ayumi/innovation/#history1971>.

35. An internal document estimated the number of ATMs in Japan for 1974 as negligible. Source: Asami (circa 1986, 127). See also Endo Teuro, 'Japan Experiences Rapid Growth in Cash Dispensers', *The Magazine of Bank Administration*, 1974: 12–14. Another source claims that 12 city banks and the Bank of Tokyo had 2,463 offices, deployed 2,943 cash dispensers, and issued 9.5 million cards in 1975. This source does not specify the type of card. See Maixé-Altés (2017, 18).

36. See Maixé-Altés (2017, 18).

37. For instance see 'Donald C. Wetzel: Biography', *Engineering and Technology History Wiki*, accessed 7 April 2016, <http://ethw.org/Donald_C._Wetzel>.

38. Palm (2016).
39. Billings and Booth (2011, 167).
40. Essinger (1987, 3).
41. David K. Allison, 'Interview with Mr Donald Wetzel', *National Museum of American History*, 21 September 1995, accessed 30 November 2016, http://americanhistory.si.edu/comphist/wetzel.htm.
42. David K. Allison, 'Interview with Mr Donald Wetzel', *National Museum of American History*, 21 September 1995, accessed 30 November 2016, <http://americanhistory.si.edu/comphist/wetzel.htm>.
43. David K. Allison, 'Interview with Mr Donald Wetzel', *National Museum of American History*, 21 September 1995, accessed 30 November 2016, <http://americanhistory.si.edu/comphist/wetzel.htm>.
44. Essinger (1987, 4).
45. David K. Allison, 'Interview with Mr Donald Wetzel', *American History*, 21 September 1995, accessed 16 April 2007, <http://americanhistory.si.edu/comphist/wetzel.htm>.
46. 'ATM Inventor', *Atmmachine*, accessed 7 April 2016, originally at: <http://www.atmmachine.com/atm-inventor.html/>.
47. Cornelis Robat, 'ATM: Automatic Teller Machines', accessed 6 February 2008, <http://www.thocp.net/hardware/atm.htm>.
48. Peter Hartlaub, 'Behold, One of the Bay Area's First ATMs from 1971', *The Big Event*, 9 April 2014, accessed 1 November 2016, <http://blog.sfgate.com/thebigevent/2014/04/09/behold-one-of-the-bay-areas-first-atms-from-1971/>.
49. 'First ATM', *AP Images*, accessed 1 November 2016, <http://www.apimages.com/metadata/Index/Watchf-Associated-Press-Domestic-News-Californi-/5c1e26570f8b4 14f90d675176350c996/49/0>.
50. 'First ATM', *AP Images*, accessed 1 November 2016, <http://www.apimages.com/metadata/Index/Watchf-Associated-Press-Domestic-News-Californi-/5c1e26570f8b4 14f90d675176350c996/49/0>.
51. In 1971, Diebold advertised the 'MD 200 Currency Dispensing' model, which used 'special cards which [were] retained for later processing by the bank' and the 'MD 400 Automatic Teller System', which was 'compatible with present (sic) credit cards'. The description of these devices corresponds to Chubb's MD2 and MD4. Source: Zimmer (1971).
52. Interview (telephone) with Tom Graef, a developer for Diebold, by B. Bátiz-Lazo, 26 March 2013.
53. Palm (2016).
54. Arfvidson (2007).
55. The IBM machine was also connected to the NCR series 4200 machines. These devices were connected via modem to an IBM2701 data adapter. The 4200 class could be an accounting machine or a cash register, depending on its construction. It later became an electronic data input machine to output to punch tape and punch cards and then became an electronic calculating machine known as a Post-Tronic.

56. Personal communication (email) from Lars Arfvidson, Previous Head of R&D at Metior, with B. Bátiz-Lazo, 12 June 2012.

57. Datasaab was at the start of its collaboration with Leif Lundblad and his Stockholm-based Inter Innovation Company. Lundblad had developed its own cash-dispensing mechanism to accommodate the differences between dollar notes and European currencies. The experience of Datasaab with the Docutel machines, combined with Lundblad's dispensing mechanism, led to the decision to develop a Datasaab ATM. However, before a working machine could be presented, Datasaab became a part of Ericsson Information Systems. A number of Datasaab's machines were produced and installed around the world.

58. Thodenius (2008, 22).

59. See further Arfvidson (2007); Maixé-Altés (2015).

60. At this point Datasaab was a subsidiary of Ericsson Information Systems and had developed its own machines in collaboration with Omron. See Thodenius et al. (2011). See also 'ATM (Automated Teller Machine)', *DATASAABs Vanner*, accessed 13 April 2016, <http://www.datasaab.se/Bildarkiv/S2100/ATM/atm_eng.htm>.

61. It is worth noting that by 1971, Metior had achieved a dominant position in Switzerland (where De La Rue had left the market). Also in 1972, it entered the French market in collaboration with Transac, a division of Compagnie Industrielle des Telecommunications (CIT). Given the success of the Bankomat in French banks, production relocated to France. See Michaud (2004, 30).

62. See the case of the Midland Bank documented in Booth (2004).

63. Personal communication (email) from Sir Anthony Cleaver, former CEO of IBM, with B. Bátiz-Lazo, 18 April 2016.

64. 'Counter Revolution', *Lloyds Bank News*, No. 50, February 1971: 5.

65. Bátiz-Lazo et al. (2011b); Bátiz-Lazo and Smith (2016); Maixé-Altés (2012, 2015).

66. Martin (2011, 2012).

67. Anonymous, 'IBM Backs the Dark Horse', internal IBM document provided by Sir Anthony Cleaver, Former CEO of IBM UK, 29 April 2013.

68. Lloyds Banking Group Archives, HO/DP/Pla/6, *Bank System Study*, Lloyds Bank—IBM, 1964, vol. 1: 1.

69. The proposed system considered 677 branches throughout England and Wales and planned to save the cost of 1,350 ledger machine operators. The proposal excluded 47 branches operating with two or more accounting or desk-top accounting machines and handling 67,000 accounts, because of their 'isolated location and consequent high transmission cost' and 533 with one accounting or desk-bookkeeping machine (*Bank System Study*, vol. 1: 11 and 12).

70. The Lloyds-IBM study of 1964 called for additional equipment, namely, two IBM7010 for record maintenance and two 1460s to handle the input/output. These would be supported by an IBM1050 Data Communications System located at each branch and IBM7740 Communications Control Systems 'switches' in London, Manchester, Birmingham, and Bristol (*Bank System Study*, vol. 1: 11, 12, and 20).

71. *Bank System Study*, vol. 1: 3.

72. *Bank System Study*, vol. 1: 161.

73. The study estimated 12 man-years to develop the programs for the 7010 and 5 man-years for the 1460 or a team of 10 programmers working for two years (*Bank System Study*, vol. 2: 275).

74. The General Post Office became the communications monopoly in 1912. The telephone and digital communications arm was floated as a separate company, British Telecommunications plc (today BT Group), in 1980.

75. *Bank System Study*, vol. 2: 274–5.

76. With the exception of the Pall Mall branch, the bank aimed to service no more than 15,000 customers per branch (and would open a new branch nearby when this number was exceeded). This was important, in that it determined the numbering of customer accounts per branch. Source: *Outline for Development*, 'Account Numbering': 164–7.

77. 'Bank Scores "First" in Branch Computer Link-up', *Lloyds Bank News*, 47 (November) 1970: front page.

78. Unless otherwise stated, this paragraph borrows freely from Anonymous, 'IBM Backs the Dark Horse', Internal IBM document provided by Sir Anthony Cleaver, 29 April 2013 and 'Computer "First" for Lloyds Bank', press release, Lloyds Bank Ltd, 26 October 1970.

79. Following IBM's standard nomenclature, '39' and '29' denote a special, non-standard engineering product. IBM developed the 3940 at the Hursley Laboratories (near Winchester, England) and manufactured it in Greenock, Scotland.

80. Unless otherwise stated, this paragraph borrows freely from 'Branch Computer Link-up', *Lloyds Bank News*, 50 (February) 1971: and 'Bank Scores "First" in Branch Computer Link-up', *Lloyds Bank News*, 47 (November) 1970: front page.

81. Ackrill and Hannah (2001, 322–4).

82. This would be between £312.50 and £822.70 million in 2014. See: 'Purchasing Power of British Pounds from 1270 to Present', *Measuringworth*, accessed 9 April 2016, <http://www.measuringworth.com/ppoweruk/>, accessed 18 October 2013, <http://www.measuringworth.com/ppoweruk/>.

83. For the response of other British banks to the digitalization of Lloyds see Bátiz-Lazo et al. (2014b).

84. 'Technology', *Lloyds Bank News*, March/April 1979 (number 123): 2.

85. 'Lloyds Bank: Customer Statistics June 1976' and (unnamed) internal IBM document provided by Sir Anthony Cleaver, former CEO of IBM UK, 29 April 2013.

86. 'Branches were unable to cope with end of the week business as Friday lunchtime was seeing people queuing outside the door'. Interview with Sir Anthony Cleaver, former CEO of IBM UK, by B. Bátiz-Lazo, London, 13 April 2013.

87. Lloyds Banking Group Archives, HO/IT/Pla/2, *Outline for Development: Information Services*, Lloyds Bank—IBM, 1969: Letter to R. A. Barber (Manager Banking District), 21 July 1969.

88. This feature was also present in many other devices by 1975, as suggested in the specifications of the Diebold, LeFebure, Mosler, and NCR in Zimmer (1975).

89. Interview with Sir Anthony Cleaver, former CEO of IBM UK, by B. Bátiz-Lazo, London, 13 April 2013.

90. 'Purchasing Power of British Pounds from 1270 to Present', *Measuringworth*, accessed 10 April 2016, <https://www.measuringworth.com/ppoweruk>. According to the Office of National Statistics, the median gross annual earnings for 2013–14 was £22,044 for all employees and £27,195 for full-time employees and the average annual income in 1969 was £1,607.16. Both nominal and present value measures result in a 2.8 cost to salary ratio.

91. Born in 1938 and graduating from Trinity College, Oxford in 1962, he joined IBM UK as systems engineer in 1962 and eventually became its Chief Executive and Chairman, later to head the UK Atomic Energy Authority. His knighthood was announced in the New Year's Honours List, 1991. See further: 'Anthony Cleaver', *Wikipedia*, accessed 14 April 2016, <https://en.wikipedia.org/wiki/Anthony_Cleaver>. Unless otherwise stated, this paragraph borrows freely from the interview with Sir Anthony Cleaver, former CEO of IBM UK, by B. Bátiz-Lazo, London, 13 April 2013.

92. Personal communication (email) from Sir Anthony Cleaver, former CEO of IBM UK, with B. Bátiz-Lazo, 18 April 2016.

93. 'John Fairclough', *Wikipedia*, accessed 18 May 2016, <https://en.wikipedia.org/wiki/John_Fairclough>.

94. In August 1973 Chubb purchased all of Smiths Industries' manufacturing, assets, patents, and stock in cash dispensing for £218,000.

95. Stearns (2011, 74) notes that the American Bankers Association (ABA) 'publicly endorsed the magnetic stripe (often abbreviated "magstripe") in early 1971 as the preferred method for making the cards machine-readable and defined a format for encoding the account information upon it. As a result, a number of manufacturers began producing [point of sale] terminals in 1971 designed to read the ABA format and transmit the card data across standard telephone lines.' Cash machine manufacturers were also prompt to comply.

96. The comments and clarification from Alan Konheim, Philip Lippard, and Jonathan Rosenne on magstripes and ATM standards are much appreciated.

97. Constable (2015, 6).

98. Konheim (2015, 14).

99. Developed in 1929 by Lester S. Hill. Konheim (2015, 12).

100. Regarding these developments US patent 3956615 (filed in June 1974 and published November 1976), refers to the use of the Lucifer code, specifically stating that this was not a 'critical' choice for the invention but making reference to Horst Feistel's original article in *Computer Design* and the original patent (US 3798359 published March 1974). A second patent for the IBM machine (US 4186871, filed in March 1978 and published in February 1980) cites the previous patent's use of the Lucifer cipher in the paragraph beginning line 67, column 5, and on p. 12. In this case the reference is once again to the flexibility of the machine's use of ciphers and states that the Lucifer code is no longer used, giving way to a National Bureau of Standards Algorithm (DES or Data Encryption Standard). According to Konheim (2007, 329 [part 9.20]) another patent of relevance for the development of the cipher was that awarded to Roy Alder (US 4255811, filed in March 1985 and published in March 1981).

101. Personal communication (email) from Alan G. Konheim, with B. Bátiz-Lazo, 18 April 2016. See also Attalla's biography here: 'Martin Atalla', *Wikipedia*, accessed 15 June 2016, <https://en.wikipedia.org/wiki/Martin_Atalla>.

102. Interview (telephone) with Irwin Derman, former executive of Visa, by B. Bátiz-Lazo, 6 July 2016.

103. See further Konheim (2015, 2016).

104. Towards the end of the 1970s international standards for the physical and technical characteristics of credit cards were enacted. The first version of ISO 3554 standard relating to the magnetic stripe encoding for tracks 1 and 2 (as well as character embossing) of credit cards was published in 1976. Then came ISO 4909 or the standard detailing magnetic stripe data content for track 3 in bank cards in 1978. See: 'ISO 3554: 1976 Credit Cards—Magnetic Stripe Encoding for Tracks 1 and 2', International Organization for Standardization, accessed 6 July 2016, <http://www.iso.org/iso/home/store/catalogue_ics/catalogue_detail_ics.htm?csnumber=8957&ICS1=35&ICS2=240&ICS3=15>.

105. Konheim (2015, 19).

106. Interview with Sir Anthony Cleaver, former CEO of IBM UK, by B. Bátiz-Lazo, London, 13 April 2013.

107. 'New "Robot" Cashier to Help Staff', *Lloyds Bank News*, 54 (June) 1971: front page.

108. The bank had dispensers installed at branches in the West End of London (3); the Home Counties (9); and the Birmingham area (12) ('On Line Ready Cash', *Lloyds Bank News*, (September) 1970: front page).

109. 'Run-up Begins for Cash Point Launch', *Lloyds Bank News*, 69 (September) 1972: front page.

110. 'Lloyds New Cash Dispenser', *The Banker*, February 1973: 225.

111. 'New "Robot" Cashier to Help Staff', *Lloyds Bank News*, 54 (June) 1971: front page. However, the team at Speytec (which by that time had become a subsidiary of Burroughs in the UK) already had a couple of years' experience in developing a cash machine operated by a card and magnetic stripe (Bátiz-Lazo and Reid 2008). Although the earliest patent and application of a magnetic stripe seems to date back to Omron-Tateisi as a transport solution for Tokyo, the common wisdom points to the patents and applications by IBM. See for instance Stearns (2017).

112. 'New "Robot" Cashier to Help Staff', *Lloyds Bank News*, 54 (June) 1971: front page.

113. 'Lloyds New Cash Dispenser', *The Banker*, February 1973: 225.

114. 'Lloyds New Cash Dispenser', *The Banker*, February 1973: 225.

115. 'Run-up Begins for Cash Point Launch', *Lloyds Bank News*, 69 (September) 1972: front page.

116. Interview with James Adamson, former CEO of NCR Dundee, by B. Bátiz-Lazo and R. Reid, Edinburgh, 18 June 2008.

117. Lloyds TSB Archive, Index cards on ATM.

118. Personal communication (email) from Eve Richards, with B. Bátiz-Lazo, 16 October 2017.

119. Lloyds Bank acquired the in-store branches of Lewis's and Selfridges in the early 1970s. It was evident from the staff magazine (*Lloyds Bank News*) these were operated as an integral part of the bank rather than at arm's length.

120. Anonymous, 'Lloyds Bank: Customer Statistics June 1976', internal IBM document provided by Sir Anthony Cleaver, Former CEO of IBM UK, 29 April 2013.

121. Data were sourced from *Evidence of the London Clearing Bankers to the Committee to Review the Functioning of Financial Institutions (General memorandum of evidence to the Wilson Committee—November 1977)* (London: Committee of London Clearing Bankers, 1978): 37.

122. Lloyds TSB Archive, Index cards on ATM.

123. Interview with Sir Anthony Cleaver, former CEO of IBM UK, by B. Bátiz-Lazo, London, 13 April 2013.

124. Personal communication (email) from Jonathan Rosenne, former engineer IBM Israel, with B. Bátiz-Lazo, 29 March 2013.

125. Personal communication (email) from Philip Lippard, former engineer IBM USA, with B. Bátiz-Lazo, 12 April 2016.

126. 'A Coders Chronology', *Plippard*, accessed 14 July 2012, <http://www.plippard.com/page/a-coder-s-chronology>; personal communication (email) from Philip Lippard, former engineer IBM, with B. Bátiz-Lazo, 11 August 2012; and 'IBM 3624', *Wikipedia*, accessed 15 August 2012, <http://en.wikipedia.org/wiki/IBM_3624>.

127. Personal communication (email) from Robert Rosenthal, former IBM engineer, with B. Bátiz-Lazo, 3 August 2016.

128. Dale Dooley, former President and CEO Shazam/ITS, ATM Industry Association, Orlando, 15 February 2017.

129. The remainder of this paragraph was sourced in 'A Double Milestone', *Lloyd Bank News*, December 1988: 3.

130. Personal and confidential letter to W. C. Paxton, IBM Charlotte, NC from Jonathan Rosenne, Tel Aviv, 15 April 1984.

131. Interview with Sir Anthony Cleaver, former CEO of IBM UK, by B. Bátiz-Lazo, London, 13 April 2013.

132. Personal communication (email), from Jonathan Rosenne, former IBM engineer, with B. Bátiz-Lazo, 16 April 2016.

133. Unless otherwise stated, this paragraph draws on the interview with James Adamson, former CEO of NCR Dundee, by B. Bátiz-Lazo and R. Reid, Edinburgh, 18 June 2008.

134. Personal communication (email) from Jonathan Rosenne, former engineer IBM Israel, with B. Bátiz-Lazo, 16 April 2016.

135. e.g. Gandy (2013).

136. e.g. Campbell-Kelly (2003).

137. Pardo-Guerra (2013).

138. In 1974 Docutel reached the zenith of its penetration when it acquired a 70 per cent share of the US ATM market (Essinger 1987, 43). The demise of Docutel was also influenced by the recession that followed the oil embargo of October 1973 and Docutel's lack of diversification.

139. Personal communication (email), from Jonathan Rosenne, former engineer IBM Israel, with B. Bátiz-Lazo, 16 April 2016.

140. 'ISO 8583'. *Wikipedia*, accessed 19 May 2016, <https://en.wikipedia.org/wiki/ISO_8583>.

5

The Network Becomes the Core of the ATM

5.1 Embedding the ATM in the Banking Organization

This chapter deals with the growth of shared ATM networks during the 1980s, to explain how the rise of reciprocity and sharing effectively marked the end of the proprietary ATM network. For instance, until the advent of the Iowa Transfer System (ITS) in Iowa or the Money Access Center (MAC) network in Pennsylvania, all ATMs in the USA were accessible only to customers of the bank that owned them.[1] The Iowa network was of further significance because it was the first to use the single message format for authorization and settlement, a concept that revolutionized the payment industry and the genesis of ANSI X-92 and later ISO 8593.[2] Hence, a characteristic of the early days of the ATM and other self-service banking technologies was that there were no true communication standards. This was also the case of the magnetic stripe.[3] Its content varied between institutions and what their host processing systems were expecting to read. Engineers had then to figure out both the online format (stored in the magnetic stripe's second track, Track 2 for short) as well as the offline format (Track 3). All this changed with the advent of true shared (also called interchange or switched) ATM networks. They brought about not only the demise of offline transactions (and therefore, the need for Track 3 encoding) but impinged on standard communication protocols and made possible the globalization of cash withdrawals and electronic fund transfers at point of contact payments.

This chapter describes how shared ATM networks and interconnection standards emerged together with the competitive and political dynamics that framed these processes. This, in turn, will allow us to document, first, how changes in the retail banking industry impacted on the ATM in as much as the evolution of this device permitted depository institutions to articulate their strategic plans; and second, how during this period bankers begin to lose hope that applications of computer technology could deliver competitive advantage in retail banking.

5.2 An Alphabet Soup in the USA

5.2.1 *The Tipping Point*

From the late 1970s to the early 1980s the concept of automated cash distribution had proved viable and the technology sufficiently mature to facilitate commercial exploitation. Competition in the ATM's design moved away from proving its feasibility and turned to focus on operational issues. This move built on the likes of the IBM Customer Information Control System (CICS), a family of mixed language applications designed to support rapid, high-volume online transaction processing.[4]

The CICS was initially designed for utility companies, but banks and credit card companies pushed for a cost-effective interactive system that enabled them to move away from batch processing and punched cards. By the early 1970s, the CICS middleware allowed COBOL programs to support large terminal networks. These formed the basis for several ATM management software systems and enabled the device to proliferate. For instance in 1982 ACI Worldwide Inc. introduced its BASE24 software. This was designed to support the payment systems used by large financial institutions and was quickly taken up by many of the largest banks.[5]

Supporting this growth one often found high availability, fault-tolerant computer equipment (also called 'NonStop')—which was first introduced by Tandem Computers in the late 1970s and proved to be particularly adept at handling high volume repetitive tasks. This was the case, for instance, of the NYCE automated teller machine network. Owned by the New York Switch Corp., based in Hackensack, NJ and established by eight New York area banks in 1984, NYCE initially shared 750 ATMs amongst 2.5 million proprietary access card holders and more than 2 million 'qualified' Visa and MasterCard users in the area.[6] NCYE linked banks to a Timplex Corp. multiplex located in its Fort Lee, NJ headquarters through a dedicated 2,400/bit per sec line, which then used a 9,600/bit per sec dedicated line to connect to the network switch in Berlin, WI, which consisted of a Tandem Nonstop II computer.

Orders for new devices piled up between 1978 and 1980. This after a dearth of interest in cash machines in the mid-1970s as a result of the energy crisis. Manufacturing ATMs then emerged as one of the few industries (if not the only one) that were growing in the recession that followed the energy crisis of the early 1980s. At the time, one source estimated that 120,000 machines were to be installed between 1981 and 1985—tripling the number of devices in operation worldwide.[7] The USA hosted about half the world's installed devices and the appetite for them among American banks made the business case for expecting growth. The industry then coined the term 'vendor' to describe the partnerships that aimed to compete with the worldwide marketing muscle of IBM and NCR. These vendors included Italy's

Olivetti marketing and servicing of Docutel machines outside North America while Eindhoven-based Phillips marketed those of Chubb and Diebold. Yet the biggest manufacturer at the time, Omron, continued to sit quietly at home in Japan.

5.2.2 The Importance of Magnetic Stripes

If the 1980s was a period of rapid growth for ATMs so it was for the shared ATM networks. That was certainly the case in the USA.[8] Still, some forces limited ATM growth. For instance, the competitive nature of US banking meant that even large banks had limited geographic territory for expansion. But at the same time, other forces fuelled ATM growth. The two most important ones were, first, a ruling of the US Supreme Court, before which the new ATMs set up by banks and savings banks in Pennsylvania, for instance, had to go through the same authorization procedure as branches. But in 1985 the ruling settled the issue of the ATM's organizational nature by siding with the view that they were not subject to the same regulatory considerations as 'bricks and mortar' branches.[9] Consequently bankers, particularly those in multi-branch states, had greater freedom to decide on location and the sharing of ATMs across state lines was able to proceed.

A second development, just as important, was the introduction of state laws to mandate sharing.[10] These laws led to the emergence of shared ATMs, mostly along geographic lines, as early as 1972.[11] One of these initial interchange networks was built around Huntington Bankshares, a holding company with affiliates in Ohio. In 1973, Huntington coordinated a three-way interchange agreement amongst its affiliates to allow individual customers with cards issued by Huntington or MasterCharge (later MasterCard) to receive cash advances from ATMs at any of its banks.[12] Another early shared network was Iowa Transfer System (ITS) Inc. It was established in 1974 and became operational on the back of NCR devices in 1976.[13] Its aim was to allow Iowa community bankers to evolve beyond proprietary ATMs and point of sale terminal services into a state-wide electronic fund transfer network.[14] Iowa being a unit bank state, sharing was imperative. By 1982, some $50 million had been invested in ATMs and other collectively deployed hardware around ITS. This enabled a population of approximately 2.8 million customers evenly distributed across the state and including a large number of commuters to the metropolitan areas of Des Moines and Cedar Rapids to be serviced.

Withdrawal limits in offline systems would typically rely on 'shop floors' stored on magnetic stripes. But solutions based on the offline 'Track 3' limit were subject to error and loss. An alternative was a direct link between computer centres. In the absence of standards for inter-bank networks, early consortia shared the design and specification of several important parameters for everyday operation. These included the format of messages, data elements, and code values in the communication between the device and the data centre (such as institution identification number, the method of applying for codes, the method of obtaining lists of codes, etc.).[15] John Chamberlin, an engineer involved in developing switched networks in Arkansas, recalled the challenge in making communications work:

> Data rates achieved in the 1970s and 1980s were abysmal compared to today's. In some countries the data communication lines were from the national post, or another government agency. In the USA they were mostly from AT&T. Modems came from the network vendor. The ASCII terminals connected at data rates of 10 characters per second (cps) or maybe even 30 cps. IBM terminals might use synchronous modems of 1200 baud, 2400 baud or 4800 baud, where you can roughly divide by ten to get a cps equivalent. The cost of synchronous modems was roughly a dollar per baud![16]

The early 1980s, then, was a world that had cards with magnetic stripes. In some countries and financial institutions, banking computers stored comprehensive account databases. These computer systems were capable of online access where the ATM sat as the terminal of a larger system while systems had the communications infrastructure to support more devices.

But interconnection for ATM networks relied on agreements not only on technological specifications but also on ways of distributing the cost of running the network. These reciprocity agreements were often negotiated on a bilateral basis and were not only cumbersome but could generate conflicting incentives. For instance, individual members of a group could try to increase profits by violating the agreement that other members were honouring.[17] Ultimately the agreement could disintegrate. Alternatively, the potential growth of the network was limited, given the prohibitively high cost of an ever-larger number of bilateral negotiations.

Towards the end of the 1970s and during the 1980s, cooperation evolved towards the establishment of joint venture companies that would enable some or all of the members to share equity ownership as well as control of the decision-making process (on such matters as membership access, organizational structure, and specific details of network operation). An important feature of these joint ventures was a central data centre, called a 'switch', which routed transactions between customers of different banks—giving rise to the term 'switched transaction network'.

Figure 5.1 depicts the flow of information and charges generated by a withdrawal transaction in a shared ATM network. The transaction begins when the customer of Bank Ω uses his/her PIN and card while looking to withdraw cash at an ATM which is owned by Δ. Let us assume that there is a significant geographical distance between Bank Ω and Δ, which might be a convenience

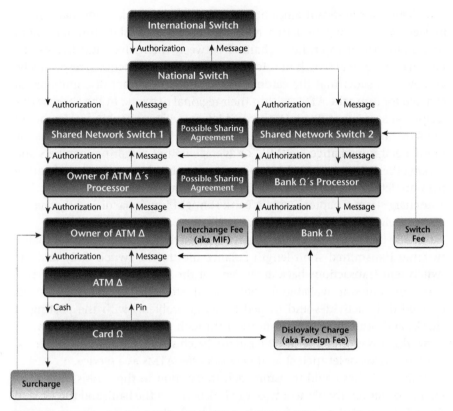

Figure 5.1. Flow of authorization messages in a shared ATM network

Source: Author's own analysis based on Hayashi et al. (2006) and McAndrews (1991).

store, airport, or casino; and for the sake of brevity let's also assume that the owner of ATM Δ is a depository financial institution.

Figure 5.1 depicts the flow of essential information to finalize the transaction. In one direction, the flow of information will ask for approval and, if funds are available, the opposite flow will authorize the ATM to dispense the money. Transaction information will be routed to a central computer (i.e. a switch) by the owner of ATM Δ, or its payment processor. The lower the daily transaction volume of ATM Δ's owner, the more likely it would be to use a third-party processor (see Independent ATM Deployers (IADs) in Chapter 7). The larger the volume of network transactions generated by ATM Δ's owner, the more options there are to choose the most cost-effective option amongst different switching fees (where each interchange network determines the price for its services). In the USA, for instance, it was the case that very large banks were members of multiple interchange ATM networks, while in the early days, interconnection between regional ATM networks in the USA served as a national switch.

If there is a significant amount of traffic between Bank Δ and Bank Ω (or between regional switches), they may establish a reciprocal sharing agreement that allows them to create a channel between themselves and bypass the national or regional switch in interregional or local transactions, respectively; and even consider that the cardholders of Ω and Δ are not discriminated or charged for using the ATMs within their regional network. In the absence of a reciprocal agreement, Bank Ω, the card issuer, will pay Bank Δ, the owner of the ATM, an interchange fee set by the network. This fee is also known as the multilateral interchange fee (MIF) or average cost of acquiring members and making their machines available to card issuers. In addition, Bank Δ as part of the transaction might collect a fee for servicing the customer of Bank Ω (called a surcharge—see Chapter 7) while Bank Ω might impose a 'disloyalty charge' (aka a foreign fee) to its customer for not using Bank Ω's ATMs.

Initially there were two types of network switch: batch and online.[18] Batch switches transmitted short-length balance files to the switch daily and the switch sent transactions back at the end of the day. 'Floor limits', that is, a maximum amount available for withdrawal, stored in the magnetic stripe, enabled daily activities and helped to avoid problems with the posting of checks and other forms of verification through rather slow communication networks. It was often the case that many batch switch participants either did not have ATMs or let their shared network offer ATMs as a service.

Online switches could transmit each transaction to the card-issuing bank for authorization, thanks to a two-way link between the bank and the ATM. If the ATM accepted a card from its own bank this was known as 'on us' transactions or 'intercept processing', meaning the bank intercepted its own transactions and authorized them, so as to avoid network fees. When the ATM accepted cards from other banks, these transactions were routed through the network. Different network fees would then apply to the bank and the customer. As mentioned, some banks had sufficient volume to link to multiple switches, sending transactions to the most cost-effective network.

Initially each switch could have its own data formats, handshakes, transaction sets, and processing rules. This required different modules for each variant but the data communications protocols were usually easier. Many switches used the IBM 3780 communications protocol or treated the bank computer as a terminal.[19] Passing transactions through the network added delays, causing rules to be set that would speed up response times. Part of coming live with a network was a highly organized certification procedure, testing the transaction set in many sequences, errors, and timing. Over time, more standard switch specifications emerged, such as the ISO 8583 bit oriented data format in 1987.[20] Introduced as the international inter-bank message standard, ISO 8583 was implemented across new and existing networks as they expanded.[21]

5.2.3 *The Role of the Card Companies*

An early example of a switch ATM transaction network was the TYME consortia. TYME was an acronym of 'Take Your Money Everywhere' and the network was established in Milwaukee, WI, by member banks in December 1976 as a non-stock and non-profit corporation.[22] By 1979 TYME was a 24-hour, seven day a week network that offered state-wide access to ATMs and point of sale terminals. TYME was composed of eight independent data processing centres, a switch, and an undisclosed number of intercept processors. The latter enabled some banks to deal with 'on us' transactions (for their own bank or correspondent banks) without having to rely on the switch, whereas those banks without an intercept processor relied on the switch to do the work for their own bank and its correspondents. Together this ensemble handled six different types of ATM and point of sale terminals. Individual banks made their own decisions for tailored marketing campaigns, as well as for purchases and the location of individual devices. The joint venture owned the TYME trademark. Through a system of one member, one vote it established standards (e.g. magnetic card encoding and plastic card dimensions) as well as levels of performance and capacity for the data centres. By 1979, TYME was handling an average of 360,000 transactions per month through the switch and was expected to handle up to 800,000 per month by the end of 1980 and through 'some of the millions of dollars [invested] in [developing their] own systems', the directors of TYME were looking to sell their systems to Arizona banks. They were also discussing with banks in other states how a national network could be created.

TYME is thus an example of the early move of a regional network which attempted to go country-wide. But, before proceeding to discuss national networks in the USA, two caveats are worth making. First, by 1980 a third of banks of all sizes in the USA were involved in some form of ATM sharing arrangement.[23] This meant there was experience and willingness around sharing in some corners of US banking. Second, a contemporary banker estimated that in 1982 only 2 to 5 per cent of customers required a national cash withdrawal service frequently.[24] Indeed, a survey by the Operations and Automation Division of the American Bankers Association in the spring of 1981 reported that on average, three-quarters of the surveyed banks of all asset sizes had neither installed nor had any plans to install point of sale terminals.[25] This shows how minuscule the debit cards' transaction volume and cardholder base were before the 1990s. Instead, cash withdrawals in the 1970s and 1980s used an ATM card, meaning the credit card sized plastic card which prompted the ATM to debit a current account when withdrawing cash. The ATM card prohibited interoperability across a point of sale terminal. ATM withdrawals also resulted from credit card advances (see also Chapter 6).

The modest demand for national cash withdrawals, together with the low penetration of payments with debit cards suggests that the service providers were the ones that were insisting on a national ATM network, hoping to recuperate some of their investments and lower the cost of operation.

A watershed moment for the idea of a national network in the USA took place in July 1981, when a press communiqué from Visa USA informed everyone 'that members could now use its computerized authorisation and billings systems to interconnect local proprietary and regional *non*-Visa, shared ATM networks... [and this] caught bankers, regional ATM operators and even card association rival MasterCard International by surprise'.[26] At the time, Visa's announcement was also seen as a reaction to third party switching services emerging in the USA alongside other joint ventures and bank-owned proprietary networks.[27] The significance of the announcement, however, was that Visa had proven organizational and technological capabilities to deal with large numbers of banks exchanging information and money across state and international boundaries.

Since the dawn of the bank credit card systems in the 1960s, Visa had offered a cash withdrawal facility to inter-state and international cardholders.[28] It was called the 'Cash Disbursement Service' and involved using credit cards for cash withdrawals at tellers of retail branches (regardless of bank and location). Through the 1981 announcement, Visa now wanted to replace these tellers by ATMs at member banks. This idea was called the Automated Cash Disbursement Service or ACDS. To implement the ACDS, staff at Visa began to develop message and PIN sharing formats (using DES encryption). The latter would enable Visa to have the systems in place to transmit ATM transactions through its communications networks, regardless of location. The business proposition had value given that the Cash Disbursement Service generated lucrative fee income for banks while the proliferation of ATMs (and the possible closure of retail branches) threatened this line of income.[29] Initially Visa aimed to start by attracting one major bank per state.[30] But instead participants came from states such as Iowa or Wisconsin where banks were used to sharing ATMs and wanted more volume through them. The ACDS strategy was ultimately unsuccessful, however, because the network remained small in terms of both volume and number of devices until 1987, when Visa became part owner of Plus System Inc. Similarly, MasterCard launched 'MasterTeller' in 1982 but it met the same fate as Visa. Even American Express' 'Express Cash' service, established as a pilot in 1979 and a national service from 1981 onwards, grew more than Visa and MasterCard's shared ATM networks in the USA.[31] Instead, the backbone of national shared ATM networks emerged from the establishment in the early 1980s of two interchange networks called Cirrus and Plus.

Plus was born in 1982 to link the subsidiaries of the Colorado National Bank (Denver, CO), through its credit card processing arm, the Rocky Mountain

BankCard System.[32] Plus won immediate recognition in less than a year by signing up big players such as Chase Manhattan Bank (New York, NY), First Bank System (Minneapolis, MN), and Bank of America (San Francisco, CA).[33] Meanwhile, Cirrus was established in 1983 by a group of banks spearheaded by First Interstate Bank (Los Angeles, CA) and including heavyweights Manufacturers Hanover Trust (New York, NY), Mellon Bank (Pittsburgh, PA), and BayBank (Boston, MA).[34] MasterCard acquired Cirrus in January 1988, while Cirrus absorbed the small staff operating MasterCard's 'MasterTeller' ATM sharing program. The acquisition of Cirrus consolidated MasterCard's position in the USA while Cirrus might have been the nucleus for a worldwide ATM network—a network that had been expected to consist of at least 30,000 machines in more than a dozen countries by 1990.[35]

Note how the initial success of Plus and Cirrus relied on attracting large banks in different states. This illustrates how ATM capabilities were viewed by bankers across the USA: as a way for banks to outperform local competitors— the greater the ATM fleet, the greater the convenience to the customer. As noted above, ATMs were also seen as instrumental in reducing costs at and customer queues within retail branches. But this proposition required substantial investment. Sharing the cost of running the network with others was therefore attractive. More so as proprietary ATM networks had not been decisive in changing market share.

An illustration of the competitive pressures on shared ATM networks in the USA can be found in events that took place in 1991, when Citicorp decided to join Cirrus.[36] Up to this point Citicorp had been building its own network, and had even designed and manufactured its own ATMs.[37] But after the deal the bank opened 75 per cent of the 1,200 ATMs that it operated in the New York City area to other members of Cirrus. Altogether the link was able to give Cirrus members access to 1,430 Citicorp ATMs throughout the USA and 500 ATMs worldwide. At the time, however, Citicorp had not yet joined any regional network, such as NYCE which then owned some 5,000 ATMs in the New York City area and included all other major banks with large consumer operations in this area. Through Cirrus, Citi's customers gained access to the ATMs of Chemical Bank and Manufacturers Hanover Trust, two of Citi's biggest competitors. According to reports in the press, Citi's change of mind responded to growing customer complaints requesting access to NYCE or any other stronger regional ATM network. Another cause of customers' alienation was that Citi's network did not have point of sale capabilities. A Citicorp spokesperson claimed that the move was part of a plan with much bigger scope, which aimed to give its customers access to any ATM across the globe.

Cirrus, Plus, and other shared networks grew to be significant players in the US market even while technological and organizational issues were being sorted out. The first dealt with protocols, such as the specification of the encoding in the magnetic stripe (including the number of digits in the account and in the PIN), on which a common communications platform depended. 'Protecting the PIN and keeping things moving was a technological problem we all had [in constructing an ATM network]' said Irwin Derman, vice-president in charge of Visa's global ATM program in the 1980s.[38] Organizational issues included drafting agreements for the types of service that the switch would provide, sharing the cost of running the network (i.e. the interchange fees), and the conditions and costs of the reciprocal use of a device by non-domestic cardholders (i.e. surcharging).

The emergence, growth, and success of Plus and Cirrus seem to contradict the apparent intention behind the domestic ATM networks promoted by Visa and MasterCard, especially considering that the card companies were not-for-profit organizations, consortia owned by member banks—many of which were otherwise local competitors.[39]

According to Derman and to research on credit cards by David Stearns, the apparent contradiction of investing in both Visa and alternative ATM consortia is explained by the deep political and cultural divide that permeated retail banking during the 1970s and 1980s.[40] To begin with, the asset side (where credit cards sat) was making increasing contributions to the bottom line. Yet some bankers still considered the credit card a questionable venture, attractive only if it could translate into increased deposits. Seldom did a career in credit cards lead bank staff to executive positions, to the extent that credit card operations were often allocated remote, undesirable, and sometimes derelict premises. Of course, this view was not universal but progressive, innovative banks were the exception rather than the rule.

Nevertheless, the liability side had traditionally been the route to the top. Here is where 'real' banking took place by attracting more deposits (which could be converted into larger commercial loans). It also involved managing retail branches and buttressing contact with key customers. In this context, Visa and MasterCard use was based on the idea that a decal on a plastic card could give the customer who wielded it access to national and international banking services—including cash advances at tellers of retail branches. But extending these services to cash withdrawals through ATMs ran counter to and combated the strategy of using ATMs to build competitive advantage in the local market. To little surprise 'the people in the debit (i.e. checking account) side of the bank didn't want to talk to Visa [whose credit card sat on the other side of the balance sheet]'.[41] These dynamics between banks and within the banking organizations, therefore, not only obstructed the sharing of ATMs through Visa and/or MasterCard, but also the way in which the credit card organizations at first tried to deploy debit cards. Instead, it made more sense to recoup the investment in ATMs and offer nationwide ATM access by sharing with banks in other states through a joint venture or third party service—provided the latter had rules to exclude other local competitors and, therefore, could keep competitive pressure in the immediate market intact.

5.3 Meanwhile in Canada

5.3.1 A Sui Generis North American

Although briefly, it may be useful to outline the development of the Canadian shared country-wide network, because, for some industry insiders, Canadian ATMs 'operated in a fundamentally different environment'.[42] The reasons included Canada's significantly different climatic and physical structure and its relatively small, dispersed, but affluent population. All this made it quite challenging to deploy the logistics for distributing enough ATMs. At the same time, the Canadian case lets us take a first look at the creation of international ATM networks.

In Canada it all started in Toronto in 1969.[43] This first device was a British made Chubb MD2 deployed through Chubb-Mosler and Taylor, the joint venture between Chubb & Son (UK) and Mosler Safe Co. (USA), at a branch of the Canadian Imperial Bank of Commerce (CIBC).[44] To meet CIBC's needs, the device had been changed so much that it was 'regarded more of a saver of teller's time than solely a dispenser of cash'. Before the end of 1969, Chubb had sold two more cash machines to banks in the Canadian mid-West (which placed orders for three more) and an order for twenty in Quebec had been met. By 1978 there were 250 automated banking machines (as they called them) in operation.[45]

The territorial area of Canada is approximately 10 million km^2. In 1983, this country had 25.5 million inhabitants (a 6 per cent increase from 1978), of which 19.4 million or 76 per cent lived in urban areas (a 7 per cent increase from 1978).[46] There were five nationwide banks and 12,938 retail branches of deposit-taking institutions (a 2 per cent decrease from 13,151 offices in 1978), resulting in 1,496 inhabitants in urban areas per banking office (an 8 per cent increase from the 1,381 in 1978).[47] The country had over 23 million credit cards in circulation in 1983. By this time, the number of cash machines had increased to 1,960 devices or almost seven times the total in 1978, while the number of urban inhabitants per device decreased from 72,669 in 1978 to 9,875 in 1983.[48] Chartered banks had taken the lead in deploying ATMs: in 1983 Royal Bank of Canada had 588, Toronto Dominion had 321, Bank of Montreal had 255, and Bank of Nova Scotia had 114.[49] However, nearly half the banks' cash machines were located in the province of Ontario.[50] This is not surprising, given that Ontario in 1981 housed 8.6 million inhabitants or 35 per cent of the total Canadian population, 82 per cent of whom lived in urban areas.[51] Meanwhile, trust companies were competing aggressively in the retail market through extended hours of service, a selling point that could be undermined by the round-the-clock availability of ATMs.[52]

Given its population growth and uneven geographical distribution, it is not surprising that in the early 1980s Canada saw abundant speculation regarding a country-wide ATM network shared by banks, trust companies, and credit unions.[53] By 1984, the five major banks owned 2,055 devices (out of approximately 2,600 in operation throughout the country), while some of the large trust companies had none. Financial institutions thus faced significant capital costs if they wanted to build a respectable presence.[54]

Initially the Bank of Nova Scotia and the National Bank of Canada signed a reciprocity agreement—called 'Idéal'. At the same time, several non-financial companies set up shared ATM networks while trying to capitalize on the fear among smaller institutions. These included Access Banking Network Inc. of Toronto, Canada Systems Group, also based in Toronto, and Pacific Network Services Inc. of Vancouver (which had acquired the rights to British Columbia from The Exchange Systems Inc., a US-based shared ATM service set up in the 1970s in the nearby state of Washington).[55] However, these services had 50 or fewer machines each. Only Co-operators Data Services Ltd., which serviced credit unions in Ontario, Saskatchewan, and British Columbia, with its 200 devices was of any significance. Yet in 1984 only 2 per cent of all the cash machines in Canada were being shared.[56]

The main limitation on small participants' spreading their ATM capacity was the significant investment required to adopt an industry-specific innovation. At the time, the cost per ATM ranged between $35,000 and $50,000 Canadian dollars and it was estimated that a machine had to handle 6,000 transactions to be cost-effective.[57] This led some observers to think it was unlikely that regional networks would succeed there. The view of Norman White, an assistant president of Canada Trustco Mortgage Co. of Ontario, was representative: 'There is going to be a winner. I don't see the candidates for multiple shared networks,' he said.[58]

Table 5.1 summarizes the resulting change in overall outlook when some large banks came together to form a shared ATM network in 1984. First, the 700 ATMs of the Royal Bank of Canada, the country's largest financial institution, formed a shared network by joining forces with the 'caisses populaires' of Quebec and three other major banks, namely Canadian Imperial Bank of Commerce, Nova Scotia, and Toronto Dominion.[59] Initially each member of the consortium, called 'Interact' (also known as the Interact Association), contributed 50 devices to articulate a network of 250 out of their 1,900 machines combined. These were to be spread out throughout Canada's major cities and in key locations such as shopping malls. All of the institutions in the joint venture 'offered Visa marquee credit cards and that seemed to have been a factor in making it easier for them to meet and put together a deal'.[60]

Table 5.1. Shared ATM networks of major Canadian banks, 1986 (by size of ATMs in the network)

Institution	Name of system	Number of machines	Shared networks Canada	Foreign (USA)
Royal Bank of Canada	Personal Touch	1,134	Interact	Plus
Bank of Montreal	Instabank	653	Interact, Circuit	Cirrus
Toronto Dominion Bank	Green Machine	550	Interact	
Canadian Imperial Bank of Commerce	Instant Teller	500	Interact	
Bank of Nova Scotia	Transaction (Cashstop)	216	Interact, Idéal	Electron-Visa
National Bank of Canada	Day-Night Teller	150	Interact, Idéal	Master Teller (MasterCard)

Source: Own estimates, based on Elder (1986).

The Interact network is another good example of the many regional or national networks that emerged in the 1980s, which saw a fragmented approach, with bilateral or multilateral ATM-sharing schemes, often limited to a number of 'compatible' large banks.

In a similar move to that of the five banks behind Interact, Bank of Montreal used its 430 devices as the basis to create 'Circuit', attracting Access Magibank, a number of western credit unions and trust companies (such as Royal Trust, National Victoria and Grey Trustco, Guaranty Trust of Canada, Premier Trust, and The Bay/Simpson's) as partners.[61] Interestingly the Montreal allowed customers of other financial institutions whose cards displayed carried a MasterCard logo to use any of its machines.

In 1986, Interact opened up to organizations other than the major banks.[62] In 1994, after some trails, Interact also launched a scheme to allow its members' cardholders to use their plastic cards at point of sale terminals. Interact also extended its franchise by allowing non-bank Independent ATM Deployers or IADs into its switched network in 1996 and at the same time allowed limited surcharging (details of IADs and surcharging are discussed in Chapter 7).

The number of interchange networks remained stable in Canada until the end of the 1990s, when the advent of IADs resulted in a new spurt of growth. In 2000 IADs helped to propel the number of networks to 71. The number of devices also grew, almost doubling from 17,690 in 1995 to 31,922 in 2000.

The total population of Canada was just short of 31 million in the year 2000, while the proportion of the urban population reached 79 per cent of the total (24.5 million inhabitants). In the previous decades, the number of urban inhabitants per ATM dropped from 3,715 in 1987 to 1,289 in 1995 (a 65 per cent reduction). Then, as a result of the entry of IADs to Canada, density again dropped to 766 urban inhabitants per device in the year 2000 (a reduction of 41 per cent from 1995 or an accumulated 80 per cent since 1987). In other words, the density of the ATM network in Canada was comparable with that of other densely ATM-populated countries such as Japan, Spain, and the USA (which had provided 695, 685, and 741 urban inhabitants per ATM respectively in the year 2000), but the number of devices grew so fast between 1987 and 2000 that there were almost four times more ATMs per person in Canada than in these other countries at the turn of the millennium.[63] The role of IADs in this process cannot be underestimated.

5.3.2 *Canada Dry: Growing across the Border*

In tandem with domestic developments, large Canadian banks joined US-based ATM interchange networks, in the process articulating the first cross-border links for US networks. Specifically, the Royal Bank became part of Plus System Inc.[64] Plus was already one of the main players in the USA, with 3,800 shared devices and 1,300 member banks. Cirrus was another large US-based network which entered Canada through the Montreal's Circuit[65] and thereby Cirrus serviced the top eighteen largest Canadian metropolitan areas.[66] The Montreal and the Royal Bank were to act as principal acquirer respectively for Cirrus and Plus while the National Bank of Canada became a member of MasterCard's Master Teller, which gave its customers access to 4,000 devices throughout the USA.

The move by the Montreal and the Royal Bank signified not only a first cross-border service for Cirrus and Plus but the basis for a Canadian national network. This became possible because the Montreal and the Royal Bank were the largest players in the country while the consortia around the other major banks effectively eclipsed previous moves in the direction of a Canada-wide shared ATM network. For instance, in 1986, Interact pooled together nearly 4,000 ATMs belonging to banks and credit unions across Canada while Circuit had approximately 750 devices.[67] There was little doubt in the media that the advent of shared ATM networks increased customers' convenience and the ease of getting cash, because interchange networks let customers using an ATM or a credit card withdraw funds no matter what their bank and as quickly as if it had been their own. Some shared machines provided account balances but none served to make deposits or transfers. Customers, however, had to be wary of fees. For instance, both the Montreal and the Royal Bank charged their clients one Canadian dollar per withdrawal or cash advance (plus a surcharge by the issuing bank for the use of the credit card). The same fee applied to other-bank transactions through Interact and Circuit. The Canadian Imperial Bank of Commerce charged C$ 0.75 per transaction, whereas depository financial institutions with smaller proprietary networks charged no withdrawal fee.[68] Meanwhile, there was an even C$2 fee per cross-border transaction with the USA. Not surprisingly, transaction fees and surcharges incentivized small regional networks to continue—at the end of 1987 there were forty of them—when the number of ATMs was estimated at 5,480 devices.[69] Interact effectively became the Canadian national network, acting as the main switch for smaller interchange networks.

In summary, the shared approach of Canadian financial institutions to cash machines was critical for their operation and for surmounting the challenges of the terrain they faced. The Canadian case is interesting in that many financial institutions were trying to work out at first how to build a national shared ATM network. It built fast around the five major banks, with an uncanny resemblance to the system used to process cheques and clear credit cards. But this did not hamper the emergence and growth of regional players. Meanwhile, excess capacity and a search for economies of scale help to explain the cross-border growth of US switched networks into Canada.

5.4 The Path to a Single ATM Network in the UK

5.4.1 *The Nature of European Consortia*

The approach in Europe to shared ATM networks was somewhat different to that of Canada, Japan, and the USA—where multiple networks coexisted for a long time. In Europe, shared networks were not only much smaller in number than in North America and Japan but they quickly gravitated to a single national network. A case in point is Sweden, where two consortia formed in the early 1970s with the idea of sharing investment and maintenance costs.[70] As mentioned in Chapter 2, one of these consortia was the Automatic Cash Dispenser Centre (Bankomatcentralen), established by the Swedish Bankers Association (Svenska Bankföreningen), the Post Office Bank (Postgirot Bank), and the Federation of Swedish Rural Credit Societies (Sveriges Jordbrukskasse-förbund); this brought down the costs of running, maintaining, and upgrading the devices.

The remainder of this section looks in greater detail at the formation of a single shared network in the UK as an exemplar of countries observing high concentration in ATM ownership. This will help to understand how a global ATM network emerged from developments in Europe rather than in North America or Japan.

5.4.2 *Unstrapping the Unbanked in British Banking Markets*

Since the 1950s, bankers in Europe and North America had been clear that one of the best ways to persuade people to open a bank account was to pay them through the banking system.[71] New customers typically were of working-class origin, people who had perhaps some financial literacy, thanks to their

117

dealings with savings banks, or hire purchase and mortgage specialists but who had not been concerned with (nor of interest to) commercial banks.[72]

Michael McQuade, at the time sub-branch manager for the Leicester Trustee Savings Bank, remembered how sometime in the 1970s wages from workers in a nearby factory began to be paid directly into their savings account passbook.[73] Of their own initiative, McQuade and the branch manager started to migrate these people from passbooks to their own current account. The idea was to tell the customer this would speed up their time at the branch. This move was instrumental to eliminating the queue of customers coming out of the branch on Fridays, and yet they 'had the same number of people coming through the door [while] the other banks were happy living with their queue'. McQuade also mentioned that not long after, they again took the initiative to offer the customers of his branch 'Auto-Teller cards'. At the time, there was no cash machine at his branch but there were a couple of them in branches of the same bank at city centre locations. Slowly but steadily, he recalled, 'people were drawing cash on their [ATM] cards, and it became just a gradual thing and then people started to move into automation'.

McQuade's experience clearly illustrates the processes at branch level for coping with large pools of people brought into the banking system in many developed countries during the late 1970s and early 1980s. This strategy built on the emergence of the service economy and the growth in the size and diversity of business organizations. In turn, these resulted in the cash payment of a weekly wage to manual and agricultural labourers giving way to the stability of the monthly salary paid directly into a current account. As the latter accelerated, retail banks found that the ATM was a device that could help ease congestion at 'bricks and mortar' branches. Individual banks then aimed to develop their own networks of cash machines that they expected to generate sufficient transactions to support the fixed costs of managing a large and often geographically diverse proprietary network. In turn, this would be an advantage over banks with small networks or even no cash machines at all.

By the early 1980s, the strategy of growing by attracting the unbanked had had some positive results in Britain. For instance, the proportion of wages and salaries paid in cash in the UK dropped from 58 per cent in 1976 to 42 per cent in 1981, while direct to account deposits grew from 22 to 33 per cent by giro credit and from 5 to 8 per cent by weekly cheque (with monthly cheques remaining unchanged at 7 per cent).[74] In 1981, 75 per cent of British adults aged 25 to 35 had a current account, whereas the percentage in 1976 was below 55. Moreover, 45 per cent of the over 65s in 1981 had one, compared with less than 30 per cent in 1976. Meanwhile about 6 per cent of all Britons in 1981 had a plastic card (namely a credit card, cheque guarantee card, or ATM access card) but the average Briton made only three payments by credit card per year, as opposed to twenty payments per year in the USA. Almost a third of

British adults with a current account had no plastic card in 1981. Instead they managed using personal cheques at an average rate of 36 cheques per person per annum. This was significantly below the 74 in Canada and 154 in the USA. In 1981, 88 per cent of all payments in the UK above £1 in value were made in cash, compared with 94 per cent of all payments over 50 pence in 1976 (which prices were roughly half the 1981 levels).[75] However, while in the same year all Swedish adults had a bank account of one sort or another, there was a large market potential in the UK, 36 per cent of the British adult population (approximately 6 million people) being 'unbanked'; that is, they had no bank current account, building society, or saving bank account of any kind.[76] Competition to attract new customers then ensued between banks and building societies. To support this move they deployed a number of technologies, including ATMs, home banking, and terminals for the transfer of money at the point of sale (also known as EFTPOS).[77]

5.4.3 Competition from Building Societies

Building societies were deposit accepting mortgage specialists, first established in the late eighteenth century.[78] For most of their history, building societies captured retail deposits in the form of sight accounts and savings accounts, but were excluded from offering current accounts and advances other than mortgages.[79] This changed with the Building Societies Act of 1986, which set them at par with clearing (i.e. commercial) banks.[80] As a result of this regulatory innovation, the adoption of ATMs by building societies was a key factor adding to both the 'bancarisation' of Britons and the growth of the ATM stock in the UK during the 1980s.

Table 5.2 shows the growth of building societies in the provision of out of hours cash distribution. Initially the number of ATMs attached to building societies was modest, given that most societies had a significantly smaller branch network and customer base than banks—making it hard for senior staff to justify investment in ATMs. However, the Halifax, for most of the twentieth century the biggest building society in terms of assets, was the first to deploy six cash machines in 1978 and 1979. These aimed to experiment with the technology while servicing a small group of customers who had access to cheque accounts.[81] The first machine in 1978 was an IBM 3614 at head office and five IBM 3624 were deployed in different retail branches throughout 1979.[82] Alliance & Leicester followed shortly after, also installing IBM machines.[83] The timing of these developments is interesting because they took place before the Building Societies Act of 1986. This meant that societies were limited to accepting deposits and lending only for house purchase; they were unable to offer overdraft facilities. As a result, they had to

Table 5.2. ATM deployment by British banks and building societies, 1975–1990

Year	Banks (a)			Building Societies (b)			Sum	
	ATMs	Annual growth	Per cent of total		Annual growth	Per cent of total	Annual growth	
1975	568		100%				568	
1976	676	19%	100%				676	19%
1977	875	29%	100%				875	29%
1978	1,004	15%	100%	1		0%	1,005	15%
1979	1,178	17%	99%	6	500%	1%	1,184	18%
1980	1,707	44%	100%	n/a			1,707	44%
1981	2,807	65%	100%	n/a			2,807	64%
1982	4,061	45%	100%	n/a			4,061	45%
1983	5,628	39%	98%	112		2%	5,740	41%
1984	6,524	16%	96%	291	160%	4%	6,815	19%
1985	8,193	26%	93%	652	124%	7%	8,845	30%
1986	9,044	10%	88%	1,286	97%	12%	10,330	17%
1987	10,320	14%	83%	2,072	61%	17%	12,392	20%
1988	11,326	10%	81%	2,654	28%	19%	13,980	13%
1989	13,168	16%	84%	2,578	−3%	16%	15,746	13%
1990	14,083	7%	83%	2,921	13%	17%	17,004	8%

Notes:
(a) Excludes first-generation cash dispensers and trustee savings banks.
(b) Abbey National was the first building society to convert to a bank. It was included in the total of banks from 1989 onwards.

Source: Own estimates, based on data from UK Payments (formerly Association for Payment Clearing Services), Building Societies Yearbook (several years) and Barrie (2006).

develop online, real-time capabilities before they could offer automated with-drawals from savings accounts.[84]

Table 5.2 shows how the deployment of ATMs up to 1990 by building societies positioned theirs at 17 per cent of the total number of devices in the UK. For much of this period the smaller societies were keen to share while the Halifax, the largest, wanted to build a proprietary network. As mentioned, the earliest Halifax machines date back to 1978 and 1979. The Halifax's initial encounter was said to have been useful for learning about the 'frailties' of IBM cash machines.[85] Not satisfied with the IBM devices, when the time came to install a large ATM fleet in 1983, this society deployed 100 Phillips devices; that is, Diebold cash machines manufactured in the USA but distributed under licence while incorporating De La Rue banknote dispensing capabilities.

The decision against IBM equipment was said to have been made largely on technical grounds and was long in the making.[86] Evidence of this showed that the Halifax had installed an IBM 3980 Bank Teleprocessing System through-out its branches in 1971, but by the late 1970s this society was buying 'from other suppliers such as Amdahl, Memorex and Phillips because of significant cost savings coupled with better performance and reliability'.[87] The decision not to deploy IBM ATMs, however, reflected a deepening disagreement between the Halifax's IT management and IBM about ways of supplying society's needs with regard to ATMs and other matters.[88] In fact the decision not to deploy IBM ATMs led Edwin Nixon (1925–2008), chairman of IBM UK (1979–90), to visit Raymond Potter (1916–93), chairman of the Halifax (1974–83), at the society's London flat with the intention of regaining the society's custom.[89] During this meeting 'Potter politely listened to Nixon... [and then told him] that the Society's [sic] board were quite happy to let technical decisions be made by the organization's technical staff'.[90]

This episode at the Halifax is somewhat typical in showing how middle managers often play a key role in the adoption of new technology for organizations. The encounter further suggested that there was room to suspect that political rather than purely technical elements had informed the Halifax's decision not to deploy IBM ATMs (see also Chapter 6).

Meanwhile, cash machines at building societies grew to 112 in 1983 and 291 in 1984.[91] The trend intensified with the passing of the Building Societies Act in July 1986, which allowed the societies to diversify their business portfolio, while aiming to put them on the same footing as the clearing banks. As shown in Table 5.2, the number of devices at building societies grew from 652 or 7 per cent of the total in the UK in 1985, to 1,286 in 1986 (12 per cent of the total) and to 2,072 in 1987 (17 per cent of the total). By 1988, before the first large building society demutualized, the societies were managing almost one in four of the total number of active devices in the UK. Interestingly, in the course of this process the societies, most of which had started their computerization on the back of IBM systems, were no longer loyal to 'Big Blue' and purchased the more cost-effective NCR cash machines—which emulated the IBM ATM operation, IBM's security and encryption key management and systems by Siemens and Burroughs.[92]

At the time, membership of Visa required that any device should accept a Visa card, but the large banks were 'not playing by the rules'.[93] As a result, some societies and other non-bank participants in retail financial markets had to consider whether there was more to be gained by creating their own shared network than by developing a fleet of ATMs organically. The dilemma faced by John Hardy, head of strategic planning at National Girobank, in 1982 is typical in this regard. Indeed, many medium and small depository institutions were challenged to offer an increasingly popular technology while lacking the funds, volume, and a big enough 'bricks and mortar' branch network to support it.[94] Hardy estimated that to remain competitive while servicing some 1.3 million customers evenly distributed through the UK, his bank had to invest in approximately 1,000 ATMs. But the size of this expenditure was out of the question. Management was willing to purchase only a couple of hundred machines while Hardy estimated that transaction volume would be low and would not justify a four-digit ATM fleet.

Partly out of necessity and partly influenced by developments in the USA (specifically the actions of Western Trust and Savings, Chicago, IL), Hardy continued to call the large banks to ascertain their views on sharing their ATMs, but found that they were not interested. Instead a small group of like-minded executives from other small and medium-sized financial providers stepped in. As a result, in February 1985, Abbey National (the second biggest society in terms of assets and the first to demutualize in 1989), Nationwide Building Society (the third largest in terms in assets), National Girobank, the Co-operative Bank, American Express, and some smaller societies created an inter-bank switch network called LINK.[95]

LINK was established as a joined owned company that invested in computer technology to articulate a central platform for an ATM network. The company was chaired by John Hardy from its inception until he retired in 2005. The leverage gained through a shared network was self-evident for some members which, like the National Girobank, were making their first machine operational.[96] Others such as Abbey National, the single biggest contributor, installed 200 machines between February and May 1985 in its retail branches, as well as some retail stores, such as House of Fraser and 7-Eleven stores.[97] But thanks to the LINK network, Abbey's six million depositors had access to five times more (1,000 machines) by the end of 1986.

A second ATM network called 'Sharing Group' was built by bringing together a small group of building societies but it was short-lived and amalgamated with LINK within two years.[98]

5.4.4 *MATRIX: A Network Reloaded*

A third network was launched in March 1986 when building societies were starting to implement their own ATM networks and needed to compete with the banks. This initiative was led by Leeds Permanent, traditionally the fourth or fifth largest in terms of assets (which merged with the Halifax in 1995).[99] The Leeds attracted others from the ten largest building societies in terms of assets to the MATRIX consortium. These included Anglia (merged with Nationwide in 1987) and Bradford and Bingley (demutualized in 2000 and acquired by Santander UK in 2010). Later other large building societies became members, including Alliance & Leicester (formed by the merger of the Alliance and the Leicester in 1985, demutualized in 2000 and acquired by Santander UK in 2008), National Provincial (formed by the merger of the Provincial and the Burnley in 1982, merged with Abbey National in 1996), and the Co-operative Bank.

MATRIX's biggest contributor was the Woolwich Equitable Building Society (today part of Barclays), traditionally the fourth or fifth largest in terms of assets, demutualized in 1997 and acquired by Barclays in 2000. The Woolwich had launched its 'Cashbase' dispenser in August 1985. This was for the exclusive use of the 150 staff at head office who had opened a 'Cashbase' (i.e. current) account. A couple of months later, in October 1985, the project was extended to the general public in greater London and the south-east of England (i.e. the Woolwich's longest trading areas).[100] The name 'Cashbase' was chosen 'after market research among target customers' and was supposed to be 'simple, memorable and...would not date'.[101] 'Cashbase' machines offered a range of services, namely, up to £250-per-day cash withdrawals and deposit and balance enquiries.[102] When the Woolwich joined MATRIX, at the end of 1986, it gave 8.1 million individual customers access to a network of 346 machines.[103] Robert Rosenthal, an IBM engineer who had helped create MATRIX, recalled:

> This network was designed, implemented and hosted by IBM and designed in conjunction with its users. A switch in the centre of the network provided individual links to each society's central systems for them to not only accept transactions from their own ATMs but from those of others. Transactions accepted from cardholders of other societies were routed across the MATRIX network to the cardholder's society for authorisation. Likewise, transactions from other ATMs for a society would be routed across to them for authorisation. Full security of transactions and customer's PIN were maintained, together with strict rules on processing, message formats and security across the network. 'End-of-Day' settlement reports were also produced and made available online by MATRIX together with others detailing availability and performance statistics.[104]

Despite the apparent disadvantage of a smaller network for the Woolwich, the rolling out of MATRIX and the 'Cashbase' account were key to converting customers from holders of passbook-operated deposit accounts to current accounts. Growth for MATRIX, however, was relatively slow because, for one thing, the Woolwich did not reach the 100 devices mark until October 1987, and installed its and MATRIX's first non-branch ATM at a Sainsbury's retail store in September 1988. At the same time, LINK had grown in size and credibility. Table 5.3 shows how on the back of MATRIX and LINK the value of ATM withdrawals at building societies by the end of the 1980s had grown to 10 per cent of the total.

Two critical events took place in 1989 as building societies were increasing their share of the retail deposit market. First, LINK absorbed MATRIX. Second, the Halifax joined LINK and made its 1,200 ATMs available to all customers of banks that were members of LINK. However, the Halifax introduced a 50 pence 'disloyalty charge' (paid when using a non-Halifax ATM) in order to encourage its customers to use the society's ATMs whenever possible. As we will see, surcharging was to become a point of contention in the UK (see Chapters 7 and 8).[105]

Table 5.3. Volume and value of cash withdrawals at British banks and building societies, 1975–1990

Year	Number of withdrawals			Value of withdrawals	Number of ATM cards issued
	Banks (millions)	Building societies (millions)	Sum (millions)	(£millions) (a)	(000's) (a,b)
1975	8		8	111	583
1976	12		12	177	895
1977	17		17	281	1,515
1978	25		25	460	2,325
1979	36		36	733	3,094
1980	55		55	1,316	4,732
1981	96		96	2,540	7,131
1982	157		157	4,290	9,424
1983	228	1	229	6,597	12,254
1984	325	3	328	9,751	16,023
1985	396	8	404	12,401	19,801
1986	480	16	496	15,590	22,517
1987	566	61	627	18,848	24,731
1988	666	88	754	24,320	27,443
1989	796	87	883	31,948	36,833
1990	900	92	992	38,474	37,067

Notes:
(a) Data for building societies were unavailable.
(b) The number of issued ATM cards considered both single function withdrawal cards and multi-function debit cards with a PIN. Estimates excluded credit cards.

Source: Own estimates, based on data from UK Payments (formerly Association for Payment Clearing Services), Building Societies Yearbook (several years) and Barrie (2006).

5.4.5 Banks Become More Confident of Sharing their ATMs with Other Banks

Before the creation of LINK and MATRIX, large banks signed reciprocal sharing agreements with one another. Some of these agreements presupposed conjunction with IBM expertise, for the engineers at 'Big Blue' had continued to develop inter-bank payment systems. These systems helped banks feel more confident about sharing their ATMs with other banks, since they provided, among other things, secure transaction authorization against central account databases.[106] The first of these bank sharing ATM networks in the UK comprised four clearing banks, namely Lloyds, Barclays, Royal Bank of Scotland, and the Bank of Scotland.[107] This network was informally known as the 'four bank reciprocity' network; it consisted of multiple individual links between the banks and was designed collectively by the four banks with support from IBM. The design included specifying message standards and security within the network.[108] Another reciprocity agreement to share ATMs amongst banks was built around Midland (today HSBC), NatWest, and the TSB Group. Initially NatWest and Midland signed a sharing agreement through which customers could insert their cards in either bank's machines to withdraw cash as long ago as 1983.[109] The TSB joined them shortly afterwards.

The main difference between banks' sharing agreements and building societies was that the banks had wired their mainframes directly rather than to a central computer acting as network switch. In contrast, and in the same way as MATRIX, LINK's central computer would act as a clearing house by receiving and transmitting transactions between the member that ran the ATM and the member hosting the customer's account. However, in the early 1990s early adopters of ATM technology such as Midland Bank with a 2,000-strong network of machines in operation, abandoned sharing agreements that involved wiring mainframes directly to each other because these had proved cumbersome to manage and were found to have limited capacity to increase their scale. As direct wiring networks ceased, these banks joined LINK to extend the shared use of ATMs by their customers.

5.4.6 Colonizing Non-Branch Locations

The possibility arose to make it attractive to share facilities at locations away from the retail bank branch where space was sometimes at a premium. A move in this direction was made by NatWest when it fitted an ATM in the courtyard of J. Sainsbury's Crystal Palace retail store in 1983.[110] At the time this was heralded as the first off-branch location of any British bank. However, one of Lloyds Bank's 'Cashpoints' was operational at the retail branch of Lewis's store in Birmingham in December 1974 (see Chapters 4 and 7).[111] This gave Lloyds the prestige of having operated the first cash machine in a non-banking site, almost ten years before others.[112]

The move to non-banking sites, however, was not immediate or swift. This was because as late as 1986 there was room to improve the provision in retail branches of banks by installing second and third machines in high-usage sites, as Citibank had done in New York City since the late 1970s, as well as enhancing the reliability and convenience of installed machines (e.g. by extending online services from all devices to 24 hours a day).[113] In fact, it was not until 1994 that NatWest embarked on an active programme to operate cash machines in non-branch locations. These included high-traffic sites at Boots the Chemist, J. Sainsbury's supermarkets, and railway stations.[114] Other attractive sites included hospitals, airports, petrol stations, and motoring services. Barclays went even further and installed cash dispensing machines in the House of Commons (1990), the House of Lords (1996), and even a 'drive in' at Hatton Cross near Heathrow airport (1998).[115]

In the process of optimizing locations at retail branches, some banks also reintroduced Saturday opening. Barclays was the first in August 1982 and

NatWest followed in April 1983.[116] This while banks continued to make more of automation and move away from routine paper processing.

Although slowly, the move of greater connectivity continued as cost containment gave way to fee income generation through interchange fees. The interchange fee (also known as terminal income), is the amount paid to the owner of an ATM by the network member bank whenever that member's cardholder uses the owner's ATM (see Chapters 4 and 7).[117] Although exact figures were unavailable, between 1980 and 2000 these fees seem to have oscillated in the UK between 25 and 45 pence.[118] Anecdotal evidence suggests that these may have been two or three times higher for transactions involving international network switches such as Visa and MasterCard.

During this period, moreover, the average withdrawal almost doubled in nominal value. For NatWest the average withdrawal (in nominal value) grew from £28.64 in 1986 to £47.00 in 1997.[119] It is likely this was not unique to NatWest, but part of a trend where retail banking customers responded to a greater number of available machines and locations (the discussion returns to this issue in greater depth in Chapters 7 and 8). For the likes of Midland, NatWest, Halifax, the TSB, and Barclays, which had the largest proprietary networks and managed the most attractive off-branch sites (such as the busiest railway stations and forecourts of the largest supermarkets), reciprocity agreements were a way to generate fee income.

Generating fee income offered the possibility of reducing the high sunk (i.e. irrecoverable) costs of setting up proprietary networks by achieving economies of scale in their running costs. The increase in the number of withdrawals provided incentives for those with larger networks to increase the number of reciprocity agreements that would make their fleet available to others. Finally, when in 1998 Barclays joined LINK, there was only a single ATM switch network in the UK; the participants in British retail finance had by then developed full interoperability for cash withdrawals around a single common platform.

5.5 I Will Share Your ATM, but the Hard Part is Sharing Mine with You

During the 1980s many banks had the determination to become so-called global, universal financial supermarkets.[120] But this ambition proved fruitless and by the end of the twentieth century only a handful of global players had emerged. Most of the others had changed focus and wanted now to provide a diversified offering within their domestic markets.[121] A key element of these processes was office mechanization and the automation of service provision on the back of computer technology.[122] In this context, the growth of the

ATM in the 1980s responded to two mutually excluding competitive strategies: shared networks and a proprietary fleet.

This chapter discussed the competitive effects around the perception of proprietary ATM networks as a source of competitive advantage for financial institutions. The persistence of proprietary networks explains why interconnectivity was slower to develop in Europe than in North America. Sharing ATM networks made sense for smaller banks (in terms of assets) to resolve apparent scale disadvantages. At the same time, economies of scale and the potential for the machines with greater traffic to make net fee income contributions, seem to have been key reasons for those with larger proprietary networks to support the emergence of domestic interconnectivity. When interchange networks replaced proprietary networks the ATM became a 'threshold competency' in retail finance; that is, automated cash dispensing services became not so much a source of competitive advantage as an element in being a credible competitor. The replacement also indicates the emergence of standardized, high volume, low margin retail financial services, such as the commoditized services of cash withdrawal and balance enquiries.

The strategic shift from proprietary to shared networks was reinforced by the presence of network externalities. These occur when the value of the network increases as new users join it. As more members join, the network becomes more valuable to each individual user. Network externalities result in 'increasing returns', that is, as the network continues to grow, it becomes easier to attract additional users. A larger number of users in the expanded network makes the deployment of an ATM more profitable, which further enhances its accessibility to existing members. But as the case of the ATM suggests, it is hard to reach the point where network externalities kick in. Reaching this point takes time, investment, and, as is evident in Chapter 8, effort to persuade users to adopt the innovation. On the flip side, when the externalities kick in, it is hard to adopt new technologies even if these are more effective and efficient than the established solution.[123] Participants are also said to find barriers to innovation because of the strong incentives to protect the status quo.[124]

Mandatory sharing laws in the USA were another important incentive for the development of switch (i.e. shared) network transactions, a technological and organizational model that was replicated elsewhere, as the shared networks in Canada and the UK show. But competitive dynamics also influenced the formation and shape of interchange networks. In the USA, for instance, building a joint venture came naturally to states which had sharing laws (e.g. Iowa) but at the same time, in other states where there was fierce local competition (e.g. California and New York), sharing with locals was anathema to the strategic objective of deploying greater numbers of ATMs through proprietary networks (while aiming to outperform other local competitors).

Although slowly, the creation of greater connectivity continued as cost containment gave way to fee income generation through interchange fees. This again changed the nature of competition as the number of ATM networks in the USA reached a 'saturation' point around the mid-1980s, after which they declined. By the early 2000s, a handful of shared networks controlled almost all the traffic in North America.

As Chapter 6 details, Visa and MasterCard eventually became the backbone of transaction authorization around the world. Once the PIN management system was in place, creating a global switched network while making regional and national interchange networks technologically redundant was straightforward, but it was important first to create standards for the global interoperability of ATMs. This was impossible until the internal politics within and between banks had been sorted out.

Notes

1. On the formation of the Money Access Centre (MAC) network see Clemons (1990).
2. Personal communication (email), from Dale Dooley, former President and CEO Shazam/ITS, with B. Bátiz-Lazo, 18 February 2017.
3. Personal communication (email), from Christopher D. Klein, Sr., former NCR engineer and Atlantic Bank director, with M. Lee, 31 January 2017.
4. 'Customer Information Control System (CICS)', *Wikipedia*, accessed 15 June 2016, <https://en.wikipedia.org/wiki/CICS>.
5. Personal communication (email), from Jonathan Rosenne, former engineer IBM Israel, with B. Bátiz-Lazo, 16 April 2016.
6. Member banks were Bank of New York, Barclays Bank of New York, Manufacturers Hanover Trust, National Westminster Bank USA, Goldome Bank, Union Trust Co., and Marine Midland Bank. Interestingly the switch was not operated by the consortia but by a specialist company called A. O. Smith Data Systems. Source: James Connolly, 'N.Y.-Area Banks to Tie ATMs into a Single Net', *Computerworld*, 26 November 1984: 30.
7. 'Automated Banking: European Battler', *The Economist*, 13 December 1980: 66. A Nilson Report quoted in this article estimated the following worldwide sales as of November 1980: Omron 6,250 (worldwide market share 15.6 per cent, US sales as a percentage of total 0 per cent), NCR 6,140 (15.3 per cent, 33.4 per cent), Diebold 5,800 (14.4 per cent, 99.1 per cent), Docutel-Olivetti 5,320 (13.3 per cent, 92.5 per cent), IBM 5,100 (12.7 per cent, 75.5 per cent), TRW-Fujitsu 4,300 (10.7 per cent, 34.4 per cent), Other 7,230 (18.0 per cent, n.a.), Total 40,140 (100 per cent, 47.5 per cent). In its first study, RBR London included 13 countries in Western Europe, covering 11,844 of the 12,500 ATMs in the region in 1982. The five largest ATM manufacturers that year were IBM, NCR, Transac, Dassault, and Docutel. Source: 'RBR's ATM Research Follows the Market to Asia', *Linkedin*, 4 August 2016, accessed 4

August 2016, <https://www.linkedin.com/pulse/rbrs-atm-research-follows-market-asia-dominic-hirsch?trk=hb_ntf_MEGAPHONE_ARTICLE_POST>.

8. For a thorough and detailed review of shared networks in the USA see Hayashi et al. (2006) and McAndrews (2003).

9. 'Independent Bankers Association of New York State Inc.', *Justia US Law*, accessed 18 February 2017, <http://law.justia.com/cases/federal/appellate-courts/F2/757/453/425988/>. Unconfirmed reports point to the Bank of New York deploying ATMs in Connecticut as the first bank to test the limits of Depression-era restrictions on inter-state growth using technology.

10. Hannan and McDowell (1987); Peffers (1991).

11. According to Peffers (1991, 68–9), in 1979 there were 12 states that combined limited bank branching or unit branching laws and mandatory ATM sharing laws, namely, Colorado, Illinois, Iowa, Kansas, Michigan, Minnesota, Montana, Nebraska, New Hampshire, North Dakota, Oklahoma, and Wisconsin. According to the same source, there were eight states that allowed state-wide branching and imposed mandatory ATM sharing laws, namely, Delaware, Hawaii, Idaho, Maine, Oregon, South Dakota, Utah, and Washington.

12. 'Three Ohio Banks Arrange Automated Cash-advance Interchange', *Autotransactions Industry Report*, March 1975: 12–13.

13. Dale Dooley, former President and CEO Shazam/ITS, ATM Industry Association, Orlando, 15 February 2017.

14. 'What's the Real Significance of National ATM Networks?', *ABA Banking Journal*, September 1982: 40.

15. Personal communication (email) from Robert Rosenthal, former IBM engineer, with B. Bátiz-Lazo, 3 August 2016.

16. Personal communication (email) from John Chamberlin, founder of Arkansas Systems (ArkaSys), with B. Bátiz-Lazo, 12 July 2016.

17. Laderman (1990b, 2).

18. I appreciate the comments made to clarify the working of network switches from John Chamberlin. Source: Personal communication (email) from John Chamberlin, founder of Arkansas Systems (ArkaSys), with B. Bátiz-Lazo, 12 July 2016.

19. To over-simplify, the ASCII world was asynchronous—characters in a signal were defined by the mark and space technology that came from telegraph technology via the teletype terminals. IBM felt they could get faster and more accurate transmissions by including a clock and synchronizing the signals. They called this 'bisynchronous communications' because the two devices were synchronized. IBM had a remote terminal that supported a card reader/punch and a printer called a 3780. The bisync variant that connected this machine to IBM mainframes was also known as 3780. Again I appreciate the comments to clarify the working of network switches from John Chamberlin. Source: Personal communication (email) from John Chamberlin, founder of Arkansas Systems (ArkaSys), with B. Bátiz-Lazo, 12 July 2016.

20. 'ISO 8583:1987', International Organization for Standardization, accessed 3 August 2016, <http://www.iso.org/iso/home/store/catalogue_ics/catalogue_detail_ics.htm?csnumber=15870>.

21. Personal communication (email) from Robert Rosenthal, former IBM engineer, with B. Bátiz-Lazo, 3 August 2016.

22. Unless otherwise stated, the reminder of this paragraph draws from Paul F. P. Coenen, 'Banks Put TYME on their Hand', *ABA Banking Journal*, May 1979: 40–2. See also the formation of the MAC network in Pennsylvania documented in Clemons (1990).

23. 'Latest Figures for ATMs and Other Retail Services', *ABA Banking Journal*, March 1982: 111.

24. Paul F. P. Coenen, 'Banks Put TYME on their Hand', *ABA Banking Journal*, May 1979: 40–2.

25. 'Latest Figures for ATMs and Other Retail Services', *ABA Banking Journal*, March 1982: 112.

26. Bill Streeter, 'Will Bank Card Networks be the National Switch?', *ABA Banking Journal*, September 1981: 165. Italics in the quotation and the article's title are in the original.

27. 'Latest Figures for ATMs and Other Retail Services', *ABA Banking Journal*, March 1982: 110.

28. Bátiz-Lazo and Del Angel (2016); Stearns (2011).

29. Interview (telephone) with Irwin Derman, former Visa executive, by B. Bátiz-Lazo, 6 July 2016.

30. Bill Streeter, 'Visa and MasterCard: Self-evaluations', *ABA Banking Journal*, September 1982: 48–60.

31. American Express' Express Cash programme was launched as a pilot in late 1979. It was exclusively available to Gold Card customers through devices in individual banks and major ATM networks (while American Express' own ATMs only issued travellers' cheques).

32. 'The Premier ATM Network: 1982–1992', *ABA Banking Journal*, January 1992: n.p.

33. 'The Premier ATM Network: 1982–1992', *ABA Banking Journal*, January 1992: n.p.

34. 'What's the Real Significance of National ATM Networks?', *ABA Banking Journal*, September 1982: 38–47.

35. Jeffrey Kutler, 'Head of Cirrus Resigns, Gives MasterCard Time to Tighten Grip', *American Banker* June 1988: 114.

36. Unless otherwise stated, this paragraph draws from Susan Weeks, 'Citibank goes Global', *ABA Banking Journal*, May 1991: 78.

37. See Glaser (1988).

38. Interview (telephone) with Irwin Derman, former Visa executive, by B. Bátiz-Lazo, 6 July 2016.

39. MasterCard and Visa were floated as independent companies in 2006 and 2008 respectively. See: Robin Sidel, 'MasterCard Stages Solid IPO', *The Wall Street Journal*, 26 May 2006, accessed 29 July 2016, <https://www.wsj.com/articles/SB114857228165563097> and Ben Steverman, 'Visa's IPO Victory', *Bloomberg*, 20 March 2008, accessed 29 July 2016, <http://www.bloomberg.com/news/articles/2008-03-20/visas-ipo-victorybusinessweek-business-news-stock-market-and-financial-advice>.

40. Unless otherwise stated, the remainder of this section borrows freely from the interview (telephone), with Irwin Derman, former Visa executive, by B. Bátiz-Lazo, 6 July 2016. See also Stearns (2011, 171–2).

41. Interview (telephone) with Irwin Derman, former Visa executive, by B. Bátiz-Lazo, 6 July 2016.

42. Interview (telephone) with David Cavell, former director Co-op Bank and management consultant, by B. Bátiz-Lazo, 14 July 2016.

43. Unless otherwise stated, the paragraph sources are in LMA CLC B 002: 01 07 035 'Chubb-Mosler and Taylor', Letter from R. S. Euston (Chubb-Mosler and Taylor) to L. W. Dunham (Chubb & Son), dated 28 August 1969.

44. Chubb & Son started a Canadian sales office in Toronto in 1954. At the same time, the Cincinnati, OH-based Mosler merged its Canadian operations with those of J & J Taylor. Soon after, they entered into talks and Chubb took a 51 per cent ownership of the combined Chubb-Mosler & Taylor while developing local manufacturing capabilities (source: LMA CLC B 002: 01 07 035 'Chubb in Canada', signed LWD/JG, dated 6 August 1974). Meanwhile Mosler (USA) designed and marketed its own cash machines in the US market. In 1978, TRW purchased the rights to manufacture and sell the 6000 and 8000 series of ATMs from Mosler (USA) and moved the manufacturing to Orlando, FL. Source: Harper and Bátiz-Lazo (2013, 106).

45. Banking data were sourced from Bank for International Settlements (1985) *Payment Systems in Eleven Developed Countries* (Red Book), Basle: 29–32. This is the earliest cross-country systematic study of the retail payment system, with data for 1978 and 1983.

46. Population data were sourced from the World Bank's *World Development Indicators*, 1960–2014.

47. The 'Red Book' of 1985 estimated Canada's total population as 23.6 million in 1978 and 25.0 million in 1983. As a result it estimated 1,779 inhabitants per office in 1978 and 1,934 in 1983. Using World Bank's population estimates, its total inhabitants per office were 1,828 in 1978 and 1,968 in 1983 (an 8 per cent increase). Likewise the 'Red Book' estimated the number of inhabitants per machine to be 94,580 in 1978 and 12,755 in 1983. My estimates were 96,144 and 12,988 respectively.

48. The number of devices per 100,000 urban inhabitants increased from 1.38 in 1978 to 10.13 in 1983.

49. Enchin Harvey, 'Cost Slows Move to ATM Network', *The Globe and Mail*, 16 March 1984: B1.

50. Enchin Harvey, 'Cost Slows Move to ATM Network', *The Globe and Mail*, 16 March 1984: B1.

51. 'Rural and Urban Population Changes Since 1851', *Statistics Canada*, accessed 2 February 2018, <http://www12.statcan.gc.ca/census-recensement/2011/as-sa/98-310-x/98-310-x2011003_2-eng.cfm>.

52. According to the Canadian Bankers Association: 'Canada's banks are federally incorporated. Unlike banks, trust companies can be incorporated and regulated at either the federal or the provincial level. By law, only trust companies are allowed

to provide trustee functions. Banks can do this only through a separately created trust subsidiary. The other difference is that a bank has full commercial lending powers, whereas trust companies must have more than $25 million of regulatory capital to receive full lending powers with the approval of the Office of the Superintendent of Financial Institutions (OSFI).' Source: 'What is the Difference Between a Bank, a Trust Company and a Credit Union', Canadian Bankers Association, accessed 22 July 2016, originally at <http://www.cba.ca/en?view=article& catid=72%3Ageneral&id=170%3Awhat-is-the-difference-between-a-bank-a-trust-company-and-a-credit-union&Itemid=0>. See also 'Rob Special Report: Trust Firms Face Major Shift in Lending', *The Globe and Mail*, 12 November 1982: B1; Settlement, 'What Kinds of Financial Institutions are There?', 2 February 2018, <https://settlement.org/ontario/daily-life/personal-finance/banks/what-kinds-of-financial-institutions-are-there/>.

53. According to the Canadian Bankers Association: 'Credit unions are different from banks and trust companies in that they are fully provincially regulated . . . Credit unions are owned by their members and are typically established to serve a particular group of people based on geographic area, ethnic background or employer.' Source: 'What is the difference between a bank, a trust company and a credit union', Canadian Bankers Association, accessed 22 July 2016, <http://www.cba.ca/en? view=article&catid=72%3Ageneral&id=170%3Awhat-is-the-difference-between-a-bank-a-trust-company-and-a-credit-union&Itemid=0>.

54. Unless otherwise stated, this paragraph borrows freely from Martin Mittelstaedt, 'B of M Plan to Join U.S. ATM Network Complicates Picture', *The Globe and Mail*, 12 September 1984: n.p.; and Martin Mittelstaedt, 'Financial Firms Discuss Shared Automation', *The Globe and Mail*, 13 August 1983: B1.

55. By 1987, The Exchange network 'had 4,500 active ATMs in 36 states and Canada. The network was run from Clifton, NJ, over lines with speeds of between 9.6 kbit/s and 19.2 kbit/s. They were multiplexed at 35 sites using a Racal-Milgo Omnimux. There were 47 Tandem NonStop II computers at Clifton powering the network in addition to doing other tasks.' Source: John T. Mulqueen, 'Industry Watch Consolidation Could Boost Traffic, Lower Per-transaction', *Data Communications*, 16 (11), 1 October 1987: 85.

56. The 'Red Book' of 1985, p. 33.

57. Harvey Enchin, 'Cost Slows Move to ATM Network', *The Globe and Mail*, 16 March 1984: B1.

58. Martin Mittelstaedt, 'Financial Firms Discuss Shared Automation', *The Globe and Mail*, 13 August 1983: B1.

59. Martin Mittelstaedt, 'Banks Agree to Share Automated Tellers', *The Globe and Mail*, 22 November 1984: P1.

60. Martin Mittelstaedt, 'Banks Agree to Share Automated Tellers', *The Globe and Mail*, 22 November 1984: P1.

61. 'Shared Bank-machine Systems Convenient but Watch for Extra Fees', *The Montreal Gazette*, 10 November 1986: B6.

62. Data in this paragraph draw on Cavell (2003, 18).

63. The number of devices per 100,000 urban inhabitants in 1987 was 26.91, 77.59 in 1995, and 130.53 in 2000. This represented a 188 per cent increase between 1987 and 1995, a 68 per cent increase between 1995 and 2000, and a 385 per cent increase between 1987 and 2000. In the year 2000, Japan, Spain, and the USA had 143.98, 145.97, and 134.96 ATMs per 100,000 urban inhabitants.

64. Martin, Mittelstaedt, 'Royal Bank Joins ATM Network,, *The Globe and Mail*, 25 October 1984: B3.

65. The deal meant that customers visiting one country would receive its currency but the account would be debited in the customer's domestic currency.

66. Richard Ringer, 'Cirrus Adds 8 New Members, 2,900 ATMs', *American Banker*, 19 June 1986.

67. Unless otherwise stated, the remainder of this paragraph borrows freely from 'Shared Bank-machine Systems Convenient but Watch for Extra Fees', *The Montreal Gazette*, 10 November 1986: B6.

68. Smaller networks included those of Toronto Dominion Bank, Bank of Nova Scotia, National Bank of Canada, Montreal City & District Savings Bank, and Caisses populaires Desjardins as well as the Idéal reciprocal system.

69. Bank for International Settlements (1988) *Payment Systems in Eleven Developed Countries* (Red Book), Basle, p. 298.

70. Bátiz-Lazo et al. (2014b); Bátiz-Lazo and Maixé-Altés (2011b); Ekebrink (1974); Maixé-Altés (2015).

71. Bátiz-Lazo et al. (2014b).

72. Bátiz-Lazo et al. (2014b); Booth (2007).

73. The rest of this paragraph draws on the interview with Michael D. McQuade, branch manager and group director TSB, by B. Bátiz-Lazo, Leicester, 6 March 2008.

74. Unless otherwise stated, the reminder of this paragraph is sourced from 'The Revolution in Retail Banking', *The Economist*, 4 December 1982: 90–1.

75. It was not until the end of 2014 that cashless payments overtook the use of notes and coins in the UK for the first time. Source: Kevin Peachey, 'Cashless Payments Overtake the Use of Notes and Coins', *BBC News*, 21 May 2015, accessed 14 February 2017, <www.bbc.com/news/business-32778196>.

76. 'The Revolution in Retail Banking', *The Economist*, 4 December 1982: 9. This number may have overestimated the size of the British population without access to a bank account, in view of the popularity and use of other depository financial institutions such as the Post Office Bank, trustee savings banks, and building societies. Given these and the collapse of the hire purchase banks in the 1970s one may safely assume that the banking culture in the UK was much bigger than this estimate suggests.

77. Chemical Bank (New York, NY) launched a service called 'Pronto' in 1981. It allowed customers to use home computers to check their balances and make payments. This is the first recorded home banking service. Within a year similar experiments were on the way in California, Texas, and Florida. A similar but earlier service was launched in (West) Germany using videotext. Source: 'Banking on the Inhuman Factor', *The Economist*, 27 March 1982: 85; and 'Cash from the Other

Fellow's Tap', *The Economist*, 18 September 1982: 94. See further Bátiz-Lazo and Woldensenbet (2006); Pennings and Harianto (1992).

78. Price (1959).

79. Davies (1981).

80. Boléat (1986).

81. The amalgamation of the Halifax Equitable and Halifax Permanent in 1928 resulted in a legacy of 11,000 deposit cheque accounts serviced through four branches (Halifax, Huddersfield, Bradford, and Sheffield). These accounts were the target for the deployment of a small number of IBM 3624 cash machines in 1978. Source: Interview, with Richard Barrow, Halifax by B. Bátiz-Lazo and C. Reese, 19 May 2008 and Barrow (2006, 82).

82. Barrow (2006, 72 and 82).

83. Disregarding the small experiment by the Halifax, Alliance & Leicester (later part of Santander UK) made claim to be the first in the field. It is not clear whether its machines were IBM 3614 or IBM 3624. Source: Personal communication (email) from Nigel Hardman, Group Archives, Alliance & Leicester, with B. Bátiz-Lazo, 3 May 2007.

84. The other large competitor for retail deposits in the UK, the trustee savings banks (TSB), took a slightly different path in the adoption of ATMs. On the automation of the TSB, see Bátiz-Lazo et al. (2014b); Moss and Russell (1994); Moss and Slaven (1992).

85. Barrow (2006, 72 and 82).

86. Barrow (2006, 73–4).

87. Barrow (2006, 73).

88. Personal communication (email) from Robert Rosenthal, former IBM engineer, with B. Bátiz-Lazo, 24 October 2016.

89. Bernardo Bátiz-Lazo, 'Nixon, Sir Edwin Ronald (1925–2008)', *Oxford Dictionary of National Biography*, Oxford University Press, Jan. 2012; online edn., Sept. 2012, accessed 31 October 2016, <http://www.oxforddnb.com.ezproxy.bangor.ac.uk/view/article/99499>, doi:10.1093/ref:odnb/99499); and Stephen Cockroft, 'Obituary: Sir Raymond Potter', *Independent*, 24 November 1993, accessed 31 October 2016, <http://www.independent.co.uk/news/people/obituary-sir-raymond-potter-1506370.html>.

90. Barrow (2006, 74).

91. A survey by Gourley (1999, 4.46) attributes the first ATM in a building society to the Halifax in 1983 and claims the Alliance & Leicester had 16 in operation in 1983 (making a total of 17 for all building societies).

92. Personal communication (email) from Robert Rosenthal, former IBM engineer, with B. Bátiz-Lazo, 24 October 2016; and interview with James Adamson, former CEO of NCR Dundee, by B. Bátiz-Lazo and R. J. Reid, Edinburgh, 18 June 2008.

93. Personal communication (email) from David Cavell, former director Co-operative Bank, with B. Bátiz-Lazo, 24 January 2017.

94. Unless otherwise stated, the remainder of this paragraph borrows freely from an interview with John Hardy, founder and former CEO of LINK, London by B. Bátiz-Lazo and C. Reese, 21 November 2007.

95. 'Building Society in Cash Link', *The Times*, 16 February 1985: 3, Issue 62064, col. A. On the computerization of the National Giro see Billings and Booth (2011).

96. Personal communication (email) from Nigel Hardman, Group Archives, Alliance & Leicester, with B. Bátiz-Lazo, 3 May 2007.

97. The first machine installed in a British rail station took place in 1970, when a cash machine of the National Provincial Bank became operational in London's Victoria Station (shortly before the bank's brand name changed to National Westminster Bank or NatWest). This was, however, within the premises of the bank's Victoria branch. Source: RBSGA—NW/B1239, National Westminster Bank, photograph of a member of staff using the cash machine at Victoria Station Branch of National Westminster Bank. During the 1980s, small 7-Eleven convenience stores were common in the larger towns and cities of the south-eastern UK. The first shop opened in London, in Sydenham, south-east London in 1985. The company ceased trading operations in 1997, but resumed trading in the UK in 2014. Source: '7-Eleven', *Wikipedia*, accessed 31 October 2016, <https://en.wikipedia.org/wiki/7-Eleven#British_Isles>.

98. Interview with John Hardy, founder and former CEO of LINK, London, by B. Bátiz-Lazo and C. Reese, 21 November 2007.

99. In its internal newspaper, the Woolwich claimed to have led the consortium. See: 'Countdown to Cashbase', *Woolwich World*, vol. 8, no. 7, July 1985: 3.

100. 'Cashbase: Switch-on at Head Office', *Woolwich World*, vol. 8, no. 8, August 1985: 1.

101. 'Cashbase Set for Launch Later in the Year', *Woolwich World*, vol. 8, no. 7, July 1985: 1.

102. Renewing the offer of envelope deposits by Cashbase in the mid-1980s was interesting. As noted in Chapter 2, this was the central feature of the Simjian machine in 1960 and as noted in Chapter 4, during the 1970s US banks insisted that cash machines include envelope deposits as evidence of their interest in capturing core deposits. In the UK, Barclays explored the possibility of accepting envelope deposits via cash machines as early as 1976, but found that transactions involving withdrawals were ten times more frequent. Indeed, in December 1976 the Management Services Department reported that 43,670 Barclaybank cards had been issued in the four weeks to 27 November. While there had been 6,983 withdrawals (at an average of £21 per withdrawal) there were only 663 deposits (average amount not disclosed). Although Barclays eventually discontinued the service in the 1970s, it was reintroduced as 'Express Deposit' with new Barclaybank machines using 'Barclay's Connect' cards in 1991. Source: BSA—Automation Committee Minutes: 415/156—'Use of Machines', 15 December 1976; Personal communication (email) from Nicholas Webb, Barclays Group Archives, with B. Bátiz-Lazo, 23 June 2007.

103. Initially there were 120 cash machines. The number was expected to increase to 400 by the end of the year and to 1,000 installed machines within two years. See further 'Scotland Joins Cashbase Link', *Woolwich World*, vol. 9, no. 10, September 1986: 1 and 'Matrix Gets Off to a Flyer', *Woolwich World*, vol. 9, no. 3, March 1986: 1.

104. Personal communication (email) from Robert Rosenthal, former IBM engineer, with B. Bátiz-Lazo, 23 July 2016.

105. Barrow (2006, 98).

106. Unless otherwise stated, this paragraph borrows freely from the personal communication (email) from Robert Rosenthal, former IBM engineer, with B. Bátiz-Lazo, 23 July 2016.

107. BGA, 'Barclays Fact Sheet—Cash Machines', undated. Note that an internal document, also compiled by the Barclays Group Archives, claims: 'Barclays joins a consortium of five banks sharing ATM facilities' in April 1983. The latter probably refers to the West of England Building Society—a small player—who joined the four bank network in 1988.

108. Personal communication (email) from Robert Rosenthal, former IBM engineer, with B. Bátiz-Lazo, 3 August 2016.

109. RBSGA—unpublished research note in Group Archives.

110. RBSGA—NWB/914/12, NatWest, news release 288/98, 1 December 1988.

111. Lloyds TSB Archive, Index cards on ATM.

112. Lloyds Bank acquired in-store ATMs in the branches of Lewis's and Selfridges in the early 1970s. It was evident from the staff magazine (*Lloyds Bank News*) that these machines operated as an integral part of the bank rather than at arm's length.

113. RBSGA—NWB/1358, NatWest, 'NatWest Update' circular, no. 56,'Developing Technology', January 1986.

114. RBSGA—unpublished research note by Group Archives.

115. BGA, 'Barclays Fact Sheet—Cash Machines', undated. Note by Barclays Group Archives. Interestingly, Barclays' 'drive in' came some twenty years after similar facilities had been tried and tested in other countries. Some of these remained part of everyday life (i.e. USA, Saudi Arabia) while others were very short-lived (i.e. Mexico, Belgium).

116. BGA, 'Barclays Fact Sheet: Cash Machine', undated.

117. McAndrews (1991, 4).

118. Barrie (2006, 74).

119. RBSGA—NWB/914/12, NatWest, news release 288/98, 1 December 1988. The UK's Retail Price Index (base 13 January 1987), was 160.0 at the end of December 1997 (Source: Office for National Statistics, accessed 7 June 2007, originally at <http://www.statistics.gov.uk/rpi>). The deflated value of NatWest's average withdrawals in 1997 is then £28.20 or 2 percent below £28.62, observed at the end of 1986.

120. Channon (1988); Walter (1997).

121. Bátiz-Lazo and Wood (2000); Canals (1993, 1997).

122. Bátiz-Lazo and Wardley (2007); Fincham et al. (1994).

123. David (1985, 2000). See also the critique of path dependence in the seminal articles by Liebowitz and Margolis (1990, 1994, 1995) and Cusumano et al. (1992).

124. Bátiz-Lazo and Reese (2010).

6

A Global Network

6.1 The Sharing Economy of ATM Consortia

6.1.1 *International Comparative Growth of ATM Stock*

This chapter illustrates the importance of understanding the local foundations of global events by explaining how interconnecting one national network with another enabled people to access cash in local currency regardless of location. This global network came into being thanks to the proliferation of domestic shared ATM networks in many countries. This chapter thus takes a step back to compare the growth of ATMs across selected economies and then discuss the formation of international switches on the back of Visa and MasterCard.

To explain the construction of a global ATM network, Figure 6.1 offers a timeline of the key events treated in this chapter. These milestones include: a first attempt at an international network by Visa in 1981; a pilot project and successful launch of a shared ATM network in Europe in 1984 and 1987, respectively; 'duality' or an agreement enabling bank customers across the world to use their Visa or MasterCard cards in point of sale terminals and ATMs alike, and with no additional fee; the establishment of a computer centre in Europe to clear cross-border credit and debit card transactions; and the maximum point of adoption of ATMs by a selected group of countries in 2011. It is important to note here that the emergence of global shared networks around Visa and MasterCard, with their own message encryption protocols (see Chapter 7), makes regional and national shared networks redundant. The chapter finishes with a brief reflection on the resilience of a global ATM network to hacker attacks such as that of WannaCry in 2017.

Throughout this chapter the significance of these key events is explained alongside changes in the stock and, subsequently, the density of cashpoints in a small sample of countries. Hence, Figure 6.1 summarizes and compares the growth of the ATM stock across Japan and representative countries in Europe and North America.[1] Note that Figure 6.1 makes no distinction between the

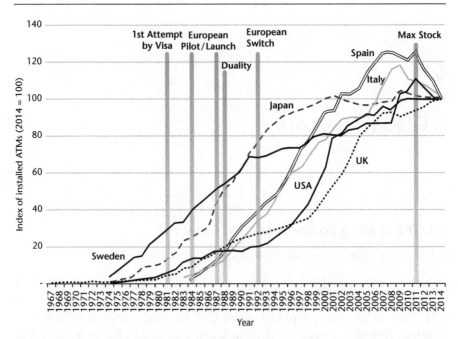

Figure 6.1. Growth of cash machine and ATM stocks in selected countries, 1967–2014 (Index 2014 = 100 percent)

Source: Author's own estimates, based on Asami (*c*.1986); Bank for International Settlements (Red Book, 1985–2014); Banca d'Italia; Bátiz-Lazo and Maixé-Altés (2011b); Endo (1974); International Monetary Fund; World Bank; Maixé-Altés (2013); Lipis et al. (1985); Peffers (1991); RBR; Thodenius et al. (2011b); Zimmer (1971).

early (strictly offline) cash machine and the ATM, because it was up to individual banks to begin operating their devices online and many used them offline well into the 1980s, despite being connected to a larger computer system.

Figure 6.1 presents the growth of cashpoints in four early adopters of the ATM (Japan, Sweden, the UK, and the USA) and two late adopters (Italy and Spain). These countries shared a cautious uptake of cashpoints throughout the 1970s, reaching a combined deployment of 29,746 devices in 1979 or 4 per cent of the stock held in 2014 (latest date for which comparable data were available). In 1980, Spain and Italy had yet to deploy cashpoints in significant numbers; the UK had accumulated 3 per cent and the USA 4 per cent of the stock observed in 2014, whereas Japan had 11 per cent and Sweden 25 per cent of the stock they held in 2014. The 1980s for the first time saw ATMs grow in significant numbers across all six countries. By 1989, the USA had accumulated 18 per cent of the stock observed in 2014, the UK and Spain had 23 per cent and 25 per cent respectively, and Italy 19 per cent (with the rate of adoption being steeper for Spain and Italy as 'latecomers'); while Japan and Sweden had a staggering 55 per cent and 58 per cent respectively. Together the

ATM stock of these six countries was 192,437 devices in 1989 (26 per cent of the stock in 2014) but almost six times that of a decade before. In the USA alone the number of devices grew five and a half times from 13,995 in 1979 to 78,136 in 1989. Figure 6.1 also shows that for most countries the stock of ATMs continued to grow throughout the 1990s and 2000s, until it peaked in the six named countries at 745,332 machines in 2011. This maximum was about a third of the total world stock in 2014.[2] Growth then levelled or started to shrink in individual countries and as a result the stock in 2011 was 11,079 units or 1 per cent higher than in 2014.

This evidence suggests the period between 1980 and 2011 was one of great success for the ATM, growing not only in selected countries but across the world. The period coincided with the transformation of the cash machine into the ATM as a terminal of a larger computer system. The prolixity of this process of adoption bears witness to the embedding of the ATM in the retail banking organization and implicitly suggests how much time and effort organizations had to be invested to assist non-expert users to develop a basic understanding of new applications of computer technology and the skills to deal with it, while making these applications part of everyday life.[3]

6.1.2 Standardized International Comparison of ATM Density

To compare changes in the density of ATMs, Figure 6.2 summarizes the trends in ATM growth, recalibrating the data in Figure 6.1 by the size of the urban population.[4] Urban numbers were deemed more appropriate than the number overall for two reasons. First, the cost of servicing ATMs in rural locations is significantly higher than in urban spaces, particularly for off-branch devices. Indeed, the cost of servicing remote locations has been identified as one of the two main challenges to the widespread use of ATMs in developing countries.[5]

Second, the proportion of urban inhabitants rose in all countries in the sample. Urban dwellers as a proportion of total inhabitants varied from 63 per cent in Spain and Italy in 1967, to 93 per cent in Japan in 2014—with an (arithmetical) average of 77 per cent (standard deviation, hence forward st. dev., of 3) for all six countries during the 1967 to 2014 sample period. Figure 6.2 also shows the combined proportion of total inhabitants in sample countries, from a minimum of 71 per cent in 1967 to a maximum of 83 per cent in 2014.

The apparent correlation between the size of the urban population and the rate of adoption of ATMs is also evident in late-to-industrialize countries where the mass adoption of ATMs was more recent. For instance, when their deployment was first taking place in Brazil (at Brandesco in 1983), China (Bank of China, 1980), and India (HSBC, 1987), ATMs had already been deployed in their thousands in developed countries; estimated ATM numbers

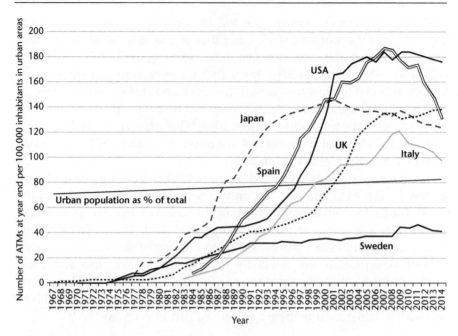

Figure 6.2. Density of cash machines and ATMs per capita in selected countries, 1967–2014 (Number of devices per 100,000 urban inhabitants)

Source: Author's own estimates, using population data from the World Bank.

in 1984 were 58,960 for the USA; 36,168 for Japan; 6,794 for the UK; 2,217 for Italy; 1,960 for Canada; and 1,295 for Sweden. Other countries introduced them even later, for instance Poland (1990), Egypt (1994), Ukraine (1996), Pakistan (1998), Belarus (1998), Afghanistan (2004), Vietnam (2006), and Kazakhstan (2007). The adoption data thus suggest that ATMs appeared earlier and diffused much faster in industrialized nations with a high and increasing proportion of urban inhabitants—which probably also had a higher proportion of salaried people, mostly working in the service sector.[6] Quantitative empirical studies even after taking account of the numbers of on- and off-retail bank premises, have also found that ATMs tend to be located in urban areas.[7] This is because of lower deployment, security, operation, and maintenance costs as well as the higher demand for cash withdrawal services.

Given the above, we can conclude that the ATM is an urban technology that facilitated banking for salaried people (those paid by cheque or bank transfer to their account). To compare the growth of ATMs in different countries, it is better to adjust the size of the ATM fleet by the urban population and compare the changes in the density of ATMs than to adjust for the total population.

Admittedly greater accuracy would be possible using the number of adults or age groups in urban areas.[8] But however desirable, there are no consistent data for the number of adult urban inhabitants during the 1967–2014 period. As a result, ATM deployment was adjusted only by the overall size of the urban population, as shown in Figure 6.2.

The result of recalibrating the data suggests that the deployment of ATMs during the 1980s and 1990s far exceeded the growth of the urban population in different countries—except for Sweden where they remained relatively stable (as far as population growth was concerned). Peak adoption in Sweden was observed in 2011 with a maximum number of 47 ATMs per 100,000 urban inhabitants (ATM/100UI); for the period 1967 to 2014 the average was 28 ATM/100UI (st. dev. 12.60). Sweden's average deployment was well below that of Spain (112 ATM/100UI, st. dev. 59.96); Japan (93 ATM/100UI, st. dev. 52.25); the USA (82 ATM/100UI, st. dev. 71.76); Italy (69 ATM/100UI, st. dev. 39.33); and the UK (52 ATM/100UI, st. dev. 50.89).

Most countries in the sample illustrated by Figure 6.2 observed a clear 'S shaped' pattern or curve of adoption as would be expected by the so-called 'Diffusion of Innovation Theory'.[9] Accordingly the first country to reach maximum deployment was Japan in 2001 with 146 ATM/100UI. Japan, however, observed a curious development in that the number of devices continued to grow, from 142,700 in 2001 to 147,202 in 2009 (equivalent to 139 ATM/100UI). This behaviour would suggest that the size of the Japanese urban population grew faster than the number of ATMs between 2001 and 2009, which is unlikely; it perhaps corresponds to an error in the estimates of installed capacity reported by the Bank of Japan to the Bank for International Settlements.

The peak for Japan was followed by one for Spain in 2007 at 187 ATM/100UI; Italy's apex was 120 ATM/100UI in 2009, the USA's 185 ATM/100UI in 2010, and finally the UK with 138 ATM/100UI in 2014. In other words, the trends in Figure 6.2 suggest that ATM deployment reached a peak and then contracted during the 2000s and 2010s, particularly for Japan, Italy, and Spain—the rate of initial adoption and subsequent elimination of ATMs in these three countries seems to have been at rates above the average of the other countries in the sample. Other signs of industrial maturity in the cash distribution sector were the messianic news of a cashless economy in the Scandinavian countries and amalgamation leading to greater concentration amongst ATM manufacturers. Chief amongst the latter was the merger in 2016 between two long-standing and leading ATM providers, namely, US-based Diebold which took over Wincor-Nixdorf of Padeborn, Germany for 1.7 billion euros (1.8 billion US dollars).[10] The resulting Diebold Wincor became a new SP 500 company while raising competition concerns in the UK.[11]

In spite of the apparent saturation of ATM provision in some countries suggested above, the ATM network continued to expand worldwide. Table 6.1 shows that in Brazil, the fifth-biggest country in the world in terms

Table 6.1. Diffusion of cash dispensers and ATMs in selected countries, 1967–2015 (alphabetical order)

	Year of first adoption of a cash machine	Estimated total units at apex of adoption	Units per capita at apex of adoption
	(Bank)	(Year)	(ATM/100UI)
Brazil*	1983 (Brandesco)	175,000 (2012)	102
China*	1980 (Bank of China)	415,600 (2012)	59
India	1987 (HSBC)	193,768 (2015)	45
Italy	1983(?) (Not available)	48,549 (2009)	120
Japan	1969 (Sumitomo Bank)	147,700 (2001)	146
Korea	1979 (Chohong Bank)	124,236 (2013)	301
Russia*	1989 (Sberbank)	172,000 (2012)	163
Spain	1968 (Banesto)	58,536 (2007)	187
Sweden	1967 (Uppsala Savings Bank)	3,566 (2011)	47
United Kingdom	1967 (Barclays Bank)	69,000 (2014)	138
USA	1969 (Chemical Bank)	431,000 (2010)	185

Note: * = Estimates available only for 2008 to 2012.

Source: Own estimates.

of total population, the ATM fleet grew from 158,400 devices in 2008 (97 ATM/100UI) to the third largest in 2012 with 175,000 devices (102 ATM/100UI).[12] A much more impressive growth took place in Russia. This country had 75,000 devices in 2008 (71 ATM/100UI), which expanded by 129 per cent to 172,000 devices in 2012 (163 ATM/100UI). Meanwhile India, the second largest country in terms of total population, more than doubled the size of its ATM stock from 87,355 devices at the end of 2011 (22 ATM/100UI) to 193,768 devices in 2015 (45 ATM/100UI).[13]

In 2012, although the USA remained the largest deployer with 432,500 devices, its stock was contracting. At the same time, China, the world's most populated country, was fast catching up and overtaking the USA in terms of the stock of ATMs. Chinese deployment grew 148 per cent from 167,500 units in 2008 to 415,600 units in 2012. But Chinese ATM density remained below that of the USA, Japan, and many European and some Asian countries. The density of cashpoints in China increased between 2008 and 2012 from 27

ATM/100UI to 59 ATM/100UI respectively, while the USA observed 181 ATM/100UI in 2012.

The Republic of Korea offers another interesting example of diffusion.[14] Chohong Bank deployed the first cash dispenser in November 1979, at a time when 55 per cent of the population lived in urban areas. The same bank also deployed the first ATM in its Myeong-dong branch (in the centre of Seoul) in 1990; and by 1992, 61 ATMs were in operation. By then, too, 76 per cent of the South Korean population lived in urban areas, where the (mainly commercial) banks had installed 9,659 cash dispensers. A cash dispenser in Korea is a device operated by a card or passbook that allows consumers to withdraw cash and make account transfers and balance enquiries. An ATM not only performed the functions of a cash dispenser but also accepted cash and cheque deposits and other self-service transactions, such as purchasing insurance or paying taxes. Figure 6.3 shows the growth of cash dispensers and ATMs in the South Korea since 1992—the earliest that data were available for comparison.[15]

Figure 6.3 depicts the deployment of cash dispensers and ATMs in South Korea by commercial banks, the Post Office bank, and domestic offices of foreign banks since 1992—the first year that data were available. Trends

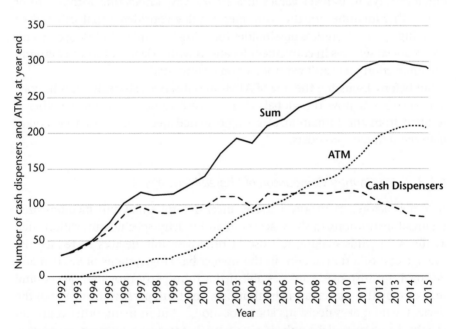

Figure 6.3. Dispersion of cash dispensers and ATMs in the Republic of Korea, 1992–2015 (Number of devices per 100,000 urban inhabitants)

Source: Author's own estimates, based on Bank of Korea statistics, using population data from the World Bank.

143

suggest that the ATMs numbers grew to 87,274 or 210 ATM/100UI in 2014, while cash dispensers peaked at 48,283 devices or 119 ATM/100UI in 2010. Taking the sum of cash dispensers and ATMs, as it was taken for the other countries discussed above, then 2013 was the year when adoption peaked in Korea at 124,236 units or 301 ATM/100UI. But while the number of ATMs seems to have formed a plateau, cash dispensers have shrunk to similar levels to those observed in the early 1990s. These estimates suggest that, although the South Korean market accepted levels of penetration above those in North America, Europe, or elsewhere in Asia, it also reached a point of saturation— certainly in the case of cash dispensers.

In short, there was potential for the continuing global expansion of ATMs but in specific countries and regions rather than worldwide, and this expansion would probably be slower than before. As is discussed in Chapter 7, one potential source of growth (or lower attrition) in the ATM stock within developed countries is the great potential within an established base of conveniently located machines to do more things than simply distribute cash. Paul Stanley, former managing director of Moneybox, commented on how providers ought to think in terms of self-service rather than solely on ATMs.[16] The technology that is deployed within these devices, he said, can be used in different ways to transfer values in a secure way, interacting with a card or some other identifier for the consumer. Stanley considered that this way of thinking opens up endless possibilities for going forward by 'offering convenient financial services in convenient locations with a degree of security around the interaction you can't get from a home computer'.

But before discussing the role of ATMs in self-service strategies, it is important to consider how the global ATM network came about and whether it resulted from the formation of a single shared network or interoperability between different providers.

6.1.3 *Cross-Country Comparison of Shared Networks*

As noted before, there was a strong incentive for small and medium-sized financial institutions to share access to an industry-specific innovation such as the ATM, thus making full use of otherwise idle devices to reduce the average cost of a transaction. In the smaller banking systems of Sweden and Portugal, for instance, banks established a third-party provider, owned and managed by the participating institutions. The third party is the owner of the devices, who makes decisions about location.[17] But in many other countries the third party would act only as a 'switch', that is, a computer system routing transaction information from the device to the customer's bank.

In most cases ATMs are owned, managed, and maintained by individual banks, which have established a joint venture with other banks to make full use of these assets and to share the set-up and running costs of the network. This enables a customer of one member of the consortium to use the same plastic card to activate cash machines associated with other members of the network and process similar transactions through them.

Sharing ATMs, however, was not the only form of collaboration between retail financial institutions. High investment expenditures commonly involved collaboration as illustrated by cheque clearing in many countries and by teleprocessing and bureau services during the early days of computerization in the 1950s and 1960s. The very nature of teleprocessing and bureau services involved individual banks coming together to rent assets owned by someone else—a third-party provider.[18]

At this point it is worth remembering that some parts of the US banking industry were particularly prone to collaborating in activities involving high capital investment and specialist skills. For most of the twentieth century the USA had no national banks because of restrictions on banking across state lines. In many states (particularly in the Midwest) banks could not branch across county lines. This led to a system with many small community banks— at least one or two per county—that depended on larger banks in nearby cities to clear their cheques and credit card receipts, help provide loans, and, of course, share computer technology. Regulatory constraints to geographic diversification, therefore, made the use of third-party providers particularly attractive, given the atomistic nature of American banking.

Initially at least, the idea of bank alliances for electronic clearing was somewhat troubling to politicians in the USA. To address these concerns a coordinated effort by the Federal Reserve, the Comptroller of the Currency, and the Deposit Insurance Corporation lobbied in favour of collaboration within banking so as to create an electronic fund transfer system or EFTS.[19] The view of these US regulators was informed by developments in Europe in the mid-1970s, most notably those around automated cash dispensing by British and Swedish savings banks.[20] Politicians' concerns eventually receded and by the end of the 1970s the construction of an automated clearing house to process batches of credit and debit payments electronically was well under way.

Alongside this development and as noted in Chapter 5, only a few shared ATM networks existed in the 1970s in the USA, but the number quickly grew, right up until the late 1980s, when amalgamation eliminated more than half of them.[21] In 1985 the top three networks in the USA were processing 11 per cent of the volume, but by 2001 a steep contraction had resulted in five ATM consortia controlling 78 per cent of transactions.[22] The factors that led to the decline of shared networks in the USA included a lower number of entrants as well as the amalgamation of banks and networks. But far more important was the 1985 ruling by the Supreme Court upholding the view that ATMs did not represent bank branches.[23] This made it easier for banks to own ATMs across state lines and therefore easier for bank-owned networks to merge with out-of-state networks.[24] Of course, economies of scale and amalgamation amongst the networks themselves also played an important part in explaining the decline in numbers in the USA.

Consolidation thus allowed the remaining networks to expand both geographically and in terms of the number of devices, as a result improving the availability and quality of service to bank customers. The anti-trust implications of this process, however, were closely monitored by state and federal agencies.[25] Table 6.2 summarizes the evolution of shared ATM networks in the USA, while also providing a comparison with similar developments in a small sample of industrialized nations.

Table 6.2 depicts a similar process across all the countries in the sample: an expansion of shared networks reaches its zenith towards the mid-1980s and contracts thereafter. Individual networks varied in size and transaction volume, since some were local, others regional, and a few national.[26] Once shared networks were established, the number of devices involved was significant. For instance, in 1983 there were five consortia in Japan involving 39 per cent of the total number of (still active) cash machines and ATMs.[27] At the same time there were three in the UK and 250 in the USA, accounting for 47 per cent and 40 per cent respectively. By the year 2000, one network controlled 100 per cent of transactions in the UK and Sweden, while the top five networks in the USA controlled approximately 80 per cent of transactions.

Table 6.2 also presents for comparison a sample of countries whose experience seems to have drawn from opposite extremes. On the one hand, there was a modest number of shared networks in Sweden and the UK. On the other, there were many shared networks in Japan, Canada, and the USA. As the case of the UK in Chapter 5 shows, connectivity in Europe arrived at roughly the same time as in North America. However, Europe had fewer networks—whereas large banks had many times over the number of retail branches observed in the USA. At the same time, individual networks in Europe

Table 6.2. Shared ATM networks in selected countries, 1978–2000

Year	Canada	Japan	UK	USA	Sweden
1978	0	1	0	10	2
1983	1	5	3	250	2
1988	40	68	6	130	5
1993	40	23	3	65	2
1998	43	16	3	45	1
2000	71	10	1	30	1
Maximum (year)	71 (2001)	75 (1990)	7 (1987)	250 (1983)	5 (1987)

Source: Own estimates, based on Bank for International Settlements (Red Book, 1985–2001) and Ekebrink (1974).

connected more devices than an average-sized shared network in North America did. As described below, linking all these otherwise independent networks in different countries produced a global network.

6.2 The Global Network

6.2.1 *Duality in Cash Machines and Point of Sale Terminals*

The combination of developments in the USA and Europe help to explain the genesis of a global ATM network built around Visa and MasterCard. A first important move took place in 1981, when Visa International announced plans to invest $15–20 million in upgrading its international data-transmission system to allow member banks to connect their ATMs across the world.[28] MasterCard, its main rival, thought the idea of interconnecting across borders 'too grandiose... [since an] American tourist [for example], would be unable to understand an ATM in Japan'.[29] Visa International's plans soured when most of the banks in North America opted out of sharing their ATMs through the credit card company (i.e. Visa's Automated Cash Disbursement Service). Their argument was that cash advances at tellers, though small in volume, generated lucrative fee income for both the bank issuing the card and the bank advancing the cash; however, US banks were said to prefer investing in other important projects. Eventually, as detailed in Chapter 5, banks in North America came to share their ATMs, but did so through the likes of Plus and Cirrus. In a way, this early start gave North American banks an advantage over European banks through having already developed the skills, knowledge, systems, and protocols to implement bank interchange networks—albeit in a domestic environment and proportionally smaller networks.[30]

Meanwhile in Europe domestic and cross-border cash advance service businesses were growing thanks to the influx of tourists.[31] European bankers around Visa were the first to see an opportunity to automate the cash withdrawal service for credit, but the beneficiaries were mainly debit card customers using Visa's card and communication networks to share ATMs across borders. Banks in four countries came together to finance the initial project. The participants in this experiment were based in net-tourism-exporting Scandinavia (i.e. Finland, Norway, and Sweden) and net-tourist-importing Spain. This pilot project helped Visa sort out marketing material, computer programs, message protocols, PIN interchange formats, and other technological changes necessary to display Visa's decal on participants' ATMs. Once in place the programme started to generate revenue by enabling ATMs in Spain to collect fees for cash advances on credit cards issued in a Scandinavian country (and ATMs in other Scandinavian countries to do the same). The apparent success of this programme attracted the interest of other European banks. By 1987 and three years after the pilot project had begun, the Automated Cash Disbursement Service had grown to 19,023 machines in twenty-one countries, making Visa International the largest bank-owned ATM network in the world.[32] American Express reported that 23,795 machines were available in twenty countries through its Express Cash network, making it bigger than Visa's global system. But American Express owned only 135 devices; the rest were owned and operated by banks that had signed an interchange agreement with the financial services conglomerate.

In 1987, MasterCard's Master Teller network had only 9,462 online devices, spread across eleven countries. This was to change with the acquisition of Cirrus in 1988 through which MasterCard gained critical scale in the US market. Cirrus then superseded the Master Teller concept by incorporating the existing devices of member banks into its network. Having acquired Cirrus, MasterCard sought to emulate Visa's international network, which by the end of 1988 had grown to 31,000 machines in thirty-three countries.[33] The target was to give MasterCard cardholders access to 35,000 ATMs by the end of 1990 while, at the same time, MasterCard quietly adopted a resolution allowing its ATMs to accept cards from its rival.

Meanwhile, Cirrus and Plus first announced plans to open their ATMs to each other in 1985.[34] The idea was to extend this agreement and also share point of sale terminals. But while Plus had put in place an encryption standard and other measures to guard against wiretapping and other fraud, Cirrus had not. This was the main point of contention—at least as far as media reports were concerned.[35] Other arguments were also put forward, such as the lack of meaningful communication and the possibility that interconnection would reduce competition for new machine locations which, in turn, could invite anti-trust investigation and possible regulation of the bank-owned networks as a public utility. In any case, the bankers who comprised the Cirrus board were not interested. They initially rejected Plus' invitation to form a reciprocal interchange of transactions with Cirrus. In the meantime, the absence of an interchange arrangement between the national networks resulted in regional ATM networks creating direct links with each other to allow transactions to flow. This in effect raised the cost to banks that were members of these regional networks as well as in Cirrus and Plus.

Following the acquisition by MasterCard, Cirrus acquiesced and agreed to share ATMs with Plus. This meant reaching an agreement for a common standard at both the ATMs and point of sale terminals in the USA, delivering on Visa's and MasterCard's strategies to be low-cost providers of transaction processing. Moreover, Visa and MasterCard struck a competitive blow at the networks assembled by American Express (Express Cash) and Sears (Discover), each approaching 20,000 ATMs in 1988. Edward Hogan, a twenty-year MasterCard staff veteran and president of Cirrus at the time,[36] highlighted the significance of reciprocity between the major ATM networks: 'MasterCard-Visa duality at ATMs is no different from the ability to use either card at points of sale.'[37] Hogan's comment points to the importance of the Visa–MasterCard 'duality', which refers to individual banks issuing cards with the marquee of either or both of the card companies, a practice that became widespread in the USA during the 1970s. Credit card duality allowed the card companies to cooperate so that member banks could interchange transaction data when they found it useful. This led critics to warn that it would diminish competition between the two card brands, but they need not have worried. In the late 1980s Visa and MasterCard were judged to have remained highly competitive.[38]

It thus took quite a long while for duality in credit and debit cards to apply to the national ATM networks. The main limitations were political and strategic rather than technological. But in the 1970s, when duality came, D. Dale Browning, president and founder of Plus, president of the Colorado National Bank, Denver, and a chief advocate of reciprocity between the ATM networks, was ironically also one of its strongest critics.

6.2.2 Assembling the Parts

Competitive dynamics around Plus and Cirrus were also important in articulating the global network and should not go unnoticed. As previously described in Chapter 5, by the late 1980s Cirrus, Plus, and other shared ATM networks had saturated the demand and left no chance of further organic growth in the USA.[39] This resulted in a wave of amalgamation which, together with regulatory innovations, drastically reduced the number of individual shared ATM networks during the 1990s. With the prospect of saturation, Plus and Cirrus started to look for growth in international markets—while aiming to emulate the success that Visa and MasterCard were having beyond North America. But they did not find it.

Asking banks' boards of directors for permission to invest significant sums in building worldwide communication networks made little sense to bankers who had also been involved in and had funded the international operations of the credit card companies. It was simply too expensive to have multiple sets of equally functional worldwide communications networks. Instead, a deal was made through which the acquisition of an equity stake in Plus by Visa and a takeover of Cirrus by MasterCard channelled the international traffic of these organizations through the communication networks and clearing channels that Visa and MasterCard had put in place.

Two important issues remained, however, before full worldwide interoperability could be delivered. These were the physical location of the network switch and the message encryption standards. First, once the message management and organizational infrastructure for the global network were in place, it was not the ATM that drove the development of a computer centre for clearing transactions based in Europe,[40] since the volume of cross-border ATM transactions, at the time, was minuscule, compared with that of credit cards. Yet European banks did not like the idea of having to switch through California or McLean, VA, to run the worldwide network. As a result, in order to contribute a European presence, a third computer super-centre for the credit card business which would also act as international switch for ATM transactions was built in the UK (in Basingstoke, Hampshire) in 1992.[41]

A second important hurdle for articulating the global ATM network was related to the absence of inter-bank standards. As noted in Chapter 5, this resulted in bank interchange networks defining their own protocols for messages and encryption between ATMs and banks' computer centres. Specifically, North American networks used a nineteen-digit Primary Account Number (PAN) and four- to six-digit Personal Identification Number (PIN). Meanwhile the international community had been built around a sixteen-digit PAN and a four-digit PIN. The difference in specification of PIN and account number was far from trivial; PIN and PAN were essential to secure encryption and therefore to the secure exchange of information between the ATM and the bank's data centre.

Although a PIN became a binding form of authentication between customer and bank, a PIN is not unique to a person. This is because, whether a PIN is chosen by the customer or is randomly assigned, it is made of only a finite number of possible combinations; and customers in any case tend to use date-related PINs,[42] causing many duplications even in a small bank.[43] The PIN becomes unique only in combination with the PAN. Initially the PAN was encrypted with a key, the first four digits of which became the PIN assigned to an individual customer. The advent of a customer-selected PIN required the introduction of an off-set, resulting from the difference between the customer's *assigned* PIN and the customer's *selected* PIN.[44] As previously noted in Chapter 3, the IBM 3614 and 3624 ATMs were amongst the first devices to implement a facility that could handle different bank specification (including different PINs and account numbers) within a bank interchange network.[45] But it was the introduction of an international standard definition for inter-bank messages (ISO 8583) in 1987 that helped to move things forward by its ability to support different account numbers and PINs of different lengths and to support encryption keys in a bank's own ATM network that were not the same as in the interchange network(s).

But even though ATMs could accommodate a system to manage PINs, whoever had chosen them, and different sizes of PIN and account number, banks had to update their internal systems to comply with these variations.

The result was that while the global shared networks were being built, card-holders from the USA, for example, often could not use their cards overseas.

Meanwhile, it was not easy to persuade member banks of Cirrus and Plus to invest and modify their standards in order to give US cardholders access to the international network. Updating ATM software can be costly and time consuming; sometimes even requiring technicians to visit each machine physically.[46] In addition, central authorization systems and databases also had to support the new standard. Gradually the international inter-bank message standard (ISO 8583) was introduced across the new and existing networks as they expanded.[47] This incurred migration and/or implementation costs for domestic and international banks taking part in an interchange network (e.g. ATMs and point of sale terminals). However, it was the growing use of debit cards in the 1990s rather than ISO 8583 that ultimately resulted in the boards of Cirrus and Plus acquiescing and agreeing to conform to the Visa debit card protocol as standard for security in transactions.[48] From this point on, it was no longer a technological issue but strictly a business decision for banks around the world to display Plus, Cirrus, Visa, and/or MasterCard decals on their machines. Hence differences in the priority of business goals and costs ultimately explain why the global ATM network was introduced in stages.

Irwin Derman, vice-president in charge of Visa's global ATM program in the 1980s, recalled the transition while stating that Cirrus, Plus, and the banks within them changed their standards when the Visa debit card started to make significant inroads.[49] According to Derman, they conformed to the international credit card standards and suddenly compliance was no longer a problem of technology, he said, it was a problem of marketing only. According to Derman, Visa never really made an effort to make Plus an international program, but it was a big effort for Visa to make the debit card an international program. 'It was not Plus but the Visa debit card which really took over', Derman said.

To illustrate the growing importance of the debit card in the 1990s, consider that in November 1993 Visa announced plans to take over the remaining 70 per cent of Plus by 1996.[50] The acquisition of 101,000 Plus terminals in forty countries took the Visa total to 160,000, with plans to increase the total to 250,000 by 1996 by absorbing other bank-owned ATMs into the system. MasterCard's Cirrus, by contrast, had 143,565 machines. At the time an unnamed source at Visa said that 'the expansion of the [Visa] ATM network [was] in part a move to expand the use of [our] debit cards... [In fact the] availability of ATMs internationally... [will] enhance the attractiveness of Visa debit cards.' Visa had 68 million debit cards on issue in 1993, compared with 318 million credit cards. Its plan was to expand the number of debit cards to 220 million by the end of 1995.

The growth in ATMs and of point of sale (POS) terminals mirrored that of debit cards. Both these physical points of entry to the payment system also provided the cardholder with access to its liquid assets. But note that ATM transactions and POS transactions have opposite effects, since the use of debit cards at ATMs increases cash withdrawals while the use of debit cards at POS reduces cash holdings for purchasing purposes.[51] Cost considerations notwithstanding, the card companies were indifferent whether cardholders used an ATM or a POS, for both would generate fee income for them. The banks of course saw things differently and they invested strongly in ATMs leaving retailers to control the POS terminals.

6.3 Some Scattered Thoughts on the Global ATM Network

6.3.1 *Cheque Guarantee Cards: The Albatross around the ATM*

In 1999, when it fell victim to debit cards and the advent of the single European currency, Eurocheque, a 31-year-old payment service, started a two-year winding down process. The decision 'was widely recognized within the banking sector as the best way to address the decrease in Eurocheque usage',[52] while member banks decided to discontinue this service to focus resources on the introduction of euro notes and coins, and the increasingly popular MasterCard-marquee Maestro debit card.

Eurocheque was born in the late 1960s, as Western European banks bet on cheque guarantee cards while US banks backed credit cards. Cheque cards were an incremental innovation, particularly in countries which had a well-functioning cheque clearing system, though banks in other countries adopted it too. In Spain, for example, Eurocard was launched in 1970 when the volume of personal cheques was minuscule.[53] The cheque guarantee card appeared as a response to help bank customers cash cheques when not at their own branch and thus avoid the hassle of advance arrangements or lengthy telephone calls.[54] To make the card more acceptable to retailers, standards for agreed terms and design were introduced, but more important, so was a guarantee that individual cheques up to a certain amount would be honoured. For instance, in the UK the guarantee was up to £30.00 per cheque in 1965 (the equivalent of approximately £560 in 2017).[55]

With increased use of domestic cheque guarantee schemes, it was natural that a number of bilateral arrangements began to spring up as banks in different countries agreed to cash each other's cheques (if supported by a domestic guarantee card). A European clearing arrangement, called Eurocheque, was established in 1968 by fifteen European banks.[56] Although the clearing system was successful, it was the subsequent development of uniform cheques and cards in 1972 that made it a major force in retail payments. One source placed the Eurocheque as 'the most widely used payment system in the world [in 1985], in terms of transaction volumes and retail outlets'.[57] However, by 1997 the growing maturity of the ATM network in Europe and the considerable increase in the acceptance of the Maestro debit card contributed to a 19 per cent decline in Eurochque transactions and a 22 per cent fall in their value.[58]

For customers, access to Eurocheque privileges only required an additional annual fee. For financial institutions, cheque guarantee cards were projects less demanding in terms of new skills, and required less capital investment than credit cards or a network of cash machines. Although cheque guarantee cards and specifically Eurocheque cards were routinely used long before there was any serious discussion regarding a single European currency, their adoption in countries such as Germany, where they were particularly successful, helps to explain a lag in the adoption of credit cards and ATMs in some Western European countries. This delay clarifies another reason for the slow formation of a global ATM network during the 1990s. Interestingly, some observers believed that continental Western European banks were using a purposeful strategy in promoting the use of Eurocheques but boycotting the adoption of ATMs well into the new millennium.[59]

Whatever the reason, the end of the Eurocheque system brought to light the incapacity of European-based payment networks to make a dent in global payments and, simultaneously, the success in articulating a global payments network around US-based Visa and MasterCard.

As for the future, whether Visa and MasterCard would remain the dominant players in retail payments was being questioned at the time of writing. For one thing, Visa and MasterCard have struggled to get a foothold in China. At the same time, many Americans who previously thought their Discover card, a third US-based payment network, was useless outside the USA, found that this was not the case in China[60] thanks to Discover's long-term partnership with China's state-controlled card-payment monopoly, UnionPay.[61] Even more interesting for consumers, Discover did not charge its 3 per cent transaction fee, as most of the Visa, Mastercard, and American Express cards had done for foreign transactions. Nor did Discover exact a currency exchange fee. The link with the Chinese plus its attractive trading conditions may then position Discover or indeed, UnionPay, as a third global payments network.

How likely is this scenario? Beyond China, the recognition of Chinese brands, especially in finance, was very low. However, in the fifteen years to 2015, UnionPay not only developed international ambitions for Africa and Asia, but also became the largest bank card group in the world by value of transactions, taking 37 per cent of the $21.6 trillion global payments market in 2015.[62] But the jury may be out for a decade before coming back with a decision on the success of UnionPay and other Chinese networks, such as

Rupay, to become significant players in global payments. Meanwhile in China, the rapid growth in the number of users and transaction functionality of mobile payments networks like Alipay and Weechat undermined the business model based on plastic cards, point of sale terminals, and ATMs.[63]

6.3.2 A Brief Word on Global ATM Standards

This chapter has largely focused on the way in which a global ATM network grew on the back of common communication protocols and the deployment of ATMs by banks within national borders. This, however, obscures a degree of heterogeneity in operation. Although the final consumer had unvarying access to ATMs for many years (in the form of a standard plastic card operating by means of a magnetic stripe or a chip on the card), as late as 2017, ATMs were far from being devices that could work perfectly when first used or connected, without reconfiguration or adjustment to the systems of a financial institution.

Differences existed at even a low level of software, such as the operating system. The industry adopted IBM OS/2 from 1987 onwards as manufacturers replaced proprietary microprocessors by Intel-powered microchips.[64] This took place at roughly the same time as Windows-based personal computers arrived in bank branches and head offices. Figure 6.4 illustrates the use of Windows computers in ATMs while showing the back of an unidentified ATM device—for which its manufacturer requested anonymity when the image was captured. One can see the distinctive box of a Windows-based personal computer in the top left corner. In other words, the adoption of a Windows-based processor in an ATM translated into physical adjustments being made to house actual personal computers alongside a security vault (safely storing cassettes with banknotes), a cash dispenser mechanism, printer and paper tape with the record of transactions, video display unit (VDU), etc.

But while other parts of the bank kept up with developments in technology, change was slower at the ATM. For instance, by the mid-1990s OS/2 became the primary operating system for ATMs.[65] Yet, by one estimate, 58 per cent of all ATMs in the USA were running in OS/2 as late as 2006.[66]

Meanwhile some financial institutions in and outside the USA had migrated from OS/2 to Windows XP. But Microsoft's policy to end issuing updates and patches for Windows XP in 2014 placed ATMs as one of the devices (if not *the* very device) most affected by the end of general support to XP.[67] The industry response to the XP fiasco was to promote the adoption of Windows 10 in 2020—the proposed date to cease its extended support for Windows 7.[68] However, by one estimate, 60 per cent of the ATMs surveyed in the summer of 2015 still operated in XP, with the transition still continuing in 2017.[69] Another estimate was that at least 1 million out of the 3.6 million in operation

Figure 6.4. Storage of Windows-based computer in an ATM, 2017
Source: Author at ATM Industry Association, London.

in 2016 were still working on Windows XP in 2016.[70] The point being that regardless of estimate, the number of ATMs on Windows XP is significant. Indeed, Figure 6.5 shows the screen of an ATM in the process of resetting and clearly displaying the Windows XP logo. I captured this image by pure chance while walking in Amsterdam in 2017.

Graham Mott, of the LINK network in the UK, spoke of the challenges of system migration for ATM management.[71] He described the heterogeneity of operating systems coexisting within the ATM stock at any one time and this, he said, has to do with the age of the machines across the different members of the network. Some of these machines will be brand new and some will be seven or eight years old. So, for instance, Mott continued, at any one point there will be machines which are multicolour, running on the latest version of Windows, which can do many things; sitting alongside others which are running systems that are fifteen or twenty years old, two colour screens, very difficult to do graphics and very expensive to change. As a result, he said, you do not have thousands of universal terminals and neither can you plan for the average age or capability in the network because the reality is a

Figure 6.5. Evidence of Windows XP in ATMs, 2017
Source: Author at Rembrandt Square, Amsterdam.

jigsaw of different capabilities within the network. In Mott's view, this issue is acerbated as the number of members of the shared ATM network grows.

Although the industry (due to the lack of options) standardized to Windows, the differences noted above remained, largely due to the cost of having to fit new hardware and software throughout the almost 3.5 million devices available worldwide in 2017.[72] Adjusting for the adoption of polymer banknotes or important software updates can require physical access to devices, which is a costly proposition.

The response of managers overseeing large ATM fleets has been to minimize upgrade costs by securing patches (such as extended-extended cover of XP purchased from Microsoft) while migrating to better hardware and software as old devices were decommissioned. This was the case with the newer operating systems, which often require more powerful hardware.[73] And it was also the case in the USA with the introduction of EMV compliance. EMV stands for Europay, MasterCard, and Visa—a global standard for payment cards that uses computer chips to authenticate (and secure) chip-card transactions. Rather than specifying the nature of devices, compliance meant interoperability between the chips, the ATMs, and the POS terminals. This was part of a set of new rules to determine liability in case of fraudulent transactions. Failure to have terminals ready would shift the cost to the ATM owner or merchant originating the transaction (known as 'chargeback' or 'back charge').

In Europe the process of adopting EMV, or 'chip and pin' in the vernacular, started with the publication of the standard and roadmap in the mid-1990s (the standard was originally written in 1993–4), with the liability switch for POS on 1 January 2006 and 1 January 2008 for ATMs.[74] By 2017, 100 per cent of ATMs and POS in the UK were EMV compliant.[75]

The deadline for EMV compliance in the USA was initially set for 1 October 2015 (later extended to 21 October 2016).[76] The announcement of the new rules was a strong incentive to upgrade ATMs and POS terminals in the USA from 2014 onwards, because older models would need new card readers and Windows 7 would be better suited to implementing security protocols.[77] Hence, as newer devices with greater capacity and critical features for operation come to market, ATMs migrate to newer operating systems (such as XP, Windows 7, Windows CE, and Windows 10 sometime in the future). However, it was estimated that by 2017 only half of all ATMs and POS in the USA were EMV compliant, while the number was about 20 per cent in India and much lower in Latin America.[78]

Differences in ATMs could also be found at higher levels of operation. These differences stem from vendors maintaining features which were unique to their make and model, causing issues of interoperability. To some extent these differences incentivize the adoption of devices from the same vendor. In this regard, Aravinda Korala, CEO of the biggest non-hardware provider to the industry, explained how many banks have solutions that are tied to the different models in their network.[79] But if the financial institution wants to change the functionality, he continued, it has to change the software multiple times depending on what hardware capabilities exist within the ATMs.

Mr Korala emphasized that allowing the hardware vendor to determine the software that will manage it is a costly way of running the ATM network. An alternative to lower the cost of running this network is to use a single hardware vendor across the network. But this was not a viable solution for banks which wanted to maintain a wide choice of hardware vendors. Therefore the software application to control ATM networks would either have to be developed in-house or use vendor-agnostic software. Says Korala:

> if a bank integrates its ATM software into what is known as a single 'multi-vendor' software solution that runs on ATMs from multiple vendors, then low-cost, and rapid updates become possible, and this contributes to improved customer service.[80]

These software applications enabled financial institutions to run ATMs from different vendors in the same network. The downside, however, is that there is no central body to referee and coordinate the development of CEN XFS, the protocol used by most vendor-agnostic solutions, while, as noted, vendors can be creative with implementation causing more than one issue of interoperability (while blaming devices from competitors as the source of the problem).

In short, almost fifty years since the deployment of the first cash machines and while there is a global network as far as end users are concerned, there is much more variety and heterogeneity than standard sign posting and familiar displays on ATM screens would suggest.

6.3.3 *ATMs Resist a Global Malware Attack—This Time*

On Friday, 12 May 2017, the WannaCry cyber-attack affected more than 200,000 computers in 150 countries, affecting government, healthcare, and private company systems.[81] This sent shivers down the ATM industry's spine given that there were at the time over 3 million ATMs, compared to 1.1 million retail bank branches, worldwide. At the same time, a very high number of ATMs were still running Windows XP in 2017 (with some estimates placing up to 70 per cent of Indian ATMs still running on XP) plus the fact that any computer running XP with TCP port 445 open was vulnerable to the malware. Not surprisingly, several Indian banks pulled their ATMs out of service.[82]

Their fears, however, failed to materialize. A week after the attack, the ATM Industry Association Global Security Expert confirmed that no ATM systems had '[gone] down as a result of the recent ransomware attack'.[83] Several explanations are possible for the unlikeliness of networks and ATM (devices and networks) falling victim to this or possible future ransomware. First, Microsoft, in an unusual move, released a new patch for Windows e-attacks on XP to help prevent further attacks.[84] This meant that banks could roll out this patch and ATMs running on XP were at risk only if they had not been patched. Second, although ATMs can deliver services using TCP/IP protocols (the same as those which fuel the Internet) since 1997,[85] as has been documented in the current and previous chapters, banks and security experts have worked since the 1970s on delivering resilient protocols for ATMs to communicate and exchange information with their owner and throughout the network. The ransomware is very unlikely to use the ATM to get into the owner's (or an ATM shared network) system because the exchange is, as mentioned, not only encrypted but very specific in its demands: from the ATM to its owner, the customer's account information and a request to withdraw a certain amount; while the return message is either to authorize the withdrawal, decline it, or withhold the customer's card. Third, that some ATMs use TCP/IP protocols does not imply that the devices are connected to the Internet. Fourth, some experts inferred that 'hackers are looking for systems that are so widespread and so large that [in comparison] ATM networks, or individual ATMs, just aren't a big enough target for them to worry themselves with'.[86]

Indeed, skimming (i.e. physical access) remains the biggest threat to ATMs.[87] In this regard, eliminating plastic cards or enabling contactless transactions at ATMs would be an advantage as it would reduce both opportunities for skimming and the number of moving parts within the machine, and increase customer convenience. However, the large variation in the adoption of EMV compliance amongst banks and between countries meant that the industry was still some way from beginning to fear an attack that leveraged the total interoperability between ATMs.

6.4 Long-Term Questions, Short-Term Responses

European banks drove the demand for global ATM interconnectivity. Yet having the USA on board was critical, given that by 2001 the global total of ATMs reached 1.142 million, of which '345,000 were located in the USA, a number that exceeded the machine population of any other region'.[88] The creation of a worldwide switch for ATMs was quite a feat but, as noted above, the globalization of after-hours, automatic, cross-border, cash withdrawals was neither sudden, nor a major revolution in connectivity; it was a staged, political process. Indeed, once the PIN management system was in place, creating a global network had more to do with bringing about change within and across organizations (and organizational groups) than with any technological challenge. This evidence further endorses the idea that, although engineers and engineering firms may be the primary shapers of new technology, the potential to realize an original vision very much depends on the commercial setting and the interaction of interested groups.[89] In this regard it is important to bear in mind that it was domestic depository financial institutions that were chiefly responsible for deploying ATMs in the 1980s and early 1990s. Indeed, in spite of global interconnectivity, 'the global ATM market is still not a single entity but a group of individual markets that have retained and developed their own distinct characteristics'.[90] Thus, understanding local dynamics (as was the case with Cirrus, Plus, Visa, and Master-Card in the USA) is important in analysing when and how domestic and international interconnectivity emerged and evolved into a global network.

It should not escape our attention that the globalization of automated cash withdrawals was built upon fragmented payments markets where the banks and the two main credit card companies were the main gatekeepers. These markets were characterized by different payment standards, formats, services, and market practices that were closely connected to the geopolitical borders of sovereign states, the development within the European Union of the Single Euro Payments Area (SEPA) initiative in 2002 being a case in point. In fact, the advent of the single currency in 2000 was followed by the creation of the European Payments Council (EPC) and from here the idea of SEPA emerged.[91] These institutions encapsulated the political vision of integrating a Single Market for Payments.[92]

Two elements stand out from the process of delivering SEPA regarding the global ATM network. First, among the efforts to remove fragmentation, serious consideration was given to developing a pan-European ATM switch by linking domestic inter-bank networks. This also posited an alternative to clearing through Visa and/or MasterCard.[93] The idea was to allow ageing platforms to 'starve' while organically deepening the integration in regional or pan-European platforms. But this initiative has yet to show signs of success.

A second indicator was that one of the European-based global banks considered replicating Citibank's internal global platform.[94] This was to sidestep developments around SEPA by developing a strategic advantage through the creation of an internal network for international payment clearing that would have charged customers less than Visa, MasterCard, or a possible pan-European network for the same service.[95] These efforts, however, were fruitless. The exact reason is obscure, but most probably it was because profitability (and thus individual bonuses) went on being allocated by geography rather than product line. It is likely that country-specific managers had few incentives to cooperate.

At the same time, however, there were issues of capacity and processing costs.[96] In 2017, for instance, to stay solvent Visa Germany required an average capacity of 2,500 transactions per second (trx/sec), with peaks of up to 8,000 trx/sec; while back-end communication in global clearing in the banking system would need a sustained capability of 2,000 trx/sec. Etherium, a cutting-edge distributed ledger application, could only offer 200 trx/sec, which perhaps was sufficient bandwidth for a smart contract application but clearly inadequate for the average retail payment ecosystem in a developed country.

Finally and as has been documented in this and previous chapters, up to the mid to late 1990s, domestic depository financial institutions were chiefly responsible for deploying ATMs. However, there was a new spurt of growth in the late 1990s and early 2000s which resulted from the combination of multi-vendor software (which enabled devices from different manufacturers to coexist within the same bank), wireless ATMs, low-end devices, an increased use of debit cards and the advent of a new change agent, namely the so-called Independent ATM Deployer (IAD). Together they increased ATM density in the USA, the UK, Canada, Germany, and other countries. Indeed, between 1997 and 2011 (the maximum point of adoption), the five countries discussed in this chapter deployed almost half a million units or 54 per cent of the joint stock in 2011. Chapter 7 will describe how this growth took place and the role of IADs and low-end ATMs in the process.

Notes

1. Additional sources: 'Statistical Database', Banca d'Italia, accessed 9 March 2017, <https://infostat.bancaditalia.it/inquiry/#eNorLqhMz0ksLtYvSazIt3IOdXINdg2x DQh1cvKJNzCogTHiDQxrQlycDA2MDE10PENcfYNdfVyj%0AbGFC8YbmBg YWBkY6%2FgGufrZpiTnFqfplmanlYAM9XYIxFOoDAJyDIkw%3D>; 'Financial Access Survey 2015', International Monetary Fund, accessed 14 June 2016, <https://www.imf.org/en/News/Articles/2015/09/14/01/49/pr15455>; 'Urban Population', The World Bank, accessed 14 June 2016, <http://data.worldbank. org/indicator/SP.URB.TOTL>.

2. RBR London estimated there were more than 2 million ATMs worldwide in 2009, which grew to 3 million in 2014 and 3.5 million in 2017. My estimates suggest that ATM deployment had yet to peak in the USA and the UK but in 2009 it had reached a maximum of 147,202 units in Japan. Later on, Spain had 58,536 devices and Sweden had 3,566 in 2011.

3. Bessen (2015a, 2015b).

4. 'Urban Population', The World Bank, accessed 14 June 2016, <http://data.wor ldbank.org/indicator/SP.URB.TOTL>.

5. Fees and surcharges are the other main challenges. See for instance, Bernardo Bátiz-Lazo, 'The Challenge of Digital Micropayments in Mexico', *The Cashless Society*, 3 September 2013, accessed 25 October 2017, <https://cashlesssociety.wordpress. com/2013/09/03/the-challenge-of-digital-micropayments-in-mexico/>.

6. The urban population of Brazil grew from 53 per cent in 1967 to 85 per cent in 2014. For that same period the urban populations of India and China grew from 19 per cent and 17 per cent in 1967 to 32 per cent and 54 per cent in 2014, respectively.

7. See further French et al. (2012); Lee (2004).

8. Moldova ranks top of the list in per capita terms with three ATMs per 1,000 adults as estimated by Oliwia Berdak, 'The Country with the Most ATMs Per Capita? The Contest Re-Opens', *Oliwia Berdak Blog*, 8 January 2014, accessed 1 March 2017, <http://blogs.forrester.com/oliwia_berdak/14-01-08-the_country_with_the_most_ atms_per_capita_the_contest_re_opens>. However, this eminence is less impressive when recalibrated by the size of the urban population. According to the National Bank of Moldova, the country had 982 ATMs at the end of 2013. With an adult population of 2.8 million, its rate of 0.34 ATMs per 1,000 adults was less than Ms Berdak calculated. This remains the figure when one reflects that 57 per cent of the total Moldovan population was living in an urban area at the time. In fact, the result of this adjustment is a ratio of 62 ATMs per 100,000 urban inhabitants—well below many other countries in our sample.

9. See further Gourley (1999); Lozano (1987); Rogers (1976, 1995).

10. Patrick McGee, 'ATM Maker Diebold Wins Vote to Take Over Wincor', *Financial Times*, 24 March 2016, accessed 2 March 2017, <https://www.ft.com/content/ 0b606157-62b5-3886-ad5b-6aa4370e6863>.

11. Joel Lewin, 'UK Watchdog will Probe ATM-Maker Merger', *Financial Times*, 30 August 2016, accessed March 2017, <https://www.ft.com/content/a200cac0- 400d-3209-af14-2832d67b736b>.

12. Deployment data sourced at: Committee on Payment and Settlement Systems, 'Red Book Basle', Bank for International Settlements, accessed 1 March 2017, <http://www.bis.org/cpmi/publ/d112p2.pdf>.

13. Data for India were sourced from: 'Bankwise ATM/POS/CARD Statistics', The Reserve Bank of India, accessed 1 March 2017, <https://rbi.org.in/scripts/atm view.aspx>. On Brazil see: Mona Chalabi, 'Where are the World's Cash Machines?', *The Guardian*, 17 December 2013, accessed 1 March 2017, <https://www.theguardian.com/news/datablog/2013/dec/17/where-are-the-worlds-cash-machines-atms> and the international comparison here: Oliwia Berdak, 'The Country With the Most ATMs Per Capita? The Contest Re-Opens', 8 January 2014, accessed 1 March 2017, <http://blogs.forrester.com/oliwia_berdak/14-01-08-the_country_with_the_most_atms_per_capita_the_contest_re_opens>.

14. Research assistance on the Republic of Korea by Jungsik Son is greatly appreciated. In 1967 only 35 per cent of the South Korean population lived in urban areas. Rapid industrialization resulted in 76 per cent of the country's population living in urban areas in 1992 and 82 per cent in 2014.

15. 'Urban Population', The World Bank, accessed 14 June 2016, <http://data.worldbank.org/indicator/SP.URB.TOTL> and 'Search in Statistical Calculation', Economics Statistics System, accessed 20 May 2017, <http://ecos.bok.or.kr/flex/EasySearch_e.jsp>.

16. The rest of this paragraph draws on the interview (telephone) with Paul Stanley, founder and former managing director of Moneybox, by B. Bátiz-Lazo, 11 December 2007.

17. Ekebrink (1974).

18. Hayashi et al. (2003, 119) define a third-party provider as one not having a principal relation in the banking transaction (between the bank and its customer). A third-party provider might be owned by or be part of a financial institution.

19. Sprague (1977, 29).

20. On the automation of savings banks see Bátiz-Lazo et al. (2014b); Bátiz-Lazo and Maixé-Altés (2011a, 2011b); Maixé-Altés (2012, 2013, 2015).

21. McAndrews (1991, 2).

22. Hayashi et al. (2003, 22).

23. Sienkiewicz (2002, 3).

24. Hayashi et al. (2003, 19).

25. Hayashi et al. (2003, 19).

26. According to Hayashi et al. (2003, 20) transaction volume is taken to include the total number of deposits, withdrawals, transfers, payments, and balance enquiries performed in the network, whether or not these transactions are transmitted through the network data centre. The measure is relevant because interchange fees are usually estimated and paid on the basis of transaction volume.

27. Unless otherwise stated, data in this paragraph were sourced from Group of Experts in Payment Systems, *Payment Systems in Eleven Developed Countries* (Basle: Bank for International Settlements, 1985).

28. 'Electronic Banking: Cash from the Other Fellow's Tap', *The Economist*, 18 September 1982: 94 and 96.

29. 'Electronic Banking: Cash from the Other Fellow's Tap', *The Economist*, 18 September 1982: 94 and 96.

30. Personal communication (email) from Robert Rosenthal, former IBM engineer, with B. Bátiz-Lazo, 3 August 2016.

31. Unless otherwise stated, the remainder of this paragraph borrows freely from the interview (telephone) with Irwin Derman, former Visa executive, by B. Bátiz-Lazo, 6 July 2016.

32. Jeffrey Kutler, 'Visa Reports its ATM Network is Largest Bank-owned System', *American Banker*, vol. 152 (August) 1987: 159.

33. Unless otherwise stated, data in this paragraph draw on Jeffrey Kutler, 'Card Issuers Link ATMs Abroad but in US, Cirrus Still Resists Connection to Plus', *American Banker*, vol. 153 (December), 1988: 243.

34. Michael Weistein and Molly Hooper, 'Plus System to Begin Accepting Cirrus Cards', *American Banker*, 2 May 1985: 3.

35. Unless otherwise stated, the remainder of this paragraph borrows freely from Jeffrey Kutler, 'Card Issuers Link ATMs Abroad But in US, Cirrus Still Resists Connection to Plus', *American Banker*, vol. 153 (December), 1988: 243.

36. Bruce A. Burchfield founded the Cirrus System Inc. in 1982 and built it into a nationwide network of 21,000 automated teller machines with 81 million cardholders in 1988. He resigned as president of Cirrus six months after it was acquired by MasterCard International Inc. (January 1988). Edward Hogan, a consultant to MasterCard oversaw Master Teller, negotiated the Cirrus takeover, and was the acting president of Cirrus from July 1988 until January 1989, when John O. Smith was appointed his permanent successor. See: William Gruber, 'He's Cutting Out After Cutting Back', *Chicago Tribune*, 13 June 1988, accessed 3 August 2016, <http://articles.chicagotribune.com/1988-06-13/business/8801070245_1_products-severance-offer-chicago-board-options-exchange> and Kim Ross, 'Cirrus Approves Duality', *Business Wire*, 27 February 1989.

37. Jeffrey Kutler, 'Card Issuers Link ATMs Abroad but in US, Cirrus Still Resists Connection to Plus', *American Banker*, vol. 153 (December) 1988: 243.

38. Jeffrey Kutler, 'Cirrus Spurns Rival's Proposal to Offer Joint Access to ATMs', *American Banker*, vol. 153 (February) 1988: 33.

39. This paragraph draws on the interview (telephone) with Irwin Derman, former Visa executive, by B. Bátiz-Lazo, 6 July 2016.

40. Unless otherwise stated, the remainder of this paragraph borrows freely from the interview (telephone) with Irwin Derman, former Visa executive, by B. Bátiz-Lazo, 6 July 2016.

41. 'VISA Super centers Now Fully Operational', *PRNewswire*, 24 November 1992, accessed 4 August 2016, <http://www.thefreelibrary.com/VISA+SUPER CENTERS +NOW+FULLY+OPERATIONAL-a012892390>.

42. Bonneau et al. (2012).

43. More so as customers tend to use date-related PINs. See Bonneau et al. (2012).

44. The off-set was stored in the card's magnetic stripe in order to validate the PIN while still providing encryption of the PAN. After the PIN was entered, it was encrypted with a 'PIN key' and then became part of the transaction authorization

request message. This message would be further encrypted with a 'Message Key' before being sent to the central database for authorization. So a PIN transmitted on the network was encrypted twice, each time with different keys. I appreciate the clarification on PIN encoding by Robert Rosenthal. Source: Personal communication (email) from Robert Rosenthal, former IBM engineer, with B. Bátiz-Lazo, London, 2 August 2016.

45. Personal communication (email) from Robert Rosenthal, former IBM engineer, to B. Bátiz-Lazo, 3 August 2016.

46. Steve Hensley, 'Highlights From the "2016 ATM Software Trends and Analysis" Guide', *ATM Marketplace Webinar*, 2 August 2016, <https://www.atmmarketplace.com/whitepapers/live-webinar-2016-atm-and-self-service-software-trends/>.

47. Personal communication (email) from Robert Rosenthal, former IBM engineer, with B. Bátiz-Lazo, 3 August 2016.

48. Interview (telephone) with Irwin Derman, former Visa executive, by B. Bátiz-Lazo, 6 July 2016.

49. This paragraph draws on the interview (telephone) with Irwin Derman, former Visa executive, by B. Bátiz-Lazo, 6 July 2016.

50. Unless otherwise stated, the remainder of this paragraph borrows freely from Richard Waters, 'Visa to Buy Plus ATM Network', *Financial Times*, 3 November 1993: 26.

51. Carbo-Valverde and Rodríguez Fernández (2016).

52. Jeffrey Kutler, 'Eurocheuqe, a Pioneer, Falls to Debit Cards', *The American Banker*, 24 June 1999: 18.

53. See the brief discussion of the Spanish cheque guarantee card in Bátiz-Lazo and Del Angel (2016). For the use of personal cheques in France see Effosse (2017). For personal cheques in the USA see Jaremski and Mathy (2017).

54. Frazer (1985, 39).

55. Richard Browning, 'Historic Inflation Calculator', *MailOnline*, accessed 4 October 2017, <http://www.thisismoney.co.uk/money/bills/article-1633409/Historic-inflation-calculator-value-money-changed-1900.html>.

56. Because of exchange rate regulations, customers of British banks were able to cash personal cheques abroad after 1970.

57. Frazer (1985, 44).

58. Jeffrey Kutler, 'Eurocheuqe, a Pioneer, Falls to Debit Cards', *The American Banker*, 24 June 1999: 18.

59. Personal communication (email) from Micheal Lafferty, Chairman Lafferty Group, with B. Bátiz-Lazo, 30 August 2017.

60. I appreciate Micheal Lafferty's thoughts around these ideas. Personal communication (email) from Micheal Lafferty, Chairman Lafferty Group, with B. Bátiz-Lazo, 30 August 2017.

61. Stefan Krasowski, 'Is Discover the Best Credit Card for China?', *Rapid Travel*, 12 December 2012, accessed 4 October 2017, <http://rapidtravelchai.boardingarea.com/2012/12/28/is-discover-the-best-credit-card-for-china/>; 'For Americans, Discover Card is the Usable in China as Unionpay', *Lonelyplanet*, accessed 4 October 2017, <https://www.lonelyplanet.com/thorntree/forums/asia-north-east-asia/china/for-americans-discover-card-is-the-usable-in-china-as-unionpay>.

62. Don Weinland and Gabriel Wildau, 'China's Fight with Visa and MasterCard Goes Global'. *Financial Times*, 24 April 2017, accessed 4 October 2017, <https://www.ft.com/content/a67350fa-1f6f-11e7-a454-ab04428977f9>.

63. Gabriel Wildau, 'Ant's Alipay Challenges China Unionpay's Dominance', *Financial Times*, 31 July 2016, accessed 5 October 2017, <https://www.ft.com/content/5204bb48-56e4-11e6-9f70-badea1b336d4>.

64. Eric de Putter, Payment Redesign Consulting, ATM Industry Association meeting, Orlando, FL (14 February 2017); Harper and Bátiz-Lazo (2013, 34).

65. Personal communication (email) from Aravinda Korala, CEO KAL ATM Software, with B. Bátiz-Lazo, 21 February 2017.

66. Harper and Bátiz-Lazo (2013, 84).

67. Sarah Mishkin, 'End of Windows XP Support Puts ATMs at Risk', *Financial Times*, 17 March 2014, accessed 18 February 2017, <https://www.ft.com/content/300c8788-abcd-11e3-90af-00144feab7de>.

68. 'ATMIA Position Paper', ATM Industry Association, 1 June 2015, accessed 18 February 2017, <https://www.atmia.com/news/atmia-position-paper-recommending-migration-to-windows-10/2607>.

69. Personal communication (email) from Eric de Putter, Payment Redesign Consulting, with B. Bátiz-Lazo, 21 February 2017.

70. Tom Hutchings, RBR London, ATM & Cyber Security Conference, London, 10 October 2017.

71. This paragraph draws on the interview with Graham Mott, LINK, by B. Bátiz-Lazo and C. Reese, London, 30 July 2008.

72. The distribution of operating systems is quite heterogeneous. In the USA, for instance two-thirds of all operational devices in 2017 were run by Independent ATM Deployers largely using Windows CE. In Brazil approximately 20 per cent of all ATMs are run with Linux, like some banks in India and Bangladesh. But the performance of Linux has been unconvincing and banks are moving away from it. Source: Personal communication (email) with Aravinda Korala, CEO KAL ATM Software, with B. Bátiz-Lazo, 21 February 2017; and personal communication (email) from Eric de Putter, Payment Redesign Consulting, with B. Bátiz-Lazo, 21 February 2017.

73. Hardware requirements to run XP were a 300 MHz/32 bit processor, 128 MB RAM memory, 1.5 GB hard disk, and Super VGA graphics card. Hardware requirements to run Windows 7 were a 1 GHz/32 or 64 bit processor, 1 GB RAM, 16 to 20 GB hard disk, and a MS DirectX 9 graphics device with WDDM driver. Requirements for Windows 10 included 1 GHz 32 or 64 bit processor, processor support (PAE, NX or SSE2), 2 GB RAM, 50 GB hard disk, and a MS DirectX 9 graphics device with WDDM driver. At the time of writing, manufacturers still had to deliver the first Windows 10-compatible devices in 2017. Source: Eric de Putter, Payment Redesign Consulting, ATM Industry Association meeting, Orlando, FL, 14 February 2017.

74. I appreciate the clarification by Tony Gandy on this. Personal communication (email) from Anthony Gandy, independent management consultant, with B. Bátiz-Lazo, 27 March 2017.

75. Tom Hutchings, RBR London, ATM & Cyber Security Conference, London, 10 October 2017.

76. 'Deadline Extended', *NationalLink*, accessed 21 April 2017, <http://www. nationallinkatm.com/deadline-extended-atm-emv-liability-shift/>.

77. On contactless payments and EMV see for instance: 'Swipe and Go', *Daily Mail*, 6 January 2009, accessed 1 March 2017, <http://www.dailymail.co.uk/sciencetech/ article-1106645/Swipe-Bank-launch-contactless-debit-card.html>. On ATM migration to Windows 7 as a response to EMV see: Taylor Armerding, 'Why have Most Merchants Missed the EMV Deadline', *CSO Online*, 8 October 2015, accessed 22 February 2017, <http://www.csoonline.com/article/2990207/data-protection/ why-have-most-merchants-missed-the-emv-deadline.html>. On the slow uptake of EMV in the USA see for instance: Taylor Armerding, 'Why have Most Merchants Missed the EMV Deadline', *CSO Online*, 8 October 2015, accessed 1 March 2017, <http://www.csoonline.com/article/2990207/data-protection/why-have-most- merchants-missed-the-emv-deadline.html>.

78. Tom Hutchings, RBR London, ATM & Cyber Security Conference, London, 10 October 2017.

79. Interview (telephone) with Aravinda Korala, CEO KAL ATM Software, by B. Bátiz-Lazo, 6 October 2015.

80. Interview (telephone), with Aravinda Korala, CEO KAL ATM Software, by B. Bátiz-Lazo, 6 October 2015.

81. Matthew Wall and Mark Ward, 'WannaCry: What Can You Do to Protect Your Business', *BBC News*, 19 May 2017, accessed 20 May 2017, <http://www.bbc.co.uk/ news/business-39947944>.

82. 'WannaCry Ransomware Attack', *Hindustan Times*, 15 May 2017, accessed 20 May 2017, <http://www.hindustantimes.com/india-news/wannacry-ransomware-attack-some- atms-in-india-shut-on-precautionary-ground/story-z287s1PWV5ynod8BVK-wPBM. html>.

83. Personal communication (email) from Michael Lee, CEO ATM Industry Association, with B. Bátiz-Lazo, 19 May 2017.

84. Tom Warren, 'Windows XP Patch to Prevent Massive Randomware Attack', *The Verge*, 13 May 2017, accessed 20 May 2017, <https://www.theverge.com/2017/5/ 13/15635006/microsoft-windows-xp-security-patch-wannacry-ransomware-attack>.

85. 'KAL World Firsts', *KAL ATM Software*, 17 February 2017, accessed 20 May 2017, <http://www.kal.com/en/kal-knowledge/kal-world-firsts>.

86. Tina Orem, 'CU ATMs Safe from WannaCry Hack', *Credit Union Times*, 17 May 2017, accessed 20 May 2017, <http://www.cutimes.com/2017/05/17/cu-atms-safe- from-wannacry-hack-for-now?&slreturn=1495300878>.

87. Tina Orem, 'Beware The New Generation of Card Skimmers', *Credit Union Times*, 16 October 2016, accessed 20 May 2017, <http://www.cutimes.com/2016/10/16/beware- the-new-generation-of-card-skimmers>.

88. Cavell (2003, 1).

89. Latour (2005).

90. Dominic Hirsch, 'RBRs ATM Research Follows the Market to Asia', *Linkedin*, 4 August 2016, accessed 4 August 2016, <https://www.linkedin.com/pulse/rbrs-atm-research-follows-market-asia-dominic-hirsch?trk=hb_ntf_MEGAPHONE_ARTICLE_POST>.

91. Wandhöfer (2010, 2016).

92. SEPA covers all EU member states, as well as Iceland, Liechtenstein, Monaco, Norway, San Marino, and Switzerland. The idea behind SEPA is that all transactions (domestic and cross-border) offer the same conditions of ease, efficiency, and security. The main trigger for SEPA was the Payment Services Directive (PSD) of 2007. The first steps towards SEPA were undertaken in January 2008 when the so-called SEPA Credit Transfers were put in place. This aim was to enable credit transfers to be carried out under the same operative and technical standards and conditions within the EU. This was followed by the launch of the SEPA Direct Debit—also setting homogeneous standards for these transactions—in 2009. A revision of the PSD in July 2013 led to the passing of the Second Directive on Payment Services (PSD2) in October 2015. Source: Carbo-Valverde and Rodríguez Fernández (2016).

93. Interview with John Hughes, CEO LINK, by B. Bátiz-Lazo and C. Reese, London, 11 July 2008.

94. Glaser (1988).

95. Bátiz-Lazo and Reese (2010).

96. This paragraph was sourced from Bátiz-Lazo (2017b).

7

Independent ATM Deployers

7.1 There's a New Kid in Town

This chapter explores the advent of the Independent ATM Deployer (IAD) as illustrated by events in Britain and the USA. The arrival of the IAD came hand-in-hand with the rise of disloyalty fees, charges for withdrawals (also known as 'surcharging'), and the emergence of the low-end ATM. Together these developments suggest the greater contestability of retail finance at the time. The latter was also evident, for instance, in the appearance of a secondary market for ATMs that included refurbishing or reselling old models.

The IADs appeared at a time when competition between proprietary networks had placed ATMs from different banks side by side in the same off-branch locations.[1] This strategy was expensive to maintain, uneconomical as an option for growth, and supported only by either exclusivity deals or the location of the ATMs in places with the most footfall. Reciprocity between financial institutions on the back of shared ATM networks eased some of this pressure, but still left unpopulated many places where bank customers wanted convenient access to cash. Colonizing these sites required significant investment, which financial institutions were reluctant to make. IADs took on the task of populating these and many other spaces, at the same time bringing cash withdrawal services to a host of non-bank branch locations. During this process, the IADs were instrumental in further standardizing and innovating the services at ATMs and also helped to capture greater network effects. More recently, IADs have developed outsourcing services for the management of ATM networks on behalf of financial institutions and retailers. Greater specialization has resulted in IADs becoming more cost-effective operators of ATMs than some banks and credit unions have been.

In brief, this chapter documents the long-term changes in the industrial organization of the ATM industry—an important segment of the global retail payments ecosystem. The discussion begins by recalling the emergence of a community of like-minded people built around the ATM Industry Association

(ATMIA), whose annual conferences and other events created a space to discuss and address the common concerns of banks, IADs, payment consultants, and ATM manufacturers. The story of ATMIA thus enables us to highlight some of the social aspects of this sector that would otherwise remain internal and out of sight. The discussion then steps back to recall and account for the genesis of the IADs at the start of surcharging in the USA. This took place with the emergence of the low-end ATM. We then look at the dynamics of off-branch ATM locations in the USA and the UK. Before concluding, we discuss the political storm that broke in the UK by questioning the morality of ATM surcharges.

7.2 The Formation of an International Community of Practitioners

7.2.1 Thick as Thieves, Hand in Glove

Grand inventions earn glorious references in school textbooks, but it is the diffusion and servicing of a technology that contributes to economic growth, a process that relies on the development of relevant human capital. As discussed in Chapter 9, the advent of the ATM and other forms of automation in retail banking was accompanied by a substantial transformation in the skill set of bank staff, followed by adjustments in the size of the bank workforce. Outside the banking organizations, however, the changing industrial organization of retail finance markets which saw the emergence of the IAD, also witnessed changes in skills and human capital that were quite profound.

As discussed in earlier chapters, the advent of forms of automatic cash distribution, known early on as 'robot cashiers', was an early step in the empowerment of consumers—and in the ability of banks to get customers to shoulder some of the workload of staff at bank tellers (see Chapter 2). This took place in the 1960s and 1970s, a time when relevant markets in the background for designing, installing, and servicing cash machines were rather 'thin' in Europe and North America, and probably non-existent elsewhere.[2] Here 'relevant markets' means trading activity and the knowledge behind computers, advanced electronics, cryptography and other specialized engineering, actuarial, mathematical, and banking skills needed to keep the machines and ATM networks operational (see Chapters 3 and 4). In this context, 'thin' means very limited in the number of specialists and specialist vendors.

By the 1980s and 1990s, however, the markets for these same skills and knowledge were much 'thicker', leading to a shift towards the deployment of retail payment technologies in looser, inter-firm networks, such as cross-border shared ATM networks. This 'thickness' was also evident around the growth in the numbers of people staffing an increased population of IADs in

North America and Europe (see Chapter 5 and this chapter). The increasing 'thickness' of markets is generally regarded as one reason why firms may wish to disintegrate vertically and adopt other models for coordinating production.[3] Thick markets make firms less susceptible to the so-called 'hold up' problem.[4] Moreover, regulatory changes plus the falling costs of the relevant technology allow firms with less capital and fewer liquid resources to begin participating in the market, in this case, the processes for automated cash withdrawals and other self-services through ATMs.

7.2.2 Common Language and Signposting

The emergence of the IAD can thus help us trace how communities of practitioners, working inside and outside the financial institutions, developed a common understanding about the fine details of cash distribution and other services through ATMs. These communities can be identified by the specific threats they faced and a unifying set of knowledge manifested through common terminology, the acceptance of certain conventions and standards, and a common understanding of the ways to undertake particular activities (that can increase productivity).[5] This is important because a unifying set of skills, a specific language, understanding, and knowledge make possible a more advanced division of labour.

The formation and activities of the ATM Industry Association (ATMIA) is a good example of a community of practitioners that formed around IADs in particular and automated cash withdrawal in general. This community, as noted above, transgressed the boundary of the banking firm. The emergence of this shibboleth was somewhat slow, however. The chief reason for a dilated development was that the adoption of ATMs, as well as the computer equipment and software applications that supported them, followed variable rates of penetration at individual banks and across countries. It was also the case that only a few countries had implemented the regulatory changes that enabled non-financial participants to enter retail financial markets.

By 2016, ATMIA had 6,278 individual members across the world.[6] The biggest individual membership groups were ATM hardware vendors (2,876 members, 46 per cent of the total), IADs (1,140 members, 18 per cent), ATM software vendors (473 members, 8 per cent), and banks (324 members, 5 per cent); with 21 other categories (1,465 members, 23 per cent) accounting for the remaining of a very diverse membership. Table 7.1 summarizes key moments in the formation of this community.

The roots of the ATM industry body can be traced to the mid-1980s. By this time, a handful of annual tradeshows had been held, bringing together bankers and ATM manufacturers.[7] Firm evidence has yet to ascertain the first of these trade shows, its exact nature and composition. Nevertheless, these

Table 7.1. Milestones in the development and establishment of the ATM Industry Association, 1997–2017

Year	Milestone
1997	Established as a not-for-profit trade association in the USA, initially as the ATM Operators Association, by Tom Harper in the wake of the liberalization of surcharging, which led to the growth of independent ATM operators (IADs), then known as ISOs (independent sales organizations); ATMOA launches ATM insurance programme and changes name to ATMIA.
1999	First 'ATMs in Europe' conference launched by SMI co-chaired by Tom Harper and organized by Michael Lee, SMI's Market Research Manager.
2000	US chapter grows to just under 90 members. London-based ATMIA Europe launched by Michael Lee.
2001	The first annual ATM Security conference.
2002	ATMIA begins expanding its range of products and services, including advocacy, and establishes new chapters in Canada, Australia, and Hong Kong.
2003	ATMIA establishes the Global ATM Security Alliance (GASA), later renamed the ATM Security Forum, to draft international best practices for the ATM lifecycle and to issue fraud alerts.
2008	ATM Cash Council established to present a picture of global cash demand in response to the anti-cash campaigns of global card associations.
2010	ATMIA Consulting and Training practice as a vehicle for independent consultants in the ATM and retail payments space.
2012	Chapters and conferences in Latin America, the Middle East, and India.
2015	ATMIA changes its logo in an international rebranding exercise.
2016	Global membership reaches 6,000 in 66 countries.
2017	ATMIA celebrates its 20th anniversary, while commemorating the 50th ATM anniversary.

Source: Own design, based on Harper and Bátiz-Lazo (2013) and *ATM Marketplace*.

gatherings were still regularly held a decade later. But this time they took place in the context of the liberalization of retail banking markets in the USA and, of particular importance, under the cloud of the surcharging ban now being enforced (see section 7.3). By the mid-1990s, therefore, ATM industry shows were common and well enough attended to spark off the idea of an industry body.[8]

In tandem, Tom Harper had teamed up with his father-in-law, Alan Fryrear, to produce a printed catalogue of spare parts on sale for ATMs. These were also the early days of the commercial Internet. Soon after, the catalogue became *ATM Marketplace*, an online-only outlet which grew into the most authoritative news source for the industry. After attending Faulkner & Gray's Advanced ATM Conference in San Diego, CA, Harper and Fryrear led a group of like-minded people to establish the 'ATM Owners' Association' (ATMOA) in late 1997 as a for-profit organization, with no staff (except Harper), a zero budget, and only a handful of members.

The first official ATMOA planning meeting took place on 9 October 1998.[9] The group voted in Lyle Elias as the new president, ratified a motion to change their name to the 'ATM Industry Association', and formed several committees. They also talked about launching their own conference to compete with the one they had attended in San Diego. At this time, what members wanted most was insurance. Their machines were under intense physical attack—thieves were breaking into machines, threatening cash handlers, stealing hardware. And with so many ATMs around, heavily involved deployers faced more risk of catastrophic loss from natural disasters every day. In collaboration with Mark Coons of American Special Risk, Charlotte, NC, ATMIA's International ATM insurance programme was born. During the next few years, the cash flow from the premiums enabled ATMIA to take off.

In 2000, Michael (Mike) Lee joined ATMIA as their European executive director. By then, ATMIA had up to 100 members, all in the USA, and only one member benefit scheme—the ATM insurance programme.[10] Within a year, Lee generated enough revenue in Europe through memberships, sponsorships, and conferences to cover the chapter's operating expenses. In 2001, Lee initiated an international design contest to create a graphic that would be instantly recognizable worldwide as 'ATM here', regardless of the local language or culture. The winner of this competition was Andy Kitt, formerly of the NCR Corporation. His design is depicted in Figure 7.1 and became the 'Official Global Pictogram' for the ATM.[11] The design was registered as an international public sign in 2007 (ISO 7001: PI CF 005).

Progress in bringing industry participants together resulted in the *The New York Times* nominating ATMIA as 'the leading trade group' in the global cash distribution industry in 2003.[12] In the following year, 2004, Lee was named chief executive officer and board member in recognition of his work in expanding membership, founding the Global ATM Security Alliance, and steering the association to a healthy level of profitability. To articulate the expansion of ATMIA's conference division, Dana Benson was appointed Director of Conferences in 2000. Together Benson and Lee took ATMIA's

Figure 7.1. Official global pictogram for the ATM, 2001
(Registered as international public sign in 2007)
Source: Courtesy of ATM Industry Association.

conferences beyond North America to cover Africa, Asia, Australasia, and Europe. In 2003, also, Sharon Lane was appointed Global Finance and Membership Services Director. She promoted the growth in the association's membership, which in 2016 reached over 6,000 individuals worldwide and organizations in 66 countries.

7.2.3 Pursuing Common Interests

As many other industry bodies past and present have done, ATMIA became active in different forums to represent the interests of its membership. For instance, it became a vocal advocate of the fundamental right to choose the best payment method for on-the-spot transactions.[13] In this regard, ATMIA represented its membership before financial authorities and regulators across the world to recommend a series of drastic actions to take when financial security and freedom of choice are threatened.[14] In Sweden, for example, ATMIA Europe fought for greater choice of ways to pay, including the use of cash—efforts which encompassed position papers on the economics of using banknotes and coins. This action helped persuade the Swedish central bank to support the mandate on banks to provide cash services for population groups which worked and lived in a cash economy, particularly those in the lower income bracket and other vulnerable consumers (see also Chapter 8).[15]

ATMIA and its members also approached legislators directly, for example, to encourage them to rein in anti-competitive actions. In the United States, for instance, ATMIA and the Electronic Funds Transfer Association (EFTA) worked with Congressman Blaine Luetkemeyer (Republican, MO) to counteract the negative business and economic impacts of the so-called 'Operation Choke Point', through which financial institutions were limiting access to banking services for otherwise *bona fide* business organizations.[16]

In summary, over its first twenty years ATMIA grew across the world and throughout different constituencies, developed a full range of products and services (including industry best practice manuals, regulatory monitoring and advocacy, international conferences, webinars, certified online training, endorsed consultancy practice, etc.), and in collaboration with Accenture, introduced a global ATM benchmarking service.[17] The emergence and coming of age of ATMIA also points to a growing international community of practitioners, as illustrated by the pictorial sign in Figure 7.1 and the growth and regularity of its annual conferences. Here the growth and diversity of its membership base should be emphasized; this included not only IADs, but ATM manufacturers, software vendors, security specialists, card companies, and the biggest retail banks in the world, from all five continents. In this, ATMIA and its membership were truly representative of all sectors within the industry.

As will be evident in the remainder of this chapter, however, ATMIA and its membership were also united through a common language, exemplified by unique terms such as 'pay to use' and 'free to use' ATMs, 'up time', 'availability', 'merchant replenishment', 'low-end ATM', and other usages, to which the discussion now turns in discussing the emergence and growth of the IAD.

7.3 The Surcharging Ban Sunset in the USA

The event that sparked the birth of IADs is known in the vernacular as the 'end of the surcharging ban'. Up to the mid-1990s, national ATM networks in the USA took advantage of their pre-eminent position to operate and enforce an agreement under which disloyalty or withdrawal charges for ATM use was forbidden. However, a successful legal challenge to this ban forced the networks to change their rules and, in April 1996, the two largest networks, Cirrus and Plus, allowed ATM owners to charge a fee when a customer withdrew cash (i.e. a surcharge). The move was followed by nearly all the regional networks and by 1998 most of the ATMs in the USA surcharged.[18]

According to one estimate, in 1999 the average surcharge was $1.22 at ATMs served by the ten largest networks, with Arkansas bearing the highest average surcharge at $3.05 and Iowa the lowest at $1.16 per transaction. A survey by PSI Global of Tampa Bay, FL in the spring of 1999 reported that only 15 per cent of respondents had limited their use of ATMs due to surcharging, 40 per cent of respondents avoided fees by using their own financial institution's ATMs, while only 11 per cent used ATMs that did not surcharge.[19] The survey results thus suggested that surcharge fees did not deter consumers from using ATMs and the introduction of surcharging resulted in relatively small cost to both ATM networks and member banks in the form of lost customers.

Surcharging had a positive effect on the stock and availability of ATMs, providing evidence that surcharging might in fact have increased customer access and convenience. Indeed, between 1996 and 1997 the number of ATMs in the USA increased 18.5 per cent, the fastest growth rate in fifteen years.[20] Specifically, ATMs installed in the USA went from 123,000 in 1995 to 165,000 in 1997 'with a forecast that the number of ATMs could reach 220,000 by the year 2000'.[21] Large depositary institutions such as Bank of America and Banc One led the pack with 7,500 and 7,350 units deployed, respectively. Each aimed to have between 9,000 and 10,000 ATM terminals in service within the following two years.

These numbers confirm that, from their inception until the early 1990s, ATMs in the USA were owned and operated by financial institutions. But although they were the dominant player, banks alone did not account for all new ATMs in the USA following the end of the surcharge ban. A substantial proportion of growth in the stock of ATMs during the late 1990s and early 2000s resulted from their deployment by IADs.[22] IADs were primarily responsible for the significant increase in the number of machines located in off-branch premises, an expansion that was largely financed by the fee income gained from surcharging. Indeed, additional fee income could amount to significant earnings for ATM owners, given that approximately 1,700 interchange transactions took place at an average ATM every month in the USA at this time, while ATM transaction volume rose steadily every year from 9.7 billion in 1995 to over 12 billion in 1997.

By 2003 more than 88 per cent of ATMs in the USA were 'pay to use' for users whose access cards were not associated with the ATM's owner, a practice that had virtually been unheard of ten years before. As shown in Table 7.2, surcharging was not the only type of fee paid by banks or their customers in shared ATM networks.[23]

The categories in Table 7.2 aim to illustrate how ATM services entail two types of fee: wholesale fees, which are paid by banks to other banks or the network administrator; and retail fees, which are paid by the people making the transaction (i.e. the customer) to their bank or the ATM owner. The exact

Table 7.2. Types of fee paid in ATM networks by depository institutions and their customers

Category	Frequency	Fee	Set by	Description
Retail	Periodic	Annual	Cardholder bank	Paid by cardholder to his/her bank for ATM services.
		Card	Cardholder bank	Paid by cardholder to his/her bank upon issuance of ATM card.
	Per Transaction	Foreign	Cardholder bank	Paid by cardholder to bank for a withdrawal made on an ATM not owned by the cardholder's bank.
		Surcharge	ATM owner	Paid by the cardholder to the ATM owner. Typically not charged if the owner is the cardholder's bank.
		On-us	Cardholder bank	Paid by the cardholder for a withdrawal on an ATM owned by the cardholder's bank.
Wholesale	Periodic	Membership	Network	Paid by new members upon joining the network.
		Monthly/ Annually	Network	Paid periodically by members. Usually tied to the sales volume of the card programme.
	Per Transaction	Switch	Network	Paid by cardholder's bank to network for routing transaction information.
		Interchange	Network	Paid by cardholder's bank to ATM owner for deploying and maintaining the network.

Source: Own design, based on Hayashi et al. (2003).

175

nature and amount of the fee paid by the customers is contingent on the agreement between the terms of service of the customer's bank as well as that between the bank and the network switching the transaction (see Chapters 5 and 6). For instance, in the wholesale market, the ATM acquirer charged the card issuer for the withdrawal. Acquirer and issuer were mainly banks, while the issuer bank might or might not have passed on the charge to the cardholder.

Interchange fees emerged as a way for shared ATM networks to allocate the cost of operating the switch between the banks which were members of the network. The introduction of surcharging on the retail side of the transaction meant that the ATM owner charged the cardholder directly (in some instances the interchange fee plus a disloyalty penalty imposed by the issuer). This had the additional effect of transforming the cash withdrawal transaction from a complementary service of a current account to one which resembled any other within a retail business space, where the provider of the service charges the recipient directly, at the time, and in the exact place where the service is provided.

The result of the twilight of the surcharge ban combined with the dawn of national ATM networks was to unleash the demand for reasonably-priced, off-premises ATM locations. But to satisfy that demand required affordable devices. However, banks had a hold on ATM manufacturing because the machines had been designed to suit the self-service needs of large and medium-sized financial institutions. This made the ATMs bulky (especially the early models), heavy and unbalanced (the top stored an increasing number of components), and very dangerous to move (as engineers found through the cycles of replacement).[24] All this ignored the space and self-service needs of small businesses and small financial institutions. A host of new manufacturers then appeared to fill the low-end transaction vacuum.

7.4 About the Low-End ATM

Units in the low-end ATM market segment (also known as the stand-alone, walk-up ATM) originated as cash-only dispensers. They were quite simple compared to the machines in bank branches, which accepted deposits and performed sophisticated self-service functions. As depicted in Figure 7.2, the low-end machine emerged as a versatile stand-alone device designed for installation in many different types of location (provided it could be plugged into electricity and communication lines). Another characteristic was being bolted to the floor of the site, rather than being built into a facility such as a drive-through lane or the wall of a bank. To cut costs, the low-end ATM typically incorporated more plastic in the outer structure, but the internal vault and security devices provided a high level of safety for the banknotes inside.

Figure 7.2. Triton 9500, circa 1995
Source: Courtesy of Triton Inc.

The pioneer of the low-end ATM was Triton Systems Inc., Long Beach, MS. It was known in the industry as one of the 'Three T's', together with Tranax Technologies and Tidel Technologies. Triton was established in 1979 by Frank Wilhem, formerly of Texas Instruments and NASA's Stennis Space Center, jointly with Ernest Burdette and Robert Sandoz.[25] Wilhem and his friends grew their $1,500 cash investment into a $100 million company with 400 employees. At one point it was the largest manufacturer of ATMs in the world but in 2012 it ranked fourth. By this date, Triton had shipped 100,000 units around the world, rising to more than 200,000 by 2011. The company won the Inc. 500 award three years in a row, rating as high as 30th out of 500. Triton was sold to Dover Industries in March 2000.

Originally Wilhem and his partners launched Triton to develop and manufacture sophisticated electronic systems by working closely with customers such as General Electric, Exxon, Magnavox and the US Navy. Triton diversified its product line in 1984 when its bank expressed an interest in a device for training customers on the use of the ATM. In response, Triton developed the 'ATM Jr' (see Figure 7.3), the world's first battery-powered portable device for

Figure 7.3. ATM Jr, circa 1984
Source: Courtesy of Triton Inc.

training consumers to use ATMs. In 1994, Triton began shipping the 9500, its first low-end, stand-alone, cash-only-dispensing ATM (see Figure 7.2).

Tranax entered the US market in 1998 as a distribution channel for Hyosung Computer, the South Korean manufacturer. Now called Nautilus Hyosung, the company supplied components for Tranax ATMs, which were assembled by Tranax in Fremont, CA. Nautilus Hyosung developed cash-dispensing ATMs for banks in 1993 and full-function ATMs in 1994, while launching its retail-line, low-end ATMs in 1997. It began exporting ATMs to the USA through Tranax the following year. South Korean manufacturer Hantle bought Tranax in 2008 and in 2010 Tranax changed its name to Hantle USA to reflect the change in ownership.

In 1992, Tidel Engineering, a subsidiary of Tidel Technologies based in Carrollton, TX, pioneered dial-up ATM technology with the 'AnyCard' machine. Then in the late 1990s, Tidel launched the 'Chameleon', one of the first Internet-capable ATMs designed for additional functions, such as buying airline tickets and booking hotel rooms. By 2000, according to the Nilson Report, Tidel was fifth in the ranking of ATM manufacturers in the world, shipping 13,523 units that year.[26] Tidel ended the fiscal year 2000 with a net income of $9.2 million or a 212.3 per cent increase over 1999 while its stock value peaked at $12.50 before the year ended.

In 2001, however, the Credit Card Center, a large independent sales organization (ISO) and Tidel's biggest customer, was declared bankrupt. This exposed Tidel's reliance on the ISOs. The downfall of the Credit Card Center forced Tidel to write off $25 million in 2001, and eventually led the company to borrow \$6.7 million from Laurus Master Fund Ltd.—a debt that increased by nearly \$2 million because Tidel could not meet its loan payment obligations. Tidel then faced financial ruin. After years struggling to pull itself from the depths of the debt incurred after the Credit Card Center debacle, NCR purchased Tidel Engineering's ATM assets for \$10 million in 2006.[27] Soon the Tidel name disappeared from the ATM marketplace, although many of the company's machines remained in service long after.

Well-established manufacturers also entered the low-end segment—but they found it hard to penetrate building organically. For instance, in 1998, NCR collaborated with TBS First Inc. to assemble 'The Cash', a dial-up cash dispenser designed to offer a look and feel that users would perceive as dissimilar to the devices in large financial institutions. This arrangement ended in 1999, when NCR introduced a low-end ATM designed in conjunction with WRG Services Inc. of Willoughby, OH. However, NCR developed a significant presence in the low-end segment only after it acquired Tidel in 2006 and rolled its assets into an independent operating company called NCR EasyPoint ATM. This subsidiary integrated NCR's own EasyPoint product line with Tidel's 3000 series.[28]

In short, Triton was the first to market a low-end, off-premises ATM. This segment grew as 'the Three T's' moved to the top of the manufacturing ranking. This growth testified further to the popularity of off-branch ATMs. Several other makers of low-end ATMs have come and gone over the years. More recently manufacturers have sprung up in China, South Korea, and India, each delivering machines for other brands in addition to their own as well as building devices to serve their unique dynamic markets.

7.5 Off-Premise ATM: From ISO to IAD

7.5.1 *A Brief Overview of the Economics of Off-Branch Locations*

In 1997, Triton launched the 9600 series ATM, which quickly became known as the industry workhorse for the off-premises market. Grocery and convenience stores were among the first locations to benefit from installing these on-premises ATMs. As illustrated in Figure 7.4, supermarkets had seen cash dispensers on their premises since at least the mid-1970s. Figure 7.4 captures the pioneering mood in 1975 of Dahl's Foods of Des Moines, IA, the first supermarket to install an ATM in its stores.[29] This installation was possible thanks to Iowa's early readiness to share an ATM network. But Dahl itself was exceptional. Very few other supermarkets owned ATMs and hardly any banks had operated these devices in a supermarket court before 1985.[30] But what explains the dearth of off-premise devices? On the one hand, before the growth of shared networks, there were no in-lobby ATMs that would meet

Figure 7.4. Early use of an ATM at Dahl's Foods supermarket, circa 1975
Source: Courtesy of Diebold-Wincor Inc.

federal guidelines for off-premise installation.[31] On the other, deploying non-bank and off-premise ATMs in large numbers before the end of the surcharge ban was considered unprofitable.

The position in the late 1990s, however, was different. As mentioned, the trend to deploy off-bank premise ATMs originally started in both supermarket chains and small convenience stores. Reasons for this growth and why small stores could be interested include, first, that owners believed that people were more likely to return and visit frequently once they found a store where they could not only purchase food and soft drinks but also get cash.[32] Research by the Tower Group in 2000 for the USA and independently by NCR in 2003 for the UK, respectively estimated that as much as 20 per cent of the cash withdrawn at a store machine would be spent in the host store, with the average withdrawal amounting to $40 and £45.[33]

Second, retailers could use ATMs to save on operating expenses. For example, about three-quarters of all supermarkets in the late 1990s sold postage stamps, typically with no mark-up.[34] This customer service was delivered entirely at cost and generated no direct income. However, an ATM could offer the same service and amass revenue for the store. Third, the store owner generated income not only from the customers' purchases but also from lease payments of the cash machine or from a share of the revenue from the interchange or surcharge fee.[35]

By one calculation almost 22,000 or 85 per cent of the almost 26,000 devices installed in 1997 were in non-bank sites. By the early 2000s, approximately half of all global ATMs were located away from a bank branch, with 67 per cent of ATMs in the USA found off-premises.[36] RBR London estimated that by the end of 2007, approximately 808,000 devices or slightly fewer than half the ATMs worldwide were not at a bank branch.[37] The expansion in the off-premise market began as the revenue stream from surcharges created the economic incentive to develop an independent ATM-deployment industry.

7.5.2 The Dawn of the Planet of the IADs

Originally known as Independent Sales Organizations (ISOs), they were designed to provide and in some cases maintain card-processing devices to independent retailers, small businesses, and small banks. They also acquired payment card receipts on behalf of small merchants, who were often not serviced by bank acquirers. However, the emergence of the low-end ATM, the proliferation of interconnections between the processing networks, and the ability to surcharge created incentives for ISOs to diversify. The lines between ISO activities blurred as they began to process card payment transactions on behalf of their clients. They also began to own and lease ATMs and point of sale terminals and maintain and restock cash and materials or contract with others for these activities.[38]

The term 'Independent ATM Deployer' (IAD) was then used to denote institutions which, like banks, could provide ATM operating services. Some IADs went as far as developing their own manufacturing capabilities, packaging off-the-shelf components into machines to serve specific markets. For instance, Midwest Bancard Corp. began to manufacture a cost-effective, through-the-wall ATM designed to be accessed from the rear for cheque-cashing stores. Hence some IADs owned ATMs, leased them to others, sold ATMs outright, and also operated their own fleets of ATMs.

The IAD interacted with merchants in designing operating strategies. These included detailing such issues as ownership, compliance with operating regulations, maintenance (including technical servicing, supplies, insurance, and cash management), operations management, insurance, monitoring, security, and signage and advertising materials.[39] During negotiations the IAD and its client specified the placement and location terms of the devices, staff training, the sharing of compensation, and type of connection. Some ATM networks required IADs to be sponsored by a financial institution already in the network. In other instances, IADs were members of the ATM network in their own right and acted as representatives of their clients.

The range of ISO/IAD activities has been quite diverse. For instance, EDS, headquartered in Plano, TX, was the first payment processor to expand into providing ATM network services after its acquisition of the MPACT network in the late 1980s. EDS continued to expand and purchased at least six other ATM networks, such as TX, ACCEL/Exchange, and Exchange International.[40] Another sign of consolidation and enlarged operational scope in this part of the industry was the move of electronic processing firm eFunds Corp., Scottsdale, AZ, into the ISO/IAD business through its acquisition of Access Cash in 2001. This was followed by the acquisition of Hanco Systems, the Samsar ATM Company, and Evergreen Teller. As a result, eFunds in 2006 became one of the largest IADs in North America with 12,000 ATMs. More recently following a strategy of acquisitions, Cardtronics of Houston, TX became one of the largest players in the industry with a fleet of over 230,000 ATMs in 2017 (16,812 of which were located in the UK) which dwarfed the 12,000 or so machines at a large US bank or 7,812 devices in the ATM fleet of the Royal Bank of Scotland in the UK.[41]

In short, the rapid growth of off-premises ATMs went hand-in-hand with the expansion of IADs because they could provide ATM-operating and payment processing services more cheaply than financial institutions could. In many instances, these services were provided on behalf of a bank or credit union with the IAD owning and managing the ATMs but branding them as if owned and managed by the financial institution. The importance of the IADs for the industry is self-evident: in 1998, they owned or had under contract 9 per cent of the ATMs in the USA. By 2006 their share had increased to 17 per cent. This growth initially helped to dilute the concentration of ATM ownership. However, a wave of amalgamations within the IAD and third-party processor industries resulted in banks and IADs owning over half of the ATMs in the USA in 2017. But even though banks had only 40 per cent of the machines, they had over 70 per cent of the volume of transactions.

The concentration of ownership within IADs showed that expanded scope and ownership concentration were not limited to shared ATM network services. At the same time, the concentration of ATM ownership worried leaders of small depository institutions, such as credit unions, lest their members fled to other financial institutions that offered a large network of ATMs where consumers could get surcharge-free cash.[42] These fears, however, failed to materialize and credit unions engaged in 'selective surcharging' alliances with IADs.[43]

7.6 Return to the Planet of the IADs

7.6.1 *Brummie and Home-County Roots*

The very first off-bank site ATM to collect a convenience fee in the UK was operational in December 1998 in a franchised store of the Dutch multi-national company Spar, located on the outskirts of Birmingham. The ATM was installed and managed by the British subsidiary of Euronet Worldwide.[44] At the time, the subsidiary was under the general management of Harry Smart. But following a management buyout in 2003, this subsidiary was renamed Bank Machine.

When a BBC correspondent interviewed customers at that very first off-bank branch, surcharging ATM, he found they did not object to the £1 fee: 'a bus ticket to the nearest alternative would have cost more', he reported.[45] Within a couple of years TRM, Moneybox, and Hanco ATM Operating Systems (Hanco) had all joined Euronet to do business in the UK. Others such as CashCard, CardPoint, Securicor, and Infocash would soon follow, thanks to the implementation of the recommendations prepared for H.M. Treasury in the Cruikshank Report of March 2000.

At the time, it was felt that the limited competition for locations by banks and building societies had resulted in the available ATMs clustering together. Terry Turner, co-founder of Hanco in the UK and early Triton distributor in Britain, recalled the 1980s and 1990s, days when ATMs were linked to only one of three national processing networks. 'If you wanted to cover all card-holders, you had to have three ATMs [in each location], which meant you could only put them in train stations or big supermarkets,' he said, 'or [customers] had to go along to your bank branch.'[46] This situation helped to explain why there were only around 6,000 off-bank premises ATMs or approximately 25 per cent of the 24,728 in operation in 1998.[47]

Industry pioneers such as Euronet/Bank Machine and Moneybox were sponsored by the Woolwich, one of the bigger building societies, which demutualized and converted into a bank in 1997. The Woolwich had secured a contract to populate Post Office retail branches with ATMs and entered into a contract with Euronet/Bank Machine to install 'pay to use' ATMs in low foot traffic Post Office branches where 'free to use' Woolwich ATMs would be uneconomical.[48] But the Woolwich was then acquired by Barclays Bank and did not carry out the installations at the Post Office.[49] Euronet/Bank Machine, however, entered into a direct contract with the Post Office and deployed a significant number of full-service NCR ATMs in Post Office branches between 1998 and 2004. The supply of banknotes for these ATMs was possible through a deal with Alliance & Leicester, another demutualized building society, which provided cash for 'hire' to many organizations; that is, the recipient paid a fee for the service plus an interest charge for borrowing the money.[50]

As IADs entered the market there was a feeling that there were large 'deserts' or areas not already serviced by either a branch or a bank-owned ATM. Incumbents, particularly NatWest, were already at top tier sites such as big airports, the busiest railway stations, and big supermarkets. But most banks were reluctant to make a major commitment to off-branch sites. This resulted in a high degree of frustration within the British retail community at the turn of the millennium, and opened the door for the likes of Euronet/Bank Machine and Moneybox to make plans for installing a combined total of 1,200 ATMs between 2001 and 2002.[51] In fact, the expectation at the time was that IADs could deploy up to 35,000 new ATMs in the UK by populating unattended locations such as medium-sized and small railway stations, shopping malls, independent convenience stores, petrol stations, cinemas, other retailers, and even military bases.[52]

The acquisition of the Woolwich by Barclays, however, could dampen IAD's plans. The bank was not interested in fulfilling the commitment with the Post Office nor in sponsoring IADs.[53] Barclays' attitude threatened the viability of the emerging industry because none of the other thirty-two members of LINK at the time was willing to sponsor IADs. But a change of rules in 2001 allowed Euronet/Bank Machine and other IADs to become members of the LINK network in their own right.[54]

When LINK opened to new entrants there was a rush to colonize untapped locations. But the *quid pro quo* for opening LINK to the IADs was that they could either receive the interchange fee or the surcharge (the amount of which had to be clearly displayed on the ATM screen before the withdrawal took place), but could not receive both interchange fee and surcharge at the same time for the same transaction.[55] The same applied to financial institutions such as Halifax, Woolwich, HSBC, and NatWest, which received large sums in disloyalty fees when their own customers used other banks' cash machines—as much as £65 million a year for the Halifax and £37 million for HSBC.[56]

There were indeed many opportunities for new deployment. But since many new entrants tried to seize the best sites, there was also the possibility that the price of those prime locations would rise. It was also unrealistic and indeed unfeasible to expect that ATMs would pop up in each and every shop or fast-food restaurant. Moreover, the model under which IAD-owned or managed ATMs would be replenished by a security company (known in the industry as cash in transit or CIT) required over 300 transactions per month to break even. During an interview in 2004, Ron Delnevo, then managing director of Bank Machine, said: 'At this moment in time, I don't think many retailers want to spend thousands of pounds buying [an ATM], thinking it will only do a few hundred transactions a month.'[57]

The intervention of Hanco, however, somewhat changed the competitive dynamics of the market. Some IADs had already offered 'merchant replenished' ATMs in the UK but Hanco was the one to popularize this business model. Originally established in Atlanta, GA, by Tom Hannon, Hanco was one of the pioneers of the off-premises ATM industry in the USA.[58] Hannon exported its otherwise successful business model to build around the deployment of low-end, merchant replenished ATMs in Britain.

Turner remembered the early days of Hanco as they established the company headquarters in Milton Keynes.[59] He described how they started trading in July 2000 after investing about half a million pounds, most of which went into legal fees, plus securing £1.5 million pounds' worth of leasing. He stated that by that point in time the £1 surcharge had become the standard in the industry and on that basis they estimated the break-even point at 300 transactions per month per machine. As a result, they recruited independent sales agents with the task of placing machines into independent retailers. In recalling Hanco's success, he said: 'In no time, we were averaging 450 transactions per month per machine. All of our customers were very happy.'[60]

Turner also recalled that they could buy Triton ATMs at £3,000 and sell them to retail merchants for £7,000 per device.[61] In the early days of off-premises ATMs, the company would hope to sell five or six ATMs a day. 'There was no one really selling Tritons in the United Kingdom, and Triton had no presence here at all really, so we had to do it from scratch anyway,' Turner said.[62] Learning from its experience in the USA, alongside the salesforce Hanco invested in a 24-hour/seven-day-a-week help desk for its merchant customers, with engineers who travelled throughout the UK helping customers with problems.

Hanco and later some other American, Canadian, and British IADs largely replicated the business model developed in North America, where low-end ATMs were sold or leased to retailers on the basis of potential increases in foot traffic that would, in turn, increase the sales and profitability of their existing business. Restocking an ATM with banknotes from its own cash register was attractive to small merchants because it offered an alternative to banking the cash. Hanco and other IADs also argued that merchant replenished IADs would benefit end-customers as it was positioned to significantly increase the availability of the ATM; while for the IAD, merchant replenishment could reduce the ATM operating costs by up to 75 per cent, primarily by eliminating the need for a cash in transit solution and the costs associated with 'hiring' the cash.[63]

But the model of a merchant replenished ATM purchase also had its downside. On the one hand, the replenishment providers sometimes seemed more interested in making a profit on the sale and installation of ATMs than on the actual continuing business of servicing and keeping transaction volume high. Moreover, the notion that merchant replenished ATMs increased availability (also known as 'up time') failed to materialize. It fact, some IADs reported that merchants failed to replenish and those ATMs were often unable to dispense cash for long periods of time, sometimes days.[64] It was also evident that their vision of being in every shop was too optimistic to be true.

At the same time, there was criticism that ATM replenishment was open to money laundering. There were also rumours that ATM replenishing facilitated the distribution of counterfeit banknotes. Quantifying the potential for either was hard as there were no objective data, and the evidence adduced was mostly anecdotal.[65]

However, in the near future, the use of cash recycling ATMs will easily answer these concerns, for merchants and their customers will both be able to feed their cash into recycling ATMs, which are also fitted with the technology to identify counterfeit banknotes. Recycling ATMs provide an effective barrier to potential counterfeiting, and because they are fed banknotes through the door that also dispenses the cash, they relieve the merchant from having to open the machine (which, in turn, may reduce the risk of tampering or the merchant's accidentally damaging the components).

7.6.2 Performance of Alternative Business Models

Figure 7.5 illustrates the growth of IADs in the provision of cash distribution in the UK. In Figure 7.5 the number of devices deployed by IADs is shown to have increased from 200 in 1999 to 3,898 in 2000, suggesting that overnight the IADs occupied 12 per cent of the total stock in the UK. The reason for this steep start was that, as mentioned, the IADs had initially been sponsored under LINK and were thus effectively invisible to the ATM network—because the transactions were seen as coming from the sponsor.[66]

Figure 7.5 illustrates the number of devices under third-party control which grew much faster than those of the banks and building societies. In 2003 there were 14,436 devices or 31 per cent of the total owned or managed by IADs; 34,788 (43 per cent) in 2006; and 39,781 (57 per cent) in 2016. In other words, the number of machines owned or managed by IADs grew almost ten times between 2003 and 2016. Ron Delnevo, managing director of Bank Machine,

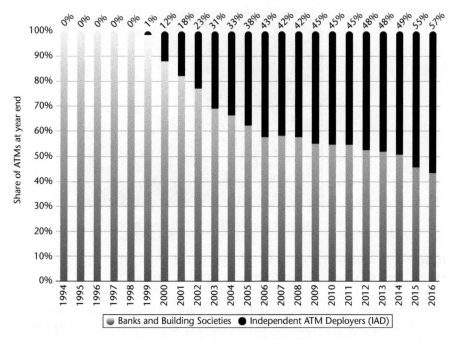

Figure 7.5. Share of ATMs in operation at year end owned or managed by incumbents and new participants in British retail finance, 1994–2016

Source: Author's own estimates, based on data from LINK, Payments Council and Statista.

the company that pioneered the move of IADs into operating 'free to use' ATMs, recalled fond memories of those years:

> [After the management buyout in 2003] we grew that business organically for the next nine years, and every single year we had double digit revenue growth largely through the installation of 'free to use' ATMs. We often took sites over from banks and increased transaction numbers by 10 per cent through superior operating standards.[67]

Meanwhile, devices in banks and building societies grew from 28,750 (88 per cent of the total) in 2000 to 30,239 (43 per cent) in 2016. This was a 5 per cent increase in the sixteen years to 2016.

Figure 7.6 captures the diversity in the organizational ecology of cash distribution by illustrating how in its origins the location and the business model of the IAD were quite different to those of banks: while banks largely placed their ATMs in the lobbies or 'through the wall' of their branches, IADs mostly sought internal, off-branch locations; and while banks relied on banknotes being delivered by security distribution companies such as G4S (cash in transit or CIT), the IADs sourced their cash from a combination of CIT deliveries and the merchant's own till.

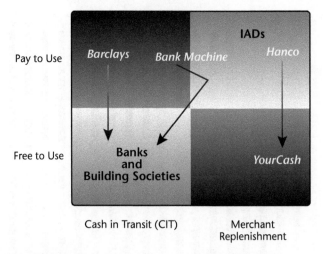

Figure 7.6. Transformation of the IAD business model, 1998–2016
Source: Author's own design, as suggested by Jenny Campbell, YourCash.

The labels 'banks' and 'IADs' in Figure 7.6 are, of course, broad generalizations. The nuance of evolution may be more evident when tracing the development of individual firms. For instance, Barclays is depicted in Figure 7.6 following the 'pay to use, CIT' model. This is to reflect the short-lived introduction by Barclays and other large banks of disloyalty fees (to customers using ATMs other than those of the issuing bank) and surcharges (to non-customers) in the late 1990s and early 2000s.[68] But banks abandoned 'pay to use' ATMs (i.e. surcharges and disloyalty fees) after a political storm that broke in the early 2000s around 'pay to use' ATMs (see section 7.7). Companies such as CashZone and Moneybox are examples of IADs following the 'pay to use, CIT' model.

Figure 7.6 captures the evolution of Bank Machine, starting as the first IAD to populate the 'free to use, CIT' model, which competed with the banks head on. This was a significant development since Bank Machine had previously deployed CIT and merchant replenished 'pay to use' ATMs.[69] It was some time before any other British IADs replicated Bank Machine's strategy. Instead, companies such as Hanco, InfoCash, and PayPoint continued to use the 'pay to use, merchant replenished' model, before moving down in some ways to the 'free to use, merchant replenish' model. In the case of Hanco, this went hand-in-hand with its transformation into YourCash.

The move by Hanco and others partly reflected saturation in the market; independent retailers were now aware of diverse and more cost-effective low-end ATMs, making them more discerning in terms of purchasing equipment at a premium. At the same time, some IADs began to target large corporates for a 'free to use' proposition. These included medium-sized and discount supermarket chains (e.g. Poundland, One Stop); pubs (e.g. Wetherspoons, Green

King); and betting shops, bingo halls (e.g. Mecca Bingo), and casino operators. A managed or tenanted pub company, for instance, could have up to 5,000 different outlets in its portfolio. As a corporate it was likely to have machine department which looked after the drinks dispensers, jackpot machines, pool tables, etc. This gave the IAD sales representative the opportunity to talk to people who understood about machines, their servicing and maintenance requirements, and more importantly had a procurement budget.

Some indigenous British IADs also tried growing overseas but with mixed results. For instance, Hanco was the only one to have a presence in Belgium, Ireland, and the Netherlands in 2017. Meanwhile in the domestic market, many British IADs began to follow Bank Machine in moving laterally to the 'free to use CIT' model in Figure 7.6. The new strategy often resulted in an ATM stock that combined 'free to use' and 'pay to use' ATMs. Sometimes this was by design, but more often a result of acquisitions.[70] At the end of this journey many IADs continued to manage small, self-filled, internal but merchant replenished ATMs while abandoning the 'pay to use' alternative, that is, most IADs steered away from the capital intensive external devices.

The case of Hanco is also representative of the transformation in the IAD business model. After being established by its US parent company in 2000, Hanco was purchased by the Edinburgh-based Royal Bank of Scotland Group in 2004; changed its name to YourCash, following a management buyout in 2010; and was then acquired in 2016 by Euronet Worldwide.[71] In the ten years that followed the first sale of the business in 2004, Hanco transitioned from approximately 6,000 'pay to use' ATMs in the UK to 4,000 machines, of which 2,500 were 'free to use' and 1,500 were 'pay to use' ATMs.[72] Purposely Hanco only kept a quarter of the 'pay to use' machines that had previously monopolized its stock. The strategic shift involved disposing of unprofitable locations that had been deployed in the 'land grab spree' and building the scale of the business, while replacing these sites by more strategically located and strictly profitable 'free to use' ATMs. This transformation, however, was more complex than simply a flick of the switch. For instance, a 'pay to use' machine might require daily replenishment of £500 in £5, £10, and £20 banknotes, whereas the same but 'free to use' ATM might require £1,500 in cash per day. Clearly, these were very different servicing propositions that required some form of cash in transit solution.

Other IADs, however, included top-end devices in their fleet from the start. Such was the case of Moneybox after it signed outsourcing agreements with small depositary institutions.[73] These included building societies such as the Norwich and Peterborough or building societies turned banks, such as the Bradford & Bingley. Moneybox also purchased ATMs and their locations from building societies turned banks, for example, Abbey National and HBOS.[74] These ATMs would display the bank or building society brand in the surround of the fascia, while the screen of the machine would display the Moneybox name and logo.

A wave of consolidation also swept the IADs concurrently with the changes in their business model. In 2007 there were 39 participants in LINK, 23 of them depositary financial institutions, which together owned 31,151 ATMs or 49 per cent of the 63,924 total in the UK. In the same year there were 13 IADs which together owned or managed 31,823 ATMs, i.e. 50 per cent of the total (three other providers controlled 950 machines or 1 per cent). By 2017 there were 31 participants and the total number of ATMs had increased 10 per cent to 70,536 machines. The number of depositary financial institutions and ATMs under their control remained largely unchanged at 22 institutions and 30,573 machines, respectively. But these now represented 43 per cent of the total ATMs in the UK. Meanwhile the number of IADs halved to 6 while the number of devices under their control increased 24 per cent to 39,584 machines or 56 per cent of all ATMs in the UK (three other participants, notably G4S and Travelex, now controlled only 379 machines).

7.7 Uproar and Controversy: The Surcharge Saga in the UK

7.7.1 *Clouds Gather, Winds Change, Tumbleweeds Roll*

As briefly noted earlier in this chapter, retail financial institutions in Britain abandoned surcharges and disloyalty fees in the early 2000s. Rather than by design or resulting from the pressure of competitive forces, the retraction followed a political storm that broke with the advent of 'pay to use' ATMs.

There was no single alarm before this episode, but the tempest that engulfed the industry was brewing throughout the 1990s. As described in Chapter 4, the first ATM interchange networks between major banks in the UK appeared in the 1980s. After this LINK and Matrix (both mainly populated by building societies and a few smaller banks) merged as British financial institutions came together to form a single ATM interchange network around LINK, while in the late 1990s and early 2000s IADs deploying 'pay to use' ATMs began to be established.

In this context came the publication in 1999 of a survey by Nationwide Building Society, then the UK's largest mutually-owned mortgage lender.[75] According to the survey, 91 per cent of the British public did not believe that people should be charged for withdrawing their own cash. Nearly three-quarters of those questioned felt that banks' motivation for charges was simply to increase profits. The survey of 984 people also found that nearly 50 per cent of respondents would stop using certain cash machines to avoid surcharges, and 26 per cent would look for alternatives such as cashbacks from supermarkets, which were provided free. At the time six financial institutions—Barclays, Lloyds TSB, NatWest, HSBC, Abbey National, and Halifax—made up 75 per cent of the UK's network of 27,525 ATMs in operation at the end of 1999.[76]

From a strictly economic perspective, the willingness to pay for a good or service is indicative of the value placed on the item. One would then be led to assume that, all else being equal, a consumer's willingness to pay a surcharge should reflect the value to that customer of this payment method, in relation to any alternatives.[77] Indeed, IADs often argued that the surcharge should be seen as the cost of convenient access to cash.[78]

The problem, however, is that the cost of using alternative payment methods is obscure for most consumers in most countries. For instance, since the inception of bank-backed payment cards in the 1950s and before a 2013 court ruling banning 'non-discrimination' clauses, merchants in the USA were unable to steer customers to cheaper forms of payment or impose discounts or surcharges on payments with plastic.[79] In other words, for decades, and regardless of the cost to the merchant or the issuing bank, customers paid the same price whether they used plastic, cash, or personal cheque. The lack of transparency plus the fact that in many countries, including the UK, customers were seldom charged for services relating to the use of their current account (while depositary institutions paid a very low or zero interest rate on liquid balances), goes some way to explaining why British consumers wanted free access to their money. Meanwhile in the USA, bank customers paid an average flat fee of \$1.14 per transaction to use any of the 73,000 off-premise ATMs, 40,000 of which were located at convenience stores in 1999.[80]

To be fair, the use of ATMs in Britain at the turn of the millennium was somewhat confusing.[81] As mentioned in Chapter 5, the Halifax, for instance, a former building society turned bank, introduced a 50 pence 'disloyalty charge' (paid when using a non-Halifax ATM) in order to 'encourage Halifax own customers to use the society's ATMs whenever possible'.[82] Customers of HSBC could get money from any of the ATMs in the LINK shared network but were charged £1 by HSBC unless the ATM belonged to NatWest, Clydesdale, or Ulster banks (the former ATM network partners of HSBC). Customers of Lloyds TSB were at the greatest disadvantage because the TSB was a member of LINK before being taken over by Lloyds in 1998, before Lloyds became a member of LINK. This meant that in the year 2000, a former customer of Lloyds would be charged £1.50 by Lloyds TSB when withdrawing from any ATM other than those of Lloyds TSB, Barclays, Royal Bank of Scotland, and Bank of Scotland, but a former customer of the TSB could withdraw without penalty from Lloyds TSB from any ATM.

Evidently the formation of a single shared ATM network in the UK had developed a labyrinthine complexity of charges. Added to this was the absence of a robust warning system for disloyalty charges. Customers could easily forget which ATMs were free of charge to them and discover nothing until their monthly bank statement arrived—always assuming of course, that customers checked their bank statements. There was thus an economic incentive for customers to avoid ATMs.

The solution of Barclays, Woolwich, and some other financial institutions to this mess, was to reverse the disloyalty concept and charge all non-customers a flat fee of £1 for taking money from an ATM. Others such as Lloyds TSB introduced a 50 pence surcharge. The latter move was seen as somewhat pointless because the interchange fee at the time was 40 pence per transaction.[83] Meanwhile, NatWest was the only big bank that remained undecided; it was said to be inclined to keep its disloyalty fee and oppose surcharges.

Adding to the mix was Brian Davies, CEO of Nationwide, who took to the airwaves against disloyalty charges and found a sympathetic ear in the media. Amongst Davies' arguments was that a disloyalty charge would mean other institutions deciding a levy on Nationwide customers. The chief villain in his row was Barclays—which claimed that the sums it might derive from disloyalty fees or surcharges would not cover the £180 million per annum it spent on installing and running its ATM network. Louise Footner, press officer at Barclays, went on record as stating that:

> There has to be an incentive for us to maintain this [ATM] network . . . Some of the building societies have made the decision not to invest in an ATM network, but their [customers] are able to use ours for free.[84]

Nationwide's response was to make public threats of legal action against Barclays.[85] But Nationwide also received criticisms from within the industry, specifically, that it was fuelling consumer dissatisfaction in order to reinforce its brand image of being fair, low cost, and different thanks to its status as the last large mutual.[86]

Consumer groups believed that disloyalty fees and surcharges would be the start of a soft process that would end 'free banking' for those in credit. Political concerns about social exclusion also emerged, since it was felt that a disloyalty fee or surcharge would hit hardest those who could least afford it: people on low incomes, who tended to withdraw small amounts; while people in rural areas would be forced either to pay a fee or travel some distance to the nearest free cashpoint.

7.7.2 An Arrangement for Post-Apocalyptic Survival

Bowing to media pressure, customer complaints, and claims of being arrogant, Abbey National was the first to desist from charging a disloyalty fee of £1.50 to its own customers when they used ATMs not owned by this former building society.[87] Others such as Halifax, Nationwide, Bank of Scotland, and the Co-operative Bank made public promises to charge nothing for cash withdrawals. Even Barclays was forced to acquiesce. The move by financial institutions, however, was insufficient to rein in politicians. Investigations continued, followed by more in 2004 when Royal Bank of Scotland (RBS) acquired Hanco.[88] Meanwhile politicians escalated the dispute at the same time making a case against all 'pay to use' ATMs. To place these discussions in context, Figure 7.7 illustrates the trends in the stock of 'free to use' and 'pay to use' ATMs in the UK.

The data in Figure 7.7 show 'pay to use' machines growing from 200 units in 1999 to a maximum deployment of 27,100 devices in 2007 (42 per cent of the total). This trend was primarily fuelled by the IADs' deployment of surcharge machines, and included a number of ATMs charging up to £5 per withdrawal.[89] Figure 7.7 also depicts a plateau where 'pay to use' machines reach a maximum of 43 per cent of the total stock of ATMs in 2005 and 2006. This stasis is seen shortly after the acquisition of Hanco by RBS in 2004 and the consequent parliamentary enquiry in 2005. Since then 'pay to use' machines have decreased and in 2016 represented only 23 per cent of the total.

The data in Figure 7.7 suggest that the acquisition of Hanco by RBS was an important event in the performance of 'pay to use' ATMs in the UK. Three other reasons that help to explain the significance of the Hanco deal were,

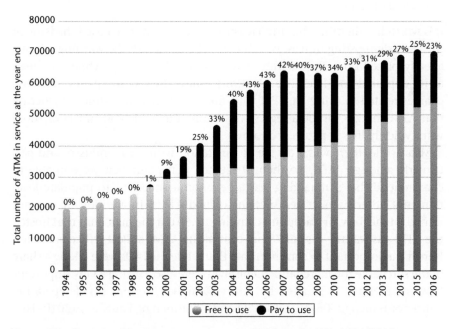

Figure 7.7. Growth of free to use vs. pay to use ATMs in the UK, 1994–2016

Source: Author's own estimates, based on data from LINK, Payments Council and Statista.

first, that the RBS paid \$143 million (£80 million) for Hanco's UK operations or approximately \$20,000 (£11,500) per ATM under Hanco's control—which Hanco had purchased at approximately \$5,500 (£3,000) each.[90] Second, the RBS already had the single largest ATM network in the UK before the Hanco acquisition. About half these machines were located at the bank's retail branches, with the other half in non-bank sites (such as railway stations and stores of the supermarket Tesco). Suspicion that the deal would increase the RBS's market power led the Competition and Markets Authority to examine the acquisition of Hanco.[91] Third, some observers, from a rather cynical standpoint, believed the acquisition of Hanco gave politicians a large corporate to target in the apparently growing public unease with 'pay to use' ATMs.[92]

Although the Hanco acquisition was cleared and not remitted to the Competition Commission, the Treasury Select Committee, under the chair of John McFall, ploughed on and began an enquiry into all cash machine charges, justifying their action as follows:

> At the time of the Cruickshank Report in 2000, only a tiny proportion of cash machines involved a direct charge. The proportion now [in 2004] is 37%. Cash machines are the most important method of cash withdrawal in the UK, used by millions every week. Concerns arise about: the principle of charging and the increasing prevalence of charging machines; the clarity of presentation of these charges to the consumer; the impact that the spread of charging may have on financial exclusion.[93]

It is worth highlighting that the Treasury Select Committee raised the issue of the clear signposting of fees, which many ATMs lacked: the warning stickers already placed on cash machines were often hidden away, while on-screen alerts appeared too late. The Committee also drew a sharp line between charges related to using an ATM with financial inclusion, while considering that ATM charges can be a regressive tax on vulnerable consumers or those who typically live in a cash economy.

Meanwhile, there was a degree of frustration within the industry and particularly amongst IADs. To them it seemed that politicians were unable to comprehend that surcharging was an economic incentive to populate locations not otherwise serviced by bank-owned ATMs. In addition, it was not Hanco, Moneybox, or Cardpoint charging £1.50 but the merchant that hosted the ATM—as was the case of 75 per cent of the ATMs at Post Office branches. Here it was important to communicate that while the IADs were taking a share of the surcharge the merchants themselves were also earning a very important flow of revenue. As recalled by Jenny Campbell, former Chief Operating Officer of Hanco (2006–10) and CEO and Chairman of YourCash (2010–16):

> The customer case for independents was that the surcharge is a convenience charge, but unlike American and Australians most British people saw it as a distress

charge. Even when people pay for their current account or in their debit card, they still hate having to pay at an ATM.[94]

The enquiry's recommendations included early alerts of charges on the ATM screen before a withdrawal and standardized external charging notices in the surround of the ATM fascia. Another result was that Gordon Pell, then chief executive of retail markets at Royal Bank of Scotland, promised in 2006 to deploy between 300 and 500 'free to use' ATMs in rural and socially deprived communities.[95]

The proposed deployments by Hanco/RBS were independent of and extra to those of LINK's Financial Inclusion Programme. The latter was established by LINK and its members in 2006, while also aiming to improve access to cash for consumers in the most deprived areas of the UK and to put most of the adult population within a one-kilometre radius of an ATM.[96] The program identified 1,700 deprived areas in need of a 'free to use' ATM in 2006 and changed its rules to generate a premium supporting the provision of these machines. By 2011 a 'free to use' ATM was in operation in 1,329 (78 per cent) of the deprived areas identified five years earlier.

In response to the publication of the enquiry's recommendations in 2005, ATM operators went on public record in 2005 stating that fewer than 4 per cent of total withdrawal transactions involved 'pay to use' machines, and that these ATMs accounted for four out of ten machines.[97] Table 7.3 shows the trends in withdrawal volume between these two types of ATM.

Table 7.3. Withdrawal volume in free to use and pay to use ATMs, 2001–2015

	Cash withdrawals (millions)			Pay to use as % of total
	Free to use	Pay to use	Sum	
2001	2,135	39	2,174	1.8%
2002	2,215	53	2,268	2.3%
2003	2,293	80	2,373	3.4%
2004	2,432	96	2,528	3.8%
2005	2,591	108	2,699	4.0%
2006	2,634	118	2,752	4.3%
2007	2,723	113	2,836	4.0%
2008	2,765	101	2,866	3.5%
2009	2,735	92	2,827	3.3%
2010	2,700	86	2,786	3.1%
2011	2,793	81	2,874	2.8%
2012	2,842	73	2,915	2.5%
2013	2,832	67	2,899	2.3%
2014	2,769	62	2,831	2.2%
2015	2,738	59	2,797	2.1%

Source: Own estimates, based on data from LINK.

Table 7.3 shows that withdrawal volume at the 'pay to use' ATMs peaked at 4.3 per cent of total transactions in 2006. Together, the trends in Table 7.3 and Figure 7.7 suggest that political pressure over the 'pay to use' ATM led to a revision of the IAD collective strategy and helps to explain the downward trend in 'pay to use' ATMs since then.

7.8 The Consequences of Greater Specialization

Cash distribution and other services in an ATM (such as balance enquiries and purchasing airtime for mobile phones) are commodities. They are highly standardized, high volume, low value transactions. However, most people take out cash, consult their balance, or purchase airtime on their way to do something else. This may be a restaurant meal, a journey home, the purchase of petrol, or a meeting with friends. Visiting an ATM is an interruption of this journey, a loss of time that they could do without. In other words, like many other banking services, cash withdrawals and other services offered through ATMs are a means to an end.

In this context, depository financial institutions remain at the centre of the payments universe.[98] They assemble and deliver the value proposition for the consumer; they store and secure the value entrusted to them by the consumer.[99] But they have increasingly delivered a broad range of utilities such as transaction services. The cash withdrawals and the other services offered through ATMs are a good example of this.

What, then, is the role of IADs from this perspective? There are two possible views of the interaction between IADs and financial institutions: it is either confrontational or complementary. The confrontational view is driven by efficiency considerations which see cash distribution and ATMs as an outright cost of operation for depositary institutions and merchants. Accordingly, banks see ATMs as an extension of the services offered to their customers through the retail branch network and specifically as a 'loss-leader' marketing strategy (i.e. an instrument to articulate initiatives in managing relationships with customers).[100] In this view, ATMs and other components of the cash distribution value chain are a business opportunity for the IADs, to the extent that levying regulatory changes enable IADs to provide a cost-effective service to financial institutions, merchants, or directly to bank customers. It is deemed confrontational because IADs and financial institutions cannot occupy the same space, within the market, at the same time.

The interaction between IADs and financial institutions can, however, be seen instead as complementary.[101] As suggested by its name, this view considers that IADs and financial institutions collaborate and share space within the market. In this outlook, financial institutions were unable or unwilling to take ATMs to the vast number of off-branch locations that their customers demanded. Instead financial institutions used interchange fees and withdrawal charges (also known as 'surcharges') as an incentive to attract investments that would increase the density of ATMs while implementing banks' distribution strategies. IADs thus enabled financial institutions to offer greater convenience to their customers without the pain of having to fund and manage vast numbers of off-site ATMs. But once this exchange of value had saturated the off-branch opportunities, fee income will contract while the IADs will start a dual process of consolidation and finding new ways to evolve their business model while continuing to collaborate with financial institutions.

The extent to which the confrontational or complementary view is better at explaining the emergence and evolution of the IAD is an empirical question. Evidence in this chapter would tend to suggest there is more complementarity than confrontation between financial institutions and IADs.

It is a common dictum of economics that greater scale through specialization can bring increasing financial rewards. This chapter illustrated this proposition in discussing the origins of the IAD and how they created a business model around fee income generation, installing ATMs in non-bank branch locations and providing convenient access to cash. The emergence of the IAD meant that owning, managing, and maintaining ATMs was no longer the sole remit of banks. This evidence would then suggest a necessary confrontation between banks and IADs.

The IADs, however, evolved while simultaneously competing and cooperating with merchants and financial institutions. Key developments for this transformation included regulatory changes, the emergence of the low-end ATM, and the competitive effects of surcharging. Before surcharging, the benefits of increasing the availability of ATMs flowed directly between the user and the cardholder's bank, but the introduction of surcharges allowed new players to capture a share of these benefits to a networked industry. But it should be recalled that it was only after changes in regulation in response to local legal and political events that a door opened to a new type of organization: the IAD.

The IADs' core activities began by servicing the retail environment, such as small grocery stores, petrol stations, and even garden centres.[102] Initially they built to a radically different business model to that of banks, as far as the operation of cash withdrawal services was concerned, because the IAD income stream was based on surcharging and conveniently located ATMs, with a strong preference for internally located, low-cost machines. Banks, however, primarily preferred 'through the wall', bank branch located ATMs, with the possibility of implementing surcharges and disloyalty fees.

But the IAD core activities changed within a couple of decades after they first appeared in the mid to late 1990s. By 2003 the IAD had begun to develop alternative revenue streams including banks' outsourcing parts (such as first-line support, help desks, software development, or event monitoring and diagnostics) up to the total management of ATM networks.[103] It would then be wrong to assume organizational homogeneity within the IAD sector. Nevertheless, the long-term competitive result was that a number of banks reassessed and rationalized their commitment to ATMs.

The past and present of the IAD further illustrate the domestic aspects of an otherwise globalized industry. As documented in this chapter, the evolution of the IAD explains a new spurt of growth in the ATM estate in the late 1990s and early 2000s, at a time when domestic and international IADs grew by installing remotely located devices in countries such as Canada, Germany, the Netherlands, the UK, and the USA. These trends support the view that the globalization of automatic cash withdrawals (discussed in Chapter 5) did not automatically provide equal opportunity to all participants.

One ought also to consider that during the late 1980s and early 1990s a handful of companies such as IBM, NCR, Diebold, and Wincor Nixdorf dominated the manufacturing of ATMs. The emergence of the IAD, however, brought a new group of players ranking side by side with previous industry titans, namely the low-end ATM manufacturers.

The rise of the IAD thus tells a story about who owns, operates, and maintains the device. This story is part of the tale underlying the globalization of the ATM as well as understanding how the device itself evolved. In other words, the story behind IADs involves considering both how ATM networks were transformed into a global payments platform and the fundamental importance of maintaining a technological backbone. For instance, in most European countries, IADs are connected to Visa and MasterCard, through a sponsoring organization or through a direct connection to these international schemes, that is, another IAD such as Euronet.

But for all the details of the industrial organization of IADs offered in this chapter around the evolution of the IAD, its story remains incomplete. This chapter has also explained how the IAD and the practice of surcharging were both caught in a political storm, in which it took some skill to make politicians understand the benefits of convenient access to cash.

Notes

1. Interview with Terry Turner, former CEO of Hanco UK, by B. Bátiz-Lazo, Milton Keynes, 4 December 2007. Although there are several more recent surveys of Hoteling's spatial competition models, interested readers could begin their exploration of this topic through Stokes (1963).

2. This conceptual discussion borrows from Bátiz-Lazo and Smith (2016).

3. Lamoreaux et al. (2003); Langlois (2003).

4. Che and Sákovics (2008).

5. Brown and Duguid (1991); Håkanson (2010); Wenger et al. (2002).

6. Total membership for 2016 was 6,911 since 633 company memberships were included, of which the biggest number were IADs (147 members, 23 per cent), security solutions (60 members, 9 per cent), and banks (60 members, 9 per cent) while 20 other categories made up the rest of a very diverse membership (366 members, 59 per cent). Personal communication (email) from Sharon M. Lane, Global Director—Finance & Member Services, ATM Industry Association, with B. Bátiz-Lazo, 19 September 2016. Also available at: 'Membership Composition', ATM Industry Association, accessed 2 August 2017, <https://www.atmia.com/about-us/overview/membership-composition/>.

7. Interview with James Adamson, former CEO of NCR Dundee, by B. Bátiz-Lazo and R. Reid, Edinburgh, 18 June 2008.

8. Unless otherwise stated, this section borrows freely from Harper and Bátiz-Lazo (2013, 45–51). It also benefits from numerous emails and conversations with Mike Lee and Tom Harper between June 2016 and July 2017.

9. 'ATMOA Planning Meeting Announcement', *ATM Marketplace*, accessed 23 August 2016, <http://www.atmmarketplace.com/news/atmoa-planning-meeting-announcement/>.

10. Personal communication (email) from Mike Lee, CEO ATM Industry Association, with B. Bátiz-Lazo, 2 August 2017.

11. Melissa Hutcheson, 'Global ATM Pictogram', *NSA Field Service Solutions*, accessed 23 August 2016, <http://www.nsa.bz/atm_pictogram.php>. See also: 'Online. Browsing Platform', International Organization for Standardization, accessed 19 July 2017, <https://www.iso.org/obp/ui#iso:grs:7001:PI_CF_005>.

12. Walt Bogdanich, 'Criminals Focus on A.T.M.'s, Weak Link in Banking System', *The New York Times*, 3 August 2003, accessed 23 August 2016, <http://www.nytimes.com/2003/08/03/us/stealing-code-con-men-cash-machines-criminals-focus-atm-s-weak-link-banking.html>.

13. 'In Face of Mobile Money Onslaught, ATMIA Makes Pro-cash Rallying Cry', *Finextra*, 27 October 2014, accessed 23 August 2016, <https://www.finextra.com/newsarticle/26627/in-face-of-mobile-money-onslaught-atmia-makes-pro-cash-rallying-cry>.

14. Rian Boden, 'Central Bank Calls for Access to Cash to be a Legal Right in Sweden', *NFC World*, 21 March 2016, accessed 23 August 2016, <http://www.nfcworld.com/2016/03/21/343432/central-bank-calls-access-cash-legal-right-sweden>.

15. 'What Can We Learn From Sweden's Domestic Payment System Quandary?', *Banking Technology*, 29 March 2016, accessed 23 August 2016, <http://www.bankingtech.com/464312/what-can-we-learn-from-swedens-domestic-payment-system-quandary/>; 'Swedish Central Bank Calls Halt on Moves to a Cashless Economy', *Finextra*, 18 March 2016, accessed 23 August 2016, <https://www.finextra.com/newsarticle/28635/swedish-central-bank-calls-halt-on-moves-to-a-cashless-economy>; 'Legal Requirement for the Banks' Cash Service', *Sveriges Riksbanken*, 16 March 2016, accessed 23 August 2016, <http://www.riksbank.se/en/Press-and-published/Notices/2016/Introduce-a-legal-requirement-for-the-banks-cash-service/>; Dan Hyde, 'Free

Cash Machines Outside Shops to Disappear "Within a Year"', *Telegraph*, 14 August 2015, accessed 16 July 2017, <http://www.telegraph.co.uk/news/shopping-and-consumer-news/11804515/Free-cash-machines-outside-shops-to-disappear-within-a-year.html>.

16. 'ATMIA Encourages Legislators to Rein in Operation Choke Point', *ATM Marketplace*, 9 February 2016, accessed 26 September 2016, <http://www.atmmarketplace.com/news/atmia-encourages-legislators-to-rein-in-operation-choke-point/>; and 'Operation Choke Point', *Wikipedia*, accessed 19 July 2017, <https://en.wikipedia.org/wiki/Operation_Choke_Point>.

17. See for instance: 'ATM Benchmarking Study 2014 and Industry Report', *Value Partners*, 5 November 2014, accessed 23 August 2016, <http://www.slideshare.net/ValuePartners/atm-benchmarking-study-2014-and-industry-report> and 'Banking ATM Benchmarking 2016', *Accenture*, accessed 23 August 2016, <https://www.accenture.com/_acnmedia/PDF-10/Accenture-Banking-ATM-Benchmarking-2016.pdf>.

18. Spong and Harvey (1998, 12). The same source notes that some ATMs surcharged before 1996, in states that had passed laws to override the network surcharging bans. At the time, many banks also charged their own customers for ATM use in an attempt to cover the interchange fees.

19. Darla Dernovsek, 'Selective Surcharging', *Credit Union Magazine*, 66(4) (April) 2000: 64.

20. McAndrews (1998, 3; 2003).

21. Unless otherwise stated, data in this paragraph were sourced in John Asher, 'The Second ATM Revolution', *ABA Banking Journal*, May 1998: 51. According to the Bank for International Settlements' 'Red Book', the actual number of devices for year-end 1995, 1997, and 2000 was 122,706, 165,000, and 227,000 ATMs respectively.

22. Unless otherwise stated, this section borrows freely from Harper and Bátiz-Lazo (2013, 35–44). See also Hayashi et al. (2003, 11–12 and 27–9).

23. Interchange fees are usually estimated and paid on the basis of transaction volume.

24. In some instances, they even became a prison. See: 'Texas Man Trapped Inside ATM Rescued After Passing Notes Through Receipt Slot', *The Guardian*, 13 July 2017, accessed 2 August 2017, <https://www.theguardian.com/us-news/2017/jul/13/texas-man-atm-bank-of-america-escape>.

25. Unless otherwise stated, this section borrows freely from Harper and Bátiz-Lazo (2013, 35–44).

26. 'Troubles at Tidel', *ATM Marketplace*, accessed 13 January 2017, <https://www.atmmarketplace.com/news/troubles-at-tidel/>.

27. 'NCR Acquires Tidel Engineering', *ATM Marketplace*, 12 February 2006, accessed 13 January 2017, <https://www.atmmarketplace.com/top-100/ncr-acquires-tidel-engineering-2/>.

28. 'NCR Acquires Tidel Engineering', *ATM Marketplace*, 12 February 2006, accessed 13 January 2017, <https://www.atmmarketplace.com/top-100/ncr-acquires-tidel-engineering-2/>.

29. Hayashi et al. (2006, 26). Dahl's Foods was established in 1931 and closed for business in 2015. See Patt Johnson, 'Dahl's Files $41 million Bankruptcy', *The Des*

Moines Register, 10 November 2014, accessed 10 February2017, <http://www.des moinesregister.com/story/money/business/2014/11/10/dahls-bankruptcy/18791717>.

30. In the landmark US Supreme Court ruling of 1985, one of the defendants was a retailer, specifically, a store of Wegmans Food Markets Inc. located in Rochester, NY, and which was being accessed by the other defendant, Marine Midland Bank, Buffalo, NY. The Independent Bankers Association of New York State and the Canandaigua National Bank and Trust Company were the plaintiffs. See 'The Independent Bankers Association of New York State and the Canandaigua National Bank and Trust Company were the plaintiffs', *Justia US Law*, accessed 17 February 2017, <http://law.justia.com/cases/federal/appellate-courts/F2/757/453/425988/>.

31. Personal communication (email) from Christopher D. Klein, Sr., former NCR engineer and Atlantic Bank director, with M. Lee, 31 January 2017.

32. This paragraph borrows from Bill Koch, 'Deployers and Retailers Can Both Win with ATMS', *American Banker*, 163(36) (February) 1988: 16.

33. Cavell (2003, 91).

34. US banks also sold postage stamps at face value through their ATMs (initially in batches of 9, 18, and 27 stamps at a time), but the cost of preparing the 'sheetlets' meant that this was done at a loss to the bank. Equibank, Pittsburgh, PA, claims to have been the earliest experience of a bank distributing stamps through its ATMs. It did so between 1988 and 1991. Another similar claim is that of Seafirst Bank, Seattle, WA. The bank claimed to have sold 32,000 stamps as a test run through its ATMs between May 1990 and January 1991. In May 1991, the US Postal Service extended this service to all banks across the country so they could sell stamps through their ATMs in sheets of 18 self-adhesive units (which would be the same size and shape as a banknote), while the bank had the option of adding a transaction charge. Wells Fargo began selling postage stamps through its ATMs in 1994. A decade later, in 2004 it became the sixth largest distributor of stamps in the United States. By 2009 most US banks had discontinued this service. Sources: Emma Johnson, 'ATMs Aren't Just for Cash Withdrawals Anymore', 16 February 2009, accessed 11 July 2017, <http://www.creditcards.com/credit-card-news/next-generation-atms-1273.php>; 'Operations Briefs', *ABA Banking Journal*, May 1991: 78; Frank Norulak and Jim Noll, 'The Stamp Stop: A Look at ATM Innovation', accessed 3 June 2017, <https://www.atmmarketplace.com/articles/the-stamp-stop-a-look-at-atm-innovation/>; Kevin Wack and Alan Kline, 'The Evolution of the ATM', *American Banker*, 23 May 2017, accessed 3 June 2017, <https://www.amer icanbanker.com/slideshow/the-evolution-of-the-atm#slide-4>.

35. In the early 2000s the surcharge fee averaged between $0.50 and $2.00. Source: Cavell (2003, 91).

36. Harper and Bátiz-Lazo (2013, 38).

37. RBR London, *Global ATM Market and Forecasts*, London (2007).

38. Hayashi et al. (2006, 11–12).

39. 'Contract Basics for the Merchant/ISO relationship', *ATM Marketplace*, 7 January 2002, accessed 4 February 2017, <https://www.atmmarketplace.com/news/contract-basics-for-the-merchantiso-relationship/>.

40. The suite of ATM, point of sale, and transaction processing businesses of EDS was consolidated into a unit called Consumer Network Services (CNS) based in Morris Plains, NJ. CNS was sold in November 2002 to Fiserv Inc., of Brookfield, WI, for $320 million. At this point CNS processed more than 2.4 billion electronic transactions annually and operated 13,170 ATMs. The combined organization, supported by more than 850 employees, became one of the top five processors of electronic transactions in the USA. 'Electronic Data Sys (EDC)', *Investegate*, 14 November 2002, accessed 4 February 2017, <http://www.investegate.co.uk/electronic-data-sys-edc-/bus/acquisition/20021115004626B0654/>.

41. <http://www.cardtronics.com>, accessed 10 July 2017; and 'Statistics', *LINK*, accessed 21 July 2017, <http://www.link.co.uk/about-link/statistics/>.

42. Darla Dernovsek, 'Selective Surcharging', *Credit Union Magazine*, 66(4) (April) 2000: 64.

43. Participating credit unions pay no surcharge fees at ATMs that are part of the alliance. The credit union retains the right to surcharge non-members to cover the cost of placing ATMs in low volume locations.

44. Euronet Worldwide (NASDAQ EEFT) was described in 2017 as a US provider of electronic payment services with reporting headquarters in Leawood, KS and operational headquarters in Budapest, Hungary. It was established in 1994 by Michael J. Brown and his brother-in-law Daniel Henry. In 2017 it offered automated teller machines, point of sale services, credit/debit card services, and other electronic financial services. Before its acquisition of YourCash in 2016, Euronet operated nearly 26,000 ATMs across 50 countries and provided services to approximately 185,000 ATMs around the world. Euronet sold its pioneering operations in the UK involving 745 ATMs and 22 employees for $29.6 million through a management buyout to a consortium led by Ron Delnevo and financed by Bridgepoint Capital in 2003. Renamed Bank Machine it was subsequently acquired by Cardtronics in 2005 while Delnevo stayed on board until 2012. Sources: Personal communication (email) from Ron Delnevo, former managing director of Euronet in the UK, with B. Bátiz-Lazo, 10 July 2017; Interview (telephone) with Paul Stanley, founder and former managing director of Moneybox, by B. Bátiz-Lazo, 11 December 2007; 'Euronet Worldwide', *Wikipedia*, accessed 11 July 2017, <https://en.wikipedia.org/wiki/Euronet_Worldwide>; 'Euronet Worldwide buys UK ATM Operator Your-Cash', *Finextra*, 10 October 2016, accessed 12 July 2017, <https://www.finextra.com/pressarticle/66505/euronet-worldwide-buys-uk-atm-operator-yourcash>; Interview (telephone) with Ron Delnevo, former managing director of Euronet in the UK and Bank Machine, by B. Bátiz-Lazo, 17 July 2017; and 'Euronet sells UK ATM business', *ATM Marketplace*, 19 January 2003, accessed 18 July 2017, <https://www.atmmarketplace.com/news/euronet-sells-uk-atm-business/>.

45. 'On Board with ISOs', *ATM Marketplace*, 21 March 2004, accessed 17 July 2017, <https://www.atmmarketplace.com/articles/on-board-with-isos/>.

46. Interview with Terry Turner, co-founder of Hanco in the UK, by B. Bátiz-Lazo, Milton Keynes, 4 December 2007. Hanco was a US-based family business linked to ATM deployment since 1991. The business built up a network of 4,300 machines across 40 states in the USA before being sold in 2002. The company was one of the

first generation of British IADs and would typically use Triton products. Source: Cavell (2003, 92).

47. Personal communication (email) from Ron Delnevo, former managing director of Euronet in the UK and Bank Machine, with B. Bátiz-Lazo, 20 July 2017.

48. Interview (telephone) with Ron Delnevo, former managing director of Euronet in the UK and Bank Machine, by B. Bátiz-Lazo, 17 July 2017.

49. Personal communication (email) from Ron Delnevo, former managing director of Euronet in the UK and Bank Machine, with B. Bátiz-Lazo, 20 July 2017.

50. Under the contract the cash remained the property of Alliance & Leicester so that it could recover it if the recipient became insolvent. Later as Bank Machine, Delnevo added Northern Rock, another demutualized building society, as a secondary supplier of their banknotes. Source: Interview (telephone) with Ron Delnevo, former managing director of Euronet in the UK and Bank Machine, by B. Bátiz-Lazo, 17 July 2017.

51. 'Changing the Guard', *ATM Marketplace*, accessed 30 June 2017, <https://www.atmmarketplace.com/articles/changing-of-the-guard-2/> and 'On Board with ISOs', *ATM Marketplace*, 21 March 2004, accessed 17 July 2017, <https://www.atmmarketplace.com/articles/on-board-with-isos/>.

52. 'Cashpoint Revolution', *Marketing Week*, accessed 18 July 2001, <https://www.marketingweek.com/1999/01/14/cashpoint-revolution> and 'On Board with ISOs', *ATM Marketplace*, 21 March 2004, accessed 17 July 2017, <https://www.atmmarketplace.com/articles/on-board-with-isos/>.

53. The long-term links between Alliance & Leicester and the Post Office through Girobank did not result in any significant number of ATMs within the 18,000 to 20,000 or so Post Office branches. The Post Office was very concerned about this, hence the initial contract with the Woolwich. However, after the takeover by Barclays, the Post Office awarded the contract to deploy 1,000 'free to use' ATMs to the Bank of Ireland in 2005. Source: Interview (telephone) with Ron Delnevo, former managing director of Euronet in the UK and Bank Machine, by B. Bátiz-Lazo, 17 July 2017; 'Bank of Ireland inks ATM deal with UK Post Office', *Finextra*, 18 July 2005, accessed 18 July 2017, <https://www.finextra.com/news/fullstory.aspx?newsitemid=13985>. On Girobank see Billings and Booth (2011).

54. The change of rules partly responded to continuing regulatory change and partly to the wish to give LINK transparency as well as direct vetting and supervision of all members. Source: Interview with John Hardy, founder and former CEO of LINK, London, by B. Bátiz-Lazo and C. Reese, 21 November 2007; 'On Board with ISOs', *ATM Marketplace*, 21 March 2004, accessed 17 July 2017, <https://www.atmmarketplace.com/articles/on-board-with-isos/>; 'Euronet Sells UK ATM Business', *ATM Marketplace*, 19 January 2003, accessed 18 July 2017. <https://www.atmmarketplace.com/news/euronet-sells-uk-atm-business/>.

55. 'Charging ATMs "Must be Labelled"', *BBC News*, 31 March 2005, accessed 24 July 2017, <http://news.bbc.co.uk/1/hi/business/4394251.stm>.

56. James Mackintosh, 'Banks Charging Disloyalty Fees Could Forfeit ATM Surcharges', *Financial Times*, 25 March 2000: 3.

57. 'On Board with ISOs', *ATM Marketplace*, 21 March 2004, accessed 17 July 2017, <https://www.atmmarketplace.com/articles/on-board-with-isos/>.

58. Hanco was actually based in Peachtree City, GA—in the south part of the metropolitan area of Atlanta. 'In Memory of Tom Hannon', *ATM Marketplace*, 4 February 2004, accessed 18 July 2017, <https://www.atmmarketplace.com/news/in-memory-of-tom-hannon/>; 'Thomas C. Hannon—Obituary', *Legacy, The Atlanta Journal-Constitution*, accessed 18 July 2017, <http://www.legacy.com/obituaries/atlanta/obituary.aspx?pid=1861482>.

59. This paragraph draws on the interview with Terry Turner, co-founder of Hanco in the UK, by B. Bátiz-Lazo, Milton Keynes, 4 December 2007.

60. Interview with Terry Turner, co-founder of Hanco in the UK, by B. Bátiz-Lazo, Milton Keynes, 4 December 2007.

61. Interview with Terry Turner, co-founder of Hanco in the UK, by B. Bátiz-Lazo, Milton Keynes, 4 December 2007.

62. Interview with Terry Turner, co-founder of Hanco in the UK, by B. Bátiz-Lazo, Milton Keynes, 4 December 2007.

63. Interview with Terry Turner, co-founder of Hanco in the UK, by B. Bátiz-Lazo, Milton Keynes, 4 December 2007 and personal communication (email) from Ron Delnevo, former managing director of Euronet in the UK and Bank Machine, with B. Bátiz-Lazo, 20 July 2017.

64. Personal communication (email) from Ron Delnevo, former managing director of Euronet in the UK and Bank Machine, with B. Bátiz-Lazo, 20 July 2017.

65. Personal communication (email) from Ron Delnevo, former managing director of Euronet in the UK and Bank Machine, with B. Bátiz-Lazo, 20 July 2017.

66. Interview with John Hardy, founder and former CEO of LINK, London, by B. Bátiz-Lazo and C. Reese, London, 21 November 2007.

67. Interview (telephone) with Ron Delnevo, former managing director of Bank Machine, by B. Bátiz-Lazo, 17 July 2017.

68. On the formation of the UK network see Barrow (2006, 98); Bátiz-Lazo (2009); Clare Gascoigne, 'Confusion surrounds Link surcharge plan', *Financial Times*, 29 January 2000: 6.

69. Personal communication (email) from Ron Delnevo, former managing director of Euronet in the UK and Bank Machine, with B. Bátiz-Lazo, 20 July 2017.

70. Hayashi et al. (2003, 12) also report a process of 'aggressive consolidation' in the US IAD industry around the turn of the millennium; this would seem to have been delayed until the mid to late 2000s in the UK.

71. Emma Sinclair, 'How Jenny Campbell went from banking to start-ups', *The Telegraph*, 3 December 2012, accessed 8 July 2017, <http://www.telegraph.co.uk/women/womens-business/9717609/How-Jenny-Campbell-went-from-banking-to-start-ups.html>; 'Euronet Worldwide buys UK ATM Operator YourCash', *Finextra*, 10 October 2016, accessed 12 July 2017, <https://www.finextra.com/pressarticle/66505/euronet-worldwide-buys-uk-atm-operator-yourcash>; 'Acquisition of Hanco ATM Systems Limited and Hanco Automated Teller Machines B.V. by The Royal Bank of Scotland Group Plc.', Competition and Markets Authority, accessed

24 July 2017, <https://www.gov.uk/cma-cases/hanco-atm-systems-ltd-and-hanco-automated-teller-machines-b-v-royal-bank-of-scotland-group-plc>.

72. Interview (telephone) with Jenny Campbell, former Chief Operating Officer of Hanco and CEO & Chairman of YourCash, by B. Bátiz-Lazo, 22 February 2017.

73. Interview (telephone) with Paul Stanley, founder and former managing director of Moneybox, by B. Bátiz-Lazo, 11 December 2007.

74. See the saga of the merger between Halifax Building Society and Bank of Scotland, and the subsequent acquisition by Lloyds Banking Group, summarized by Ramzan Karmali, 'HBOS' Demise: How it Happened', *BBC News*, 19 November 2015, accessed 16 July 2017, <http://www.bbc.co.uk/news/business-34859067>.

75. 'Surcharge Issue Heating Up Again in the UK', *ATM Marketplace*, 16 January 2000, accessed 24 July 2016, <https://www.atmmarketplace.com/news/surcharge-issue-heating-up-again-in-the-uk/>.

76. Clare Gascoigne, 'Confusion Surrounds LINK Surcharge Plan', *Financial Times*, 29 January 2000: 6.

77. On the dispersion of consumers' willingness to pay for alternative methods see, for instance, Lam and Ossolinski (2015).

78. Interview with Terry Turner, co-founder of Hanco in the UK, by B. Bátiz-Lazo, Milton Keynes, 4 December 2007; Interview (telephone) with Paul Stanley, founder and former managing director of Moneybox, by B. Bátiz-Lazo, 11 December 2007; Interview (telephone) with Jenny Campbell, former Chief Operating Officer of Hanco and CEO & Chairman of YourCash, by B. Bátiz-Lazo, 22 February 2017; Personal communication (email) from Ron Delnevo, former managing director of Euronet in the UK and Bank Machine, with B. Bátiz-Lazo, 20 July 2017.

79. Margo Hirsch Strahlberg and Judith E. Rinearson, 'Visa/MasterCard Interchange Settlement Permits Merchants to Impose Surcharges Under Certain Circumstances', *Brian Cave LLP*, 20 February 2013, accessed 24 July 2017, <http://www.lexology.com/library/detail.aspx?g=19d27879-4c58-417e-be28-32f766c944b2>. Litigation continued until 2016, See 'American Express Can Bar Merchants From Steering Clients to Cheaper Cards', *Fortune*, 27 September 2016, accessed 24 July 2017, <http://fortune.com/2016/09/27/amex-merchants-clients-cheaper-cards/>.

80. 'Cashpoint Revolution', *Marketing Week*, 14 January 1999, accessed 24 July 2001, <https://www.marketingweek.com/1999/01/14/cashpoint-revolution/>.

81. Unless otherwise stated, this paragraph was sourced in Clare Gascoigne, 'Confusion Surrounds LINK Surcharge Plan', *Financial Times*, 29 January 2000: 6.

82. Barrow (2006, 98).

83. There was a debate over the value of the interchange fee in the late 1990s—LINK did not make this information available. Some public sources established a 30 to 60 pence boundary but it seems more likely to have been 40 pence. In any case this fee resulted from an agreement rather than from cost estimates. In the same way, there was no planning or cost estimate to determine the surcharging fee. Newcomers in the late 1990s were all surcharging at a rate of £1.00 per withdrawal, which by 2005 rose to £1.25 to £1.50 per withdrawal when operating costs increased. Interview with Terry Turner, co-founder of Hanco in the UK, by B. Bátiz-Lazo, Milton Keynes,

4 December 2007 and interview (telephone) with Jenny Campbell, former Chief Operating Officer of Hanco and CEO & Chairman of YourCash, by B. Bátiz-Lazo, 22 February 2017. A 40 pence interchange fee is also mentioned in James Mackintosh, 'Abbey Retreats from Cash Machine Surcharge', *Financial Times*, 23 June 2000: 2. On the mechanics of the LINK interchange fee see Bátiz-Lazo and Reese (2010).

84. Clare Gascoigne, 'Confusion surrounds Link surcharge plan', *Financial Times*, 29 January 2000: 6.

85. 'On Board with ISOs', *ATM Marketplace*, 21 March 2004, accessed 17 July 2017, <https://www.atmmarketplace.com/articles/on-board-with-isos/>.

86. Interview (telephone) with Paul Stanley, founder and former managing director of Moneybox, by B. Bátiz-Lazo, 11 December 2007.

87. James Mackintosh, 'Abbey Retreats from Cash Machine Surcharge', *Financial Times*, 23 June 2000: 2.

88. During a parliamentary debate John Robertson (Glasgow, North-West) (Lab), pointed to the Hanco acquisition by the Royal Bank of Scotland as sparking the Treasury Select Committee review. See 'Cash machines', *House of Commons Hansard Debates for 16 Feb 2006 (pt 1)* (Column 530WH), accessed 24 July 2017, <https://publications.parliament.uk/pa/cm200506/cmhansrd/vo060216/halltext/60216h01.htm>.

89. Phillip Inman, 'Cash Machine Operators Take £250m in Fees', *The Guardian*, 12 November 2005, accessed 24 July 2017, <https://www.theguardian.com/money/2005/nov/12/business.accounts>.

90. During an interview with Terry Turner he reckoned that Hanco had purchased Triton machines at £3,000 each in the early 2000s. Interview with Terry Turner, co-founder of Hanco in the UK, by B. Bátiz-Lazo, Milton Keynes, 4 December 2007. The 1.832895 £/$ conversion rate was sourced here: 'View Twenty Years of Exchange Data for Over 55 currencies', *OFX*, accessed 24 July 2017, <https://www.ofx.com/en-gb/forex-news/historical-exchange-rates/yearly-average-rates/>. The acquisition is described in contemporary sources here: 'Royal Bank of Scotland Acquires Hanco ATM Systems', *ATM Marketplace*, 22 September 2004, accessed 24 July 2017, <https://www.atmmarketplace.com/news/royal-bank-of-scotland-acquires-hanco-atm-systems/>; and Phillip Inman, 'Cash Machine Operators to Take £250m in Fees', *The Guardian*, 12 November 2005, accessed 24 July 2017, <https://www.theguardian.com/money/2005/nov/12/business.accounts>.

91. 'Acquisition of Hanco ATM Systems Limited and Hanco Automated Teller Machines B.V. by The Royal Bank of Scotland Group Plc.', Competition and Markets Authority, 7 September 2004, accessed 24 July 2007, <https://www.gov.uk/cma-cases/hanco-atm-systems-ltd-and-hanco-automated-teller-machines-b-v-royal-bank-of-scotland-group-plc>.

92. Interview (telephone) with Jenny Campbell, former Chief Operating Officer of Hanco and CEO & Chairman of YourCash, by B. Bátiz-Lazo, 22 February 2017.

93. 'Cash Machine Charges', House of Commons Treasury Committee, 15 March 2005 (London: HSMO, 2005), accessed 24 July 2017, <https://publications.parliament.uk/pa/cm200405/cmselect/cmtreasy/191/191.pdf>.

94. Interview (telephone) with Jenny Campbell, former Chief Operating Officer of Hanco and CEO & Chairman of YourCash by B. Bátiz-Lazo, 22 February 2017.

95. 'RBS Promises to Install Free Cash Machines', *YourMoney*, 28 September 2006, accessed 24 July 2017, <http://www.yourmoney.com/saving-banking/rbs-promises-install-free-cash-machines/>.

96. 'ATM Working Group—Cash Machines Meeting Consumer Needs', 13 December 2006 (London: HSMO), accessed 24 July 2016, <http://webarchive.nationalarchives. gov.uk/+/http:/www.hm-treasury.gov.uk/d/atm_working_group_final.pdf>; 'LINK = Financial Inclusion Program – 10 Year Anniversary', LINK Consumer Council, 2015, accessed 25 July 2017, <http://www.link.co.uk/media/1241/link-10-financial-inclusion-programme-website-flyer.pdf>.

97. 'Charging ATMs "Must be Labelled"', *BBC News*, 31 March 2005, accessed 25 July 2017, <http://news.bbc.co.uk/1/hi/business/4394251.stm>.

98. See for instance Bátiz-Lazo and Efthymiou (2016).

99. Unless otherwise stated, this paragraph borrows from Steve Rathgaber (CEO, Cardtonics), 'The Expanding Role of Independent ATM Deployers', *ATM & Cash Innovation Europe*, 13 June 2017.

100. Bátiz-Lazo and Reese (2010); Harper and Bátiz-Lazo (2013).

101. John Leehey III, CEO Payment Alliance International, presentation to ATMIA 18th Annual Conference, Orlando, FL. 14 February 2017.

102. 'Garden Centres Flourish with YourCash', *YourCash*, 22 June 2015, accessed 30 June 2017, <https://www.yourcash.com/tag/easy-ga/?lang=ga>.

103. Bátiz-Lazo and Efthymiou (2016); Cavell (2003, 20–1).

8

Earning People's Trust

8.1 Who is the Weakest Link?

This chapter explains how bank customers, that is, the ultimate or end consumers, have influenced and shaped cash withdrawals and other self-services offered through ATMs. This may at first seem odd and not straightforward. When dealing with an ATM most people interact with the payment card, keyboard, video display unit, and, of course, the cash dispensing mechanism. But as the previous chapters have shown, these are not the major part of the device.

Our initial consideration was that the cash machine gave the general public its first occasion to interface directly with complex technology. But this situation was not only new for them; it was also new for the ATM providers and the banks. More recently, the criticism has been made that trying to persuade customers to use ATMs rather than visiting a bank's retail branch was 'very high on technology and very low on people'.[1] It is also the case that the victims of ATM fraud are disproportionately elderly, poor, female, or black.[2] Moreover, before 1997, most ATMs were inaccessible to many disabled or special needs people because, among other things, they lacked hearing aid jacks or were simply too high up to be accessed by someone in a wheelchair.[3]

On both sides of the Atlantic regulations were passed to widen the use of ATMs by vulnerable consumers.[4] For instance, the Americans with Disabilities Act Accessibility Guidelines (ADAAG) in 1992 introduced specific requirements for ATMs in the USA.[5] Strict guidelines to ensure the accessibility of cashpoints to the physically disabled have also been enacted in the UK and in the European Union.[6] But in spite of costly adjustments to layouts and screens to increase usage, many vulnerable customers often avoid ATMs for fear of being exposed to assault as they make cash transactions in the open.[7] They prefer to use drive-through lanes (when they are available), telephoning, the Internet, or clerks at retail branches.

The question of how to engage with vulnerable consumers has been, is, and will be very much on the agenda for financial inclusion, as well as for the providers of cash withdrawal and kindred self-services. But the acceptance of these guidelines goes to show the importance of interaction between ATMs and the larger public, that some groups of people have at times been left behind, and, therefore, that affirmative action may be required to include them.

There are thus reasons to believe in the mutual shaping or co-evolution of technology and society.[8] From this perspective the stability of technology is fragile, in the sense that it will never be a fully finished product. There is a vast literature on the co-evolution of technology and society in financial services, which for space considerations will not be reviewed in detail here.[9] Suffice it to say that the interaction of ATMs with the larger public is a source of potential innovation, organizational learning, and necessary adjustments to the changing policies of banks, ATM manufacturers, and suppliers of related services.

Hence, people do matter; this chapter documents a couple of ways in which society left its imprint on the ATM. The first argument here is that, just as the free circulation of paper currency depended on the social construction of particular forms of trust, so did the ATMs as agents of banks.[10] This suggests that in the early days of the ATM, financial institutions had to persuade people and gain their trust and custom before investments in ATMs would pay off. As this chapter goes on to demonstrate, the issue of trust was central to the success of the ATM and other self-service technologies. Otherwise, by 'walking away', consumers could have rendered useless some of the large investments which banks made in computer infrastructure, effectively boycotting the deployment of the ATM and part or all of the broader infrastructure that it and other forms of self-service banking required.

It was a huge leap to move from automating and computerizing specific functions (such as cash withdrawal), to delivering fully online, real-time systems. There were multiple 'teething problems' as devices evolved and the supporting infrastructure was created. Thus, the second line of argument of this chapter is to show how in the process of adopting a new technology financial institutions could have easily lost customers' trust and custom. Financial institutions had to tread carefully between keeping customers satisfied and incentivizing them to use ATMs rather than tellers at branches, while bankers and engineers had, at the same time, to solve technological and organizational issues. This second argument, therefore, centres on the interaction of people with ATMs and how bad (or good) the technology was; how banks did or did not investigate incidents; how the law responded— and why there were so few cases of customers' challenging banks in the UK (as compared with Germany, where people regularly take ATM cases to court).[11] In this process, financial institutions, in the course of implementing electronic transactions, redefined their implicit and explicit contracts with their customers.

As a result, the discussion will maintain that technological infrastructures (in this case, the ATM shared network) are much more than a collection of material objects. This, as the total system architecture, reflects the values, practices, and payment habits of society. Such an idea is not new.[12] Neither is the idea that interested groups often have conflicting incentives and motivations to pursue and implement a particular technological vision.[13] But while banks, bankers, engineers, and engineering firms may remain the most influential shapers of this technology, few studies have considered how individuals (who in this case are the ultimate consumers of retail financial services) have considerable power as well.

In short, the remainder of this chapter explores the marketing attempts to win people's trust and incentivize the use of ATMs; the controversial topic of so-called 'phantom withdrawals'; and recapitulates the discussion on the importance of trust to the success of self-service technology.

8.2 Creating a Timeless Teller

8.2.1 *The Disneyization of the Cash Machine*

Trust plays an important part in building and maintaining a bank's brand.[14] Bankers of the 1950s spoke about a bank's 'reputation' rather than brand but, like the technology they used and the customers they served, this was to change. In the 1950s and 1960s, bankers, in particular those in commercial banks, had close ties with business and certain professions (such as medics, accountants, and lawyers). Bankers were 'culturally predisposed towards a custodial obsession with safety, not an entrepreneurial spirit of risk taking'.[15] The emergence of charge accounts, credit cards, point of sale terminals, and ATMs evidences the transformation that ensued between the 1960s and 1980s. This transformation was not only technological but also social, since it included moves towards more socio-economically diverse and gender inclusive provision in retail banking.

This meant that, alongside educating bankers about consumers, bank customers too had to learn how to operate the devices. Admittedly, in the early days of this technology, people were unaware of the machines' existence and purpose. Evidence of this is recorded in the Banking Marketing Association's quinquennial survey on electronic banking (called 'Payment Attitudes Change Evaluation' or PACE), which stated that in the USA only 3 per cent of respondents went anywhere near a cash machine in 1973.[16] The same survey reported that three out of four Americans were unaware what a cash machine was.

Given an initial attempt by many banks to use the ATM as a source of competitive advantage, it was common to find initiatives which aimed to create among consumers a unique identity for the services delivered through the machine, while explaining the purpose of the innovation. Very often repackaging it into a sanitized format would entail major modifications of the technology's original character.[17]

Instances of these marketing campaigns included that of the Third National Bank of Nashville, TN (today part of SunTrust Banks of Atlanta, GA) which in 1976 began airing on local TV the commercial 'Tammy the Timeless Teller'.[18] Anecdotal sources state the jingle's tune and catchphrase were quite successful and are still remembered forty years later.[19]

The ad featured a young blonde, female model (Chrissa Walsh) dressed in Tammy's distinctive dark blue waistcoat and skirt, a dark green shirt, and dark blue beret with a green pompon. The attire was accentuated by a green and blue tartan scarf, a pattern that was replicated as a stripe around the base of the beret. This colour scheme reinforced that of Third National's ATM card: three-quarters of it plain dark blue (like the beret), with a lime-green band at the top (like the shirt), displaying the bank's name in white letters and below it, in a larger font, 'timeless teller'.

The TV commercial began with the human character framed by a suburban scene, in which a young Caucasian professional in a three-piece suit, drives off to work after receiving a kiss from a housewife in night robe and pyjamas. Through the ad the Tammy character sings the virtues of a 24-hour/seven-days-a-week service while extending familiarity:

> I'm Tammy the timeless teller,
> I've always got time for you.
> I work ev'ry [sic] hour
> Ev'ry [sic] day of the year
> Weekends and holidays too!
> I treat your money
> Oh so swell!
> With ev'ry [sic] service ev'rybody [sic] loves so well
> I'm Tammy the timeless teller
> From Third National Bank.[20]

Note how the lines of the jingle emphasize availability ('I work every day of the year, Weekends and holidays too!') and customers being familiar with the transactions ('With ev'ry service ev'rybody loves so well'), thus inviting the audience to use the new service with confidence ('I treat your money, Oh so swell!').

As the advert proceeds, the suburban scene fades into downtown Nashville to show Tammy alongside two other women: one African American wearing a plain light-coloured turtle neck, plain dark jacket and trousers; and one dark-haired Caucasian, with a small black purse on her shoulder, in dark high heels and a light coloured plain dress. The three walk together towards the camera while the scene zooms out to show Third National's iconic building in the background.[21] Both these accompanying women are smartly dressed, probably pitching at the flattery of social inclusiveness and the emerging image of professional females in the workplace. The building reminds us of one of the pillars of the community, that is, a strong, solid, and trustworthy bank.

In the third and last scene, we see Tammy the person transforming into Tammy the cash machine. This scene shows the human character wrapping up the song while standing in front of an ATM. Within the camera frame and alongside her name in big lime-green letters, we see a caricature of Tammie's face (also a blue-eyed blonde, sporting the beret and tartan scarf). The character's name and the cartoon face appear at the top of the dark-blue surround of the machine's fascia. The scene then zooms out, leaving the Tammy character and the ATM framed by a brightly lit, cinema-style sign with the 'timeless teller' slogan across it. It is worth noting that the combination of this sign, the dark blue surround, and the cartoon characters were all replicated in other Tammy commercials as well as in actual ATM locations.[22]

A car is driven onto the scene. This hints that there is a drive-through service lane as well, but it is hard to be sure because the car, the ATM, and the human character are all facing the camera. But, assuming that this service was offered, it was another sign of convenience, efficiency, and modernity in the advert.

The themes of convenience, availability, efficiency, and community ties continued throughout the campaign. For instance, in another Tammy commercial she is supported by an elderly gentleman dressed as a priest, who states: 'Now Tammy what do you think of that service?' and ends the ad with his comment, 'Thank God it's so convenient' as he remains in his car. This ad was clearly pitching to elderly, religious customers. In another ad Tammy helps a couple eloping (who have run out of cash for the honeymoon) and observes: 'No matter where you are in Nashville, [Tammy] is always nearby'.[23] Use of the device was also incentivized by printing a coupon for a Baskin-Robbins' ice cream on the back of the ATM receipt.[24]

8.2.2 *Personifying the ATM*

In the next decade, the PACE survey of 1985 reports evidence of the importance of the ATM as a distribution channel for financial institutions and a degree of trust from bank consumers in using them.[25] The survey states that nearly one-third of the people in its sample used an ATM regularly. Virtually every respondent knew what they were and at least 48 per cent of the respondents had an ATM card. The respondents were said to like using ATMs because of the convenience of 24-hour/seven-day access to their accounts, the speed of service (compared with lines of people at the teller's desk), and ease of use.

Findings by the same PACE survey suggest that in spite of an increasing number of 'off-premise' ATMs, US customers in the mid-1980s overwhelmingly—86 per cent of the time—used the device that was at their financial institution.[26] The next most frequent choice was at shopping centres and supermarkets. The PACE survey also suggested that fear of technology was not an especially significant factor in the reluctance to use ATMs. Instead, the most common impediments to actively using ATMs cited by the survey were the proliferation of ATM networks, fees for using the service, and interestingly, that ATMs introduced at least one layer between the customer and the bank. In this regard, people found it confusing when their own bank participated in more than one ATM network. They said that fees often put them off (with 43 per cent of men versus 30 per cent of women refusing to pay fees) but being limited to their own bank's ATMs was deemed particularly unfair.

The results of the PACE survey seem to suggest that most customers in the mid-1980s favoured using their bank's own ATMs. As a result, the financial institutions deploying ATMs at the time were challenged to create a unique identity for this service while, at the same time, reinforcing individual bank brands and values. To address this issue some financial institutions sought celebrity sponsors and who else more suited to promoting these machines than the American singer-songwriter, guitarist, actor, and author John R. 'Johnny' Cash (1932–2003)?

In 1985 Canada Trust (today CT Financial Services) based in Toronto, and one of Canada's largest non-bank financial institutions, hired Jonny Cash when it launched a campaign to advertise its 'JohnnyCash Money Machine', a 24-hour, seven-day-a-week self-service device. Through TV commercials customers were informed of the new service by none other than the larger-than-life Country and Western singer himself—probably well known amongst rural customers of Canada Trust.[27]

Dressed in the trademark all-black attire, aided by an acoustic guitar as prop and a guitar playing in the background (a reminder of Cash's signature songs), in his distinctive deep, calm bass-baritone voice, sombre and humble demeanour, and often rebellious style, he recalled the inconvenience of bank hours: 'How many times have you been found short and the only thing between you and your money is the clock' or 'You know, friends, waiting in line for your money isn't fun'. Instead he recommends the use of the ATM service from Canada Trust (as they were): ' . . . the smart way to get to your money, because we never close'.

In other instances, some of the early model names became associated with the device itself as a result of custom rather than design. This was the case of Metior and the Swedish savings banks, which originally labelled their machines 'utbetalningsautomat' in 1967 but soon shortened it to 'Bankomat', which became a brand name for cash dispensing in Italy, Portugal, the Baltic Sea region, and Eastern Europe.[28] A similar process can be found in the former USSR, where in 1989 the state savings bank Sberbank introduced the 'Bankomat'.[29]

Other interesting instances of unusual branding included that of Pittsburgh Trust and Savings Company (today PNC Bank) of Pittsburgh, PA. The bank installed its first devices in the 1970s and branded them 'Money Access Centers' (MACs).[30] The acronym was then adopted by a shared ATM network, and the brand name and logo are still active in 2017. The result was that throughout the city of Philadelphia and across the state of Pennsylvania people often called an ATM a 'MAC'.

More intriguing was using personal names as a moniker. Socrates Sulópulos from Banco Continental (Peru) remembered when people were invited to create a name of their own choice.[31] This took place back in 1979, he said, when the bank was in government hands (during military rule). A ballot amongst all the employees' sons and daughters was set up. As a result of this ballot, said Sulópulos, the first ATM in Peru was called 'Ramón'. Sulópulos also mentioned that all machines were labelled as such until international sign-posting was adopted after the bank was privatized in 1996.

Another similar instance took place in July 2015 when Barclays Bank attempted to label self-service devices with personal names in the UK. But the initiative failed to take root amongst British customers.[32]

There is little originality in a corporate name extending to a whole product category—Hoovers are vacuum cleaners in the UK, Onesies are one-piece bodysuits, Jacuzzis are hot tubs, Kleenexes are disposable tissues, and Xeroxing is a synonym for photocopying.[33] But the case of the cash machine is interesting because a manufacturer's brand does not add value to the ultimate users, bank customers, who tend to be indifferent to alternative devices so long as their bank can provide a reliable service through that channel.

This same argument was used by the credit card companies: 'If people didn't identify the card with their bank, every time they have a problem they'd be calling us [i.e. the credit card company]. That doesn't happen. They know that their line of credit comes from [their] bank.'[34] So it is the bank's brand, not the manufacturer's, that matters to users of an ATM and this is exactly what financial institutions, as owners of the point of contact, have nurtured across time.

8.2.3 *Inclusive, Incisive, Decisive, Louder, Prouder, and Colourful*

More recently the unduly masculine, white, middle-class, and heterosexual marketing of financial services was brought to the fore through the GAYTM (as in merging gay and ATM) marketing campaign by the Australia and New Zealand Banking Group (ANZ Bank).[35] Through this campaign the ATM was transformed from the agent of a grey and ordinary experience of withdrawing cash into a branded, colourful celebration of inclusion—which helped generate a significant amount of name awareness for the bank.

ANZ, in terms of assets one of the four biggest banks in Australia and New Zealand, had been a major sponsor of Australia's Sydney Gay and Lesbian Mardi Gras since 2007.[36] In 2014, the bank elevated its sponsorship to 'Principal Partner'. The bank, seeking a canvas to demonstrate its commitment to the festival and convey its support for the event, embedded the otherwise increasingly tenuous provision of retail financial services in gay pride festivities.

The bank approached the TBWA\Melbourne advertising agency (at the time called Whybin/TBWA).[37] The advertising agency's brief asked for widespread public understanding of ANZ's support and partnership with Sydney Gay and Lesbian Mardi Gras. A successful outcome at the start of the project was deemed to be 22 million media impressions (or opportunities to see); Sydney metro newspaper coverage; and news coverage on at least one major commercial TV channel. Media coverage goals showed that the bank wanted the message from this campaign to resonate not only with ANZ employees, potential employees, customers and the lesbian, gay, bisexual, transgender, intersex, and queer/questioning (LGBTIQ) community; but also with others beyond these audience groups.[38] Note that at the time, the public perception in Australia of '"the big four" major banks [was] quite low' as banks were often perceived by the Australian public to be 'cold, callous organisations [sic] placing profits above people. They [were] also viewed as very conservative and incredibly "corporate" institutions.'[39]

The GAYTM project was a significant step forward, considering that ANZ's sponsorship had consisted of small-scale traditional media and a float in the Mardi Gras parade. 'Previous executions had always embodied the values and spirit of Mardi Gras, but never in such a tangible way,' said Kimberlee Wells, CEO of TBWA\Melbourne, in an interview.[40]

Like many other successes, GAYTMs (as the ATMs were to be known) were simple in their execution. For this the bank hired artists from the LGBTIQ community to bring in the direct inspiration of 'the gay and lesbian culture'.[41] Figure 8.1 shows that the GAYTM carrying the 'Cash out and proud' message on colourful withdrawal receipts to match the gay pride rainbow. The ATMs changed their display screens accordingly, with messages such as 'Hello

Figure 8.1. Support of ANZ Bank to Sydney Gay and Lesbian Mardi Gras, 2014

gorgeous' and 'Happy Mardi Gras!'. More important, the bank changed the colour and texture of ten ATM fascias and their surround along the Mardi Gras route. These bespoke fascias were decorated by hand with rhinestones, sequins, studs, leather, denim, and fur. From unicorns and drag queens to rainbows and tattoos, each GAYTM was a riot of colour and textures.[42]

Figure 8.1 also captures Anzabella, an ANZ bank staff member in feminine persona, who fronted the launch.[43] This unique persona illustrated how the strategy celebrating diversity, inclusion, and respect started from within the bank.

A quick image search in Google or Twitter for the #gaytm hashtag shows that the idea was a huge marketing success with a great many people posing next to the machines (whether dressed as their alter-ego or more conventionally). An industry source estimated that 'a receipt roll in the ANZ Oxford Street [Sydney] ATM normally lasts an average of one week. The first rainbow-coloured, receipt roll in the ANZ Oxford Street ATM lasted one hour.'[44]

The project generated massive media coverage inside and outside Australia. According to Peter Tilton, then Director of Digital Channels at ANZ, the GAYTM campaign accrued some 65 million impressions (three times the population of Australia), across 70 countries, including citations in British newspapers and TV coverage in the USA.[45] In June 2014, ANZ and TBWA \Melbourne were jointly awarded the Cannes Golden Lion Grand Prix in the Outdoor category.[46] The campaign thus exceeded expectations at many levels, giving the bank a 'human face' while creating unprecedented positive social sentiment, with customers being proud of their bank, others now thinking they would switch to ANZ, and some of the general public and ANZ staff writing heartfelt personal letters to senior bank staff.[47]

But for all of its achievements, criticism was aired by both the public and some politicians that the GAYTM reinforced gay stereotypes and that ANZ was profiting from civil rights issues.[48] Stereotypes are hard to deal with succinctly, however, and space considerations preclude going into any depth, as I should prefer. As for the accusation of profiteering, the bank donated an undisclosed amount equivalent to all the fees from the GAYTMs to the charity Twenty10, which works with young people of diverse genders, sexes, and sexualities.[49]

But as can be seen in Figure 8.2, the GAYTMs could not escape vandals' expressing what was initially believed to be an act of homophobia.[50] It turned out that a group calling themselves 'Queers Against Injustice' claimed responsibility for defacing the GAYTM with pink paint or 'Pinkwashing, a term... [they defined to describe] the way that institutions co-opt LGBT struggles to

Figure 8.2. Vandalized GAYTM, ANZ Ponsonby Road branch, Auckland, 2015
Source: Used with the permission of the Australia and New Zealand Banking Group Limited. All rights reserved.

217

distract from and disguise unethical behaviour'.[51] The group also claimed to have been offended by the portrayal of their action in mass media as homophobic, while describing their intent as a 'political statement' to protest against the commercialization of Pride Festival symbols by the bank. This opened a brief discussion in the local press as to whether the bank or the group was being intolerant and unethical.[52]

There is much to be said for ANZ as an organization that supported and empowered staff to deliver the GAYTM innovation. Had the GAYTM campaign gone wrong, the bank would have lost more in terms of reputation and branding than the cost of designing and implementing the GAYTM campaign. Monitoring the conversations in the social media was key to delivering the campaign and making sure that it was in tune with the otherwise 'deeply connected, deeply passionate, and incredibly well-organised [LGBTIQ community]'.[53] This, in turn, was an imposition on operational staff at the bank, who had to work around the clock monitoring the social media while the festivities lasted. But it was worth doing; the bank delivered the highest engagement rate of any Australian bank across Facebook, Twitter, and Instagram.[54]

For me, at a conceptual level, the significance of the GAYTMs was, first, that they literally required 'thinking outside the (cash) box'. For instance, it was a long time before the GAYTM that banks found limited opportunities for advertising either on the ATM screen or on the back of the receipts. Time and again market reports told of consumer distaste for general advertising around the ATM, while printing information on the back of receipts had little success in raising awareness (as well as being environmentally unfriendly). Yet the GAYTM effectively redefined both these issues.

Second, the GAYTM showed the bank being sincere with its workplace policies of diversity, inclusion, equality, and respect. In this regard, Wells noted how staff members were overwhelmed by the public statement the bank made as it 'drove home ANZ's respect for individuality, particularly when ANZ employees dressed as their drag alter-egos . . . GAYTMs unquestionably became the living social proof that ANZ could walk the walk.'[55]

If nothing else, the GAYTMs challenged other industry participants (and scholars) to look again at monetary interfaces in a more positive light. In 2017, for instance, the idea of a GAYTM was reproduced in other LGBTIQ festivals such as those in Dublin (Bank of Ireland) and Oslo (Nordea).[56] The GAYTMs tapped for the first time the potential to effectively reconceptualize the ordinary, routine, and unremarkable aspects of banking services. They opened an opportunity for creating a visual and tactile splash by making (very) visible the material point of contact between people and digital markets. The GAYTMs help us to reflect on how grey, 'subterranean, and mundane the payment rails' and other parts of the payments infrastructure's interfaces are.[57] In other words, how invisible and taken for granted ATMs and point of sale terminals usually are in everyday life. One is left to wonder if the huge success of this campaign could be duplicated in other retail financial products and services, festivals, or using other interfaces and without undue expense.

8.3 Phantom Withdrawals: Banking on the Inhuman Factor

8.3.1 *Winning People's Trust*

People's fear that ATMs presented a potential for electronic error was manifested in the PACE survey of 1985.[58] Respondents felt that resolving such transactions, particularly in a machine in a shared ATM network (i.e. owned and managed by an ATM operator other than their 'home' bank) would be more difficult than correcting problems encountered at an ATM owned by the 'home' bank or in a dialogue with a bank clerk.

Unfortunately, the fears and concerns of bank customers around electronic banking in general and ATMs in particular were (and remain) justified.[59] The initial source of the threats to ATM security came not from cryptanalysis or other sophisticated attacks, but from a careless and incompletely evaluated design policy of the ATM card issuers.[60]

An additional contributing factor has been the assignment of legal responsibility for charging bank customers for either alleged or wilful fraudulent misuse of a bank's ATM card. An article in the *New York Times* articulated this point alongside the global connectivity of ATMs stating that:

> Banks are supposed to reimburse victims of A.T.M. [sic] [transaction] theft. But unlike credit card fraud, in which banks are stuck with bills for unauthorized purchases, A.T.M. thefts take cash from consumers, who may bear the burden of proving that withdrawals were unauthorized...[Admittedly]...there are people who say they have been defrauded when they have not...[61]

Indeed, as people learnt how to operate and grew accustomed to interacting with ATMs, enhanced consumer confidence resulted in their being used far more intensively than bankers had first imagined.[62] These unexpected innovations, however, made it essential for financial institutions to balance three deals at once: dealing with fraud; the challenges to invest, implement, and maintain new technology; and customers becoming confident enough in the use of cash machines to adopt their services widely. The discussion now turns to the effects of these problems and their prevalence.

8.3.2 *A Freezing Welcome to the Phantom Forest*

Today most individuals interact regularly and readily with an ATM, certain and confident that the transaction will be finalized as expected. But this was not and still is not always the case.

So-called 'phantom withdrawals' are debited transactions that the customer has contested where the cardholder has not reported the card lost or stolen.[63] The card-issuing bank will conclude that the customer is responsible for the withdrawal(s) if staff from the bank (or its vendors) are unable to find any error on their side.[64]

Few of today's staff in a retail bank branch might remember having dealt with a phantom transaction. But they appeared at the very dawn of the cash machine in the early 1970s (as suggested in a newspaper in Singapore).[65] However, problems associated with phantom withdrawals became widespread and dominated the public's attention much later, between 1981 and 1993, in the UK. This is suggested by an examination of tabloid newspapers (e.g. *Daily Mail*), industry magazines (e.g. the *Building Societies Gazette*, *Ombudsman News*), and annual reports of organizations protecting financial consumers (e.g. the Banking Services Ombudsman, the Building Societies Ombudsman, and the Financial Services Ombudsman in the UK).[66]

A stream of public evidence discussing phantom withdrawals in Britain emerged in the form of letters written to the *Daily Mirror* starting in January 1981. These letters complained about unauthorized withdrawals ranging from £5 to £1300 in different cases. As protests mounted and following an open letter in the *Law Society Gazette* (of 15 June 1983), the National Consumer Council produced two reports focusing on consumers' complaints about ATM transactions, with details of several cases concerning phantom withdrawals.[67]

Figure 8.3 records the level of grievances dealing with ATMs as a proportion of total complaints per year logged with each of the ombudsmen. Complaints relating to phantom transactions at ATMs were the single biggest source of protest at the Banking Ombudsman Service between 1986 and 1990, and between 1987 and 1990 at the Building Societies Ombudsman. Figure 8.3, also suggests that grievances dealing with ATMs as a proportion of annual complaints peaked around 1992 and then steadily declined for both the ombudsmen.

Once a complaint was logged, staff at the Ombudsman's office would evaluate its nature, and consider whether or not it merited further action, beginning with an investigation. Trends relating to investigations are summarized in Table 8.1.

The interpretation of data in Table 8.1 should not be taken as definitive because the basis for its calculation changed a number of times between 1988 and 2001. However, the trends in Table 8.1 seem in line with data

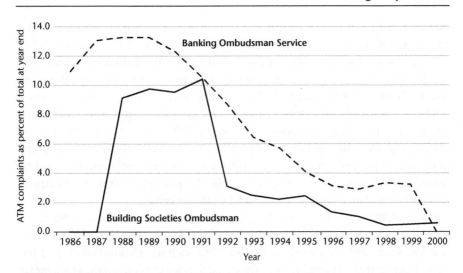

Figure 8.3. Complaints dealing with ATMs logged at ombudsmen, 1986–2000

Source: Annual reports of Banking Ombudsman Service and Building Societies Ombudsman (several years).

Table 8.1. Investigations dealing with ATMs pursued by ombudsmen, 1986–2008

Year	Number of complaints and communications		Cases investigated (% of total)		Cases relating to ATMs (% of investigated)	
	BOS	**BSO**	**BOS**	**BSO**	**BOS**	**BSO**
1986	782	*n.a.*	*n.a.*	*n.a.*	*n.a.*	*n.a.*
1987	1,748	*n.a.*	223 (13%)	*n.a.*	*n.a.*	*n.a.*
1988	2,089	980	254 (12%)	*n.a.*	*n.a.*	*n.a.*
1989	2,706	1,582	305 (11%)	*n.a.*	*n.a.*	*n.a.*
1990	3,915	2,572	475 (12%)	*n.a.*	*n.a.*	*n.a.*
1991	6,327	2,577	746 (12%)	642 (25%)	286 (38%)	86 (13%)
1992	10,109	9,525	959 (9%)	1,070 (11%)	346 (36%)	96 (9%)
1993	10,231	9,402	1,111 (11%)	1,382 (15%)	222 (20%)	51 (4%)
1994	8,691	9,100	833 (10%)	901 (10%)	132 (16%)	42 (5%)
1995	7,424	10,431	717 (10%)	1,079 (10%)	86 (12%)	20 (2%)
1996	8,044	13,219	736 (9%)	2,081 (16%)	48 (7%)	24 (1%)
1997	8,818	14,933	674 (8%)	1,692 (11%)	36 (5%)	16 (1%)
1998	11,874	15,473	741 (6%)	2,391 (15%)	59 (8%)	14 (1%)
1999	12,478	7,309	848 (7%)	1,655 (23%)	37 (4%)	5 (>1%)
2000	14,583	5,929	*n.a.*	971 (16%)	*n.a.*	2 (>1%)
Financial Services Ombudsman						
2001	414,722		31,347 (8%)			*n.a.*
2002	388,239		43,330 (11%)			26 (>1%)
2003	462,340		62,170 (13%)			114 (>1%)
2004	548,338		97,901 (18%)			128 (>1%)
2005	614,148		110,963 (18%)			190 (>1%)
2006	672,973		112,923 (17%)			279 (>1%)
2007	627,842		94,392 (15%)			291 (>1%)
2008	794,648		123,089 (15%)			883 (1%)

Source: Own estimates, based on annual reports of Banking Ombudsman Service (BOS), Building Societies Ombudsman (BSO), and Financial Service Ombudsman (several years).

documented by the Jack Committee report in 1989, which estimated that there was, on average, one disputed ATM transaction per hour across the UK.[68]

This caveat aside, the data in Table 8.1 show that the Banking Ombudsman Service received an average of 7,321 complaints and communications per annum between 1986 and 2000. The Building Societies Ombudsman received 7,926 between 1987 and 1999, while an average 565,406 p.a. were received by the Financial Service Ombudsman between 2001 and 2008. Of these complaints, the Banking Ombudsman Service investigated on average 663 grievances p.a. (9 per cent of total complaints and communications), the Building Societies Ombudsman investigated 1,386 (17 per cent), and the Financial Service Ombudsman investigated 84,514 (15 per cent).

Of the complaints that merited an investigation those dealing with ATMs represented on average 21 per cent (139 cases) for the Banking Ombudsman Service, 3 per cent (36 cases) for the Building Societies Ombudsman, and less than 1 per cent (273 cases) for the Financial Service Ombudsman. The average value of investigations suggests that complaints relating to phantom transactions at ATMs were low. However, and as illustrated in Figure 8.3, the number of investigations dealing with ATMs started as the single biggest item in the investigations of the banking and the building societies ombudsmen, and from then on showed a steep downward trend.

8.3.3 *The Spectre of Money*

There are a number of factors that could help explain phantom transactions including carelessness from the customers (e.g. writing their PIN on the card) and criminal activity. For instance, customer receipts printed by ATMs in the 1970s and 1980s included so much information that, if left behind, they enabled crooks to authorize payments through telephone banking. More important was the fallibility of the magnetic stripe.[69] One could purchase equipment for a few hundred pounds or even use a simple hot iron to 'clone' a card, that is, read and copy valid information onto a new card with a blank magnetic stripe.[70] The banks did not warn ATM users how easy it was for someone to look over their shoulder, even from a distance, and memorize the PIN as it was keyed into an ATM. Anyone with brief access to a card could clone it and use it to steal.

But sloppy consumer practices and multiple forms of fraud did not explain phantom withdrawals or how consumers could guard against the risk. The possibility of random technological malfunction was next to be considered. Geoffrey Constable, an engineer involved in the genesis of the Chubb cash machine at Smiths Industries, gave his opinion as follows:

> With a returnable card system, no token remains in the machine. The record of transactions in some cash machines was a row of printed digits produced by a tally

roll printer, and such printers occasionally made mistakes.... It is then accepted that ATMs occasionally record 'phantom' transactions.... Research undertaken at Cambridge [University] indicated that at least one transaction in 30,000 was a phantom.[71]

The possibility that technology was at fault was not lost to the government. Although it was not known how many breaches of ATM security involved a dispute at all, since only small sums were involved, it seemed reasonable to assume that machine-made phantom withdrawals could have been the source for the widespread dissatisfaction amongst consumers in their interaction with ATMs.

And here was the conundrum for bankers. On the one hand, financial institutions 'like the police, military and government, refuse to discuss security, on the grounds that publicising loopholes tells people how to exploit them'.[72] Nor were banks going to abandon the substantial sums invested to create the large-scale deployment of ATMs. On the other hand, the possibility of malfunction (either technological or administrative) questioned the viability of integrating automated cash withdrawals, electronic fund transfers, and other forms of self-service banking into the retail payments system. Indeed, '[w]ith several million cash machine transactions every day, the whole pack of [payment] cards would come tumbling down if any one bank so much as hinted that the system might be vulnerable to fraud'.[73]

Phantom transactions, therefore, not only questioned whether bankers could persuade large numbers of customers to use a machine instead of interacting with a human, but called the honesty and integrity of the individual customer into question in the way complaints were handled and consequently had the power to taint the bank's brand and reputation.

8.3.4 *A Ghost in the Legal Wires*

An issue with phantom withdrawals was always that they are typically low in value. The customer thus had little incentive to pursue matters through the justice system given that the cost of legal action would probably dwarf the accumulated value of all phantom transactions. Besides the costs of litigation, it was also the case that consumers were generally unfamiliar with the law and the legal system and lacked access to relevant information, advice, and legal services. In short, it was the consumer David against the bank Goliath. Two brief legal cases may illustrate the apparent uselessness, in this situation, of mounting a legal challenge against a bank.

One early example is that of Group Action. In 1992, Alistair Kelman and Dennis Haley were a barrister and a solicitor, respectively, representing 250 plaintiffs in a High Court action against all the UK banks and building societies on the matter of phantom withdrawals.[74] Kelman took the case on legal aid and through the assistance of the Consumers' Association, bundled up more than 2,000 people's cases into a single class action.[75] At the time, Whalley stated:

> By representing so many people, [we] hope that the banks will not be able to settle in their usual manner, that they will be forced to admit the imperfections of their systems and subsequently that they will have to improve security; something that they have been reluctant to do as yet because of the cost.[76]

The Group Action case was interesting in that it raised the issue of whether a PIN keyed into an ATM together with a card validating the account number, met the criterion of being a legal mandate from customers to banks to debit their account. But in June 1993 the banks—through the Association of Payment Clearing Services (APACS)—changed their rules. Customers became liable only for the first £50 of any disputed phantom withdrawal; the sum could be waived if the customer made a good enough case for not giving away the PIN or being careless with it. At the time, Kelman believed that the plaintiffs would settle with the banks, but they did not. Although he was dismissed, the legal plea continued, only to be ultimately denied.

Unfortunately, this event was not to be the end of phantom withdrawals. As of 2005, a website aiming to help victims documented at least twenty-one further instances.[77] One such was that of Alain Job in the UK, who sued the former building society, Halifax (later part of HBOS) in March 2007.[78]

Job was an asylum seeker from Cameroon, who came to the UK with his wife and two daughters, and was given the right to stay but not to work there. He managed financially through the help of friends, charities, and his family. But owing to the UK's immigration policy he led a fairly hectic life and relocated a number of times. Following the Home Office's dispersal policy, Job was moved to Nottingham, where he received some 350 hate mails that forced him and his family to move to Reading, where his wife subsequently died.

Eight withdrawals took place over an eight-day period from two ATMs located in Reading. Job maintained that he did not authorize anyone else to withdraw a cumulative £2100 ($3100) and that in the period of the disputed transactions he had always carried the card. In addition, the last of the questioned withdrawals was made after he had discovered the state of his bank account (but had not yet informed the bank or the police) and while he was at home watching television, with his family.[79] He decided to sue the Halifax after the Financial Ombudsman Service, where he had sought mediation, sided with the bank.[80]

As someone who had no assets, lived in rented accommodation, and by law was not allowed to take paid employment, Alain Job was, in some respects, the ideal claimant. However, his claim was rejected by the court, because he failed to provide sufficient evidence to support it. He would have had to provide evidence that he had not authorized the transactions (e.g. that no one else in his house knew his PIN—whereas some did) and that it had not resulted from gross negligence (e.g. the card had been with him at all times—which he admitted it was not; another reason for supposing he treated his card carelessly was that he had been sent no fewer than seven cards in the few years he had had an account). Meanwhile, the bank, in the judge's view, provided sufficient evidence (e.g. withdrawals stopped just before the bank was alerted) to suggest that no system error or third-party fraud could explain the withdrawals.

However disappointing the result for Job, his case attracted attention from the mass media and the academic world,[81] for the UK seldom saw an individual taking his bank to court for a relatively small sum. The case might have had implications for a significant effect on consumer protection, only these failed to materialize through the denial of Job's claim.

8.4 Trust Busting or Trust Building?

8.4.1 *Improve Security: A Lesson from Haunting Consumers*

Phantom transactions have been part of a larger debate about the security and integrity of the cash withdrawal system and have to be understood in the context of whether the customer or the card issuer would or should take responsibility for the consequences of fraud. There were technological reasons why phantom withdrawals were possible at the level of card, ATM, authorization service, and the central system, particularly in the early stages of the technology.[82] These shortcomings were ironed out gradually as the integrity of the ATM and its infrastructure improved, and as customers became more confident and used ATMs more frequently.[83]

Widespread adoption of the ATM required changes within the operational design of devices as well as within the processes, routines, skills, and procedures of financial institutions. Adaptations of particular importance were those to improve the security inside the ATM and the network's management practices. Individual banks' accounting procedures also became more robust. But here we have a typical 'chicken and egg' situation where there is no single cause and effect; customers, technology, banks, and the behaviours of the people involved interacted and co-evolved.

When confronted with the possibility of phantom withdrawals, the financial providers claimed that the transaction had to be correct because the withdrawal had been activated by card and the PIN. As noted in Chapters 4 and 6, a PIN, however, is not unique to a person. With a four-digit code there are only 9,999 possibilities, while empirical studies suggest people's choice of

PIN is highly concentrated within a limited range, not the full spectrum of possible PINs.[84] Instead, a unique identifier results only from combining the bank's own identification code with the customer's PIN and account number.

The security in most of the pioneering devices was limited to the PIN or a combination of PIN and account number. This meant that, in the absence of an electronic trail, the way for a bank to confirm a customer's claim was to assert that some anomaly had been identified during replenishment. Alternatively, branch staff could have opened the back of the ATM to reconcile the balance of banknotes issued with those in the escrow box and online transaction audit trails at the central systems. Any difference in balances would have had to be investigated. It needs no stretch of the imagination to see that the cost of offering this solution to each and every contested transaction would be very expensive for any financial institution.

Of course, ATM manufacturers responded in support of the banks and their customers. The IBM 3614 and 3624 ATM, for instance, moved security a bit further down the line.[85] Increased security was developed using encryption and secure encryption management. The system used one level of encryption to encode the PIN and account number, which was further encoded by a second level of encryption before the transmission of the transaction message between the ATM and the central authorization systems. Each level had a unique key to encrypt the information, held in secure storage within the 3614/3624 ATMs, and changed frequently in conjunction with the central system. For the system to remain robust, IBM engineers developed an application to create a new set of randomly generated master keys in a secure crypto facility within a central computer, and then update the keys in the ATMs in conjunction with the central system.

Clearly, the more the bank updated the master keys, the more secure the overall system was. In the 3624 model, for instance, the bank could choose to update keys at random, automatically at fixed intervals, or by request. This would deter any potential recording of the transaction and playback since only the crypto devices in the central system and inside the ATMs knew what the current keys were.

It is worth noting that IBM devoted a significant amount of engineering effort and hardware costs to preventing physical intrusion, on the assumption that individual machines would be left unattended.[86] These measures included all the cryptographic functions performed by hard-wired circuitry inside the most physically secure area of the machine—as opposed to a program that performed cryptographic operations. Admittedly, this design approach reduced implementation flexibility, but it still enhanced overall system security.

In spite of these innovations, however, anyone using a digital signature had to take great care to protect its key since 'even the use of cryptography cannot provide evidence of the link between the person whose primary key is used to associate a signature with a document or message, and the actual act of causation'.[87] This applies also to the recipient of the message when it cannot be verified that the sender intended to be associated with the signature.

8.4.2 *High Availability of ATMs: A Defence against the Dark Arts*

There have been nuances and country-specific responses from banks and ATM manufacturers to implement a high availability policy and deal with phantom withdrawals and/or the secure widespread uptake of ATMs by bank customers. These are all features of ATM operation that are closely related. For instance, a survey by ATM manufacturer NCR in 2012 claimed that 28 per cent of US respondents, 38 per cent of British respondents, and 70 per cent of French respondents would be very likely to switch banks if they experienced recurrent instances of ATM unavailability.[88]

Phantom transactions and security were discussed earlier in this chapter. Availability is commonly defined as the percentage of time that an ATM can dispense cash and is the most common way among ATM operators of judging ATM effectiveness.[89] Barring the consequences of extreme events, such as volcanic eruptions, the unavailability of an ATM to deliver cash to a customer can be caused by failures in the network, the central authorization systems, or the machine itself. Two of the main causes of internal failure are the build-up of dirt in the card reader mechanism and paper dust from the banknotes.

In an early effort to improve availability, IBM engineers, for instance, designed for its clients an ATM inbuilt predictive and preventive facility.[90] This system monitored the use of components (specifically moving parts) against predefined thresholds based on transaction volumes. When these thresholds were close to being reached, the system would notify the ATM operations centre, where a service call to address the problem(s) by bank staff or engineers from the manufacturer would be scheduled.

Maintenance activities would typically be organized during periods of low usage or cash replenishment, and before the device failed, so as to minimize the unavailability of the ATM to customers. In addition, the central control centre could send automated status requests to ATM(s) to address out of line situations such as unusually low or no transaction activity from a specific ATM. Where transaction levels were consistently high or when access to an ATM was not possible (e.g. overnight), the ATM operator would typically install a second or third ATM at the same site—so that if one failed or had to be put out of service the other(s) would act as back-up.

8.4.3 *Electronic Information as Evidence: A Phantom Menace*

In the UK, the Bills of Exchange Act of 1882 established that the responsibility for signature verification fell on the relying party (i.e. the bank).[91] Banks, therefore, had traditionally assumed the consequences of fraud when cashing a cheque with a false signature.[92] Yet the banks' view has been that a PIN is binding on the person who carries it as a form of authentication—although the electronic audit trail says nothing about who initiated the transaction. If so, from the perspective of the financial institutions, it is the customer's responsibility to keep the PIN safe and, when unable to prove that this has been done, assume the losses for its fraudulent use.

Legal scholars, however, have challenged this view on the basis that 'the PIN is a form of electronic signature and the law has not changed, regardless of the technology used by financial institutions'.[93] As a result, the financial institution should provide evidence that it had a mandate from the customer to debit the customer's account.

Yet few British customers are poised to mount a significant legal challenge and recoup money stolen by thieves or otherwise lost. To begin with, court proceedings generate significant associated expenses in the UK. Worse, there has been a presumption in common law in England and Wales that, in the absence of contrary evidence, computer-like devices, such as ATMs or point of sale terminals, are reliable and were in working order at the time of the event.[94]

The lack of published evidence of successful attacks or the cloning of 'chip and PIN' cards reinforces this view.[95] However, this view fails to consider that it is in the interest of criminals to conceal the power to clone chips in payment cards. It is also in the interest of financial institutions to minimize their vulnerability to fraud and transfer the loss to customers by suggesting they were careless or had attempted outright fraud. So not only is the *status quo* not challenged but judges also tend to refrain from ordering financial institutions to produce additional, detailed, contemporary evidence to prove that their technological and organizational systems were in working order at the time in question.

Meanwhile in Canada, the Financial Consumer Agency of Canada (FCAC) reiterated in 2017 its expectations that investigations of alleged unauthorized credit and debit transactions would be heard more attentively than in Britain.[96] To be specific, federally regulated financial institutions (FRFIs) must take all relevant factors into account before finding a consumer liable, regardless of the method or technology used to process the credit or debit card transaction. Consequently, FRFIs must investigate whether circumstances beyond the cardholder's control resulted in an unauthorized transaction (such as shoulder-surfing, coercion, card theft, systems malfunction, etc.). FRFIs must not rely solely on authentication technologies to curtail or prevent a comprehensive investigation of an alleged unauthorized transaction. For example, a finding of liability cannot be based solely on the fact that a transaction was completed using the correct combination of chip and PIN.

In the USA, as a result of a 1980 court decision in New York, the Federal Reserve passed regulations backing the customer unless the bank provided evidence of fraud.[97] The response of many banks was to install CCTV cameras at ATM machines to protect their interests and this seems to have had the required effect of sorting out fraud from 'abuse' (namely, a family member other than the account holder using the card and PIN, versus a stranger having effectively cloned or stolen the card and PIN).

The effectiveness of CCTV proceeds on the assumption that, if such images are offered as evidence, this can be validated,[98] for instance, by synchrony between the clock in the CCTV and the ATM. But even when internal workings cannot be validated, CCTV images can work to corroborate and reinforce evidence in combination with other devices and systems that have features attributable to a specific person (such as a licence plate or the transaction counter in the chip of a payment card).[99] It is interesting to note that CCTV is being replaced by systems that use Internet Protocol (IP) technologies and wireless IP, which will in turn cause additional expense and increase the legal complexity (such as the camera taking images in one country that are recorded or stored in another country).[100]

In Spain, the automation and self-service trailblazer *la Caixa* took a completely different approach.[101] Around 1984, this former savings bank (which in 2017 was the third largest player in the Spanish domestic market) was redesigning its branch space and looking to attract large numbers of customers to use and interact with its Fujitsu-made, bespoke-ATM, passbook-based, self-service offering. In order to attract pensioners and other possible customers who would otherwise be reluctant to trust and frequently use self-service, the bank decided that hostesses in branches were enough. Therefore, no PIN was required when pensioners and the elderly activated an ATM with a payment card or passbook.

Surprising as it may seem, the bank argued that the PIN was just another barrier in the adoption of self-service and that it was more interested in securing adoption than in limiting potential losses. The bank later reported the programme to be a success and that losses during the no-PIN operation of ATMs had been insignificant.

In summary, from the banks' perspective the issue of phantom withdrawals was one of security and system availability, whereas from the customers' perspective the issue was trust in the ATM and in the card-issuing bank. Financial institutions had a vested interest, with significant investment in ATMs' paying off. But this was contingent on winning people's trust and custom. Financial intermediaries systematically rejected the possibility of technical failure while downplaying the risk of fraud (or trying to pass its consequences on to retail customers). This was important from the standpoint of the service provider in order to maintain confidence and overall consumer trust in electronic payment systems. However, some ill feeling permeated the record of the ATM, since clients felt their honesty and integrity was being challenged—specifically when they learned that fraud and to a lesser extent technical and clerical error had indeed taken place.

It is important to realize here that secure encryption management and central system authorization resulted in higher trust in ATMs and banks and at the same time formed a basis for the development of national and world-wide ATM interchange networks, such as MasterCard and Visa (as explained in Chapter 6).

8.5 Ghosts in the Machine

Is the ATM solely responsible for consumption patterns, changes in the way we bank from strict, frugal, thrifty, and prudent cash budgeting to a culture of lavish, reckless, impromptu purchasing? 'Not entirely' is the short answer. Yet there is little doubt that cash machines have made conventional retail banking more convenient. Duncan Stance, a 74-year-old pensioner from Montreal, responded to this point: 'I withdraw what I need for the day. I am getting older and I feel more secure carrying less cash.'[102] When Bank of Montreal installed a cash machine in Stance's neighbourhood in Canada, this meant breaking a thirty-year habit of banking once a week; now he visited the ATM four times a week. Stance did miss the personal contact of the friendly cashier at the bank retail branch but the convenience of short queues, weekend banking, and improved record-keeping (through receipt slips from the machine to check against his monthly statement) more than compensated, he said.

The experience of David Stance suggests that for most people the introduction of the cash machine marked the start of banking 'where you want, what you want, when you want'; and more important, banking with the whole banking network instead of being tied to a specific retail branch of a financial institution. The cash machine signalled the end of relationship banking and the start of transactional retail financial services. But, this chapter has argued, the advent of the cash machine also meant people had to trust technology rather than a bank clerk to get things done—something today we take largely for granted, as evidenced by the growth of e-commerce and mobile banking.

As this chapter has shown, developing trust was central to the success of the ATM because banks had to win people's confidence and custom to make their large capital investments in technology profitable. But this was possible only insofar as the ATM became the agent of a bank; that is, not only serving as a cash in/cash out point but able to replicate, with confidence and certainty, a similar interaction with a human (i.e. a direct and lawful representative of the bank).[103] This chapter argues that phantom withdrawals, Tammy the Timeless Teller, and GAYTMs all questioned and brought light to bear on the nature of the agency between bank and customer through an ATM.

This chapter told of the demands by most people on their banks as part of the implicit and explicit contract to actively engage with ATMs. Failure by the banks to develop the trust and negotiate consumers' demands risks forfeiting substantial investments (to bring in large numbers of people as customers into retail financial markets). These investments included the development of widespread, conveniently located, reliable, and easy to use networks of automated cash machines. But when things did not work as expected, people had to organize action through the judiciary for their claims to be considered.

People have actively participated in infrastructure decisions around issues of accessibility for the physically disabled and, as Chapter 7 showed, the moral, ethics, and justice of surcharging vulnerable consumers. All this illustrates how citizen engagement complements technical ingenuity in the widespread use of ATMs. Moreover, the massification of retail finance effectively meant the democratization of banking. Demands for the trustworthy operation of ATMs thus reflect the transformation to fairer and more equitable access thanks to the wider infrastructure supporting the retail financial system.

Like almost any other application of computer technology, the ATM was subject to local and cultural circumstances, previous experiences, lessons learned, and idiosyncratic factors.[104] This chapter documents this impact through the episodes around the GAYTM, Tammy the Timeless Teller, and phantom withdrawals. Together with the Treasury Select Committee's investigation into 'pay to use' ATMs in the UK, and other episodes involving ATMs documented throughout this and Chapter 7, they show how infrastructure, in this case the ATM interchange network, is much more than a collection of material objects; although it is often in the background, this system architecture has an impact on and is shaped by everyday life.

Notes

1. Sam Meadows, 'Your Local Branch Has Gone and You Don't Like Online Banking. What Are Your Options?', *The Daily Telegraph*, 27 June 2017, accessed 19 July 2017, <http://www.telegraph.co.uk/money/future-of-money/local-branch-has-gone-dont-like-online-banking-options/>; Jenny Hirschkcorn, 'Connecting the Elderly with Internet Know-How', *The Daily Telegraph*, 12 June 2014, accessed 19 July 2017, <http://www.telegraph.co.uk/sponsored/finance/your-bank/10890366/elderly-help-internet.html>.
2. Ross Anderson, 'Banks Biased Against Black Fraud Victims', *Light Blue Touchpaper*, 12 January 2017, accessed 19 July 2017, <https://www.lightbluetouchpaper.org/2017/01/12/banks-biased-against-black-fraud-victims/>; Richard Spillet, 'Barclays Four Times More Likely to Deny Fraud Victims a Refund', *Daily Mail*, 14 October 2015, accessed 19 July 2017, <http://www.dailymail.co.uk/news/article-3272061/Barclays-four-times-likely-deny-fraud-victims-refund-banks.html#ixzz4nIEiBMzb: Tietelbaum (1990).
3. I was unable to locate any academic or otherwise systematic research on ATMs or financial inclusion and disabilities. On the design of the device see for instance 'Royal National Institute of Blind People Awards NCR Technology for Commitment to Financial Inclusion', *NCR*, 14 June 2017, accessed 19 July 2017, <https://www.ncr.com/news/newsroom/news-releases/financial/royal-national-institute-of-blind-people-awards-ncr-technology-for-commitment-to-financial-inclusion>.
4. Vulnerable consumers are said to include young people, old people, members of some ethnic minorities, the unemployed, those with low income, those suffering from long-term illness, or those suffering from a disability. See further Ritters (2003, 5).
5. These guidelines were extended to include headphone jacks in 1994. See: 'Americans with Disabilities Act and ATMs Accessibility History', American Bankers Association, accessed 5 July 2016, <http://www.aba.com/Compliance/Pages/DisabilitiesATM.aspx>. The first similar machine in Canada was an NCR with a retrofitted audio jack in 1997. See 'The Talking ATM', Envisioning Technologies, Disabilities Research Group, Carleton University, accessed 15 August 2017, <https://envisioningtechnologies.omeka.net/exhibits/show/the-talking-atm-innovation-a/the-talking-atm>.
6. Devlin (2005); 'Disabilities: Proposal for an Accessibility Act—Frequently Asked Questions', European Commission, 2 December 2015, accessed 5 July 2016, <http://europa.eu/rapid/press-release_MEMO-15-6148_en.htm>; and 'ATM Accessibility in Europe', *ATM Marketplace*, accessed 5 July 2016, <http://www.atmmarketplace.com/blogs/atm-accessibility-in-europe/>. For details on the passing of the Americans with Disabilities Act see Feingold (2016). On talking ATMs in the USA see 'Talking ATM Press Releases', Law Office of Lainey Feingold, 31 March 2010, accessed 19 July 2017, <http://www.lflegal.com/category/settlement-agreement-press-releases/talking-atm-press-releases/>; and for international deployment see: 'International Issues', Law Office of Lainey Feingold, accessed 19 July 2017, <http://www.lflegal.com/category/international-issues/>.
7. Bátiz-Lazo and Reese (2010).
8. e.g. Coombs et al. (1992); Pinch (2001).
9. e.g. Nagurney et al. (2007); Yates (2005).

10. Eijkman et al. (2010); Maurer et al. (2013, 55); Mihm (2007, 103ff.); Ross (2016, 2017).

11. I appreciate the comments of Stephen Mason in helping with the legal issues of electronic transactions. Personal communication (email) from Stephen Mason, barrister and speaker, with B. Bátiz-Lazo, 4 August 2017.

12. e.g. Latour (1992); Tenner (1996); Bijker et al. (1989).

13. Bátiz-Lazo et al. (2014a).

14. Although trust in banks is considered essential for an effective financial system, surprisingly little is known about what determines trust in banks. See further Fungáčová et al. (2016).

15. Vanatta (forthcoming). On the transformation of the retail bank branch manager see Vik (2017). On gender and retail financial services see Husz (2015a, 2015b).

16. Banking Marketing Association is the publishing arm of the American Bankers Association. 'Technology catches on, but people still like people', *ABA Banking Journal*, May 1986: 111.

17. e.g. Bryman (2004); Ritzer (1995).

18. See 'Tammy the Timeless Teller—Jingle', YouTube, 9 May 2015, accessed 20 July 2017, <https://www.youtube.com/watch?v=uNGr4bydMcc&feature=youtu.be>.

19. 'The Nashville I Wish I Knew, "Meet Tammy"', Facebook, 2 May 2011, accessed 20 July 2017, <https://www.facebook.com/thenashvilleiwishiknew/photos/a. 158712027526414.41100.127158557348428/158712070859743/?type=3&theater>.

20. 'Third National Bank', *Historic Nashville*, 13 January 2009, accessed 7 August 2017, <https://historicnashville.wordpress.com/2009/01/13/third-national-bank/>.

21. 'Sun Trust Building (Nashville)', *Wikipedia*, accessed 20 July 2017, <https://en. wikipedia.org/wiki/SunTrust_Building_(Nashville)>. Pictures of the interior and hall at: 'Courtyard Nashville Downtown', *Marriott*, accessed 7 August 2017, <https://www.marriott.com/hotels/photo-tours.mi?marshaCode=bnadt&pageID= HWHOM&imageID=2&roomTypeCode>.

22. See 'Tammy the Timeless Teller—Lovely Service', *YouTube*, 9 May 2015, accessed 8 August 2017, <https://www.youtube.com/watch?v=mfI4v97kIgg>.

23. 'Tammy the Timeless Teller—I Thought of Everything', *YouTube*, 9 May 2015, accessed 8 August 2017, <https://www.youtube.com/watch?v=gLtSITcN128>.

24. See 'Tammy the Timeless Teller—Baskin Robbins', *YouTube*, 9 May 2015, accessed 8 August 2017, <https://www.youtube.com/watch?v=fD84bYzOlFQ>.

25. 'Technology Catches On, but People Still Like People', *ABA Banking Journal*, May 1986: 111.

26. Unless otherwise stated, data in this paragraph are sourced in: 'Technology Catches On, but People Still Like People', *ABA Banking Journal*, May 1986: 114.

27. 'Johnny Cash Machines: Johnny Cash Stars in 1980s Commercial for ATM Machines', *Open Culture*, 21 April 2015, accessed 10 July 2017, <http://www. openculture.com/2015/04/johnny-cash-machines.html>.

28. Bátiz-Lazo et al. (2014b).

29. According to several Russian sources, the first ATM in the former USSR was a French-made 'Bankomat' deployed in 1989 by the state bank Sberbank (or Savings Bank) of the USSR. This was part of a pilot project to issue Visa credit cards. The

bank purchased four ATMs from a French company, Electronic Serge Dassault. All four were installed in Moscow: two were installed in the headquarters of Sberbank, and two in the Sberbank branch on Olympiiskii prospect (Olympics Avenue). The cards for using these ATMs were issued to the top managers of the bank and to a few employees of the branch. The pilot project pretty much died out. The next mention of the ATMs dates back to 1992 and suggests that the first 'commercial' cash machines were installed in Moscow by a (private/non-state) bank called SBS-Agro, which bought the devices from IBM (through InterBold, its joint venture Diebold). I appreciate the help of Olga Suhomlinova (Leicester) in locating this information.

30. 'Why Do People in Philadelphia Call the ATM a MAC Machine?', *Quora*, accessed 10 February 2017, <https://www.quora.com/Why-do-people-in-Philadelphia-call-the-ATM-a-MAC-machine>.

31. This paragraph draws on the personal communication (email) from Socrates Sulópulos, Banco Continental (Peru), with B. Bátiz-Lazo, 23 July 2012.

32. 'Barclays Machine Moniker Misfire Has Brits Bristling', *ATM Marketplace*, accessed 6 June 2016, <http://www.atmmarketplace.com/news/barclays-machine-moniker-misfire-has-brits-bristling/>.

33. I am grateful for the helpful comments from Sonya Hanna (Bangor) and Mark Tadajewski (Durham) on corporate branding, 1 June 2016 and 12 July 2017, respectively.

34. Russell Hogg, president and CEO, MasterCard International. Interview in B. Streeter, 'Visa and MasterCard: Self-evaluations', *ABA Banking Journal*, September 1982: 52.

35. Unless otherwise stated, this section borrows freely from Bernardo Báiz-Lazo, 'The GAY-TM: How to Make a Splash with Cash Dispensers', *Charisma blog*, 11 August 2015, accessed 10 July 2017, <http://www.charisma-network.net/finance/the-gay-tm-how-to-make-a-splash-with-cash-dispensers>.

36. 'Sydney Gay and Lesbian Mardi Gras Festival', *Sydney Gay and Lesbian Mardi Gras*, accessed 10 July 2017, <http://www.mardigras.org.au>; Alek Jenkins, 'Insight & Strategy: GAYTMs', *Contagious*, 26 August 2014, accessed 14 July 2017, <https://www.contagious.com/blogs/news-and-views/15205369-insight-strategy-gaytms>.

37. The company changed its name in 2016 following the departure of company founder Scott Whybin. See 'Scott Whybin Resigns from Whybin\TBWA', *Mumbrella*, 8 April 2016, accessed 28 July 2017, <https://mumbrella.com.au/scott-whybin-resigns-whybintbwa-358562>.

38. Note that 'Queer' and 'Questioning' are not interchangeable terms. The use of the slash is to note that in Australia the 'Q' in 'LGBTIQ' stands for 'Queer' whereas in other countries for 'Questioning'.

39. Unless otherwise stated, this paragraph borrows from 'Why and How an Australian Bank Turned ATMs into "GAYTMs"', *PR Week*, 17 February 2015, accessed 10 July 2017, <http://www.prweek.com/article/1334047/why-australian-bank-turned-atms-gaytms#RuKCozIi9cMlmHjO.99>.

40. Alek Jenkins, 'Insight & Strategy: GAYTMs', *Contagious*, 26 August 2014, accessed 14 July 2017, <https://www.contagious.com/blogs/news-and-views/15205369-insight-strategy-gaytms>.

41. Jeffry Pilcher, 'The World's First ATMs for the Gay Community', *The Financial Brand*, 3 March 2014, accessed 10 July 2017, <https://thefinancialbrand.com/37247/anz-bank-atms-for-lgbt-community>.

42. The campaign included ad hoc welcome screens. These and more detail on the ATM fascias can be seen in the video here: 'ANZ #GAYTM's 2014 Wrap-Up', YouTube, 29 May 2014, accessed 10 July 2017, <https://youtu.be/BvC6RV31PVo>.

43. Anzabella Darling, Facebook, February 2014, accessed 30 October 2017, <https://www.facebook.com/anzabella.darling>; Fran Molloy, 'Anzabella Leads the Way in Acceptance and Diversity', *ANZ Your World*, March 2016, accessed 27 November 2017, <https://www.yourworld.anz.com/social-good/anzabella-leads-the-way>; Ariel Bogle, 'The Real Reason Tech Brands are Lining Up to Sponsor Australia's LGBT Mardi Gras', *Mashable UK*, 4 March 2016, accessed 27 November 2017, <http://mashable.com/2016/03/04/mardi-gras-tech-brands/#n8KQvYW8oaq4>.

44. Alex Jenkins 'Insight & Strategy: GAYTMs', *Contagious*, 26 August 2014, accessed 14 July 2017, <https://www.contagious.com/blogs/news-and-views/15205369-insight-strategy-gaytms>.

45. Peter Tilton, 'Tapping and Fabulous', European ATMs Conference 2015, London, 16 June 2015, accessed 10 July 2017, originally at: <https://www.rbrlondon.com/events/EUATM15_Agenda.pdf>.

46. Parker Scott, 'ANZ's "GAYTMs" Wins Honours at Cannes Advertising Awards', *Sydney Morning Herald*, 18 June 2014, accessed 10 July 2017, <http://www.smh.com.au/business/media-and-marketing/anzs-gaytms-wins-honours-at-cannes-advertising-awards-20140618-3adk7.html>.

47. Carolyn Bendall, 'Five Lessons in Innovation from GAYTMs', *Blue Notes*, 21 October 2014, accessed 14 July 2017, <https://bluenotes.anz.com/posts/2014/10/five-lessons-in-innovation-from-gaytms>.

48. 'People Are Psyched For New GAYTMs To Celebrate Pride', *Buzz Feed*, 22 February 2014, accessed 14 July 2017, <https://www.buzzfeed.com/simoncrerar/delight-as-bank-unveils-gaytms-for-sydney-mardi-gras?utm_term=.cuXon2p4Y#.vs1djmyJX>; Liam Brennan, 'Lightning rarely strikes twice, but the @ANZ_AU #GAYTM campaign is back and it's still amazing #sydneymardigras', *Twitter*, 03:21 hrs, 28 February 2015, accessed 14 July 2017, <https://twitter.com/lcbrennan/status/571631348936519681>.

49. Alek Jenkins, 'Insight & Strategy: GAYTMs', *Contagious*, 26 August 2014, accessed 14 July 2017, <https://www.contagious.com/blogs/news-and-views/15205369-insight-strategy-gaytms>.

50. 'ANZ Bank "sad" over Ponsonby GayTM Attack by Vandals', *NZ Herald*, 20 February 2015, accessed 26 October 2017, <http://www.nzherald.co.nz/nz/news/article.cfm?c_id=1&objectid=11405037>; ANZ New Zealand, 'We were sad to see our NZ-designed #gaytmnz has been vandalised overnight. Clean up is in progress', *Twitter*, 19:05 hrs, 19 February 2015, accessed 26 October 2017, <https://twitter.com/ANZ_NZ/status/568497998503809024>.

51. 'Political Statement regarding "Vandalism" of GAYTM', *hashtag500words*, 21 February 2015, accessed 26 October 2017, <https://hashtag500words.com/2015/02/21/political-statement-regarding-vandalism-of-gaytm/>.

52. Nick Duffy, 'Queer Activists Vandalise "GAYTM" Cash Machine', *Pink News*, 22 February 2015, accessed 26 October 2017, <http://www.pinknews.co.uk/2015/02/22/queer-activists-vandalise-gaytm-cash-machine/>.

53. Alek Jenkins, 'Insight & Strategy: GAYTMs', *Contagious*, 26 August 2014, accessed 14 July 2017, <https://www.contagious.com/blogs/news-and-views/15205369-insight-strategy-gaytms>.

54. Carolyn Bendall, 'Five Lessons in Innovation from GAYTMs', *Blue Notes*, 21 October 2014, accessed 14 July 2017, <https://bluenotes.anz.com/posts/2014/10/five-lessons-in-innovation-from-gaytms>.

55. Alek Jenkins, 'Insight & Strategy: GAYTMs', *Contagious*, 26 August 2014, accessed 14 July 2017, <https://www.contagious.com/blogs/news-and-views/15205369-insight-strategy-gaytms>.

56. Patrick Mooney, 'Happy Pride @talktoBOI—loving the #gAyTM @DublinPride', *Twitter*, 14:13 hrs, 24 June 2017, accessed 25 October 2017, <https://twitter.com/PatrickMooney/status/878601858432065536>; <https://twitter.com/LaQuishaStR/status/841745075579236352>; Erik Esbensen, 'From #PrideBeer to #gAyTM—we are ready to start the @OsloPride week 2017 #PrideMonth #Pride #prideparade #Norway #visitnorway', *Twitter*, 08:20 hrs, 23 June 2017, accessed 25 October 2017, <https://twitter.com/EirikEsbensen/status/878150648939683840>.

57. Maurer (2006, 2012, 2015); Maurer et al. (2013).

58. 'Technology Catches On, But People Still Like People', *ABA Banking Journal*, May 1986: 114.

59. Murdoch et al. (2010).

60. According to Konheim (2016, 14), cryptanalysis refers to the study of cryptosystems with a view to finding weaknesses in them that will permit retrieval of the plaintext from the ciphertext, without necessarily knowing the key or the algorithm. For systematic evidence of ATM fraud see Anderson (1993).

61. Walt Bogdanich, 'Stealing the Code: Con Men and Cash Machines', *The New York Times*, 3 August 2016, accessed 23 August 2016, <http://www.nytimes.com/2003/08/03/us/stealing-code-con-men-cash-machines-criminals-focus-atm-s-weak-link-banking.html?_r=0>.

62. John Fisher, 'What's the Real Significance of National ATM Networks', *ABA Banking Journal*, September 1981: 43.

63. Bátiz-Lazo and Reese (2010); Essinger (1987, 23).

64. Konheim (2016, 14).

65. 'Banks Cash Dispenser That Would Not Deliver', *The Strait Times*, 21 December 1974: 7; and 'Instant Cash Cards and Magnetic Stripes', *The Strait Times*, 16 January 1975: 10.

66. As part of a series of market reforms as well as the increase in the size of retail banking custom, the British government in conjunction with the financial services industry appointed in the mid-1980s an official (commonly known as an ombudsman, from its Swedish origins) to investigate individuals' complaints against banks and another against building societies (established 1986). They were appointed in 1985 and 1986 respectively. Following the Financial Services Market Act of 2000, these were integrated into the Financial Ombudsman Service in 2000. The ombudsmen provided a regular complaints procedure.

67. National Consumer Council (1983): 'Banking Services and the Consumer'. National Consumer Council (1985): 'Losing at Cards, An Investigation into Consumers' Problems with Bank Cash Machines'. These reports were based on 60 cases of which a selection was investigated in depth and all facts were counter-checked.

68. Jack (1989, 79 and 83).

69. For a detailed contemporary case of phantom withdrawals in the early 1990s see Barry Fox, 'Phantom Card Tricks', *New Scientist*, 1885, 5 August 1993, accessed 15 August 2017, <https://www.newscientist.com/article/mg13918855-300-forum-phantom-card-tricks-barry-fox-becomes-a-victim-of-the-credit-system/>.

70. Because the ATM would only read the data on the strip and not check for the features of the card.

71. Constable (2015, 5).

72. Barry Fox, 'Phantom Card Tricks', *New Scientist*, 1885, 5 August 1993, accessed 15 August 2017, <https://www.newscientist.com/article/mg13918855-300-forum-phantom-card-tricks-barry-fox-becomes-a-victim-of-the-credit-system/>.

73. Barry Fox, 'Phantom Card Tricks', *New Scientist*, 1885, 5 August 1993, accessed 15 August 2017, <https://www.newscientist.com/article/mg13918855-300-forum-phantom-card-tricks-barry-fox-becomes-a-victim-of-the-credit-system/>.

74. A barrister is the attorney arguing cases in front of a judge.

75. Arthur Charles, 'How ATM Fraud Nearly Brought Down British Banking', *The Register*, 21 October 2005, accessed 11 July 2016, <http://www.theregister.co.uk/2005/10/21/phantoms_and_rogues/>.

76. 'Group Action Aims to Bring Scandal of Phantom Cashpoint Withdrawals to a Head', *Computer Business Review*, 13 July 1992, accessed 11 July 2016, <http://www.cbronline.com/news/group_action_aims_to_bring_scandal_of_phantom_cashpoint_withdrawals_to_a_head/>.

77. A large list of resources in this area is found in Ross Anderson's 'Phantom Withdrawals: On-line Resources for Victims of ATM Fraud', accessed 11 July 2016, <http://www.phantomwithdrawals.com>. The case is documented in greater detail in *Job v. Halifax Plc (not reported) Case num 7BQ00307*, Nottingham County Court, accessed 4 August 2017, <http://sas-space.sas.ac.uk/5520/1/1905-2673-1-SM.pdf>.

78. Konheim (2016, 14).

79. As recent anecdotal evidence in the press suggests, banks may not act swiftly even after being informed of questionable withdrawals or potential evidence of fraud. See Paul Thomas, 'Hero Who Tracked Bank Fraudsters to Win Back £20k They Stole from Him', *Mail Online*, 8 August 2017, accessed 9 August 2017, <http://www.dailymail.co.uk/money/beatthescammers/article-4772748/Hero-tracked-bank-fraudsters-win-20k.htm>; Miles Brignall, 'Why Are Britain's Banks Blaming Customers for Online Banking Fraud?' *The Guardian*, 8 August 2017, accessed 9 August 2017, <https://www.theguardian.com/commentisfree/2017/aug/08/banks-online-banking-fraud-ross-mcewan-rbs>. See also Mason (2014, 79).

80. One key difficulty for anyone wishing to litigate against a UK bank has been the risk of the bank seeking costs—and hounding the litigator into the ground with attachments of earnings, charges on homes, and other incidentals.

81. Ross Anderson, 'Chip and PIN on Trial', *Light Blue Touch Paper*, 9 April 2009, accessed 9 August 2017, <https://www.lightbluetouchpaper.org/2009/04/09/chip-and-pin-on-trial/>.

82. Interview with Robert Rosenthal, former IBM engineer, by B. Bátiz-Lazo, London, 23 July 2016.

83. As one example of customer distrust in the early days of the ATM in South Africa, for instance, customers would verify their balance before the withdrawal, proceed with the withdrawal, and then verify their balance again, to make sure the ATM had done its job properly. Source: Interview with Robert Rosenthal, former IBM engineer, by B. Bátiz-Lazo, London, 23 July 2016.

84. Bonneau et al. (2012).

85. This paragraph is sourced from interviews with Robert Rosenthal, former IBM engineer, by B. Bátiz-Lazo, London, 23 July 2016 and 27 July 2017.

86. Yeh and Smith (1991, 203).

87. Mason (2003, 482).

88. 'Rethinking ATM Availability as a Measure of Success', *ATM Marketplace*, accessed 1 August 2017, <https://www.atmmarketplace.com/whitepapers/rethinking-atm-availability-as-a-measure-of-success/>.

89. 'Rethinking ATM Availability as a Measure of Success', *ATM Marketplace*, accessed 1 August 2017, <https://www.atmmarketplace.com/whitepapers/rethinking-atm-availability-as-a-measure-of-success/>. High availability is strictly based upon the number of minutes an ATM was down and does not take into account the value of specific time periods of high usage versus low usage windows.

90. This paragraph is sourced from the interviews with Robert Rosenthal, former IBM engineer, by B. Bátiz-Lazo, London, 23 July 2016 and 27 July 2017.

91. For a compendium discussing the discovery, production, and admission of electronic information as evidence in different jurisdictions see Mason and Seng (2017).

92. The Bills of Exchange Act, however, said nothing about stolen cheques. Banks responded by overprinting cheque stock as 'not negotiable'.

93. Mason (2017, 216 (par 9.2)).

94. Mason (2014, 76–7).

95. For a detailed discussion of the technological possibilities of attacking smart cards see Steven J. Murdoch, 'The Pre-Play Vulnerability of Chip and PIN', *Light Blue Touchpaper*, 19 May 2014, accessed 18 August 2017, <https://www.lightbluetouchpaper.org/2014/05/19/the-pre-play-vulnerability-in-chip-and-pin/>.

96. This paragraph is sourced from a personal communication (email) from Brigitte Goulard, Deputy Commissioner Financial Consumer Agency, with Ross Anderson, 27 July 2017. I am grateful to Ross Anderson for sharing this information. See also: 'B-6 Investigations of Unauthorized Credit and Debit Card Transactions', Financial Consumer Agency of Canada, accessed 1 August 2017, <https://www.canada.ca/en/financial-consumer-agency/services/industry/bulletins/investigation-unauthorized-transactions.html>.

97. Konheim (2016, 14).

98. Mason and Seng (2017, 92 (par 5.11)).

99. Mason and Seng (2017, 198 (par 7.11)).

100. Mason and Seng (2017, 314 (par 9.73)).

101. This paragraph was sourced from Maixé-Altés (2012, 288–89 and 98–9).

102. Matthew Elder, 'Machines are Changing the Way We Bank', *The Montreal Gazette*, 10 November 1986: B4 and B6.

103. Eijkman et al. (2010); Maurer et al. (2013, 55).

104. Alberts (2010); Maixé-Altés (2016); Misa (2007).

9

A Bank Branch in a Box

9.1 The Rise of the Machines

Some studies have suggested that the automation of cash handling tasks has resulted in the displacement of routine-based occupations at bank retail branches.[1] For instance, in the Federal Reserve's Tenth District states, depository institutions declined by 40 per cent between 1985 and 1998.[2] This decline, however, was accompanied by a significant increase in the number of bank branches and facilities, including ATMs. Two studies from 1978 and 1980 by the Federal Deposit Insurance Corporation (FDIC) predicted that US banks would be subject to drastic cost cutting when ATMs replaced branches and staff, but by 2002 branches had actually increased in number and the number of bank clerks had dipped only slightly.[3]

The research mentioned above and other similar studies consider the ATM to be the 'paradigm case' of technology replacing workers because, during the 1970s and the early 1980s, this device evolved as bankers and engineers sought to replicate different forms of repetitive, labour-intensive transactions otherwise undertaken by bank clerks (called tellers in the USA). The ideas that drove this type of change were consistent with the pervasive Tayloristic ideology in industrial revolution(s).[4] But, at the same time, it was a process embedded in its particular historical circumstances. A recent op-ed in the *Financial Times* reminds us that '. . . new inventions do not appear in isolation . . . Instead, as we struggle to use them to their best advantage, [we shape them and] they profoundly reshape the societies around us.'[5]

Routinized physical and cognitive activities—such as cash distribution through retail bank branches—were some of the easiest and first to be automated by depositary financial institutions.[6] But even when this was the case, as will be evident below, the reduction in branch employment lagged behind the adoption of computer technology, and more specifically, the introduction of ATMs. Clearly the simple notion that ATMs eliminated bank clerks is wrong.[7] Yet it is also evident in the press that bank staff and retail branch numbers were shrinking in 2017.

Although our focus in the ensuing discussion will be on technological change, other forces also modified the internal workings of depositary financial institutions and reduced the totals of bank staff and retail branches. Also of importance for these processes, for instance, were regulatory innovations, particularly those around branch banking in the USA. Feminization was another such force; the gendering of clerical work, added to mechanization, was said to have diminished the otherwise buoyant position and salaries of male clerks. But again, they largely occurred during the 1980s and before the onslaught of ATMs from 1995 to 2005.

In short, the discussion that ensues changes the overall emphasis of previous chapters, which underlined for depositary financial institutions those features of ATMs that helped to clarify the changes in the boundary between banking organizations and the market. This chapter instead emphasizes the impact of computer technology inside banking organizations. To do so it explores the transformation of work in retail branches through assessing the long-term cost-effectiveness of ATMs for banks in terms of transaction volume at the machines, and changes in the number of staff and retail branches. Together they reflect one of the most notable features of the emergence of self-service banking. The discussion also speculates on the future of the ATM within banks' self-service strategies, focusing not on obsolescence but on a narrative of maintenance and reinvention.

9.2 The Robot-Cashier: Somewhere between Seven of Nine and C-3PO

The long-term success of the ATM embodied possibilities of transferring work done by humans to a device. The idea was not new to bankers and pre-dated the arrival of the cash machine in the late 1960s. Indeed, between the late 1870s and 1890s, clerical work was transformed from an artisan occupation and possible route to a partnership, into a proper career with its own structure and employment market where banking, insurance, and civil service clerks, mostly based in London, were referred to as the 'clerical aristocracy' of the white-collar sector since they had the highest pay and status in their profession.[8]

During the *belle époque* (1870–1914), London was the pre-eminent global financial centre, a position that the City has not held before or since.[9] The period also witnessed a substantial growth in the size of enterprises across the Atlantic, particularly in the case of financial institutions. For instance, in the 1870s even the largest banks had only a few branches, and most bank clerks worked in head offices. By 1910, the largest British banks had hundreds of branches and most clerks worked in small to mid-sized branches.[10] These trends suggest how, as banks grew, work and other value-adding activities became located in branches and sub-branches.

The clerical market in Britain also saw the introduction of women, young people, foreigners, its first unions, and office technology. Office mechanization in retail banks was not much different to other clerical work and included the adoption of typewriters, paper clips, steel filing cabinets, pneumatic tubes, addressographs, and adding machines, among others. Women and men were recruited as school leavers, but while men could work their way up to branch accountant, cashier, branch manager, or even progress to director at head office, women had to leave upon marriage.[11]

The nature and effects on clerical skills and pay of the innovations taking place at the end of the Victorian era and the Edwardian period form a contested subject.[12] But the fact remains that retail banks in Britain and many other countries created and maintained dual internal labour markets and continued to adopt (albeit at different times and degrees of intensity) mechanical, electromechanical, and even digital technology throughout the twentieth century.[13]

During the inter-war period, banks in many countries began to install telephones across their retail branches, while at central offices they adopted electromechanical devices such as tabulators. Figure 9.1 illustrates the presence of some devices used for office automation within a bank retail branch in the years after the Second World War. The large amount of space that back office operations required is notable, as well as some of the gender-specific roles within the retail branch. For instance, it was customary to find that the branch manager was male, sitting far from the reception area (in a corner or in a separate office), while female staff tended to clients but mostly performed routine tasks (the latter illustrated in the photograph in Figure 9.1). In some banks, female staff were not even allowed to be in contact with customers.

Starting in the mid to late 1950s, the first computers were used to increase the efficiency of specific processes such as the weekly payroll or annual interest payments to savings accounts.[14] It then became increasingly common to see people working alongside punched-card readers.

9.3 Transaction Volume and the Emergence of Self-Service Banking

9.3.1 *A Key Variable to Assessing Performance*

For most bankers in the 1960s, automation was, then, a fact of life. This is further illustrated in a speech by Ray R. Eppert (1902–86), chairman of the Burroughs

Figure 9.1. Office mechanization at Rabobank, circa 1959
(Interior of Coöperatieve Boerenleenbank 'Baarn')
Source: Jen Zandvoort (photographer). Courtesy of the sons of Jen Zandvoort and Rabobank Bedrijfshistorie.

Corporation (1958–67), a large supplier of computer equipment to financial institutions around the world, who inaugurated the fourth American Bankers Association Automation Conference in 1966 by enquiring: 'What should we automate and why?'[15] Eppert was effectively asking his audience not whether clerical workers should be liberated by introducing mechanical, electromechanical, and digital applications, but what work they could be liberated from. Eppert and some of his contemporaries began to believe that the arrival of digital computers was about to unlock something special—such as eliminating personal cheques, banknotes, and eventually all paper from banking transactions.[16] The emergence of the cash machine was, for some, a first tangible step that reinforced his attitude to technological and social progress.[17]

But extending innovations to the point of contact with customers was somewhat slow. It was not until 1976, for instance, that Merchants National Bank, Cedar Rapids, IA, took a first step in the deployment of a fully automated branch, when it launched an office made out of three wall-mounted, 24-hour, NCR 770 ATMs. These machines occupied about a third of the space in the branch and some people were still present in other parts of the office (including new-account and loan officers and four clerks handling nine drive-up lanes).[18] Management had given a target of six months for the machines to pick up 70 per cent of the volume if the project was to continue, but within three months after the launch, the machines were handling 80 per cent of retail transactions. This new 'fully automated' branch was launched while there was a branch with 'live' tellers across the street. By 1981, the lobby ATMs in the 'fully automated' branch were replaced with three through the wall, NCR 1780s which handled an average of 6,500 transactions per month (of which 21 per cent were balance enquiries). At the time, total transaction volume was expected to grow between 10 and 15 per cent per month.

Similarly, Citibank in New York City, in 1982 had the biggest ATM network on the east coast of the USA. The bank estimated that each of its machines represented $40,000 a year in operating expenses (including depreciation and servicing).[19] The comparable cost of a human teller was $46,000 a year. The bank clerk, however, could handle an average of between 36,000 and 40,000 transactions per annum, while the ATM was said to be capable of handling twice as many.[20]

Experiences at Citibank and Merchant National substantiate the view that automation, the ATM in particular, was helping banks to reduce the volume of transactions processed by clerks at retail bank branches. But of greater relevance is that the experiences at Citibank and Merchant National Bank also highlighted how transaction volume has been (and continues to be) a key variable to assessing performance in retail banking.[21]

The relative importance of transaction volume in this task is significant for at least three reasons. First, it validates the rejection of technological determinism because the adoption of self-service devices was not inevitable for banks, nor was it limited to juxtaposing changes in transaction volume to the potential cost of particular machines. Instead the examples offer a glimpse of the process through which depository financial institutions endeavoured to assess the costs and benefits associated with the adoption of new technologies and acted appropriately to their perceptions of the business environment.[22]

Second, Citibank's and Merchant National's vignettes above show a degree of attention by bankers to transaction volume as variables of performance. This, in turn, can be interpreted as an example of Alfred Chandler's concerns with the speed and flow of goods through the large, diversified enterprise.[23] For Chandler, a key factor in the large enterprise's long-term success is the possibility that the cost advantages of investments in productive infrastructure can be realized, but only if there was a constant flow of materials to assure capacity use. Opportunities for economies of scale and scope were thus contingent on the physical characteristics of production facilities (rated capacity) and the organizational capability to exploit technological processes (throughput).

But investments in production facilities large enough to exploit rated capacity and throughput are not enough. Long-term success also requires national and then international marketing and distribution capabilities, as well as teams of lower and middle managers to coordinate the flow through production and distribution.

But while 'throughput' has been seen as the ability to coordinate and control a flow of resources, 'throughput' in turn relies and depends upon the use of an 'efficient control system' or tool of its own. Applications of computer technology have been found particularly adept at controlling the flow of information. Such systems, for instance, are said to protect information intensive organizations such as banks from 'crisis of control'.[24] Such systems thus have the potential to reduce costs without increasing size and scope as well as playing a role in the communication, coordination, and control processes that were previously performed by Chandler's hierarchies.[25]

From a Chandlerian viewpoint, therefore, when the retail bank branch was the only point of contact with individual and business customers, it was simultaneously a production facility, marketing organization, and host to most of the managerial talent and clerical support that coordinated the flow of production and distribution for retail banks. Today's banks coordinate the flow of interactions with customers from a central location (such as head office and regional branches) while the distribution network encompasses retail branches, ATMs, and other channels such as call centres, self-service kiosks, point of sale terminals, and more recently mobile phones. As these new channels came into play and were effective in taking on (or expanding) transaction volume from retail branches, investment in and maintenance of retail branches threatened to become obsolete. In other words, the advent of automation enables us to understand the extent to which ATMs not only replaced human work at retail bank branches, but also resulted in fewer of the branches themselves.[26]

Third, a number of academic studies and government reports into the workings of the banking industry (such as the Cruickshank Report[27]), took the view that depositary financial institutions had inadequate, if not poor, internal control practices.[28] However, it has also been shown that in spite of these accusations of 'backwardness',[29] depositary institutions made active use of accounting and financial information for the purposes of internal control.[30]

In what follows I show how transaction volume is yet another variable in the internal control of banks. This draws attention to the importance of transaction volume both as a previously unexplored dimension of internal control and as a key variable in assessing the performance of alternative technologies to deliver retail financial services.

9.3.2 Trends in Transaction Volume at ATMs

Table 9.1 summarizes the changes in transaction volume in the early years of shared ATM networks in the USA. When assessing these trends, one should remember that the long-term performance as regards transaction volume was assessed under the influence of the drive to achieve economies of scale by individual banks, shared ATM networks, together with the amalgamations amongst both banks and shared ATM networks.

The transaction volume in Table 9.1 is taken to include the total number of deposits, withdrawals, transfers, payments, and balance enquiries performed in the ATM network (whether or not these transactions were transmitted through the network data centre).[31] An examination of Table 9.1 reveals that monthly transactions per ATM grew from 4,204 in 1978 to 5,177 in 1988, or 23 per cent during the period. The slight growth of monthly transactions per device suggests that every new ATM between 1978 and 1988 was working at roughly the same rate as previous deployments.

Aggregate behaviour paints a different picture, however. The total number of ATMs between 1978 and 1988 grew almost seven times, while total transaction volume grew eight times and ATMs in shared networks grew almost ten times (from 10 to 90 per cent of the total). These trends demonstrate that, in the ten years after 1978, ATMs were effective in taking on a substantial amount of repetitive work and thus suggest that transaction volume was moving away from bank clerks and to ATMs.

Table 9.1. Growth of shared networks and transaction volume in the USA, 1978–1988

Year	Installed ATMs	Annual ATM growth %	Total trans per month (millions)	Trans month growth %	Trans per month per ATM	Trans per month ATM growth %	% of ATMs shared
1978	9,750	25.8	41.0	NA	4,204	NA	10
1979	13,995	43.5	63.5	54.9	4,603	9.5	13
1980	19,000	35.8	100.0	57.5	5,408	17.5	16
1981	27,295	43.7	135.0	35.0	5,235	−3.2	23
1982	36,861	35.0	167.0	23.7	5,060	−3.3	33
1983	48,118	30.5	200.0	19.8	5,000	−1.2	40
1984	58,960	22.5	261.0	30.5	4,745	−5.1	46
1985	61,177	3.8	296.0	13.4	4,933	4.0	59
1986	69,161	13.1	301.0	1.7	4,703	−4.7	76
1987	76,031	9.9	335.3	11.4	4,930	4.8	81
1988	77,084	1.4	375.3	11.9	5,177	5.0	90
Growth 1978–1988	690.6%		815.3%		23.1%		

Source: Own estimates, based on Laderman (1990a, 1990b).

Table 9.2 presents the performance of transaction volume in the UK.[32] Note that the values for transaction volume in the UK in Table 9.2 are drawn from a slightly longer period than those in Table 9.1 for the USA. These data, however, allow us roughly to compare trends across the Atlantic and also help to assess whether the behaviour of transaction volume in ATMs in the USA was unique.

In comparing the data in Table 9.1 and Table 9.2, it was somewhat surprising to find that the transaction volume in both countries behaved similarly, especially if one takes into account that Britain had far fewer shared ATM networks and, before them, much larger proprietary ATM networks than the USA had.

According to the data in Table 9.2, the total number of ATMs in the UK for the 1978–88 period grew almost nine-fold, or about the same as in the USA. But while total transaction volume grew eight times in the USA between 1978 and 1988, it grew almost 30 times in the UK. This again suggests that ATMs were effective in taking on substantial amounts of repetitive work and that transaction volume was indeed moving away from humans into ATMs on both sides of the Atlantic. These trends in transaction volume have been explored in greater depth as illustrated in Figure 9.2.

The data in Figure 9.2 furnish two approximations to the long-term behaviour of withdrawals at automated cash machines in Britain between 1975 and 2003 (the last year when comparable data were available); namely 'daily transaction value per ATM (constant prices)' and 'average cash withdrawal (nominal value)'. The latter of these approximations represents the average withdrawal throughout the year and results from dividing the total monetary value of annual transactions by the total annual transaction volume. This measure records cash withdrawals and excludes envelope deposits, balance enquiries, and other self-service transactions at ATMs.

The 'constant prices' approximation resulted from dividing the total monetary value of annual transactions by the number of installed devices. Average daily estimates of the nominal transaction value per ATM were calculated through a straight-line allocation per day. To determine constant prices these magnitudes were deflated by the Retail Price Index.[33] The 'constant prices' approximation thus captured the average volume of business per device on a daily basis after removing the effect of inflation.

Both the alternative approximations in Figure 9.2 show a growing trend, suggesting an increasing use of ATMs by bank customers. They further substantiate the success of the automation of clerical work by cash machines. Note that 'daily transaction value per ATM (constant prices)' showed a steeper incline during the inflationary period of the 1970s (when the retail price index peaked at an all-time high of 25 per cent in 1975) and continued until 1984 or about the time when building societies began to offer automated cash

Table 9.2. Growth of transaction value and volume in the UK, 1975–2003

Year	Installed ATM	Annual growth	Annual transaction volume (millions)	Annual growth	Annual transaction value (£ millions)	Annual growth	Nominal value annual transaction per ATM (£)	Annual growth	Deflated value annual transaction per ATM (£)	Annual growth
1975	1,003		8		111		110,668		2,991	
1976	1,136	13%	12	50%	177	59%	155,810	41%	3,658	22%
1977	1,324	17%	17	42%	281	59%	212,236	36%	4,440	21%
1978	1,409	6%	25	47%	460	64%	326,473	54%	6,303	42%
1979	1,547	10%	36	44%	733	59%	473,820	45%	7,806	24%
1980	2,009	30%	55	53%	1,316	80%	655,052	38%	9,371	20%
1981	2,946	47%	96	75%	2,540	93%	862,186	32%	11,011	18%
1982	4,046	37%	157	64%	4,290	69%	1,060,306	23%	12,852	17%
1983	5,617	39%	229	46%	6,597	54%	1,174,470	11%	13,515	5%
1984	6,794	21%	328	43%	9,751	48%	1,435,237	22%	15,789	17%
1985	8,892	31%	404	23%	12,401	27%	1,394,624	-3%	14,527	-8%
1986	10,313	16%	496	23%	15,590	26%	1,511,684	8%	15,178	4%
1987	12,177	18%	627	26%	18,848	21%	1,547,836	2%	14,984	-1%
1988	13,813	13%	754	20%	24,320	29%	1,760,660	14%	15,962	7%
1989	15,694	14%	883	17%	31,948	31%	2,035,682	16%	17,135	7%
1990	17,142	9%	992	12%	38,474	20%	2,244,429	10%	17,278	1%
1991	17,935	5%	1,085	9%	52,080	35%	2,903,819	29%	21,399	24%
1992	18,557	3%	1,169	8%	55,975	7%	3,016,382	4%	21,669	1%
1993	19,259	4%	1,242	6%	60,200	8%	3,125,811	4%	22,028	2%
1994	20,061	4%	1,335	7%	65,170	8%	3,248,592	4%	22,251	1%
1995	20,928	4%	1,471	10%	72,090	11%	3,444,667	6%	22,858	3%
1996	22,118	6%	1,599	9%	80,235	11%	3,627,588	5%	23,495	3%
1997	23,349	6%	1,745	9%	89,994	12%	3,854,298	6%	24,089	3%
1998	24,758	6%	1,850	6%	98,230	9%	3,967,606	3%	24,134	0%
1999	27,525	11%	1,968	6%	107,852	10%	3,918,329	-1%	23,421	-3%
2000	32,648	19%	2,027	3%	113,013	5%	3,461,560	-12%	20,102	-14%
2001	36,630	12%	2,174	7%	127,428	13%	3,478,788	0%	20,062	0%
2002	40,810	11%	2,268	4%	136,364	7%	3,341,436	-4%	18,720	-7%
2003	46,700	14%	2,373	5%	144,123	6%	3,086,146	-8%	16,818	-10%
1978–1988	8.80		29.16		51.87		4.39		1.53	
1975–2003	45.56		295.63		1297.41		26.89		4.62	

Source: Own estimates, based on data found in Barrie (2006) and UK Payments (formerly Association of Payment Clearing Services or APACS). Nominal values deflated by the Retail Price Index (1968 = 100%).

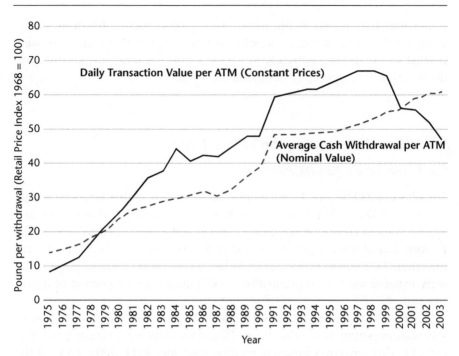

Figure 9.2. Estimates of average withdrawals per ATM in the UK, 1975–2003
Source: Author's own estimates, based on data in Table 7.3.

withdrawal services. This was also the time when the Midland Bank (now HSBC) introduced free-if-in-credit banking to Britain, thus suggesting a policy by banks to expand their customer base.[34]

Meanwhile, 'daily transaction value per ATM (constant prices)' reached its apex at £67 per daily withdrawal in 1997 and 1998. This coincided with the formation of the single network switch in the UK and with the rise in popularity of debit cards. In 2003, the end of the period of study, 'daily transaction value per ATM (constant prices)' recorded a value of £47 or roughly the same value as observed in both 1989 and 1990. Anecdotal reports in the printed media further suggested that the downward trend in average withdrawals continued well into the 2010s.[35] In short, overall trends in Figure 9.2 show that ATM stock grew as people made more use of them but, on average, individuals withdrew less cash per visit. This was a fact that, at the time, was not lost to bankers and engineers.[36]

One might conclude that the investment in ATMs (or any other labour saving device) was worth it, to the extent that the same volume of business could be handled more cost-effectively by a machine than a human.[37] Yet the fact that people made more use of ATMs but with lower amounts per transaction may question the labour saving properties of the technology, since for the same value of money withdrawn greater investments were needed to expand the network, not to mention the costs of maintenance, depreciation, and upkeep of individual machines.

9.4 Were ATMs Stealing the Tellers' Jobs?

9.4.1 *This Time is Not Different*

The effect of ATMs in replacing employees at bank branches has been widely discussed.[38] David Autor, for instance, was among those who argued that applications of computer technology, such as ATMs, tended to replace the performance of routine tasks by mid-skilled workers such as bank staff at retail branches.[39] Others went further and claimed that computers disproportionately replaced workers in occupations involving a high proportion of repetitive tasks.[40]

Whether ATM growth displaced bank clerks and even the branches themselves are important issues that have plagued the industry for many years. The extent of this concern is shown in an interview from 2011, in the midst of the economic downturn that followed the financial crisis of 2007–8: President Barack Obama illustrated how technological progress was allegedly impeding job creation by the ubiquitous ATM:

> There are some structural issues with our economy where a lot of businesses have learned to become much more efficient with a lot fewer workers. You see it when you go to a bank and you use an ATM, you don't go to a bank teller, or you go to the airport and you're using a kiosk instead of checking in at the gate.[41]

Obama's view may have some currency, given that ATMs were originally brought into bank branches to respond to cost and space constraints. Indeed, up until the 1980s, a great many routine transactions and services, such as mortgage applications or new accounts, were largely or entirely processed at the retail bank branch; whereas by the 2000s, the same transactions were being processed centrally (and in some cases, moved offshore as well).[42] Eliminating mechanical, routine transactions, cash machines and other computer terminals within branches should have freed time for clerks to interact with customers in either solving complex transaction issues or engage in sales of higher margin services. But there was at the same time a risk of annoying customers, for instance, if they were invited to apply for a new credit card every time they entered the retail branch (and more so, if they had already turned the same agent down the day or week before).

9.4.2 *The Tailor-Made Cash Machine*

The advent of ATMs and the plethora of technology changing the front office and back office of retail banks' branches may also have precipitated changes in the skills of branch staff in order to support the adoption of this and other technologies. Skills were likely to change if bank clerks were assigned to other activities. Bank clerks had to learn how to interact with and sometimes to service the new devices.

It is hard to believe that branch staff learned how to repair ATMs. The long intervals in the activity of individual machines up to the late 1980s suggest the opposite, that is, that repairs waited for the specialist engineers who were in charge of them. Yet before a full online system architecture had emerged, the machines had to be serviced every day by taking the tally of transactions at the end of the business day, replenishing banknotes, or discovering whether a customer's access card had 'fallen through the cracks'. Archival evidence and oral histories support the view that clerical staff serviced them and further suggest that, at least initially, it was the ATM which fitted bank practices and not the other way around.

The deployment of ATMs at the trustee savings banks (TSB) is a case in point. A large number of Burroughs cash machines were put into service in the 1970s and early 1980s by this group of seventy or so independent banks—which between 1970 and 1985 merged into a single financial institution.[43] Operating the ATM network was quite a challenge, since the TSB by law could not offer overdrafts and could allow customers to withdraw cash only if there were enough funds in their account; therefore the machines had to work online in real time. As stated by a former computer engineer at the savings banks, the US computer manufacturer was keen to keep the custom of the British financial intermediary.[44] He recalled how after a failed initial pitch, Burroughs engineers went away and came back with another machine. 'It was the RT650.' His team then thought of it as 'the TSB's' because all the modifications by Burroughs were made in order to meet TSB requirements.

As the statement reveals, Burroughs bespoke its devices to suit the workings of the saving banks' computer and administrative procedures. Without this move, the savings banks would not have ordered the RT650 because some senior managers at the savings banks thought that the Burroughs technology was not good enough.[45]

Figure 9.3 captures the workings of the Burroughs ATM from its rear (the image, therefore, is accessible only from inside the retail branch). Branch staff accessed the machine through a side door. The picture illustrates how banknotes for distribution were stored at the top of the device, while transactions were recorded and stored on a big tally roll immediately below. Later models replaced this paper roll with magnetic tape cassettes or floppy disks.

Figure 9.3. Detail of Burroughs RT650's rear access, circa 1975

Source: Charles Babbage Institute (CBI), University of Minnesota, Burroughs Corporation Records (Ascension 90), Product Photographs, c.1940–85 (Series 75), Box 43, Folder 6.

Each morning the dispenser was refilled, always using new notes as others would get stuck or cause the machine to malfunction, before the printed record was retrieved and balanced. The procedure was exactly the same as that used to balance the tills serviced by clerks across all TSB branches. This was designed so that any of the cashiers needed only a brief explanation to be able to service the cash machine for the purpose of routine transactions and end-of-day balance. The result of the modifications was that the day-to-day operation of the RT650 was not a challenge to the TSB's branch staff.[46]

Burroughs was not the only manufacturer to customize its machines to fit specific organizational procedures and preferences. As mentioned in Chapters 3 and 4, during the 1970s, Chubb, for instance, failed to secure economies of scale in production largely due to its policy of agreeing 'to be everything to everyone' in securing new contracts; that is, modifying its devices to suit each bank.[47] This was to change only in the early 1980s, when the likes of IBM, NCR, Diebold, and Nixdorf offered standardized (thus less costly), more resilient, and easy to maintain ATMs.[48]

9.5 Emerging Trends in Employment, Branches, and ATMs

9.5.1 *Performance in the UK*

Figure 9.4 displays ATM growth and the trends in British banks' domestic employment from the inception of the cash machine in 1967 to 2003—the last year that consistent data were available. As discussed above, these trends took place against the introduction of computer technology in both the front office and back office of retail branches. The changes included the digitalization of customer accounts as well as the introduction of machines that dispensed cash, took deposits, answered questions about balances, and accepted loan applications and the like. But rather than downsizing, depositary financial institutions began to actively manage their real estate portfolio of branches and large back office buildings, at the same time rejigging their retail branch networks in terms of closing down small branches, 'down-sizing' others, thinning out density in particular locations, and relocating offices from low frequency to high frequency use or from declining to growing neighbourhoods.[49] In other words, as the skill set of branch staff was changing, so too was the character and location of retail bank branches.

The interpretation of the data in Figure 9.4 should be taken with care. They come from a sample of depository institutions, namely, one building society, Abbey National; and four banks: Barclays, Midland-HSBC, Lloyds TSB, and NatWest-Royal Bank of Scotland. Using a sample based on internal data was

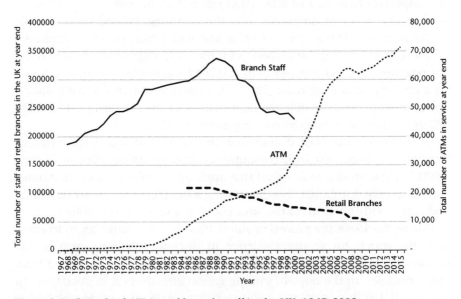

Figure 9.4. Growth of ATMs and branch staff in the UK, 1967–2003

Source: Author's own estimates, based on APACS; British Bankers Association; Barrie (2006, 92); and annual reports.

deemed necessary because other aggregate data of employment and branches (such as that of the Bank for International Settlements or the Office of National Statistics) did not discriminate between depositary institutions serving the larger domestic population and representative offices and employees servicing international financial markets in London. Meanwhile clearing (i.e. commercial) banks that would typically capture between 80 and 90 per cent of domestic deposits, reported their domestic employment and retail branches separately. However, the absence of a legal requirement to disclose this information resulted in a lack of consistency across banks, particularly because they diversified in the 1990s and 2000s, acquiring large insurance companies and former building societies. Data supporting Figure 9.4, therefore, represent a sample of the best possible effort to achieve a long-term consistent series.

Figure 9.4 depicts employment in branch staff steadily growing until 1987, then steadily dropping during the 1990s and remaining relatively stable in the early 2000s, at just below 30,000 persons. The data also show a consistent downward trend in the number of retail branches. Meanwhile the ATM stock grew continuously, albeit at different rates.

9.5.2 *The Fantastic Four*

At least four possible reasons may explain the behaviour illustrated in Figure 9.4. First, the transition through which skills for cash handling became less important than human interaction was not immediate. In Figure 9.4 the contraction in branch employment in the 1990s lags behind the large-scale deployment of ATMs in the late 1970s and mid-1980s. Trends in Figure 9.4 corroborate research by James Bessen for the USA, which also found that the introduction of ATMs between 1970 and 2013 was not immediately followed by a decimation of bank teller jobs.[50] This research contended that reducing the cost of operating retail branches actually increased the demand for bank tellers as banks responded by opening more branches.

Other authors have also documented the patterns of aggregated increased productivity associated with computer technology taking place until after 1990.[51] These studies have found that applications of computer technology were unevenly distributed, thereby creating a significant digital divide among industries, within regions of the same country, and across the globe.

During the 1980s the process of automation at retail banks began to abandon the search for greater efficiency in discrete processes—such as the accounting function.[52] Instead some activities began to be redefined from first principles, in the hope of gaining greater effectiveness in operation. To the extent that these new cross-selling activities or selling services with higher margin failed to produce the expected returns, a significant adjustment in employment and branches followed. Alongside these processes, ATMs turned into merely an additional service, which bank customers saw as intrinsic to their checking account and as an alternative to visiting a retail branch.

In short, there is an emerging consensus that the long-term productivity change associated with computer applications took place only when depositary financial institutions (as well as other companies across the economy) were prepared to reorganize to take advantage of what computers had to offer.[53] In other words, productivity-induced technological change encompasses more than simply taking old systems and adding better computers. Bankers needed to do things differently.

9.5.3 Looking for Greater Margins

A second trend explaining the behaviour in Figure 9.4 involved cash machine, computer terminals at teller counters, personal computers, automated credit scoring, and other applications of information technology that were used to leverage staff within the branches while moving them away from low margin, repetitive tasks to high margin, intermittent, sales opportunities such as mortgages and investments in the stock market.[54]

In this regard, the introduction of formal policies for relationship banking or the offering of personalization within branches and through telephone call centres, suggests that not all services at retail bank branches were susceptible to automation. In short, 'while ATMs automated some tasks, the *remaining* tasks that were not automated became more valuable'.[55]

A third trend behind Figure 9.4 was that the advent of new technology often lacked a ready-made pool of skills and knowledge in using it. In this regard, the case of the introduction of ATMs in the British savings banks is revealing.[56]

A fourth trend behind Figure 9.4 relates to the creation of a demand for ATM maintenance workers as the machines spread.[57] Their work was not only to service the machines themselves, by supplying spare parts or software and security upgrades, but also to train and develop the skills of branch staff (see the growth of ATMIA discussed in Chapter 7). It was not until the late 1980s, when branch staff in the USA and the UK began to undertake training programmes specifically tailored to articulate their skills and requirements that they were able to work effectively with ATMs as part of a branch's self-service strategy.[58]

This training involved more than meeting the casual educational needs of customers in operating a machine. Training was specifically aimed to go beyond marketing and promotion campaigns and was directed at supporting and motivating staff in order to deliver specific policy goals, such as account penetration, and acceptance and the use of self-service technology by customers. It is worth noting that, for many banks and their employees, such programmes were the first formal training courses that had proposed to support branch staff in any capacity.

The strategic drives that led to the introduction of training programmes to support branch staff were predicated on the belief that greater automation, in the form of ATMs, home banking, telephone banking, and other solutions, could be used to attract new customers and could lead existing customers to purchase high-margin products and services. But in the success of automation banks found a paradox: greater automation was desirable in that it could help to reduce costs; but operational considerations bred a new challenge: how to engage the customer (who was no longer coming into the branch) in a sales pitch?[59]

9.6 The Audacity of the ATM

As routine banking business was thrust out onto the street or the automated lobby, bank branches and their staff were transformed into sales units that attempted to engage customers in high-margin transactions. Alongside helping staff to concentrate on adding value for the bank, the automation of routine transactions also enabled branch space to be redesigned.

The purpose of introducing pods and meeting rooms, for instance, was to encourage customers to come in and discuss their financial needs. Back office space continued to shrink to the extent that in some branches it would effectively disappear. But this transition was not straightforward and depositary institutions experimented with different layouts. In the year 2000, former mortgage specialist Abbey National (today part of Santander UK), for example, introduced within branch space coffee bars for adults, Lego tables for children, and even an outlet to sell mobile phones.[60] Figure 9.5 captures the exterior of Abbey National's branch in Southend-on-Sea, a seaside resort near the Thames estuary.[61] The branch clearly displays the bank's name and logo as well as its coffee shop franchise. A sign on the branch's window invites you in: 'relax with Costa @ Abbey National'. Left to right, the image captures customers waiting inside the branch, two others using a 'through the wall' ATM, and a group of chairs and small tables where people seem to be enjoying drinks that could have been purchased inside the bank branch.

Furthermore in 2000, Bank of Scotland (now part of Lloyds Banking Group) tested a women-only banking service, 'Female2Female', where women advised women on financial matters. Halifax, another former mortgage specialist and now part of Lloyds Banking Group, went for the 'branch of the future' by decorating a bank in bright colours and allowing customers to experience 'the high street store browsing experience'.

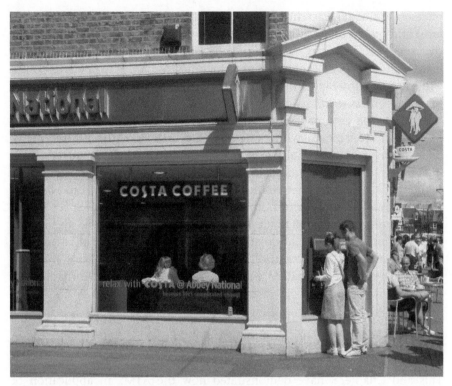

Figure 9.5. Abbey National Southend on Sea branch with Costa Coffee franchise, 2000
Source: Justin Kase (photographer). Alamy Photo (ID IY00939328).

A common thread of experimenting with coffee bars, Lego tables, mobile phone outlets, and new branch design was an attempt to turn the branch into a 'destination' rather than a required stop in a journey elsewhere. But customers saw through all these tactics. By 2006, at about the same time as Abbey National abandoned its coffee shops, its rivals were quietly withdrawing other 'new ways forward'.

The above illustrations suggest that the automation of work at retail bank branches was for a long time associated with a drive to reduce the number of routine transactions, accompanied however by a reluctance to reduce headcount. Instead, staff were retrained, while their jobs changed from process-oriented to sales-oriented activity. In this context, depositary financial institutions largely kept unchanged the number of their retail branches (indeed, in some cases, their retail branch network actually grew).

Closing retail bank branches is not always easy. In some instances, buildings were deemed to be of cultural value and were preserved by law. In others, the layout and location were so peculiar to banking that branches could not be used for anything else. At the same time, survey after survey of consumer preferences since at least the mid-1980s have nearly always shown that people most often chose their bank because it was near their home or their office.[62] In countries such as Japan, France, and the USA, another reason not to close branches too hastily has been the need for official approval to open new ones; while in Spain and like-minded countries regulation has made it very difficult to instigate mass redundancies.

In short, the automation of banks' retail branches encompasses several dimensions. In tandem with designing 'the branch of the future', many financial institutions were also exploring alternative ways to develop branches into financial service boutiques. However, it was also the case that banks found that automation often resulted in customers' never going into a branch. This led to a redefinition of both branch staff and the actual space of the branch. Indeed, to respond to President Obama's earlier quip, the installation of ATMs and computer automation has not necessarily implied massive unemployment in consequence.[63] This is because '[t]he economic response to automation of bank tellers' work was much more dynamic than many people would expect'.[64]

9.7 Tried and Trusted

This and Chapter 8 have demonstrated how the ATM, an application of computer technology, was instrumental in the transformation of the physical boundaries of deposit accepting financial institutions. There is increasing evidence, however, that the number of bank branches and ATMs in developed countries has started to decline.[65] According to figures compiled by the Federal Deposit Insurance Corporation and supplied by the American Bankers Association, the number of bank employees in the USA has remained relatively stable.[66] Employees totalled 2,110,276 in 2012 and 2,043,480 in 2016, a 3 per cent reduction for the period. But according to the same source, the number of bank branches in the USA has declined by 8 per cent from a peak of 99,540 in 2009 to 91,861 in 2016. In the same period ATMs in the USA increased 0.12 per cent from 432,500 in 2012 to 433,000 in 2016. Data would suggest that the creation of new online, self-service distribution channels rather than ATMs and call centres better explains the reduction in bank branches.

Yet despite indications of a decrease in physical operations, there are no signs that the 'bricks and mortar' presence will soon be a thing of the past. We can question the ability of bank staff to sell products such as mortgages or investment funds, but the fact remains that certain transactions require a channel in which banks are totally relied upon to accept instructions from customers. At the same time, there are some transactions that have not yet been automated, such as account opening, depositing foreign cheques (which need signing on the back), and depositing large sums in cash from shops, among others. Yet the same equipment and software applications operating in Europe or North America, which offer five or six self-service ATM transactions, can offer one hundred different transactions in China and India. Why this is so is the result of a combination of self-service strategies and customer habits. But taken together these suggest that the ATM and bank branch will remain the backbone of banks' self-service strategies.

Finally, evidence in this chapter has documented how the retail branch ceased to exist as the main 'production unit' and dominant point of contact with retail clients. Contrary to popular accounts, retail financial intermediaries began to change their mode of operation and retail customers' access to bank markets long before the advent of the Internet. This is evident, for the ATM expanded retail branch service hours, economized on labour costs, and increased customer convenience (including, for the first time, the possibility of banking at any retail branch). But ATMs have emerged as part of a purposeful strategy. This is one which from the outset has aimed to blur the physical boundaries of the banking organizations while developing retail branch and non-retail branch locations and being subject to advertising and capital budgeting. The emergence of ATM networks was key in the development of infrastructure for information technology (hardware, software, skills of individuals, and organizational learning), which later on paved the way for other spaces and ways of interaction with retail customers (such as electronic funds at point of sale terminals and telephone and Internet banking). Thus, the history of the ATM is much more than the story of a response to the 'impending needs' of a more mobile population. It is a history of technical and organizational innovation.

Notes

1. e.g. Autor et al. (2003); Chamberlin (2016); Daniels and Murphy (1994); Dos Santos and Peffers (1993); Gourley (1999); Hall and Khan (2003); Hannan and McDowell (1984); Hopkins (1986); Humphrey and Pulley (1997); Humphrey et al. (1996); Lee (2004); Lozano (1987); Peffers (1991); Saloner and Shepard (1995); Sharma (1993); Spong and Harvey (1998); Vázquez-Alanís (2007).
2. Spong and Harvey (1998).
3. 'The Surcharge: An Ironic History and Unsure Future', *ATM Marketplace*, 25 February 2002, accessed 18 November 2016, <http://www.atmmarketplace.com/articles/the-surcharge-an-ironic-history-and-unsure-future/>.

4. W. Patrick McCray, 'It's Not All Lightbulbs', *Aeon*, 12 October 2016, accessed 21 August 2017, <https://aeon.co/essays/most-of-the-time-innovators-don-t-move-fast-and-break-things>.

5. Tim Hardford, 'What We Get Wrong About Technology', *Financial Times*, 7 July 2017, accessed 26 August 2017, <https://www.ft.com/content/32c31874-610b-11e7-8814-0ac7eb84e5f1>. See further Miodownik (2013).

6. Ronald Bailey, 'Are Robots Going to Steal Our Jobs?', *Reason*, July 2017, accessed 22 August 2017, <http://reason.com/archives/2017/06/06/are-robots-going-to-steal-our>; Bátiz-Lazo et al. (2011b).

7. Tess Townsend, 'Eric Schmidt Said ATMs Led to More Jobs For Bank Tellers. It's Not That Simple', *Recode*, 8 May 2017, accessed 9 August 2017, <https://www.recode.net/2017/5/8/15584268/eric-schmidt-alphabet-automation-atm-bank-teller>.

8. Heller (2011, chap. 4).

9. Kynaston (1996); Michie (1992).

10. In 1870 there were 365 banks in England and Wales, operating 1,570 branches. Some 250 of these were privately owned and most operated from a single office. By 1913, when almost all the banks had either converted into joint stock or absorbed, there were only 29 private banks and 70 banks in total. In 1870 the number of bank branches averaged 4.3 per bank in England and Wales, while in 1913 that average was 93.9 per bank. Other depositary financial institutions also appeared during the nineteenth century, but expanded in number and retail branches at different rates. Building societies, for instance, first appeared in the late eighteenth century and by 1895 their number had grown to 3,642. Most remained single branch operations until well into the twentieth century while the largest ten in terms of assets developed 'national' branch networks in the late 1940s and early 1950s. There were 343 societies in existence in 1977 and 48 in 2011. Savings banks first appeared in 1810 and although some of the largest developed branches, they overwhelmingly remained single office operations until a change in government policy. Then the 70 or so that remained amalgamated into a single institution between 1970 and 1985. The emergence of a retail branch network for the savings banks was cautious in terms of the number of retail outlets: with 386 in 1911, reaching 1,505 in 1970 (30 for the Preston bank and 37 for the Belfast bank) and peaking at 1,650 in 1981. Sources: Capie and Weber (1985, 576–8); Davies (1981, 47); Jeremy (1998, 299); Noguchi and Bátiz-Lazo (2010) Bátiz-Lazo et al. (2014b); Horne (1947, 34); Moss and Russell (1994); Moss and Slaven (1992); Payne (1967).

11. Brian Pittman at Lloyds Bank was perhaps the last of these successful school leavers to reach the top echelons of British retail banking. See Bernardo Bátiz-Lazo, 'Pitman, Sir Brian Ivor (1931–2010)', *Oxford Dictionary of National Biography* (Oxford: Oxford University Press, 2013), accessed 29 May 2014, <http://www.oxforddnb.com/index/103/101103146>.

12. For a summary see Heller (2008); Heller and Kamleitner (2014); Seltzer (2004, 2010).

13. Bátiz-Lazo and Wardley (2007); Bátiz-Lazo and Wood (2002); Campbell-Kelly (1992, 1998, 2004); Wardley (2000, 2003); Wootton and Kemmerer (2007).

14. Bátiz-Lazo et al. (2014b); Bátiz-Lazo et al. (2011b); Heide (2009); Maixé-Altés (2012, 2013, 2015).

15. 'Obituary: Ray R. Eppert', *The New York Times*, 22 July 1986, accessed 18 November 2016, <http://www.nytimes.com/1986/07/22/obituaries/ray-r-eppert.html>; 'Unisys Corporation History', *Funding Universe*, accessed 18 November 2016, <http://www.fundinguniverse.com/company-histories/unisys-corporation-history/>; 'An On-line Conference for Real-time Achievement', *ABA Banking Journal*, July 1966: 113–17.

16. Bátiz-Lazo et al. (2014a).

17. Ted Schoeters, '1971 Target for Computer Networks', *Financial Times*, 20 October 1969.

18. Bill Streeter, 'Midwest Bank Proves an All-ATM Office Can Work', *ABA Banking Journal*, February 1981: 37–8.

19. 'Banking on the Inhuman Factor', *The Economist*, 27 March 1982: 85; Glaser (1988).

20. Another source estimated the cost of a cash machine in the early 1970s to be between $40,000 and $60,000, decreasing in nominal terms to $18,000 to $32,000 depending on model, configuration, and functionality by the mid-1980s. See Meena Modi, 'ATMs: At What Cost?', *ABA Banking Journal*, November 1987: 44–8.

21. Other contemporary figures of ATM performance would have included account penetration, card issuance, and card usage.

22. Richard Coopey (2004b) arrives at a different conclusion. He inferred that banks 'in the US or in Britain considered direct costs a minor factor of purchasing systems ... [they] had little, if any, accurate idea of the cost-benefits of computing' (p. 182).

23. Chandler (1990a, 1990b). Explorations of the banking firm using Chandler's approach include Channon (1977, 1978, 1986, 1988, 1998) and more recently Larson et al. (2011).

24. Beniger (1986).

25. Brady et al. (2001); Lescure (2016, 22); Nightingale and Poll (2000, 138).

26. A pioneering study exploring this question was that of Saloner and Shepard (1995).

27. Don Cruickshank was appointed by the Chancellor of the Exchequer in November 1998 to commission a review of the level of competition in UK banking. The report was delivered on March 2000 and resulted in an immediate referral of banking practices to the Competition Commission. Source: 'Cruickshank Report', *CMS Law Now*, 20 March 2000, accessed 2 November 2016, <http://www.cms-lawnow.com/ealerts/2000/03/cruickshank-report-on-uk-banking-results-in-reference-to-competition-commission-1?cc_lang=en>.

28. A lack of sophistication in management accounting in banks and building societies has been pinpointed in various academic studies including Bátiz-Lazo and Wardley (2007); Drury (1994, 1998); Innes and Mitchell (1997); Nightingale and Poll (2000); Soin et al. (2002).

29. Billings and Capie (2004); Booth (2001); Coopey (1999, 2004a); Jeremy (1998).

30. Bátiz-Lazo and Noguchi (2014); Bátiz-Lazo and Wardley (2007); Noguchi and Bátiz-Lazo (2010).

31. A different but related measure is switch volume, which encompasses the number of transactions that a network conveys to its members or passes on to other members. See Hayashi et al. (2003, 20).

32. Full estimates are available in the appendices.

33. 'UK Retail Price Index Since 1960', Swanlow Park, accessed 6 October 2016, <http://swanlowpark.co.uk/rpiannual.jsp>.

34. Midland claimed to have picked up 450,000 accounts with the scheme while NatWest lost 60,000 of its five million accounts to other participants offering 'free' banking. Source: 'Middle-aging Baby Boom: Customers are Getting More Choosy', *The Economist*, 22 March 1986: 9.

35. The downward trend in the use of ATMs continued well into the new century, as suggested by press reports such as: Katie Morley, 'Monthly Cash Machine Visits Becoming the Norm', *The Telegraph*, 29 August 2016, accessed 7 October 2016, <http://www.telegraph.co.uk/news/2016/08/29/monthly-cash-machine-visits-be-coming-the-norm–as-brits-rely-le/>.

36. Personal communication (email) from Bob Rosenthal, former IBM engineer, with B. Bátiz-Lazo, 23 July 2016.

37. Bátiz-Lazo (2013); Bátiz-Lazo and Wood (2000); Wood and Bátiz-Lazo (1997).

38. See for instance Humphrey (1996); Humphrey et al. (1996).

39. Autor et al. (2002); Autor et al. (2003).

40. Acemoglu and Autor (2011); Autor et al. (2008).

41. 'Obama Blames ATMs for High Unemployment', *FOX News*, 14 June 2011, accessed 22 November 2016, <http://nation.foxnews.com/president-obama/2011/06/14/obama-blames-atms-high-unemployment>.

42. Interview with Graham Mott, LINK, by B. Bátiz-Lazo and C. Reese, London, 30 July 2008.

43. Media communications of mayor deployments between 1967 and 1980 are stored at the Charles Babbage Institute (henceforth CBI), Burroughs Corp (Ascension 90), Press Releases (Series 72): Boxes 7 to 10. Another large deployment took place in South America by Banco de Colombia in 1975. But bank customers found the machines to be unreliable and largely out of service for unknown reasons.

44. Interview with Hayden Taylor, Computer Systems Controller and Director of the Computer Research and Development Unit (CRDU) of the Trustee Savings Bank (circa 1970–88), by B. Bátiz-Lazo and I. Martin, Milton Keynes, 17 July 2008.

45. This paragraph draws on the interview with Ray Neal, director TSB Computer Services and TSB Trust, by B. Bátiz-Lazo, 16 March 2008. See also Bátiz-Lazo et al. (2014b).

46. The seamless operation of humans at the branch teller or servicing the cash machine is consistent in the independent recollections of office work by Whit-more, Shipley, and McQuade. Source: Interview with Michael D. McQuade, branch manager and group director TSB (1964–2000), by B. Bátiz-Lazo, Leicester, 6 March 2008; Interview with Janet Shipley, retail branch staff—TSB (1969–2008), by B. Bátiz-Lazo, Leicester, 11 March 2008; Interview with Sarah Whitmore, retail branch staff—TSB (circa 1973–80), by B. Bátiz-Lazo, Leicester, 8 February 2008.

47. Interview (telephone) with Geoffrey Constable, director of the research laboratory at Kelvin Hughes (Smiths Industries), by B. Bátiz-Lazo, 6 November 2013, and Interview with William Chubb, 4th Lord Hayter, former shareholder and director of Chubb & Son's Lock & Safe, Monk Sherborne, Hampshire, by B. Bátiz-Lazo, 30 March 2010.

48. Interview with James Adamson, former CEO of NCR Dundee, by B. Bátiz-Lazo and R. J. Reid, Edinburgh, 18 June 2008.

49. 'Branching Out? The High Street Will Never Look the Same Again', *The Economist*, 22 March 1986: 45.
50. Bessen (2015a). A short summary focusing on ATMs is available in Bessen (2015b).
51. Brynjolfsson and Hitt (2000); Brynjolfsson and Saunders (2010).
52. Bátiz-Lazo and Wood (2002).
53. Brynjolfsson and Hitt (2000); Brynjolfsson and Khanin (2000); Brynjolfsson and Saunders (2010); Consoli and Patrucco (2010).
54. Ballarín (1985); Bátiz-Lazo and Wood (2002); Wood and Bátiz-Lazo (1997).
55. Bessen (2015b, 17; italics in original).
56. Bátiz-Lazo et al. (2014b); Bátiz-Lazo and Maixé-Altés (2011a).
57. 'Are ATMs Stealing Jobs?', *The Economist*, 15 June 2011, accessed 15 June 2011, <http://www.economist.com/blogs/democracyinamerica/2011/06/technology-and-unemployment>.
58. It is worth noting that Catherine Bond's ideas had an impact on both sides of the Atlantic; in 1987 she was invited to develop and deliver a training programme for the Co-operative Bank and separately for the former Abbey National building society in the UK. These courses lasted a number of years. Source: Interview (telephone) with David Cavell, former director Co-operative Bank, by B. Bátiz-Lazo, 14 July 2016; and Catherine L. Bond, '50 Tactical Tips Can Help ATM Programs Prosper', *Bank Systems & Equipment*, August 1987: 129 and 132.
59. Bátiz-Lazo and Reese (2010).
60. These examples borrow from Tony Levene, 'Failed Strategies', *The Guardian*, 13 June 2006, accessed 22 August 2016, <https://www.theguardian.com/money/2006/jun/13/business.accounts>.
61. 'Alamy Stock Photo', *Alamy*, accessed 1 October 2017, <http://www.alamy.com/stock-photo-southend-on-sea-seaside-resort-beside-river-thames-estuary-branch-788763.html>.
62. 'Branching Out? The High Street Will Never Look the Same Again', *The Economist*, 22 March 1986: 45.
63. Bessen (2015a).
64. Bessen (2015b).
65. Emma Dunkley, 'UK Banks shut 1,000 Branches as Customers Turn to Mobile Banking', *Financial Times*, 14 December 2016, accessed 21 August 2017, <https://www.ft.com/content/f2b66af8-c153-11e6-81c2-f57d90f6741a>; French et al. (2012); Jon Marino, 'Bank Branches are Evolving…and Shrinking', *CNBC*, 21 April 2016, accessed 21 August 2017, <https://www.cnbc.com/2016/04/21/bank-branches-are-evolvingand-shrinking.html>; 'Clydesdale and Yorkshire Banks Close Dozens of Branches', *BBC News*, 18 January 2017, accessed 18 January 2017, <http://www.bbc.co.uk/news/uk-scotland-scotland-business-38669280>; Douglas Fraser, 'Airdrie Savings Bank to Close its Doors', *BBC News*, 18 January 2017, accessed 18 January 2017, <http://www.bbc.co.uk/news/ukscotlandscotlandbusiness38669275>.
66. Thomas Heath, 'Bank Tellers are the Next Blacksmiths', *Washington Post*, 8 February 2017, accessed 25 August 2017, <https://www.washingtonpost.com/business/economy/bank-tellers-are-the-next-blacksmiths/2017/02/08/fdf78618-ee1c-11e6-9662-6eedf1627882_story.html?utm_term=.09023bb71087&wpisrc=nl_draw&wpmm=1>.

10

Epilogue: The Cashless Economy and the ATM

10.1 Automating the Past

> 'Memo to Paul Volcker: There's been a lot more technological improvement in banking since the ATM.'
>
> —Jeff Kutler[1]

This book has provided a business and technological history of innovation in retail payments with the purpose of commemorating the past of an industry that built itself around a particular machine. The aim was to keep the focus of the narrative off obsolescence and on maintenance and reinvention, while also allowing space to celebrate industry milestones. This was why the story explained how the implementation of innovations in retail payment systems encompasses more than simply number-crunching such as: 'There are 3.6 million devices around the world'. In other words, there is more to the 'hole in the wall' than establishing who the prime mover was because there is a whole network of apparatuses, there is a story to how the software applications within them came to be, as well as the standards, skills, people, organizations, jurisdictions, social understandings, and institutions supporting them.

Developing this understanding required clarity over the genesis of the technology (see Chapters 2 and 3). Hollywood movies and TV programmes portray scientists and industry-disrupting entrepreneurs as having a 'eureka moment'—that singular juncture in time when their faces change, they find the answer, and 'history is made' so that things will never be the same. It is a 'before and after' event—think Newton's apple, Alexander Fleming noticing a plate of bacteria that had been contaminated by mould, or Marty McFly telling Dr Emmett Brown about the bruise on his head.[2] Another typical feature of these fairy tales is their depiction of the entrepreneur as a young, misunderstood, college drop-out (e.g. Bill Gates or Steve Jobs) and presenting with him both the scientist and the entrepreneur hero as an altruist, middle-class, white, man (e.g. Mark Zuckerberg). Popular versions of the invention of the ATM paint a similar picture. A quick search of the Internet pops up the names of Luther Simjian, John Sheppard-Barron, James Goodfellow, and Don Wetzel all having a claim and actively competing for the accolade of 'the inventor of the ATM'. But implicit in these depictions there is a prerogative to maintain a specific gender, religious orientation, ethnicity, class, and income domain for banking and engineering.

In practice, research (and particularly research that has long-term impact) reflects a lot of persistence and teamwork. Time and again, the formula for success does not result from spontaneity but from the support of groups of people inside and outside the organization. So it is with the invention of the cash machine and its evolution into the ATM, according to the historical evidence unearthed throughout this book.

In the light of this evidence it is hard to say what vision or 'eureka moment' holds up for the transformative power of the ATM. Even disregarding prior devices performing similar services in the USA (such as Simjian's cash and cheque deposit machine) or the Japanese invention of a credit card activated machine, British and Swedish bankers independently discussed the idea of a machine substituting for bank clerks for some years before the general public began to use one. These conversations resulted in three independent teams of engineers deploying a cash machine for public use. These three deployments took place within a month of each other: one in Sweden and two in the UK. A third British team was ready to launch but delayed until 1969 because the sponsoring bank insisted on greater security (including the need for an online device, that is, the feature that distinguishes the ATM from the cash machine). At the same time, newspapers in the USA and Europe informed the general public that an automatic cash dispenser was in production (and showed pictures of alternative devices) months ahead of deployment.

Since the original motivation for this book was partly to bring clarity to 'that instance of invention' and because the absence of definitive, trustworthy, historical evidence fails to point unequivocally to the 'prime mover', it is my view that in all likelihood it was not an engineer who had the original idea but was an instance when an unidentified banker or group of bankers in Japan, Britain, Sweden, and probably the USA as well, came to a simultaneous and independent realization. But people and particularly journalists, are romantic and like the notion of the lone inventor in a garage (or, as in this case, a bath tub) revolutionizing the world in an epiphany. This is certainly more appealing than that of a room full of cigar-smoking men in bowler hats and dress suits. But however unfashionable, the available evidence, documented in this book as well as what emerged throughout the process of research, speaks of a design resulting from collective rather than individual effort, which was largely put together with standardized components and only key parts of which were bespoke (for example, the activation and dispensing mechanisms).

However, the story in this book is more than an effort to document the genesis of the cash machine. This research has shown how, in order to take shape and succeed, the ATM became a viable technology when connected to and in tune with a broader process of automation and strategic change for retail financial markets (see Chapter 8).

Neither can the cash machine be defined exclusively as a one-time response to solve the problems of greater unionization, spiralling labour costs, and congestion at retail bank branches. Instead, the main thrust of the story involved explaining the maturation of the machine, the 'great leap forward' to deliver online, real time, digital banking, as well as the efforts of several groups of people to build and maintain vast networks of conveniently located ATMs that responded to individual transactions within 30 seconds and without fail (see Chapters 3–5).

The evolution of the cash machine into the ATM was also associated with long-term changes in banking practices, organizational processes, procedures, organizational routines (including the relocation of value-added activities from branches to head office), information systems, the skills and numbers of employees in banks (even more, those in 'bricks and mortar' branches), independent ATM deployers (IADs), ATM manufacturers, and other suppliers to this industry. This evolution of the ATM and the digitalization of customer information went in step with changes in people's payment habits, sometimes creating changes in these habits themselves and at others responding to unexpected customer behaviour.

As noted in Chapter 6, globalization resulted from the interaction of a collection of otherwise independent payment systems supported by groups of engineers, bankers, payment card companies, regulators, bank customers, and others; working together to design a workable proposition, negotiate the standards that enabled interconnectivity and, more important, working to nurture and prune previous investments in applications of computer technology, that is, building new layers of the domestic and global payments ecosystem while also maintaining, repairing, using, recycling, and, as mentioned above, eventually changing working practices, the skills of branch staff, and the behaviour of bank customers.

It is superficial to believe that ATMs have a single global meaning or that the thirty years between the first operational machine and the global network can be summarized as *just* making the ATM work. Instead, the aim of this book was to depict the basic set of 'things' or common denominators that allowed convenient, reliable, seamless, and secure access to people's monetary funds through an ATM.[3]

Global ubiquity involved creating a system architecture made out of patents, regulations, computer code (such as encryption algorithms or messaging standards), and even the materiality of the activation token (a standard-sized, embossed, plastic card with a magnetic stripe on the back). And in the process of fortifying the institutions of capitalism, it brought together people, financial organizations, accreditation bodies, and many other organizations that *enabled* these machines to work and transformed the ATM into the mundane, everyday object that, as a cultural icon, is typically portrayed in the media as the omnipresent point of contact with today's otherwise digital bank.

10.2 Memo to Paul Volcker: An Agenda for Future Research

Paraphrasing Jeffrey Kutler's quotation above and, as this book has shown, there has been more innovation to the ATM and in retail banking altogether, than simply installing literally millions of copies of a machine that dispense cash in convenient locations. Previous chapters recounted how the evolution of the cash machine into the ATM was accompanied by a number of interesting developments, which included the first shared ATM networks and also took the bank closer to the point of purchase (see Chapters 4 and 5). But more important, banks sought to extend the concept of automation. In short, the arrival of the cash machine was a watershed moment and the 'firing gun' that set off retail financial institutions onto the path of self-service banking (see Chapter 8).

Self-service involves replacing labour, not only through the automation of repetitive tasks but also by relocating activities by asking customers to do for themselves what branch staff had traditionally done for them.[4] Chaper 9 explores this process. However, many of the devices implementing automatization of this kind resulted in or accompanied a process of 'disintermediation', that is, the migration of activities that had hitherto taken place inside banking organizations and now take place through transactions in the open market.

We need to better understand this process in retail finance, first, by identifying the impact on bank staff and customer habits of key devices (particularly those that were not as self-evident as the ATM, such as banknote counting machines) and information systems. Part of this process should include comparing and contrasting experiences in retail payment systems and why the latter map so clearly and neatly to sovereign borders. For instance, direct to account payment of wages and salaries was an important economic incentive for the adoption of digital banking in general and ATMs in particular; the latter were the most successful mechanism for reducing congestion at retail branches.

Research in this book has also drawn a direct connection between the emergence of bank transfer payments in Britain, Sweden, and the USA and their role in the emergence, adoption, and exportation of cash machines (see Chapters 2–4). Without a shadow of a doubt, there would not be any serious expectation of a cashless economy without the move to implement direct to account payments of salaries and wages, while allowing withdrawals through non-branch access to these liquid balances through, for instance, personal cheques, credit cards, cheque guarantee cards, and later on, electronic fund transfer at point of sale terminals. But ATMs were not only instrumental but essential to this process of digitalization.

However, important differences in payment systems across countries also led to alterations in the technology; for instance, the predominance of personal cheques in the USA leading to the development of the Bankograph by Simjian or the popularity of 'envelope deposit' boxes in ATMs.[5]

Cross-border differences are also important in the attitudes to different groups of consumers (see Chapter 8). The business and technological history of banking could work harder to understand the position and treatment of vulnerable consumers in financial institutions and retail financial markets (more below), and financial inclusion as well as financial exclusion according to sexual preference. Addressing issues of diversity, for instance, could answer such questions as how and when women (or specific minorities) broke 'the glass ceiling' and moved from performing repetitive tasks in branches to the boardroom; how the marketing of banking services to women or ethnic minorities changed; and how these groups perceived these changes. This is the sort of agenda that could link the business decisions of bankers to broader discussions in cognate areas.

The process of evolution that promised a homogeneous banking experience anywhere in the world also had its share of controversy. As documented in Chapter 7, the role of 'pay to use' fees had an important part to play—the role of regulation and regulators is critical here but discussed below.

Chapter 7 also documented how the IADs and surcharging (or other 'pay to use' schemes) allowed ATMs to spread further by creating the economic incentive to site them elsewhere than on bank premises. But it was also the case that British consumers and politicians had no appetite for surcharging and disloyalty fees, even though consumers in the USA or Canada were willing to accept them as the price of convenience.

On the one hand, ATM fees remain an issue for banks and customers. For instance, at the time of writing, a student working at a not-for-profit deposit accepting financial institution in the Caribbean, claimed her employer found that it could increase customer satisfaction, and even attract new depositors, by eliminating ATM fees and maintain or even reduce fees charged for payments by personal cheques. This apparently gave her employer a competitive advantage. For the context of this book this example in the Caribbean attests how ATM fees continue to be an issue for bankers and bank customers.

On the other hand, different customer attitudes to paying for ATM transactions question the comparability of ATM penetration and transaction volume across different countries.[6] Providing cash withdrawal and other services through ATMs comes at some cost for the bank or IAD and for the network with which they share access. Surcharging and other pay-for-use schemes aim to reimburse the provider of the service for these costs. Banks will then make savings as long as transaction volume remains the same or below that at the point of automation. Yet this is seldom the case.

In a partial equilibrium scenario, countries with no surcharging could have lower penetration (or a lower rate of growth) of ATMs, as opposed to countries that allow surcharging, disloyalty fees, and other ways to recover the cost of the service. The potential usefulness to customers in the latter countries could be greater than in countries where no fees are allowed. But it could also be the case that the fees add up to more than the economic cost of providing the service, in which case the potential usefulness to customers would be lower.

Yet any of these alternative scenarios and potential trade-offs would also be subject to the number of financial institutions and intensity of competition within the retail financial market. In Mexico and many European economies, for instance, IADs are not allowed to operate. In others where they are allowed, such as Spain and the Netherlands, they have sometimes failed to prosper. As documented in Chapter 7, IADs in Britain, Canada, and the USA have flourished—although the industry seems to be consolidating rapidly.

It may be that in the USA, which has thousands of financial institutions and IADs, it might be more efficient to allow surcharging and other fees and thereby enjoy more widespread ATMs, for individuals may encounter many situations in which they are far away from their own bank's ATMs. Meanwhile in the Netherlands and the UK, where many fewer financial institutions and IADs operate, surcharging and other fees may not be worth imposing, since many more people can, on average, locate a machine belonging to their own bank. This might explain why British and Dutch banks may agree on a broader pricing-to-share scheme, which preserves network benefits at foreign locations and compensates via interchange fees alone.[7]

It is also the case that British, Canadian, Dutch, and Belgian banking systems are highly concentrated. Some even call them an oligopoly.[8] Their business model has been to recover costs through interest on lending. In North America, the business model is somewhat different: the banks' business model is geared to recover costs through specific transactions. There are pros and cons with each approach as well as cases, such as that of Canadian IADs, that seem to be a contradiction; but more could be said about the role that business models play in explaining the timing and widespread adoption of specific retail banking technologies.

The above discussion points to the great effect that surcharging and other pay-to-use fees have had (perhaps even bigger than the strategic decisions of individual banks) on the economic and financial dynamics of the ATM industry. For this reason, it will be important for future research to determine how the business model(s) of this industry will develop. Will it converge and become a wholly fee-based market, as in the USA, Mexico, and Australia? Will fees be charged whether or not individuals use the ATMs of their own bank? Will the cost of using alternative payment methods be more transparent? Will banks continue to cross-subsidize costly current accounts and other services to keep customers happy? Or will politics and consumer resistance keep this at bay? Will IADs continue to grow their majority control of the ATM fleet in the UK, Eastern Europe, the USA, and other countries where the IAD model has been successful? And, if so, is there sufficient regulation and oversight over this industry? If innovation was always important for retail finance in the second half of the twentieth century, why in the twenty-first century has it become critical?

When discussing the emergence of the IAD, the research in this book briefly hinted at the role of knowledge management and specifically communities of practice in retail finance. Increasing interest has been shown in documenting the role of trade associations and cross-organizational bodies in implementing technological change.[9] However, most systematic studies around communities of practice have so far been found in education, policing, and health; financial services in general have not had any attention from business historians, let alone enough.[10]

Before concluding this section, a comment is necessary on two important groups of actors who are otherwise missing from the story this book tells, namely, the bank regulators and the monetary authorities. Just as there were changes in the culture and habits of retail bank customers and within the organizational milieu of financial intermediaries, automation, riding on the back of computer technology, brought about changes within central banks in terms of the supply of money (in the form of new payment methods) and monetary control (from direct control through the flow of cash to banks' retail branches up to indirect control through operations in the open market).

For instance, joint ATM networks imply the creation of protocols for electronic fund payment systems. Automation also has the potential to impact on the ratio of cash deposits and non-cash deposits, as well as on the preference for being paid in cash. The ATM has also been associated with a change from payments in cash and cheques to the predominance of plastic and digital payments. For most of the period examined in this book, the Bank of England has assumed the roles of bank regulator and (shared) monetary authority in Britain. As had been the case in the USA, 'it would be difficult to overestimate the influence of regulatory bodies and laws in the character and practices of the Financial Sector'.[11] When and how the Bank of England and other central banks became interested in computer applications and the impact they would have on monetary control and supervision of financial intermediaries (such as the challenges of auditing banks as a result of the move to digital records), but also on devices such as the ATM, the emergence of networks of point of sale terminals, the automation of clearing houses for retail payments, the competitive implications of a duopoly in payment cards, and the influence of these on larger payment systems and other aspects of retail financial markets are topics that have yet to be documented.

Evidence documented throughout this book suggests that in Europe, North America, and countries in other regions, most bank regulators engaged rather late and reactively to the ATM. Their concerns focused on either location (as was the case with some states in the USA) or more generally, on the consumer welfare implications of surcharging and other pay-to-use fees. The one exception here may be Portugal, where from the outset ATMs were considered a public utility and were managed through a central provider. But the passive attitudes of regulators across the world suggest a lack of understanding of the impact of financial technology on retail bank markets in general and payment systems in particular in the late twentieth century. These attitudes and knowledge certainly contrast with the attention to crypto currencies, distributed ledger technology, and more generally, the financial market infrastructure provided by monetary, fiscal, and banking national and supranational authorities in the early twenty-first century.

Another layer of regulation that has been overlooked is that relating to vulnerable consumers. For instance, we have yet to document how financial institutions have used devices such as ATMs to include (or neglect) people with physical disabilities. There is therefore a need to collaborate with historians of the legal system and recount how changes in legislation and specific regulation led to or resulted from internal changes within financial intermediaries.

10.3 Whenever, Wherever: The Paleo-Future of Cashless Payments

History is the study of the past, of events that have already taken place. As a result, historians pretty much leave the future to others. This can sometimes, for most people, feel lonely, as we care primarily about the future. As the image

Figure 10.1. Bernardo Bátiz-Lazo interviewed by Kevin Peachy of the BBC, 2017 (ATM & Cybersecurity Conference, London)
Source: Courtesy of RBR London.

in Figure 10.1 suggests, reservations about the nature of historical research will not deter journalists from asking questions along the lines of:

> All this history is fine and dandy. It establishes an auditable and verifiable path which challenges the accepted wisdom and sets the record straight. But what does this evidence of invention tell us about the future of the ATM? What can research into the evolution of the ATM tells us about the future of payments? How have cash machines changed consumers and will they continue to do so? What do we do today that we didn't do before the cash machine, and will this be the same with the advent of mobile payments? And how about that machine behind you, is it a 'game changer' and will it disrupt retail payments? Is the cashless society within reach? If so why do we need cash machines?

Historians and particularly those who cross into social studies of technology, tend to be reluctant to answer with tangible predictions (particularly of the kind that other business and management scholars are fond of offering), knowing from their workaday immersion in the documents of the past that predictions are almost invariably wrong.[12] Yet apocalyptic visions within mass media and fintech start-ups are all waiting for the advent of a messiah who will disrupt retail payments and deliver the cashless economy; as a result I am invariably pressed to express an opinion about the impending destiny of cash and the ATM. Not having learned my lesson, here is an attempt to answer some of the common questions about the future of the ATM.

First, visions of the future in the mass media are not only naïve but underestimate the complexity of innovation in retail payments.[13] They also airbrush out important contributors from banking and engineering in the development of key technologies. Fintech start-ups are often subject to the same views; they focus on the distinct features of their applications or devices rather than on developing an understanding of the way that the broader competitive environment came to develop specific features of its industrial organization.

Second, popular accounts of the emergence of cash machines tend to overlook the fact that their growth and widespread adoption marked the first time that technology was radically modifying services for retail customers since the beginnings of computerization in the late 1950s. Changes went beyond pre-printed stationery, mechanical annotations, or magnetic characters in cheques, all superficial concerns from a customer's perspective, and how the ATM took into account an increasingly mobile yet urban set of users who no longer wanted or had to rely on a single bank branch. In a way, the desire for this transformation is similar to today's demands by bank customers to interact with their bank whenever they choose, through the channel of their choice, and wherever they may be located around the world.

In the years after 2010 the retail banking industry began to grapple with yet another concept of self-service, namely, the so-called 'omni-channel'. This is a strategy dedicated to enabling customers to bank anywhere, at any time, whether in person or through a device. It is no secret that customers want convenience, but to get it they must be supplied with several access options. The omni-channel, therefore, challenges banks to create a platform from which the bank delivers its services in a consistent way across a variety of locations and devices—in other words, a solution that goes beyond maintaining multiple channels and actually offers the same 'look and feel' and the same transactional capabilities across all points of interaction with the customer.

The idea of an omni-channel has also been fuelled by the expectation that the bank leverages customer information so that individual customers can be reached with targeted offers. But this strategy has to allow each channel to provide multiple services and at the same time ensure that the offers or incentives are appropriate to the delivery channel. In addition, it should maintain relevance and maintain or even enhance the bank's brand.

For sceptics the idea of the omni-channel is no different from earlier propositions by universal banks. Proponents say it is not the same because its challenge is to take customer loyalty and cross-selling opportunities to higher levels while, at the same time, eliminating legacy information systems (some banks in 2017 still run their payment systems on software developed in the 1970s!). The extent to which omni-channels are a departure from the past or simply the same idea disguised under new technology is a matter of opinion and subject to future empirical studies.

Nevertheless, delivering the omni-channel has become the 'Holy Grail' of retail banking. An industry report by *ATM Marketplace* (sponsored by KAL ATM Software) estimated that in 2015 almost half of the banks sampled were in the process of developing an omni-channel strategy (while 33 per cent thought it was a long-term strategy and the rest had either given up or had never begun to attempt it).[14] This strategy envisioned a continued reliance on ATMs with 26 per cent of the survey respondents expecting to increase the size of their ATM estate both in-branch and off-site. Meanwhile, 23 per cent said they would be expanding the use of ATMs and self-service machines inside their bank branches.

These trends suggest that any serious omni-channel proposition includes greater use of self-service technology. As recalled above and documented throughout this book, the ATM has been at the centre of self-service strategies since the late 1970s and all indications are that it will continue to do so, given its proven track record as a reliable, resilient, and widespread channel. Indeed, bankers who contributed to the above *ATM Marketplace* report expected the ATM to remain central to banks' delivery strategies, while many respondents predicted that they would increase in importance as more automation realized their potential to carry further types of self-service transactions. In the report, a number of bankers were said to be already working on the integration of ATMs with mobiles and other devices.[15]

But if (yet again) the cashless economy is supposed to be around the corner, why do ATMs remain so important? There are at least four reasons for believing in the future of the ATM in banks' self-service strategies. First, the ATM, like cash and payment cards, is a trusted, reliable, and mature technology. Most of the adult population around the world knows how to use it. At the same time, access to the know-how and engineering skills that will ensure its effective deployment, together with after-sales service and maintenance, is widespread. Second, in most developed countries, ATMs have been densely deployed and are in convenient places. Not surprisingly, most customers always interact with the same five machines, more or less, in their everyday life. Third, there is a global, shared ATM network around Visa and MasterCard. So no matter where you are in the world, you are likely to have convenient access to your funds.

Fourth, looking to the future, the retail branch and the ATM are the only two channels that are fully under a bank's control—from the make and model to the location and security of transactions. These features provide an advantage over malware and fintech start-ups. This is because security concerns are higher when services are delivered over hardware which a financial institution does not control, while it is very much the case that malware is moving into mobile phones and tablet spaces.

On the one hand, ATMs and retail branches can remain channels for secure 'client present' transactions or simply to finalize transactions with a high degree of reliability. However, a higher degree of control does not offer complete protection and is no shield against attacks. Heists at banks' retail branches are the stuff of legend. ATMs are also attractive given that by their nature they provide a service while unattended.

Although ATMs attacks remain largely physical (i.e. skimming, deep insert skimming, tanking, eavesdropping, black box, detonations, etc.), ATMs were used in 2009 and 2016 as unauthorized entry points to a larger network. Fortunately, these attacks have been few and far between. It is also the case that today cybercrime is several orders of magnitude bigger than losses from ATMs or even burglaries at households.[16] However, as ATMs and other self-service devices are integrated into the 'Internet of Things', the likelihood of using these machines to put together other types of fraud (such as identity theft) could grow exponentially. How will financial institutions protect their customers from these attacks? What is the nature of their responsibility and how willing are they to protect individual customers? Such questions ought to move higher up the digital banking agenda.

To make matters worse, customer-owned devices can (and often are) more powerful and modern than financial institutions' ageing legacy systems. This would appear to open the door to disruptive innovations by new entrants in some aspects of the retail transaction space. But the reliability, trustworthiness, and security of all these innovations have yet to be tested—as opposed to the fifty-year successful track record of the ATM and even longer history of the retail branch.

In brief, what does the future hold for the ATM? As the fog clears, my crystal ball shows that the extent to which the ATM is able to support greater self-service solutions and is, therefore, central to omni-channel strategies, guarantees that it will remain the backbone of self-service distribution in retail banking. This is not to say that the ATM will remain unchanged, but it will continue to evolve incrementally through the interaction of bankers, engineers, specialist providers, monetary and fiscal authorities, and the general public as it has done for the last fifty years.

In other words, throughout their history ATMs and self-service devices have been conceived, designed, and improved upon not as the pursuit of 'the new' or to redefine banking services from the ground up, but as machines that aim to capture cost-effective gains from high volume transactions (such as cash withdrawals, balance enquiries, electronic transfers, etc.). In most instances, the success of these devices has been measured over decades while, at the same

275

time, this success allows staff in retail branches (and more recently, the real estate of retail branches themselves) to evolve and focus on high-value generating activities. Briefly, maintaining rather than disrupting is at the heart of the ATM as an innovation.

And here, then, my final thanks to you for joining me on this journey. Paraphrasing Antonio Machado, we, the wayfarers, now look back on that path that we may not set foot from now onward. I hope that, like me, you now view the history of the ATM as more than a linear story about how a bunch of nuts and bolts ended up stored on top of a safe box set behind a brick wall. Instead, this book has recounted a story of decisions about capital investments, business strategies, transaction volume and technological evolution and how these were followed by decisions dealing with legacy systems, personnel, standards, locations, and whether machines could become a source of competitive advantage in retail banking, another channel for self-service or a commodity service that could be outsourced. In short, the research in this book has presented to you the ATM as a window to internal and external changes in retail banking since the 1960s to the present.

Notes

1. Jeffery Kutler, 'Banking's Waves of Innovation', *Institutional Investor*, 28 September 2002, accessed 14 July 2016, <http://www.institutionalinvestor.com/article/3095582/banking-and-capital-markets-banking/bankings-waves-of-innovation.html#/.V4Ou9tIrK70>.
2. *Back to the Future*, directed by Robert Zemeckis (1985; Orlando, FL: Universal Pictures).
3. McCray (2012); Orr (1996).
4. See further Palm (2016, chap. 4).
5. I appreciate Lee Vinsel's reminding me of the importance of envelop deposits in the USA. Personal communication (email) from Lee Jared Vinsel, assistant professor Virgina Tech, with B. Bátiz-Lazo, 23 October 2017.
6. I am grateful to James McAndrew for raising this point. Personal communication (email) from James McAndrew, formerly at the Federal Reserve Bank of Philadelphia, with B. Bátiz-Lazo, 18 September 2017.
7. See further Hannan et al. (2001).
8. I am grateful to Mark Billings, for raising this point. Personal communication (email) from Mark Billings,, senior lecturer in accounting University of Exeter Business School, with B. Bátiz-Lazo, 18 September 2017.
9. Bátiz-Lazo and Maixé-Altés (2011a); Heide (2009); Maixé-Altés (2015, 2016); Yates (1989, 2005).
10. One exception is Bátiz-Lazo and Smith (2016). See further Scranton and Fridenson (2013, 190).

11. Cortada (2006, 15).

12. Iwan Rhys Morus, 'Future Perfect: How Victorians Invented the Future', *aeon*, 10 December 2014, accessed 21 October 2017, <https://aeon.co/essays/how-the-victorians-invented-the-future-for-us>.

13. Bátiz-Lazo et al. (2014a); Haigh and Paju (2016).

14. '2015 ATM and Self-Service Software Trends', *ATM Marketplace* and KAL ATM Software, 29 June 2015, accessed 9 August 2017, <http://www.atmmarketplace.com/whitepapers/2015-atm-and-self-service-software-trends/>.

15. '2015 ATM and Self-Service Software Trends', *ATM Marketplace* and KAL ATM Software, 29 June 2015, accessed 9 August 2017, <http://www.atmmarketplace.com/whitepapers/2015-atm-and-self-service-software-trends/>.

16. According to data from the Metropolitan Police, in 2016 one out of 43 households was reported as subject to a burglary, each most often amounting to a couple of thousand pounds. At the same time, one out of 10 were subject to some form of cybercrime (e.g. payment fraud, ransomware). Some 360,000 small and medium-sized business suffered attacks, not all of them isolated, leading to losses estimated at just short of £2 billion. Source: Tara Owens, Falcon Division—Metropolitan Police, ATM & Cyber Security Conference, London, 10 October 2017.

APPENDIX 1

List of Interviews

Date of Interview	Name	Organization (Location)	Experience / Role
8 February 2008	Sean Newcombe	Speytec and Burroughs (UK)	Pioneering Engineer
22 February 2008	Sally Hall	Bristol and West Building Society (UK)	Branch Staff
28 February 2008	Suzanne Lavelle	Scarborough Building Society (UK)	Customer Support
3 March 2008	Robin Bulloch	Royal Bank of Scotland (UK)	Director of Distribution Strategy
6 March 2008	Michael McQuade	TSB Banking Group (UK)	Branch Management
8 March 2008	Frank Chalmers	NCR Corporation (UK and USA)	Engineer
8 March 2008 and 17 July 2008	Ray Neil	TSB Computer Services and TSB Trust (UK)	Director, Computer Services
18 March 2008	Annett Bateman	TSB Banking Group (UK)	Assistant General Manager
18 March 2008	Linda Hyland	TSB Banking Group (UK)	Retail Branch Staff
26 March 2008	John Shepherd-Barron, OBE	De La Rue (UK and USA)	Pioneer and Director
27 March 2008	James Goodfellow, OBE	Smiths Industries (UK)	Pioneer Engineer
28 March 2008	Alex Blake	Sainsbury's Bank	Head of ATM Channel
3 April 2008	Dominic Hirsch	RBR London (UK)	Managing Director
1 May 2008	Don Newbold	TSB Banking Group (UK)	Engineer
1 May 2008	John Warren	Barclays Bank (UK)	Self-Service Channel
2 May 2008	Louise Carter	Alliance & Leicester (UK)	ATM Business Unit

(*continued*)

Appendix 1: List of Interviews

Continued

Date of Interview	Name	Organization (Location)	Experience / Role
9 May 2008	Stuart Miller	Barclays Bank (UK)	Head of Self-Service
19 May 2008	Mike Bullough	Halifax/HBOS (UK)	IT Systems Support ATMs
19 May 2008	Richard Barrow	Halifax Building Society (UK)	General Manager Business Information Systems
23 May 2008	John Needham	Royal Bank of Scotland (UK)	Senior Compliance Consultant
2 June 2008	John Goodfellow	Skipton Building Society (UK)	Chief Executive
4 June 2008	Jack Donald	Speytec (UK)	Pioneering Engineer
5 June 2008	Roland McGill	Santander (UK)	Head of Consumer Process Improvement
5 June 2008	Paul Robertson	Santander (UK)	Operations and ATM Channel
18 June 2008	James Adamson, MBE	NCR Corporation (UK and USA)	Pioneer and VP Financial Delivery Systems
18 June 2008	James Carden	Bank of Scotland/ HBOS (UK)	Head of IT Business Management
30 June 2008	Graham Mott	LINK (UK)	Head of Development & External Relations
11 July 2008	John Hughes	Co-op Bank (UK)	Director of Retail Banking
17 July 2008	Hayden Taylor	TSB Computer Services and TSB Banking Group (UK)	Computer Systems Controller and Director of the Computer Research and Development Unit (CRDU)
17 July 2008	Harry Read	TSB Computer Services (UK)	Director of TSB Computer Services
25 July 2008	Andrew Hutchinson	Nationwide Building Society (UK)	Head of Retail Distribution
30 April 2009	Jerome Svigals	IBM (USA)	Smart Card Development Engineer
8 September 2009	Paul Glaser	Citibank and Transaction Technology, Inc. (USA)	Engineer
22 September 2009	Manuel Barragan	HSBC (Mexico)	Head of ATM and Self-Service Channels
22 September 2009	Jacobo Viskin	Burroughs and NCR (Mexico and Latin America)	Product Leader ATM and Self-Service Channels
30 March 2010	William Chubb, 4th Lord Hayter	Chubb (Australia, Singapore, UK)	Pioneer Deployment and Director
12 July 2012	Geoffrey EP Constable	Smiths Industries & Chubb (UK)	Pioneering Engineer
23 August 2012	Gary Faulkner	Morphis, Inc. (USA)	Consultant, Marketing, and Conferences Organiser
12 September 2012	William Jackson	GRG International and Triton (USA)	Chief Technical Officer

15 October 2012	Heidi Hoo	RGR Banking Equipment (China)	Sales and Marketing
26 March 2013	James Block	Diebold (USA)	Director Global Advance Technology
26 March 2013	Tomas Graef	Diebold (USA)	Pioneer and Product Developer
1 April 2013	James Nolls	N/A (USA)	DACS Service Engineer
24 April 2013	Sir Anthony Cleaver	IBM (UK)	Pioneering Engineer and CEO
7 October 2013	Uwe Krauzmann	Wincor (Germany)	Head of Product Development
5 November 2013	David Ibbs	Smiths Industries & Chubb (UK)	Engineer
6 July 2016	Irwin Derman	Visa International (USA)	VP International Payments
13 July 2016 and 27 July 2017	Robert Rosenthal	IBM (UK and South Africa)	Engineer
14 July 2016	David Cavell	Co-op Bank (UK)	Self-service Consultant
6 February 2017	Christopher Klein	NCR Corp. (USA)	Engineering
15 February 2017	John Leehy	Payment Alliance International (USA)	Chief Executive Officer (IAD)
22 February 2017	Jenny Campbell	Hanco & YourCash (UK)	Chief Operating Officer, CEO, & Chairman (IAD)
23 February 2017	Eric de Putter	Payments Redesign (UK)	Payments Consultant
30 May 2017	David Miller	Smith Industries (UK)	Pioneering Engineer
17 July 2017	Ron Delnevo	Bank Machine (UK) and ATMIA (Europe)	Pioneering, Chief Executive Officer (IAD)
17 July 2017	Clive Nation	Travalex (UK)	Dynamic Currency Conversions
13 October 2017	Stuart McEwen Jenkins	De La Rue Instruments (UK)	Project Manager—Engineering

Technological and Regulatory Milestones

Year	Technological Turning Point	Diffussion and Adoption	Industry Developments	Judiciary and Regulatory Innovations
1959	Luther Simjian files first patent for Bankograph (a deposit accepting device).			
1960				
1961	Brief trial of Bankograph by City Bank in New York City.			
1962				
1963				
1964				
1965				
1966	In Japan the 'Computer Loan Machine' is an early cash dispenser which is activated with a credit card and money dispensed as a three-month loan at 5.5% p.a.			

	In the UK, G. Constable, A. Davies, and J. Goodfellow at Smiths Industries file patent which details the fist instance of a personal identification number (PIN) and the earliest instance of a complete 'currency dispenser system' in the patent record.	
1967	Cash machines are made operational. The first in the Enfield (London) branch of Barclays Bank (UK) and manufactured by De La Rue. This is followed two days later by an independent deployment of Asea-Metior and Swedish savings banks in Uppsala and a month later, Chubb and the Westminster Bank in London.	
1968	Cash dispenser in Malmö (Sweden) and an IBM 7714 interface connect to an IBM 360 computer in Stockholm.	First deployment in Germany, the Netherlands, Portugal, Spain, and Switzerland.
1969	In the USA, T. R. Barnes, G. R. Chastian, K. S.Goldstien, M. R. Karecki, D. C. Wetzel, J. D. White, and Docutel filed patents describing for the first time in detail a system that seems closer to the ATMs of today.	First deployment in Canada, Denmark, France, Japan, and the USA.
1970	NCR filed patent for PIN entry verified for consumer authentification.	
1971		Over 1,000 cash machines deployed globally. First cash machine in Israel.

(continued)

Continued

Year	Technological Turning Point	Diffussion and Adoption	Industry Developments	Judiciary and Regulatory Innovations
1972	In the UK, Lloyds Bank deploys a fleet of IBM 2984. A device linked to the central computer and able to check the customer's balance before withdrawal. This is the first widely deployed online cash machine (and the genesis of the ATM).	First cash machine in Mexico and Singapore.		
	In Japan, the patent of Omron-Tateisi described for the first time an 'online' method of transaction in which the system is directly connected to the user's bank account to verify funds and used a magnetic card as token.	First shared cash dispenser networks are established in the USA.		
1973	Introduction of the so called 'Atalla Box', a security system to encrypt PIN and ATM messages.	First cash machine in Australia.		
1974	Diebold introduces TABS 600, an online version of the TAB 500 which included MICR printer and CCTV.		At its zenith Docutel captures 40% of the US market.	In the USA, the Comptroller of the Currency's interpretative ruling allows bank terminals to be established without regard to geographical boundaries or locations.
	Citibank launches the pilot programme of its own desgined and patented ATM (Citicash machine)		Barclays places an advance order for 100 NCR 770 to replace its ageing DACS models in the UK.	
	NCR begins development of its first ATM.			
1975	NCR launches NCR 770 and Burroughs the TC750.	First cash machine in Colombia, Finland, and Ecuador.	In the USA, Dahl's Foods of Iowa was the first grocery to install ATMs in its stores.	

1976	Horst Feistel's Lucifer cipher (incorporated into the ATMs as DSD-1 by IBM) becomes an encryption standard for the Federal Information Processing Standard (FIPS).	First cash machine in Cyprus.
	IBM launches the 3600 Finance Communication system, which included the 3614 cash dispenser device.	
	First version of ISO3554 standard relating to the magnetic stripe encoding for tracks 1 and 2 as well as character embossing of credit cards.	
1977	Citibank launches its large-scale self-service branches including dual ATM in-branch programme (Citicard Banking Centre) in the USA.	First cash machine in Norway.
	In the UK, NatWest had 100 NCR 770 machines in operation alongside 406 Chubb MD2 and MD4 dispensers while 75,000 cards had been issued to customers.	In the USA, the Department of Justice considered that the Chubb-Diebold collaboration agreement breached US competition rules. As a result, Chubb agreed to withdraw for three years from the US market and not to enter into contact with Diebold for five years.
1978	IBM 3614 was replaced by the very successful 3624, which ushered in the online world of self-service banking for IBM.	10% of ATMs in the USA belong to a shared network.

(continued)

Year	Technological Turning Point	Diffussion and Adoption	Industry Developments	Judiciary and Regulatory Innovations
	NCR launches the 1780.	First ATM in Hong Kong, Puerto Rico, and Uruguay.	NCR relocated ATM production to Dundee, Scotland.	
	Nixdord deploys its first ATM in Cologne, Germany.			
	ISO 4909 standard detailing magnetic stripe data content for Track 3 in bank cards.			
1979		First full service office (Merchants National Bank of Cedar Rapids, Iowa).		
		First cash machine in Peru and South Korea.		
1980	NCR introduced drive-up version of the 1780.	A Nilson Report estimated there were 40,140 devices deployed worldwide by Omron (15.6%), NCR (15.3%), Diebold (14.4%), Docutel (13.3%), IBM (12.7%), TRW-Fujitsu (10.7%,), Other (18.0%).	American Express' Express Cash programme was launched as a pilot for national and international shared ATM network for Gold Card holders.	As a result of the Federal Reserve passing regulations protecting the customer unless fraud could be proved, many US banks installed CCTV cameras at ATM to protect their interests.
		Bank of China and NCR deploy the first ATM in China. Other first deployments include Honduras and Ireland.		
		First shared network in Austria and Spain.		
1981	IBM launches the 4700 Finance Communication System (which includes the 4732 cash machine). Lack of compatibility with previous systems becomes a hindrance.	First deployment in Greece, Iceland, Malaysia, Phillipines, and South Africa.	Docutel becomes part of Olivetti.	
		Diebold deploys its 6,000th TAB ATM.	Visa USA announced that members could now use its computerized	

1982	First cash recycling ATM by OKI in Japan. NCR model 5085, the first ATM with an internal hard disk drive launched.	First deployment in New Zealand and Turkey.	authorization and billings systems as a national shared ATM system. Visa International announces plans to invest $20 million to establish an international ATM shared network. In the UK, letters written to the *Daily Mirror* newspaper in January 1981 complain about phantom withdrawals ranging from £5 to £1300. Rocky Mountain BankCard System establishes Plus System Inc. in Denver, CO. Italy's Olivetti marketing and servicing Docutel machines outside of North America while Eindhoven-based Phillips those of Chubb and Diebold.
1983	NCR introduced colour displays and functional desplays keys in its models.	The number of shared ATMs reaches a maximum of 250 different networks in the USA. A worldwide record. First ATM in Brazil, Italy, and Thailand. First shared network in the UK.	First Interstate Bank (Los Angeles, CA) spearheads the establishment of the Cirrus System Inc. shared ATM network.
1984	NCR launched the 5070, considered the first full function machine which offered transfers, payments, printing of detailed statements, and envelope deposits.	First ATM in Costa Rica. Over 100,000 cash machines deployed globally.	IBM and Diebold launch their joint venture (InterBold). Out of court settlement established the priority of the Chubb-Constable-Davies-Goodfellow PIN/PAN patent.

(continued)

Continued

Year	Technological Turning Point	Diffussion and Adoption	Industry Developments	Judiciary and Regulatory Innovations
1985	IBM 4730 accepts notes and coins of different denominations and cashes cheques to the penny.	First ATM in Argentina and Ghana.		US Supreme Court upholds a lower court ruling that ATM are not bank branches.
		Building societies, Co-op Bank, and American Express establish LINK. It was to become the backbone of the single shared network in the UK.		
1986		First shared network in El Salvador, Guatemala, and Venezuela.		
1987	Citibank launches its designed and patented touch screen ATM (CAT 1).	HSBC and Diebold deploy the first ATM in India.	Visa takes minory stake in Plus System Inc.	
	First version of ISO8583 standard, used by point-of-sale devices and ATM messages containing information about the value of a transaction, where the transaction originated, the card account number, and bank sort code.			
1988		Shared networks give access to 90% of all the ATMs in the USA.		
1989	NCR fourth generation systems include single and multi-function devices, with improved ergonomics and the first intelligent deposit ATM.	First ATM deployed in Kenya, Nigeria, Russia, and Tanzania.	Visa through Plus and Mastercard's Cirrus sign duality agrement through which cardholders of either can use point of sale terminals and withraw cash through any of their shared ATM networks in the USA and globally.	The Jack Committee report estimated that there was on average one disputed ATM transaction per hour across the UK. First Texas Savings Association won arbitration against the regional PULSE ATM network to allow surcharging. Valley Bank of Nevada won a legal battle with Cirrus to allow surcharging of cardholders with accounts at other banks.

1990		There are over 300,000 ATMs in operation worldwide.	Siemens takes over Nixdorf and renamed Siemens Nixdorf Informationsyteme (renamed Siemens Nixdorf Retail and Banking in 1998).
1991	Olivetti introduces CD 64000, a device based on Microsoft 8036 chip (with 1 MB RAM), hardware included color display, capacity for 2,000 notes, and smart card reader/writer.	At its zenith there are 75 shared ATM netorks in Japan. First ATM in Poland. NCR is the first ATM manufacturer to reach 100,000 devices installed globally. A Bureau of National Affairs study estimated that 86% of ATM transactions were cash withdrawals, with cash or cheque deposits comprising 10% of transactions and account transfers and bill payment making up the rest.	
1992	NCR introduces thermal receipt printers, audio input, and signature capture in its devices.	Sepah Bank and Siemens Nixdorf deploy the first ATM in Iran. Autobank-e: first large-scale manifestation of a compley self-service branch (Standard Bank, South Africa).	In the USA, the Americans with Disabilities Act Accessibility Guidelines (ADAAG) introduce specific guidelines for ATMs.
1993	Second version of ISO8583 messaging standard.	First pop-up branches with ATMs.	
1994	Triton 9500 launched. The first low-end retail ATM.	First major self-service banking network based on ATMs. First ATM in Lebanon and Egypt. Walk in kiosk, self-service independent branches with small front ATM (Co-op Bank, UK).	

(continued)

Continued

Year	Technological Turning Point	Diffussion and Adoption	Industry Developments	Judiciary and Regulatory Innovations
1995		According to RBR London there are half a million ATMs worldwide.		Succesful legal challenges force Cirrus and Plus to start charging fees.
1996	Triton launched the 9600 series ATM, which quickly became known as the industry workhorse for the off-premises market.	First ATM in Ukraine and first shared network in Puerto Rico.	The two largest national ATM networks in the USA—Cirrus, owned by MasterCard, and Plus, part owned by Visa—announced they were dropping their long-time ban on ATM surcharges by network members. This inaugurated a new era of growth for independent, or non-bank, ATMs, based on highly accessible locations in the retail sector which employed a simple convenience fee.	
1997	KAL Software, IBM, and Canadian Imperial Bank of Commerce (CICB) introduced the first web ATM (same technology as that which powers the Internet: NT/IP technology) - displaying targeted messages to specific customer profiles. This was the world's first multivendor, browser-driven, e-commerce enabled ATM application.		InterBold is wrapped up. IBM abandons payment technology systems entirely. ATMIA established as a not-for-profit trade association in the USA, initially as the ATM Owners Association, by Tom Harper in the wake of the liberalization of surcharging, which led to the growth of independent ATM operators (IADs), then known	Sen. Alfonse D'Amato (R-NY) initiates campaign against the ATM surcharge (i.e. double charge).

1998	KAL was the world's first software company to create both an ActiveX-based componentized software platform for the XFS standard and a 'web-wrapper' that allowed banks' Internet web transactions to be delivered on XFS-compliant kiosk hardware.	There is only one single shared network in the UK and Sweden.	as ISOs (independent sales organizations); ATMOA launches ATM insurance programme and changes name to ATMIA (ATM Industry Association).
			In the UK, the first Independent ATM Deployer (IAD) joinks LINK (the single network).
			Sen. Alfonse D'Amato (R-NY) introduced bill that would have prohibited banks from collecting ATM surcharges from non-bank customers. The bill failed.
1999	San Francisco Credit Union displays the first 'talking' ATM to help the visually impared.	First deployment in Pakistan and Belarus.	In the USA, 99% of ATMs are part of a shared network.
		NCR installs the world's most southernly ATM in McMurdo Station, Antarctica.	Tranax entered the US market as a distribution channel for South Korean manufacturer Hyosung Computers.
			First ATMs in Europe' conference launched by SMI co-chaired by Tom Harper and organized by Michael Lee, SMI's Market Research Manager
			Following a buyout Siemens Nixdord Retail and Banking is renamed Wincor Nixdorf
			Rep. Maurice D. Hinchey (R-NY) introduced House Bill 1575, the Fair ATM for Consumers Act, which used the same language as D'Amato's bill. It also failed.
			Berkeley, California, became the first city in the USA to pass an ordinance banning ATM surcharges for individuals who used terminals not owned by their bank.

(continued)

Continued

Year	Technological Turning Point	Diffussion and Adoption	Industry Developments	Judiciary and Regulatory Innovations
2000	DSD encryption is replaced by the 'Advanced Encryption Standard' (AES) protocol, also known by its original name of Rijndael.	According to RBR London there are 1 million ATMs worldwide.	US chapter grows to just under 90 members; ATMIA Europe launched by Michael Lee, along with ATMIA's first European conferences.	Cruickshank Report is delivered and adopted by British government, opening the door for IADs in the UK.
2001			First annual ATM Security conference. Triton sold to Dover Industries. Mike Lee at ATMIA launches an international design contest to create a graphic that would be instantly recognizable worldwide.	
2002		Approximately half of all global ATMs were located away from a bank branch, with 67% of US ATMs found off-premises.	ATMIA begins expanding its range of products and services, including advocacy, and establishes new chapters in Canada and Australia.	
2003	Third version of ISO8583 messaging standard.	Five shared networks control 90% of transaction volume in the USA.	ATMIA establishes the Global ATM Security Alliance (GASA), later renamed the ATM Security Forum, to draft international best practices for the ATM lifecycle and to issue fraud alerts. In the UK there are 13 active IADs which owned or managed about 30% of total installed capacity.	
2004	NCR launches Personas 71, the world's first freestanding weatherized ATM.	First deployment in Afganistan.	OCBC Bank (Sinpagore) wins ATMIA Best Practice Deployment Award for its innovative use of terminal personalization and customer relationship management (CRM) in ATMs.	In the USA, ADAAG is expanded to include headphone jacks.
2005		According to RBR London there are 1.5 million ATMs worldwide. First ATM in Iraq.	ATMIA chapters launched in Asia and Latin America.	

2006	In Japan, Fujitsu launches first finger vein (biometric) authentication device ATM which was deployed in 26,500 ATMs by Japan's Post Office that same year.	First ATM in Vietnam.
2007	First ATM in Guyana and Kazahstan.	In the UK, IADs own or manage 50% of total installed capacity but only recording 5% of total withdrawals.
2008		ATMIA establishes the ATM Cash Council to present a picture of global cash demand in response to the anti-cash campaigns of global card associations.
		ATMIA registered its official global pictogram as an international public sign.
2009	According to RBR London there are 2.3 million ATMs worldwide.	
2010	Visa and MasterCard implement their common protocol for smart payment cards and for payment terminals and ATMs (also known as EMV) in Europe.	ATMIA establishes the ATMIA Consulting and Training practice for independent consultants in the ATM and payments space.
		The fist large-scale deployment of an ATM with biometric capabilities takes place in Poland.
		Large-scale deployment of contactless ATMs in Mexico and Spain.
		Harkin Amendment defeated after advocacy by industry coalition led by EFTA and ATMIA (Amendment Limiting ATM Fees Not Included in Final Bill Passed by Senate).
2011	Early cardless ATM transactions program launched by FNB in South Africa, using cell phone banking at the ATM.	

(continued)

Continued

Year	Technological Turning Point	Diffussion and Adoption	Industry Developments	Judiciary and Regulatory Innovations
2012	Solar-powerd ATM is deployed in Siberia, Russia.		ATMIA completes its globalization programme under International Director, Michael Lee (later the CEO), opening chapters and conferences in Latin America, the Middle East, and India	
2013				Common standard for greater accessibility for people with disabilities comes into effect across the European Union.
2014		According to RBR London there are 3 million ATMs worldwide.

According to RBR London China becomes the largest ATM market worldwide, surpassing the USA.

Europe's first biometric ATM shared network launched in Poland.

NCR ATMs are in over 120 countries around the globe. | In Australia, ANZ Bank launches the GAYTM campaign in support of the Sydney Mardi Gras. | |
| 2015 | EMV is introduced in the USA.

NCR SelfSer 23, the world's first 'tap and pin' deployment for ATMs as user authentication methods change. | | ATMIA changes its logo in an international rebranding exercise | At least one third of EU countries have specifically regulated on accessibility to ATMs. |
| 2016 | | | ATMIA's global membership reaches 6,000 in 66 countries.

Diebold acquires Wincor Nixdorf creating a new S&P 250 company. | |
| 2017 | | According to an estimate by RBR London, there are 3.6 million ATMs worldwide with a forecast of 4.1 million for 2020. | ATMIA celebrates its 20th anniversary, while commemorating the 50th anniversary of the origins of the ATM. | |

References

Acemoglu, Daron, and David Autor (2001). 'Skills, Tasks and Technologies: Implications for Employment and Earnings'. In *Handbook of Labor Economics*, edited by David Card and Orley Ashenfelter, 1043–171. Amsterdam: Elsevier.

Ackrill, Margaret, and Leslie Hannah (2001). *Barclays: The Business of Banking 1690–1996*. Cambridge: Cambridge University Press.

Alberts, Gerard (2010). 'Appropriating America: Americanization in the History of European Computing'. *IEEE Annals in the History of Computing* 32, no. 2: 4–7.

Anderson, Ross (1993). 'Why Cryptosystems Fail'. *Proceedings of the ACM Conference on Computer and Communication Security* 37, no. 11: 33–40.

Arfvidson, Lars (2007). 'Teknikhistoria: Den Första Bankomaten I Världen'. Stockholm: *Tekniska Museet*. <http://www.tekniskamuseet.se/>.

Asami, Hiroshi (*c*.1986). 'El enfoque japonés del "Bank Office Automation"'. Fujitsu Ltd.

Autor, David H., Lawrence F. Katz, and Melissa S. Kearney (2008). 'Trends in US Wage Inequality: Revising the Revisionists'. *Review of Economics and Statistics* 90, no. 2: 300–23.

Autor, David H., Frank Levy, and Richard Murnane (2002). 'Upstairs Downstairs: How Introducing Computer Technology Changed Skills and Pay on Two Floors of Cabot Bank'. *Regional Review* Q2: 22–30.

Autor, David H., Frank Levy, and Richard Murnane (2003). 'The Skill Content of Recent Technological Change: An Empirical Exploration'. *Quarterly Journal of Economics* 116, no. 4: 1279–333.

Ballarín, Eduard (1985). *Estrategias competitivas para la banca*. Barcelona: Ariel.

Barrie, Abass (2006). 'The Impact of Information Technology on UK Banking: The Case of Automated Teller Machines'. MSc International Finance and Banking, London South Bank University.

Barrow, Richard (2006). *Fifty More Years of the Halifax 1953–2003*. Halifax: HBOS and Richard Barrow.

Bátiz-Lazo, Bernardo (2009). 'Emergence and Evolution of ATM Networks in the UK, 1967–2000'. *Business History* 51, no. 1: 1–27.

Bátiz-Lazo, Bernardo (2013). 'Direct Line Insurance: A Case Study of Telephone Banking and Its Impact on the Competitive Performance of the Royal Bank of Scotland, 1985–1995'. *Zeitschrift für Unternehmensgeschichte/The Journal of Business History* 18: 54–72.

Bátiz-Lazo, Bernardo (2017a). 'Between Novelty and Fashion: Risk Management and the Adoption of Computers in Retail Banking'. In *Decision Taking, Confidence and Risk*

Management in Banks from Early Modernity to the 20th Century, edited by Korinna Schönhärl, 189–208. Basingstoke: Palgrave Macmillan.

Bátiz-Lazo, Bernardo (2017b). 'Is DLT the Cure for the Omni-Channel Blues? A Provocation'. Bangor, Gwynedd: Bangor University Business School (WP 17–03). <https://ideas.repec.org/p/bng/wpaper/17003.html>.

Bátiz-Lazo, Bernardo, and Gustavo Del Angel (2016). 'The Dawn of the Plastic Jungle: The Introduction of the Credit Card in Europe and North America, 1950–1975'. Hoover Institution (Economics Working Papers 16107). Palo Alto, CA: Stanford University. <https://www.hoover.org/research/dawn-plastic-jungle-introduction-credit-card-europe-and-north-america-1950-1975>.

Bátiz-Lazo, Bernardo, and Mark Billings (2007). 'In Search of a Winning Strategy: A Case Study of Strategic Change at the Woolwich Equitable Building Society (1950–70)'. Fifth Accounting History International Conference. Banff.

Bátiz-Lazo, Bernardo, and Trevor Boyns (2003). 'Automation and Management Accounting in British Manufacturing and Retail Financial Services, 1945–1968'. EconWPA—Munich Personal RePec Archive (MPRA). <https://ideas.repec.org/p/wpa/wuwpeh/0303001.html>.

Bátiz-Lazo, Bernardo, and Leonidas Efthymiou (2016). '360 Degrees of Cashlessness'. In *The Book of Payments: Historical and Contemporary Views on the Cashless Economy*, edited by Bernardo Bátiz-Lazo and Leonidas Efthymiou, 1–10. London: Palgrave Macmillan.

Bátiz-Lazo, Bernardo, and Nurdilek Hacialioglu (2005). 'Barclaycard: Still the King of Pla$tic?'. In *Exploring Corporate Strategy: Text and Cases* (7th edn.), edited by Gerry Johnson, Kevan Scholes, and Richard Whittington, 886–900. London: Prentice Hall/ Financial Times.

Bátiz-Lazo, Bernardo, and Thomas Haigh (2012). 'Engineering Change: The Appropriation of Computer Technology at Grupo ICA in Mexico (1965–1971)'. *IEEE Annals of the History of Computing* 34, no. 2: 3–16.

Bátiz-Lazo, Bernardo, and Joan Carles Maixé-Altés (2011a). 'Managing Technological Change by Committee: Adoption of Computers in Spanish and British Savings Banks (Circa 1960–1988)'. *Revista de Historia Industrial* 47: 117–50.

Bátiz-Lazo, Bernardo, and Joan Carles Maixé-Altés (2011b). 'Organisational Change and the Computerisation of British and Spanish Savings Banks, Circa 1950–1985'. In *Technological Innovation in Retail Finance: International Historical Perspectives*, edited by Bernardo Bátiz-Lazo, Joan Carles Maixé-Altés, and Paul Thomes, 137–54. London: Routledge.

Bátiz-Lazo, Bernardo, and Masayoshi Noguchi (2014). 'Disciplining Building Societies by Accounting-Based Regulation, Circa 1960'. *British Accounting Review* 46, no. 1: 1–17.

Bátiz-Lazo, Bernardo, and Claudia Reese (2010). 'Is the Future of the ATM Past?'. In *Financial Markets and Organizational Technologies: System Architectures, Practices and Risks in the Era of Deregulation*, edited by Alexandros-Andreas Kyrtsis, 137–65. Basingstoke: Palgrave Macmillan.

Bátiz-Lazo, Bernardo, and Robert J. K. Reid (2008). 'Evidence from the Patent Record on the Development of Cash Dispensers and ATM Technology'. Paper presented at the IEEE History of Telecommunications Conference, Paris.

Bátiz-Lazo, Bernardo, and Robert J. K. Reid (2011). 'The Development of Cash Dispensing Technology in the UK'. *IEEE Annals of the History of Computing* 33, no. 3: 3–15.

Bátiz-Lazo, Bernardo, and Andrew Smith (2016). 'The Changing Industrial Organization of Epistemic Communities During Hong Kong's Progression Towards a Cashless Society (1960s–2000s)'. *IEEE Annals in the History of Computing* 38, no. 2: 54–65.

Bátiz-Lazo, Bernardo, and Peter Wardley (2007). 'Banking on Change: Information Systems and Technologies in UK High Street Banking, 1919–1969'. *Financial History Review* 14, no. 2: 177–205.

Bátiz-Lazo, Bernardo, and Kassa Woldensenbet (2006). 'Product and Process Innovations in Banking'. *International Journal of Financial Services Management* 1, no. 4: 400–21.

Bátiz-Lazo, Bernardo, and Douglas Wood (2000). 'Effects of Regulatory Change on European Banks: A Case Study on the Strategy and Stock Market Performance of Lloyds Bank 1980–1993'. *Journal of European Financial Services* 4, no. 1: 31–63.

Bátiz-Lazo, Bernardo, and Douglas Wood (2002). 'An Historical Appraisal of Information Technology in Commercial Banking'. *Electronic Markets: The International Journal of Electronic Commerce & Business Media* 12, no. 3: 192–205.

Bátiz-Lazo, Bernardo, Thomas Haigh, and David L. Stearns (2014a). 'How the Future Shaped the Past: The Case of the Cashless Society'. *Enterprise & Society* 15, no. 1: 103–31.

Bátiz-Lazo, Bernardo, Tobias Karlsson, and Björn Thodenius (2014b). 'The Origins of the Cashless Society: Cash Dispensers, Direct to Account Payments and the Development of On-Line Real-Time Networks, c.1965–1985'. *Essays in Economic and Business History* 32: 100–37.

Bátiz-Lazo, Bernardo, Joan Carles Maixé-Altés, and Paul Thomes (2011a). 'In Digital We Trust: The Computarization of Retail Finance in Western Europe and North America'. In *Technological Innovation in Retail Finance: International Historical Perspectives*, edited by Bernardo Bátiz-Lazo, Joan Carles Maixé-Altés, and Paul Thomes, 3–14. London: Routledge.

Bátiz-Lazo, Bernardo, Joan Carles Maixé-Altés, and Paul Thomes (eds.) (2011b). *Technological Innovation in Retail Finance: International Historical Perspectives*. London: Routledge.

Bátiz-Lazo, Bernardo, Jarunee Wonglimpiyarat, and Douglas Wood (2002). 'Barclaycard'. In *Exploring Corporate Strategy: Text and Cases* (6th edn.), edited by Gerry Johnson and Kevan Scholes, 925–40. London: Pearson Education.

Beniger, James (1986). *The Control Revolution: Technical and Economic Origins of the Information Society*. Cambridge, MA: Harvard University Press.

Bessen, James E. (2015a). *Learning by Doing: The Real Connection between Innovation, Wages and Wealth*. New Haven, CT: Yale University Press.

Bessen, James E. (2015b). 'Toil and Technology'. *Finance and Development* 52, no. 1: 16–19.

Bijker, Weibe E., Thomas P. Hughes, and Trevor Pinch (1989). *The Social Construction of Technology*. Cambridge, MA: MIT Press.

Billings, Mark, and Alan E. Booth (2011). 'Techno-Nationalism, the Post Office and the Creation of Britain's National Giro'. In *Technological Innovation in Retail Finance:*

International Historical Perspectives, edited by Bernardo Bátiz-Lazo, Joan Carles Maixé-Altés, and Paul Thomes, 155–72. London: Routledge.

Billings, Mark, and Forrest Capie (2004). 'The Development of Management Accounting in UK Clearing Banks, 1920–70'. *Accounting, Business and Financial History* 14, no. 3: 317–38.

Boléat, Mark (1986). *The Building Society Industry*. London: Allen & Unwin.

Bonin, Hubert (2004). 'The Development of the Use of Accounting Machines in French Banks from the 1920s to the 1960s'. *Accounting, Business and Financial History* 14, no. 3: 257–76.

Bonneau, Joseph, Soren Preibusch, and Ross Anderson (2012). 'A Birthday Present Every Eleven Wallets? The Security of Customer-Chosen Banking Pins'. Paper presented at Financial Cryptography and Data Security Conference, Bonaire.

Booth, Alan E. (2001). 'British Retail Banks, 1955–70: A Case of "Americanisation"?'. In *Americanisation in Twentieth Century Europe: Business, Culture, Politics*, edited by Matthias Kipping and Nicholas Tiratsoo, 309–23. Lille: Université Charles de Gaulle.

Booth, Alan E. (2004). 'Technical Change in Branch Banking at the Midland Bank, 1945–75'. *Accounting, Business and Financial History* 14, no. 3: 277–300.

Booth, Alan E. (2007). *The Management of Technical Change: Automation in the U.K. and U.S.A. since 1950*. Basingstoke: Palgrave Macmillan.

Booth, Alan E. (2008). 'Technological Change and Gender in the Labour Policies of British Retail Banks, 1945–70'. In *Managing the Modern Workplace: Productivity, Politics and Workplace Culture in Postwar Britain*, edited by Joseph Melling and Alan E. Booth, 101–24. Aldershot: Ashgate.

Brady, Tim, Andrew Davies, and Jeremy Hall (2001). 'Capacity Utilization Revisited: Software, Control and the Growth of Large Technical Systems'. *Industrial and Corporate Change* 12, no. 3: 477–517.

Brown, John Seely, and Paul Duguid (1991). 'Organizational Learning and Communities-of-Practice: Toward a Unified View of Working'. *Organization Science* 2, no. 1: 40–57.

Bryman, Alan (2004). *The Disneyization of Society*. London: Sage.

Brynjolfsson, Erik, and Lorin M. Hitt (2000). 'Beyond Computation: Information Technology, Organizational Transformation and Business Performance'. *Journal of Economic Perspectives* 14, no. 4: 23–48.

Brynjolfsson, Erik, and B. Khanin (eds.) (2000). *Understanding the Digital Economy*. Cambridge, MA: MIT Press.

Brynjolfsson, Eric, and Adam Saunders (2010). *Wired for Innovation*. Cambridge, MA: MIT Press.

Campbell-Kelly, Martin (1992). 'Large-Scale Data Processing in the Prudential, 1850–1930'. *Accounting, Business and Financial History* 2, no. 2: 117–39.

Campbell-Kelly, Martin (1998). 'Data Processing and Technological Change: The Post Office Savings Bank, 1861–1930'. *Technology & Culture* 39, no. 1: 1–32.

Campbell-Kelly, Martin (2003). *From Airline Reservations to Sonic the Hedgehog: A History of the Software Industry*. Cambridge, MA: MIT Press.

Campbell-Kelly, Martin (2004). 'Mechanisation and Computers in Banking: A Foreword'. *Accounting Business and Financial History* 14, no. 3: 233–4.

Canals, Jordi (1993). *Competitive Strategies in European Banking*. Oxford: Clarendon Press.

Canals, Jordi (1997). *Universal Banking*. Oxford: Oxford University Press.

Capie, Forrest, and Alan Weber (1985). *A Monetary History of the United Kingdom, 1870–1982*. London: George Allen & Unwin.

Carbo-Valverde, Santiago, and Francisco Rodríguez Fernández (2016). 'The Single Euro Payment Area (SEPA): Implementation in Spain'. In *The Book of Payments: Historical and Contemporary Views on the Cashless Economy*, edited by Bernardo Bátiz-Lazo and Leonidas Efthymiou, 351–8. London: Palgrave Macmillan.

Cavell, David (2003). *Self-Service Banking and ATMs in the 21st Century*. London: Lafferty Publications.

Ceruzzi, Paul E. (2003). *A History of Modern Computing* (2nd edn.). Cambridge, MA and London: MIT Press.

Chamberlin, John G. (2016). 'Reflections on ATM and Network History'. Mimeo.

Chandler, Alfred D. (1990a). 'The Enduring Logic of Industrial Success'. *Harvard Business Review*, March–April: 130–40.

Chandler, Alfred D. (1990b). *Scale and Scope: The Dynamics of Industrial Capitalism*. Cambridge, MA: Harvard University Press.

Channon, Derek F. (1977). *British Banking Strategy and the International Challenge*. London: Macmillan.

Channon, Derek F. (1978). *The Service Industries: Strategy, Structure and Financial Performance*. London: Macmillan.

Channon, Derek F. (1986). *Cases in Bank Strategic Management and Marketing*. New York: John Wiley.

Channon, Derek F. (1988). *Global Banking Strategy*. New York: John Wiley.

Channon, Derek F. (1998). 'The Strategic Impact of IT on the Retail Financial Services Industry'. *Journal of Strategic Information Systems* 7: 183–97.

Che, Yeon-Koo, and József Sákovics (2008). 'Hold-up Problem'. In *The New Palgrave Dictionary of Economics* (2nd edn.), edited by Steven N. Durlauf and Lawrence E. Blume. Basingstoke: Palgrave Macmillan.

Clemons, Eric K. (1990). 'MAC—Philadelphia National Bank's Strategic Venture in Shared ATM Networks'. *Journal of Management Information Systems* 7, no. 1: 5–25.

Consoli, Davide, and Pier Paolo Patrucco (2010). 'Complexity and the Coordination of Technological Knowledge: The Case of Innovation Platforms'. Laboratorio di economia dell'innovazione 'Franco Momigliano'. Turin, Italy.

Constable, Geoffrey (2015). 'Review of Chubb ATM Security Measures (1967–1971)'. Mimeo. Hemel Hempstead.

Coombs, Rod, David Knights, and Hugh Willmott (1992). 'Culture, Control and Competition: Towards a Conceptual Framework for the Study of Information in Organizations'. *Organization Studies* 13, no. 1: 51–72.

Cooper, Carolyn C. (1991). 'Social Construction of Inventions through Patent Management'. *Technology & Culture* 32, no. 4: 960–98.

Coopey, Richard (1999). 'Management and the Introduction of Computing in British Industry, 1945–70'. *Contemporary British History* 13, no. 3: 59–71.

Coopey, Richard (2004a). *Information and Technology Policy: An International History*. Oxford: Oxford University Press.

Coopey, Richard (2004b). 'A Passing Technology: The Automated Teller Machine'. In *Wiring Prometheus: Globalisation, History and Technology*, edited by Peter Lyth and Helmuth Trischler, 175–92. Aarhus: Aarhus University Press.

Cortada, James W. (2006). *The Digital Hand, Vol. 2*. New York: Oxford University Press.

Cusumano, Michael A., Yiorgos Mylonadis, and Richard S. Rosenbloom (1992). 'Strategic Maneuvering and Mass-Market Dynamics: The Triumph of VHS over Beta'. *Business History Review* 66, no. 1: 51–94.

Daniels, Kenneth, and Niel B. Murphy (1994). 'The Impact of Technological Change on the Currency Behaviour of Households'. *Journal of Money, Credit and Banking* 26, no. 4: 867–74.

David, Paul A. (1985). 'Clio and the Economics of Qwerty'. *American Economic Review* 74, no. 2: 332–7.

David, Paul A. (2000). 'Path Dependence, Its Critics and the Quest for "Historical Economics"'. In *Evolution and Path Dependence in Economic Ideas: Past and Present*, edited by P. Garrouste and S. Ioannides, 120–42. Cheltenham: Edward Elgar Publishing.

Davies, Glyn (1981). *Building Societies and Their Branches: A Regional Economic Survey*. London: Fianey & Co.

Devlin, James F. (2005). 'A Detailed Study of Financial Exclusion in the UK'. *Journal of Consumer Policy* 28: 75–108.

Dicks, John (1968). 'Crying All the Way to the Giro'. *Focus: The Consumer Council Magazine*.

Dos Santos, Brian L., and Kenneth Gordon Peffers (1993). 'The Effects of Early Adoption of Information Technology: An Empirical Study'. *Journal of Information Technology Management* 4, no. 1: 1–13.

Drury, Colin (1994). *Survey of Management Accounting in UK Building Societies*. London: Chartered Institute of Management Accountants.

Drury, Colin (1998). 'Management Accounting and Information Systems in UK Building Societies'. *The Service Industries Journal* 18: 125–43.

Drury, Tony, and Charles W. Ferrier (1984). *Credit Cards*. London: Butterworths.

Effosse, Sabine (2017). 'El cheque en Francia: el lento ascenso de un medio de pago de masas (1918–1975)'. *Revista de Historia de la Economía y de la Empresa* 11: 77–96.

Eijkman, Frederik, Jake Kendall, and Ignacio Mas (2010). 'Bridges to Cash: The Retail End of M-Pesa'. *Savings and Development* 34, no. 2: 219–52.

Ekebrink, Ivan (1974). 'Cash Dispensing: A Joint Venture in Sweden'. *Magazine of Bank Administration*: 10–12 and 63.

Elder, Matthew (1986). 'Machines Are Changing the Way We Bank'. *The Montreal Gazette*, 10 November: B4 and B6.

Endo, Teuro (1974). 'Japan Experiences Rapid Growth in Cash Dispensers'. *The Magazine of Bank Administration*, August: 12–14.

Essinger, James (1987). *ATM Networks: Their Organization, Security and Future*. Oxford: Elsevier International.

Feingold, Lainey (2016). *Structured Negotiation: A Winning Alternative to Lawsuits*. Chicago, IL: Publications Board of the American Bar Association.

Fincham, Robin, James Fleck, Rob Procter, Harry Scarbrough, Margaret Tierney, and Robin Williams (1994). *Expertise and Innovation: Information Technology Strategies in the Financial Services Sector*. Oxford: Oxford University Press.

Fishlow, A. (1961). 'The Trustee Savings Banks, 1817–1861'. *Journal of Economic History* 21, no. 1: 26–40.

Frazer, Patrick (1985). *Plastic and Electronic Money: New Payment Systems and Their Implications*. Cambridge: Woodhead-Faulkner.

French, Shaun, Andrew Leyshon, and Sam Meek (2012). 'The Changing Geography of British Bank and Building Society Branch Networks, 2003–2012'. University of Nottingham. <http://eprints.nottingham.ac.uk/2199/>.

Fungáčová, Zuzana, Iftekhar Hasan, and Laurent Weill (2016). 'Trust in Banks'. In *Institute for Economics in Transition*, edited by Bank of Finland. Helsinki.

Gandy, Antony (2013). 'Book Review: Technological Innovation in Retail Finance'. *Economic History Review* 66, no. 4: 1227–8.

Glaser, Paul F. (1988). 'Using Technology for Competitive Advantage: The ATM Experience at Citicorp'. In *Managing Innovation: Cases from the Service Industries*, edited by Bruce R. Guiler and James Brian Quinn, 108–14. Washington, DC: National Academy Press.

Gourley, Adrian Robert (1999). 'The Diffusion of Process Innovation in the UK Financial Sector: An Empirical Analysis of Automated Teller Machine (ATM) Diffusion'. PhD dissertation, Loughborough University.

Haigh, Thomas (2006). '"A Veritable Bucket of Facts": Origins of the Data Base Management System, 1960–1980'. *ACM SIGMOD Record* 35, no. 2: 73–88.

Haigh, Thomas, and Petri Paju (2016). 'IBM Rebuilds Europe: The Curious Case of the Transnational Typewriter'. *Enterprise & Society* 17, no. 2: 265–300.

Håkanson, Lars (2010). 'The Firm as an Epistemic Community: The Knowledge-Based View Revisited'. *Industrial and Corporate Change* 19, no. 6: 1801–28.

Hall, Bronwyn H., and Beethika Khan (2003). 'Adoption of New Technology'. In *New Economy Handbook*, edited by Derek Jones. Bingley: Emerald Group Publishing.

Hannan, Timothy, and John M. McDowell (1984). 'Market Concentration and the Diffusion of New Technology in the Banking Industry'. *Review of Economics and Statistics* 66, no. 4: 686–91.

Hannan, Timothy, and John M. McDowell (1987). 'Rival Precedence and the Dynamics of Technology Adoption: An Empirical Analysis'. *Economica* 54, no. 214: 151–71.

Hannan, Timothy H., Elizabeth K. Kiser, Robin A. Prager, and James McAndrews (2001). 'To Surcharge or Not to Surcharge: An Empirical Investigation'. Washington, DC: Board of the Federal Reserve (WP 2001–38). <<https://www.federalreserve.gov/pubs/feds/2001/200138/200138pap.pdf>.

Harper, Tom, and Bernardo Bátiz-Lazo (2013). *Cash Box: The Invention and Globalization of the ATM*. Louisville, KY: NetWorld Media Group.

Hayashi, Fumiko, Richard J. Sullivan, and Stuart E. Weiner (2003). *A Guide to the ATM and Debit Card Industry*. Kansas City, MO: Federal Reserve Bank of Kansas City.

Hayashi, Fumiko, Richard J. Sullivan, and Stuart E. Weiner (2006). *A Guide to the ATM and Debit Card Industry: An Update*. Kansas City, MO: Federal Reserve Bank of Kansas City.

Heide, Lars (2009). *Punched-Card Systems and the Early Information Explosion, 1880–1945.* Studies in Industry and Society. Baltimore, MD: Johns Hopkins University Press.

Heller, Michael (2008). 'Work, Income and Stability: The Late Victorian and Edwardian London Male Clerk Revisited'. *Business History* 50, no. 3: 253–71.

Heller, Michael (2011). *London Clerical Workers, 1880–1914.* London: Pickering & Chatto.

Heller, Michael, and Bernadette Kamleitner (2014). 'Salaries and Promotion Opportunities in the English Banking Industry, 1890–1936: A Rejoinder'. *Business History* 56, no. 2: 270–86.

Holmes, A. R., and E. Green (1986). *Midland: 150 Years of Banking Business.* London: B. T. Batsford.

Hopkins, Deborah Ann (1986). 'Factors Affecting the Adoption of Automated Teller Machines, Direct Deposit of Paychecks and Partial Direct Deposit to Savings Where Available'. Ohio State University.

Hopton, David (1979). *Electronic Fund Transfer Systems: The Issues and Implications.* Bangor Occasional Papers in Economics No. 17, edited by Jack Revell. Bangor, Gwynedd: University of Wales Press.

Horne, H. O. (1947). *A History of Savings Banks.* London: Oxford University Press.

Howells, J., and J. Hine (1993). *Innovative Banking: Competition and Management of the Network Technology.* Padstow, Cornwall: TJ Press.

Humphrey, David B. (1996). 'The Economics of Electronic Benefit Transfer Payments'. *Federal Reserve Bank of Richmond Economic Quarterly* 82, no. 2: 77–94.

Humphrey, David B., and Lawrence B. Pulley (1997). 'Banks' Responses to Deregulation: Profits, Technology, and Efficiency'. *Journal of Money, Credit and Banking* 29, no. 1: 73–93.

Humphrey, David B., Lawrence B. Pulley, and Jukka M. Vesala (1996). 'Cash, Paper and Electronic Payments: A Cross-Country Analysis'. *Journal of Money, Credit and Banking* 28, no. 4 (part 2): 914–39.

Husz, Orsi (2015a). 'From Wage Earners to Financial Consumers: Class and Financial Socialisation in Sweden in the 1950s and 1960s'. *Critique Internationale* 69: 99–118.

Husz, Orsi (2015b). 'Golden Everyday: Housewifely Consumerism and Domestication of Banks in 1960s Sweden'. *Le Mouvement Social* 205: 41–63.

Husz, Orsi (forthcoming). 'The Emergence of Bank Identity: Banks and the Management of Identification in Sweden'. *Enterprise & Society.*

Innes, John, and Falconer Mitchell (1997). 'The Application of Activity-Based Costing in the United Kingdom's Largest Financial Institutions'. *The Service Industry Journal* 17: 190–203.

Jack, Robert B. (1989). *Banking Services: Law and Practice Report by the Review Committee.* London: Her Majesty's Stationary Office.

Janicki, Hubert P., and Edward S. Prescott (2006). 'Changes in Size Distribution of U.S. Banks: 1960–2005'. *Federal Reserve Bank of Richmond Economic Quarterly* 92, no. 4: 291–316.

Jaremski, Matthew, and Gabriel Mathy (2017). 'Looking Back on the Age of Checking in America, 1800–1960'. *Revista de Historia de la Economía y de la Empresa* 11: 41–76.

Jeremy, David J. (1998). *A Business History of Britain, 1900–1990s.* Oxford: Oxford University Press.

Kirkman, P. (1987). *Electronic Funds Transfer System: The Revolution of Cashless Banking and Payment Methods*. New York: Basil Blackwell.

Knights, David, and Darren McCabe (1998). ' "The Times Are a Changin"? Transformative Organizational Innovations in Financial Services in the U.K.' *International Journal of Human Resource Management* 9, no. 1: 168–84.

Konheim, Alan G. (2007). *Computer Security and Cryptography*. Hoboken, NJ: John Wiley.

Konheim, Alan G. (2015). 'The Impetus of Creativity in Technology'. *Cryptologia* 39, no. 4: 291–314.

Konheim, Alan G. (2016). 'Automated Teller Machines: Their History and Authentication Protocols'. *Journal of Cryptographic Engineering* 6, no. 1: 1–29.

Kynaston, David (1996). *The City of London, Vol. II: Golden Years 1890–1914*. London: Pimlico.

Laderman, Elizabeth S. (1990a). 'The Public Policy Implications of State Laws Pertaining to Automated Teller Machines'. *Economic Review: Federal Reserve Bank of San Francisco* 1: 43–58.

Laderman, Elizabeth S. (1990b). 'Shared ATM Networks: An Uneasy Alliance?' *FRBSF Weekly Letter*.

Lam, Tai, and Crystal Ossolinski (2015). *The Value of Payment Instruments: Estimating Willingness to Pay and Consumer Surplus*, edited by Reserve Bank of Australia. Sydney.

Lamoreaux, Naomi R., Daniel M. G. Raff, and Peter Termin (2003). 'Beyond Markets and Hierarchies: Towards a New Synthesis of American Business History'. *American Historical Review* 108: 404–33.

Lane, Sarah Julia (1989). 'Entry and Industry Evolution in the ATM Manufacturers' Market'. PhD dissertation, Stanford University.

Langlois, Richard N. (2003). 'The Vanishing Hand: The Changing Dynamics of Industrial Capitalism'. *Industrial and Corporate Change* 12, no. 2: 351–85.

Larson, Mitchell Jonathan, Gerhard Schnyder, Gerarda Westerhuis, and John Wilson (2011). 'Strategic Responses to Global Challenges: The Case of European Banking, 1973–2000'. *Business History* 53, no. 1: 40–62.

Latour, Bruno (1992). 'Where are the Missing Masses? The Sociology of a Few Mundane Artifacts'. In *Shaping Technology/Building Society: Studies in Sociotechnical Change*, edited by Wiebe E. Bijker and John Law, 225–58. Cambridge, MA: MIT Press.

Latour, Bruno (2005). *Reassembling the Social: An Introduction to Actor-Network-Theory*. Oxford: Oxford University Press.

Lee, Eun-Ju (2000). 'Consumer Adoption and Diffusion of Technological Innovations: A Case of Electronic Banking Technologies'. PhD dissertation, University of Tennessee.

Lee, Haywon (2004). 'Spatial Analysis of Bank's ATMs in Korea'. *Journal of Korean Geographical Society* 39, no. 5: 755–67.

Lescure, Michel (2016). 'Why Some Banks Fail to Fail?'. In *Immortal Banks: Strategies, Structures and Performances of Major Banks*, edited by Michel Lescure, 9–16. Geneva: Librairie Droz & Société Générale.

Liebowitz, Stan J., and Stephen E. Margolis (1990). 'The Fable of the Keys'. *Journal of Law and Economics* 33, no. 1: 1–25.

Liebowitz, Stan J., and Stephen E. Margolis (1994). 'Network Externality: An Uncommon Tragedy'. *Journal of Economic Perspectives* 4, no. 1: 133–50.

Liebowitz, Stan J., and Stephen E. Margolis (1995). 'Path Dependence, Lock-in, and History'. *Journal of Law, Economics & Organization* 11, no. 1: 205–26.

Lipis, Allen H., Thomas R. Marschall, and Jan H. Linker (1985). *Electronic Banking*. New York: John Wiley.

Lozano, Marvin Francis (1987). 'The Diffusion and Adoption of a Technical Innovation: The Automated Teller Machine'. University of Arizona.

McAndrews, James J. (1991). 'The Evolution of Shared ATM Networks'. *Federal Reserve Bank of Philadelphia Business Review*, May/June: 3–16.

McAndrews, James J. (1998). 'ATM Surcharge'. *(Federal Reserve Bank of New York) Current Issues in Economics and Finance* 4, no. 4: 1–6.

McAndrews, James J. (2003). 'Automated Teller Machines Network Pricing: A Review of Literature'. *Review of Network Economics* 2, no. 2: 146–58.

McCray, W. Patrick (2012). *The Visioneers: How a Group of Elite Scientists Pursued Space Colonies, Nanotechnologies, and a Limitless Future*. Princeton, NJ: Princeton University Press.

McFarlan, F. Warren, James L. McKenney, and Philip Pyburn (1983). 'The Information Archipelago: Plotting a Course'. *Harvard Business Review* 61: 145–56.

McKenney, James L. (1995). 'Developing a Common Machine Language for Banking: The ABA Technical Subcommittee Story'. *IEEE Annals of the History of Computing* 17, no. 4: 61–75.

McKenney, James L., and Amy Weaver Fisher (1993). 'Manufacturing the ERMA Banking System: Lessons from History'. *IEEE Annals of the History of Computing* 15, no. 4: 7–26.

Maixé-Altés, Joan Carles (2012). *Innovación y compromiso social. 60 años de informatización y crecimiento*. Barcelona: 'la Caixa' Group.

Maixé-Altés, Joan Carles (2013). 'La opción tecnológica de las cajas de ahorro españolas antes de Internet, circa 1950–1995' [The Technological Option of Spanish Savings Banks before the Internet, circa 1950–1995]. *Investigaciones de Historia Económica/Economic History Research* 9, no. 3: 175–86.

Maixé-Altés, Joan Carles (2015). 'ICT the Nordic Way and European Retail Banking'. In *History of Nordic Computing 4, 4th IFIP WG 9.7 Conference, HINC 4. Revised Selected Papers*, edited by Christian Gram, Per Rasmussen, and Soren Duus Ostergaard, 249–62. Heidelberg: Springer Verlag.

Maixé-Altés, Joan Carles (2016). 'Divergent Paths to a Network World: Looking at Computers through the Savings Bank Industry before the Internet'. A Coruña: Universidad A Coruña. <https://mpra.ub.uni-muenchen.de/67785/>.

Maixé-Altés, Joan Carles (2017). 'Retail Trade and Payment Innovations in the Digital Era: A Cross-Industry and Cross-Country Approach'. A Coruña: Universidad A Coruña.

Mandell, Lewis (1990). *The Credit Card Industry: A History*. Boston, MA: Twayne Publishers.

Marinc, Matej (2013). 'Banks and Information Technology: Maketability and Relationships'. *Electronic Commerce Research* 1, no. 1: 71–101.

Martin, Ian (2011). 'Britain's First Computer Centre for Banking: What Did This Building Do?'. In *Technological Innovation in Retail Finance: International Historical Perspectives*, edited by Bernardo Bátiz-Lazo, J. Carles Maixé-Altés, and Paul Thomes, 37–70. London: Routledge.

Martin, Ian (2012). 'Too Far Ahead of Its Time: Barclays, Burroughs and Real-Time Banking'. *IEEE Annals of the History of Computing* 34, no. 2: 2–16.

Mason, Stephen (2003). *Electronic Signatures in Law* (1st edn.). London: LexisNexis Butterworths.

Mason, Stephen (2014). *When Bank Systems Fail*. London: PP Publishing.

Mason, Stephen (2017). *Electronic Signatures in Law* (4th edn.). London: Institute of Advanced Legal Studies.

Mason, Stephen, and Daniel Seng (2017). *Electronic Evidence* (4th edn.). London: Institute of Advanced Legal Studies.

Maurer, Bill (2006). 'The Anthropology of Money'. *Annual Review of Anthropology* 35: 15–36.

Maurer, Bill (2012). 'Forms and Functions of Value Transfer in Contemporary Society'. *Cambridge Anthropology* 30, no. 2: 15–35.

Maurer, Bill (2015). *How Would You Like to Pay? How Technology Is Changing the Future of Money*. Durham, NC: Duke University Press.

Maurer, Bill, Taylor C. Nelms, and Stephen C. Rea (2013). '"Bridges to Cash": Channelling Agency in Mobile Money'. *Journal of the Royal Anthropological Institute* 19, no. 1: 52–74.

Michaud, André (2004). 'Contribution à L'Histoire de la Société TRANSAC—1970–1982'. In *7e Colloque sur l'Histoire de l'Informatique et des Télécommunications*, edited by Jacques André and Pierre Mounier-Kuhn, 24–37. Rennes-Cesson (France): INRIA/Université de Rennes.

Michie, Ranald C. (1992). *The City of London*. London: Macmillan.

Mihm, Stephen (2007). *A Nation of Counterfeiters: Capitalist, Con Men, and the Making of the United States*. Cambridge, MA: Harvard University Press.

Miodownik, Mark (2013). *Stuff Matters*. London: Penguin.

Misa, Thomas J. (2007). 'Understanding "How Computing Changed the World"'. *IEEE Annals in the History of Computing* 29, no. 4: 52–63.

Mitchell, Karlyn, and Nur M. Onvural (1996). 'Economies of Scale and Scope at Large Commercial Banks'. *Journal of Money, Credit and Banking* 28: 178–99.

Moss, Michael S., and Ian Russell (1994). *An Invaluable Treasure: A History of the TSB*. London: Weidenfeld & Nicolson.

Moss, Michael S., and Anthony Slaven (1992). *From Ledger Book to Laser Beam: A History of the TSB in Scotland from 1810 to 1990*. Edinburgh: TSB Bank Scotland.

Murdoch, Steven J., Saar Drimer, Ross Anderson, and Mike Bond (2010). 'Chip and Pin Is Broken'. Paper presented at the IEEE Symposium on Security and Privacy, Berkeley, CA.

Nagurney, Anna, Jose M. Cruz, and Tina Wakolbinger (2007). 'The Co-Evolution and Emergence of Integrated International Financial Networks and Social Networks: Theory, Analysis, and Computations'. In *Globalization and Regional Economic*

Modeling, edited by R. Cooper, K. P. Donaghy, and G. J. D. Hewings, 183–226. Berlin: Springer.

Nightingale, Paul, and Robert Poll (2000). 'Innovation and Investment Banking: The Dynamics of Control Systems within the Chandlerian Firm'. *Industrial and Corporate Change* 9: 113–41.

Noguchi, Masayoshi, and Bernardo Bátiz-Lazo (2010). 'The Auditors' Reporting Duty on Internal Control: The Case of Building Societies, 1956–1960'. *Accounting History Review* 20, no. 1: 41–66.

Nye, James (2014). *A Long Time in Making: The History of Smiths*. Oxford: Oxford University Press.

Orr, Julian E. (1996). *Talking About Machines: An Ethnography of a Modern Job*. Ithaca, NY: ILR Press.

Palm, Michael (2016). *Technologies of Consumer Labor: A History of Self-Service*. London: Routledge.

Pardo-Guerra, Juan Pablo (2013). 'Making Markets: Infrastructures, Engineers, and the Moral Technologies of Finance'. Department of Sociology, London School of Economics.

Payne, Peter L. (1967). 'The Savings Bank of Glasgow, 1836–1914'. In *Studies in Scottish Business History*, edited by P. L. Payne. London: Cass.

Peffers, Kenneth Gordon (1991). 'Information Technology Impact on Performance: An Investigation of Investments in Automated Teller Machines'. PhD dissertation, Purdue University.

Pennings, Johannes M., and Farid Harianto (1992). 'The Diffusion of Technological Innovation in the Commercial Banking Industry'. *Strategic Management Journal* 13: 29–46.

Pinch, Trevor (2001). 'Why You Go to a Piano Store to Buy a Synthesizer'. In *Path Dependence and Creation*, edited by Raghu Garoud and Peter Karnoe, 381–99. Mahwah NJ: Lawrence Erlbaum.

Poon, Martha (2011). 'Historicizing Consumer Credit Risk Calculation: The Fair Isaac Process of Commercial Scorecard Manufacture, 1957–circa 1980'. In *Technological Innovation in Retail Finance: International Historical Perspectives*, edited by Bernardo Bátiz-Lazo, Joan Carles Maixé-Altés, and Paul Thomes, 221–45. London: Routledge.

Price, Seymour J. (1959). *Building Societies: The Origins and History*. London: Franey & Co.

Pugh, Peter (2011). *The Highest Perfection: A History of De La Rue*. London: Aubrey Books.

Revell, Jack R. S. (1983). *Banking and Electronic Fund Transfers*. Paris: Organisation for Economic Co-operation and Development.

Richardson, Denis W. (1970). *Evolution of an Electronic Funds-Transfer System*. Cambridge, MA: MIT Press.

Ritters, Katrina (2003). *Consumer Education in the UK*. London: Trading Standards Institute.

Ritzer, George (1995). *Expressing America: A Critique of the Global Credit Card Industry*. Thousand Oaks, CA: Pine Forge Press.

Rogers, Everett M. (1976). 'New Product Adoption and Diffusion'. *Journal of Consumer Research* 2: 290–301.

Rogers, Everett M. (1995). *Diffusion of Innovations* (4th edn.). New York: Free Press.

Ross, César (2016). 'Innovating Means of Payment in Chile, 1840s–1860'. In *The Book of Payments: Historical and Contemporary Views on the Cashless Economy*, edited by Bernardo Bátiz-Lazo and Leonidas Effthymiou, 33–42. Basingstoke: Palgrave Macmillan.

Ross, César (2017). 'Chile: emisión bancaria, inflación y la constitución del nuevo mercado monetario, 1860–1900'. *Revista de Historia de la Economía y la Empresa* 11: 23–40.

Ross, Duncan M. (2002). '"Penny Banks" in Glasgow, 1850–1914'. *Financial History Review* 9: 21–39.

Saloner, Garth, and Andrea Shepard (1995). 'Adoption of Technologies with Network Effects: An Empirical Examination of the Adoption of Automated Teller Machines'. *The RAND Journal of Economics* 26, no. 3: 479–501.

Schroeder, Jonathan E. (2003). 'Building Brands: Architectural Expression in the Electronic Age'. In *Persuasive Imagery: A Consumer Response*, edited by Linda M. Scott and Rajeev Batra, 349–82. Mahwah, NJ: Lawrence Erlbaum Associates.

Scott, Susan V., and Markos Zachariadis (2014). *The Society for Worldwide Interbank Financial Telecommunication (SWIFT): Cooperative Governance for Network Innovation, Standards, and Community*. Global Institutions Series. London: Routledge.

Scranton, Philip, and Patrick Fridenson (2013). *Reimagining Business History*. Baltimore, MD: Johns Hopkins University Press.

Seltzer, Andrew (2004). 'Internal Labour Markets in the Australian Banking Industry: Their Nature Prior to the Second World War and Their Recent Decline'. *Accounting Business and Financial History* 14, no. 3: 237–56.

Seltzer, Andrew (2010). 'Salaries and Promotion Opportunities in the English Banking Industry, 1890–1936'. *Business History* 52, no. 5: 737–59.

Sharma, Sunil (1993). 'Behind the Diffusion Curve: An Analysis of ATM Adoption'. University of California Working Paper No. 686.

Shepherd-Barron, James (2017). *Hole in the Wall: Memoirs of a Cash Machine*. London: Kissyfish Books.

Sienkiewicz, Stan (2002). 'The Evolution of EFT Networks from ATMs to New On-Line Debit Payment Products'. Discussion Paper, Payments Cards Centre. Federal Reserve Bank of Philadelphia.

Soin, Kim, Willie Seal, and John Cullen (2002). 'ABC and Organizational Change: An Institutional Perspective'. *Management Accounting Research* 13: 249–71.

Spong, Kenneth, and James Harvey (1998). 'The Changing Structure of Banking: A Look at Traditional and New Ways of Delivering Banking Services'. *Financial Industry Perspectives*, May: 1–16.

Sponski, John J. (1974). 'Can Automated Teller Machines Be Cost Justified?' *The Magazine of Bank Administration*, October: 24–9.

Sprague, Richard E. (1977). 'Electronic Funds Transfer in Europe: Their Relevance for the United States'. *Savings Banks International* 3: 29–35.

Stearns, David L. (2011). *Electronic Value Exchange: Origins of the Visa Electronic Payment System*. History of Computing. London: Springer-Verlag.

Stearns, David L. (2017). 'Mag Stripe'. In *Paid: Tales of Dongles, Checks, and Other Money Stuff*, edited by Bill Maurer and Lana Swartz, 30–8. Cambridge, MA: MIT Press.

Stokes, Donald E. (1963). 'Spatial Models of Party Competition'. *American Political Science Review* 57, no. 2: 368–77.

Sullivan, Richard J. (1990). 'The Revolution of Ideas: Widespread Patenting and Invention During the English Industrial Revolution'. *Journal of Economic History* 50, no. 2: 349–62.

Tenner, Edward (1996). *Why Things Bite Back*. New York: Alfred A. Knopf.

Thodenius, Björn (2008). 'Teknisk Utveckling I Bankerna Fram Till 1985: Transkript Av Ett Vittnesseminarium Vid Tekniska Museet'. In *Trita-HST 2008:26*. Stockholm: KTH, Philosophy and History of Technology.

Thodenius, Björn, Bernardo Bátiz-Lazo, and Tobias Karlsson (2011). 'The History of the Swedish ATM: Sparfrämjandet and Metior'. In *History of Nordic Computing 3: Third IFIP WG 9.7 Conference, HINC 3, Stockholm, Sweden, October 18–20, 2010, Revised Selected Papers*, edited by John Impagliazzo, Per Lundin, and Benkt Wangler, 92–100. Berlin: Springer.

Tietelbaum, David (1990). 'Violent Crime at ATMs'. *The Business Lawyer*, June: 1967–71.

Vanatta, Sean H. (forthcoming). 'Charge Account Banking: A Study of Financial Innovation in the 1950s'. *Enterprise & Society*.

Vázquez-Alanís, Gregorio (2007). 'ATM Adoption by Banks in Mexico: Did It Lead to Performance and Network Effects?' Monterrey, NL: Instituto Tecnológico y de Estudios Superiores de Monterrey.

Vik, Pal (2017). 'The Computer Says "No": The Demise of the Traditional Bank Manager and the Depersonalisation of British Banking, 1960–2010'. *Business History* 59, no. 2: 231–49.

Walker, David A. (1980). 'Electronic Funds Transfer Cost Models and Pricing Strategies'. *Journal of Economics and Business* 33: 61–5.

Walter, Ingo (1997). 'Universal Banking: A Shareholder Value Perspective'. *European Management Journal* 15, no. 4: 344–60.

Wandhöfer, Ruth (2010). *EU Payments Integration: The Tale of SEPA, PSD and Other Milestones Along the Road*. Basingstoke: Palgrave Macmillan.

Wandhöfer, Ruth (2016). 'European Payments: A Path Towards the Single Market for Payments'. In *The Book of Payments: Historical and Contemporary Views on the Cashless Economy*, edited by Bernardo Bátiz-Lazo and Leonidas Efthymiou, 341–50. London: Palgrave Macmillan.

Wardley, Peter (2000). 'The Commercial Banking Industry and Its Part in the Emergence and Consolidation of the Corporate Economy in Britain before 1940'. *Journal of Industrial History* 3, no. 2: 71–97.

Wardley, Peter (2003). 'Perceptions of Innovation, Receptions of Change: Responses to the Introduction of Machine Banking and Mechanization in Interwar British Retail Banking'. Paper presented at the Information Systems and Technology in Organisations and Society, Universitat Pompeu Fabra, Barcelona.

Wardley, Peter (2011). 'Women, Mechanization and Cost-Savings in Twentieth Century British Banks and Other Financial Institutions'. In *A Business and Labour History of Britain: Case Studies of Britain in the Nineteenth and Twentieth Centuries*, edited by Mike Richardson and Peter Nicholls, 32–59. Basingstoke: Palgrave Macmillan.

Wenger, Etienne, Richard McDermott, and William Snyder (2002). *Cultivating Communities of Practice*. Boston, MA: Harvard Business School Press.

Wood, Douglas, and Bernardo Bátiz-Lazo (1997). 'Corporate Strategy, Centralization and Outsourcing in Banking: Case Studies on Paper Payments Processing'. *International Association of Management Journal* 9: 33–57.

Wootton, Charles W., and Barbara E. Kemmerer (2007). 'The Emergence of Mechanical Accounting in the U.S., 1880–1930'. *The Accounting Historians Journal* 34, no. 1: 91–124.

Yates, JoAnne (1989). *Control through Communication: The Rise of System in American Management*. Baltimore, MD: Johns Hopkins University Press.

Yates, JoAnne (2005). *Structuring the Information Age*. Baltimore, MD: Johns Hopkins University Press.

Yavitz, Boris (1967). *Automation in Commercial Banking*. New York: Free Press.

Yeh, Phil C., and Ronald M. Smith (1991). 'ESA/390 Integrated Cryptographic Facility: An Overview'. *IBM Systems Journal* 30, no. 2: 192–205.

Zimmer, Linda Fenner (1971). 'A Status Report on Cash Dispensing Machines and Automated Tellers'. *The Magazine of Bank Administration*, November: 112.

Zimmer, Linda Fenner (1974). 'The Status of Automated Tellers and Cash Dispensers'. *The Magazine of Bank Administration*, August: 26–9 and 74.

Zimmer, Linda Fenner (1975). 'Cash Dispensing Equipment and Automatic Tellers'. *The Magazine of Bank Administration*, May: 25–36.

Index

Data supporting the research of this book is available to download from

The Centre for Financial Stability:
http://www.centerforfinancialstability.org/hfs.php?

The European Association for Banking and Financial History:
http://bankinghistory.org/publications/eabh-papers/

Research Papers in Economics (RePEc):
https://ideas.repec.org/p/zbw/eabhps/1801.html